GEOLOGICAL ENVIRONMENT

Encyclopaedia of Geographical Science and Environment Series

GEOLOGICAL ENVIRONMENT

Edited by

Ravi Mishra

ANMOL PUBLICATIONS PVT. LTD.

NEW DELHI - 110 002 (INDIA)

ANMOL PUBLICATIONS PVT. LTD.
4374/4B, Ansari Road, Daryaganj
New Delhi - 110 002
www.anmolbooks.com

Geological Environment

First Edition, 2002
ISBN 81-261-1100-3

PRINTED IN INDIA

Published by J.L. Kumar for Anmol Publications Pvt. Ltd., New Delhi - 110 002 and Printed at Tarun Offset Press, Delhi.

Contents

Preface

Language forces us to express ourselves in a one dimensional stream of words. But nature is seldom so simple and tractable; instead, it has many different dimensions. This is particularly true of geographical environment because its subject matter includes many complexities, inter-related concepts and phenomenon involving several heads of organization. Thus, there is no such thing as an "ideal" outline or a perfect sequential order for presecutation of the subject treated here. To obtain an overview of modern geographical environment, a student needs to assimilate a great many ideas. Ideally, a reader would knew everything in this present title before beginning to read it. Perhaps the only solution is to read it twice. To help a reader follow a train of thoughts different from the authors have chosen to use here, various chapters and sections are cross-referenced.

Our approach throughout is critical and evaluative; neither old nor new theories are taken to trust but are examined rigorously and often critical; the student should be aware of what material is sound and what untested or controversial. Those principles which survive such analysis we have put together in a new and current synthesis of the 'state of the art.' We have deliberately avoided a descriptive habitat a taxonomic approach to the material, feeling that geographical environment must be shown to be quantitative exact science, with certain underlying principles and laws as fundamental as the laws of pure physics.

The present title is aimed to bring together in one place and in a simple way the fundamentals of geographical environment with special emphasis on the modern viewpoint of the science. The potential scope of this branch is very great and no attempt of any exhaustive treatment of the subject is made here.

In the preparation of such a title we have obviously had a great deal of help from a great many people. We would like to take this opportunity to thank many friends and colleagues with whom we have thrashed out the ideas. All of them are most warmly acknowledged.

We have freely consulted a large number of foreign books and journals in the preparation of the present title and also to make it comprehensive and uptodate and to that extent it is not claimed to be our original work.

Any worthwhile criticism and suggestions for improvement would be thankfully acknowledged.

Editor

Chapter 1

Igneous Rocks and Igneous Activity

Igneous rocks make up about 80% of the mass of the earth's crust. It is not surprising then, that the subject of igneous rocks holds a very prominent place in physical geology.

Igneous rock is formed from *magma,* a high temperature mixture of the chemical ingredients of silicate minerals. Magma normally included substances in liquid, solid, and gaseous states. A large proportion of most magmas consists of a hot liquid, or *melt,* present because the temperature of the magma is above the melting points of certain magma ingredients. In a melt, the metallic ions move about more or less freely, without being organized into crystal lattice structures. However, the silicon-oxygen tetrahedra probably remain largely intact and may be linked to one another in complex but irregular chains and networks. Suspended in the melt of most magmas are crystals of minerals formed during early stages of magma cooling. If the proportion of suspended crystals to liquid is high, it gives the magma some of the physical properties of a solid. It may help to visualize this mixture as resembling slush, produced by rapid melting of snow, in which ice crystals are mixed with liquid water, Slush has enough strength to hold its form on a flat pavement but contains a large proportion of free water. In addition to both liquids and solids, magma also contains various gases, which are dissolved in the melt.

Magma that appears at the earth's surface coming into direct contact with air or water, is called *lava*, and its emergence from the solid earth provideds us with sure proof that magma exists. Because lava is rapidly cooling and losing its dissolved gases, however, it can not provide us with an accurate picture of the magma that lies far beneath the earth's surface. But it is important to note that magma formed deep within the crust undergoes various chemical and physical changes as it moves upward through the crust. Some of the chemical components originally present may be separated out, while new chemical components may be added from surrounding rock with which the magma comes in contact. The study of magma inferences based on indirect scientific evidence. The study of plate tectonics has shed a great deal of light on major sources of magmas and why the composition of emerging magma often varies from place to place.

There is general agreement among geologists that magma can be formed by the melting of solid rock in certain depth zones in the asthenosphere. You will recall from chapter 1 that the asthenosphere is a soft layer of the upper mantle within which rock temperature is close to its melting point. Evidence from earthquake waves, indicates that the mantle is closest to its melting point in the depth of 100 to 200 km . It seems most probable that only a small fraction of the mantle rock at this depth range actually melts, while the larger proportion of the mass remain crystalline. This phenomenon is called *partial melting*. The melted fraction, which is a liquid less dense than the crystalline fraction, tends to rise through the sponge like crystalline mass and to collect in magma pockets at shallower depths. It is supposed that the enormous volume of mafic magma continually rising along the spreading plate boundaries collects in magma chambers near the base of the oceanic crust at a depth of 4 to 6 km below the ocean floor. Magma that rises from a location above a descending lithospheric plate at a subduction (converging) boundary is produced under quite different conditions and depths.

Temperatures and Pressures in Magma

Temperature increases rapidly with depth into the earth. This increase in rock temperature, as measured directly with thermometers in deep mines, averages about 1°C per 30 m. Downward through the crust and into the upper mantle temperatures can only be estimated. The graph showing the estimated increase in temperature with depth. Two curves are show, one typical of conditions under the continents, the other for conditions under the ocean basins. Both curves show that while the temperature increases, the rate at which it does so falls off rapidly after about 300 km. Temperatures within the asthenosphere are largely in the range from 1000 °C to 1500 °C. For comparison, the melting point of iron at the earth's surface is about 1500 °C, while molten iron in a blast furnace reaches a temperature of 2000 °C . It might seem like a simple procedure to measure the melting point of a specimen of igneous rock and, using the temperature-depth curves, find the depth at which melting is to be expected and magma to be formed.

Unfortunately, the actual relationships are not that simple. The temperature at which silicate minerals will melt depends upon several factors. Each mineral has its own melting point for a given environment. For example, in the surface environment, under the atmospheric pressure that prevails, pure olivine melts in the temperature range of about 1600 °C to 1800 °C, whereas plagioclase feldspar melts in the range from 1200 °C to 1400 °C.

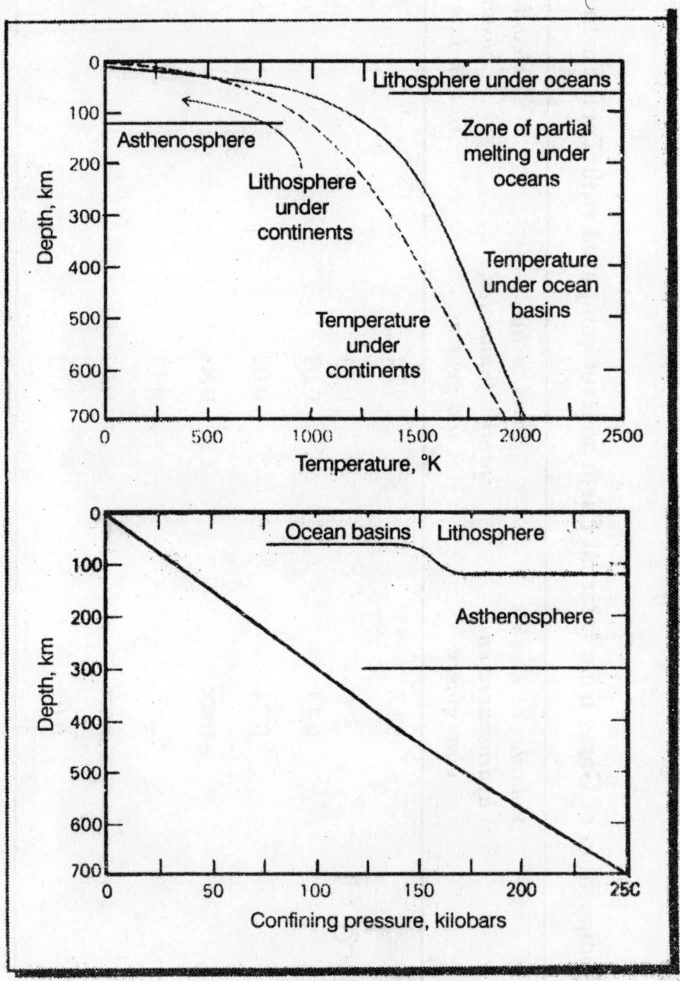

Fig. 1.1. A. Estimated increase in temperature with depth unde continents and under ocean basins. The dashed lines shows the melting point of dy peidotite., B. Estimated increase of confining pressure with depth.

Table 1.1. Composition of Gases from Internal Earth sources compared with Total Earth Volatiles.

	Volatiles of Earth's hydrosphere and atmosphere	*Gases in hot springs, fumaroles, and geysers*	*Volcanic gases from basaltic lava of Mauna Loa and Kilauea*
Water, H_2O	92.8	99.4	57.8
Total carbon, as CO_2	5.1	0.33	23.5
Sulfur, S_2	0.13	0.03	12.6
Nitrogen, N_2	0.24	0.05	5.7
Argon, Ar	trace	trace	0.3
Chlorine, Cl_2	1.7	0.12	0.1
Fluorine, F_2	trace	0.03	—
Hydrogen, H_2	0.07	0.05	0.04

Downward into the earth, the confining pressure to which all rock is subjected increases steadily under the load of the overlying rock layer. The unit to pressure used by geologists is the *kilobar,* which is equal to one thousand bars, a *bar* being approximately equal to the pressure of the earth's atmosphere at sea level- about 1kg per sq cm.The graph to show the approximate increase of confining pressure with depth. An increase in pressure causes the temperature of the melting point of a given mineral or rock to increase. For example, the melting point of iron at a depth of about 100km, under a confining pressure of 40 kb, is about 1650°C, which is 150 °C higher than at the surface.

This relationship between melting point and pressure applies only to conditions in which no water is present. In presence of water, the melting-point temperature is considerably lowered. For example, using a confining pressure equal to a depth of 20 km, a dry rock sample consisting of about 60% pyroxene and 40% calcic plagioclase feldspar has a melting point of about 1300 °C to 1400 °C. The same rock sample containing a substantial proportion of water melts at only 700 °C to 1000 °C. Thus the importance of water in magma is very great. Even a small amount of water in a magma can greatly lower the temperature at which the silicates will remain molten. A rising magma, experiencing a progressive lowering of temperature as it moves upward into cooler zones of surrounding rock, can remain molten at considerably lower temperatures with water present than if the magma consisted of the same silicates without water. Because of this effect, magma with water can reach closer to the earth's surface before solidifying, and it can pour out upon the surface as lava in greater volumes than if water were absent.

Water in magma occurs as dissolved gas, and the dissolved gases are also present. Termed *Volatiles,* these are chemical substance which remain in the liquid or gaseous state at a much lower temperature than that of the mineral-forming silicates. Thus the volatiles become separated from the magma as temperature drop and the silicate minerals crystallize. We can understand from this why, when a specimens of an igneous rock is melted in the laboratory, the melt it produces cannot be a true copy of the magma from which the rock originated.

Although we do not know a great deal about the content of volatiles in magmas at depth in the crust and upper mantle, much has been learned by sampling gases emitted from volcanoes along with emerging lava.

The emission of volatiles with magma at the earth's surface is a geological process *outgassing*; it has acted throughout all geologic time and continues today. As water is the dominant constituent of the volatiles contained in lava, we infer that it is by volume about 90% of the gas contained in an average magma. Estimates of the proportion of water in magmas show a range from 0.5 to 8%, while fresh igneous rocks commonly contain about 1% water, entrapped in small cavities within the minerals during their crystallization. Besides water, the list of volcanic volatiles includes carbon (as carbondioxide gas), sulfur, nitrogen, argon, chlorine, fluorine, and hydrogen.

Outgassing is responsible for the formation of the earth's atmosphere and hydrosphere. The *atmosphere* is the gaseous envelop that surrounds the earth, while the *hydrosphere* is the total free water of the globe, including not only the oceans but all fresh water on the land and beneath the land surfaces. Nitrogen, oxygen, argon, and carbon dioxide together make up over 99% of the atmosphere, and it is clear from Table that these ingredients reached the earth's surface through outgassing. Molecular oxygen (O_2)was formed from water and released to the atmosphere through the process of photosynthesis in green plants.

Outgassing of water was also responsible for the growth of the earth world ocean. The process was probably very rapid in the first aeon of geologic time. Salts accumulated in seawater through the decomposition of silicate minerals rich in ions of sodium, magnesium, calcium and potassium. It is thought that as early as 3 billion years ago the salinity (salt concentration) of seawater had reached a value comparable to what it is today. Chlorine, which today makes up about 55% of the total weight of all matter dissolved in sea water, and sulfur, found in much smaller proportion, were contributed as volatiles through outgassing.

Crystallization of Magmas

During the crystallization of magmas, not all minerals form simultaneously. If, for example, the magma originally has a basaltic composition, olivine, pyroxene, and calcium plagioclase will be among the earliest minerals to crystallize. Often these first-formed crystals are larger and more perfect than those formed later because, when they formed, there was ample space and an abundance of elements required for growth. Those minerals that crystallize later must fit into the remaining spaces and thus tend to be smaller and less perfect. Also, minerals enclosed in other minerals must have formed before the enclosing mineral. By using these observations of size and spatial relationships of minerals as viewed in thin sections of the rock, it is sometimes possible to make a reliable estimate of the order of crystallization of minerals in a magma.

During the first half of the present century, an eminent petrologist named *N. L. Bowen* studied the crystallization of artificial silicate melts

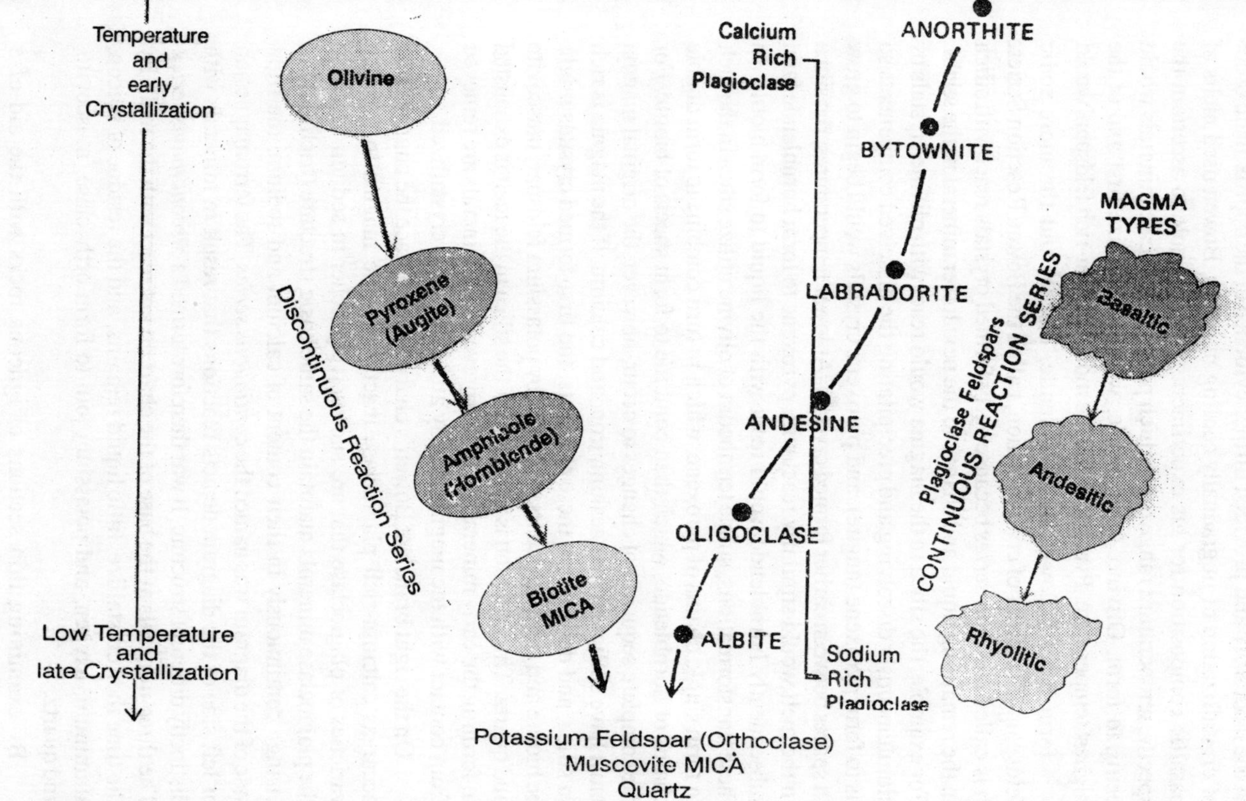

Fig. 1.2. Bowen Reaction Series. Note that the earliest minerals to crystallize from a cooling magma are olivine and calcium-rich plagioclase minerals like bytownite. As crystallization proceeds, olivine reacts with the melt to form pyroxene, pyroxene reacts to form amphibole etc. The plagioclase

in the laboratory and provided further evidence of the approximate order of crystallization of in gradually cooling magmas. Bowen used melts of basaltic composition for his experiments and was able to ascertain the specific temperature range over which particular silicate minerals would being to form. Olivine, for example, would crystallize first and at the highest temperature. Pyroxenes and the more calcium-rich feldspars would

form next, followed by hornblende, biotite, and the more sodic feldspars. The order of crystallization, called the Bowen Reaction Series. It is called *reaction series* because early formed crystals react with silica in the remaining liquid and change to the next lower mineral in the series. For example, the silica in the magma would react with olivine crystals by simultaneously dissolving and precipitating the dissolved components so as to form pyroxene (augite), and pyroxene crystals would begin to grow in spaces between earlier formed crystals. At lower temperatures, the silica in the melt would similarly react with pyroxene to form hornblende, and subsequently hornblende would react with the liquid to form biotite. In these transformations, single tetrahedra of olivine utilize silica in the melt to form single chains of pyroxene, which in turn combine to form double chains of hornblende, which then combine to form sheets of biotite. For the complete sequence of changes to occur, however, the original magma must have sufficient magnesium, iron, and calcium. If the magma is rich in silica, and deficient in these elements, the first-formed crystals might be biotite and sodic feldspars, followed by potassium feldspar, muscovite and quartz. Thus reaction is prevented if the silica in the melt is exhausted in forming the early minerals. It is also prevented if minerals are removed from contact with the magma shortly after they have crystallized.

On the right branch of Bowen's chart, one can trace the changes that occur as calcium-rich plagioclase reacts with the magma to produce varieties of plagioclase that are successively richer in sodium. Because the plagioclase minerals maintain the same basic structure (triclinic) but change continuously in their content of calcium and sodium, the right side of the diagram was named the *continuous series.* The ferromagnesian or left side of the diagram depicts reactions that result in minerals with distinctly different structure. It was therefore termed a *discontinuous series.* The three minerals at the base of the chart do not react with the melt. By the time they crystallize, little liquid remains, and the residue of silicon, aluminum, oxygen, and potassium join to form orthoclase, muscovite, and quartz.

By examining thin sections of igneous rocks with the aid of a microscope, one can often see rather direct evidence of the reactions described above. It is not uncommon, for example, to find plagioclase crystals in which the innermost layers or zones are more calcium-rich and outer zones more sodium-rich. Similarly, reaction rims of pyroxene can be observed around olivine and rims of hornblende around pyroxene.-

During the crystallization of magmas, not all minerals form simultaneously. If, for example, the magma originally has a basaltic composition, olivine, pyroxene, and calcium plagioclase will be among the earliest minerals to crystallize. Often these first-formed crystals are larger and more perfect than those formed later because, when they formed, there was ample space and an abundance of elements required for growth. Those minerals that crystallize later must fit into the remaining spaces and thus tend to be smaller and less perfect. Also, minerals enclosed in other minerals must have formed before the enclosing mineral. By using these observations of size and spatial relationships of minerals as viewed in thin sections of the rock, it is sometimes possible to make a reliable estimate of the order of crystallization of minerals in a magma.

During the first half of the present century, an eminent petrologist named *N. L. Bowen* studied the crystallization of artificial silicate melts in the laboratory and provided further evidence of the approximate order of crystallization of in gradually cooling magmas. Bowen used melts of basaltic composition for his experiments and was able to ascertain the specific temperature range over which particular silicate minerals would being to form. Olivine, for example, would crystallize first and at the highest temperature. Pyroxenes and the more calcium-rich feldspars would form next, followed by hornblende, biotite, and the more sodic feldspars. The order of crystallization, called the Bowen Reaction Series. It is called *reaction series* because early formed crystals react with silica in the remaining liquid and change to the next lower mineral in the series. For example, the silica in the magma would react with olivine crystals by simultaneously dissolving and precipitating the dissolved components so as to form pyroxene (augite), and pyroxene crystals would begin to grow in spaces between earlier formed crystals. At lower temperatures, the silica in the melt would similarly react with pyroxene to form hornblende, and subsequently hornblende would react with the liquid to form biotite. In these transformations, single tetrahedra of olivine utilize silica in the melt to form single chains of pyroxene, which in turn combine to form double chains of hornblende, which then combine to form sheets of biotite. For the complete sequence of changes to occur, however, the original magma must have sufficient magnesium, iron, and calcium. If the magma is rich in silica, and deficient in these elements, the first-formed crystals might be biotite and sodic feldspars, followed by potassium feldspar, muscovite and quartz. Thus reaction is prevented if the silica in the melt is exhausted in forming the early minerals. It is also prevented if minerals are removed from contact with the magma shortly after they have crystallized.

On the right branch of Bowen's chart, one can trace the changes that occur as calcium-rich plagioclase reacts with the magma to produce varieties of plagioclase that are successively richer in sodium. Because the plagioclase minerals maintain the same basic structure (triclinic) but change continuously in their content of calcium and sodium, the right side of the diagram was named the *continuous series.* The ferromagnesian or left side of the diagram depicts reactions that result in minerals with distinctly different structure. It was therefore termed a *discontinuous series.* The three minerals at the base of the chart do not react with the melt. By the time they crystallize, little liquid remains, and the residue of silicon, aluminum, oxygen, and potassium join to form orthoclase, muscovite, and quartz.

By examining thin sections of igneous rocks with the aid of a microscope, one can often see rather direct evidence of the reactions described above. It is not uncommon, for example, to find plagioclase crystals in which the innermost layers or zones are more calcium-rich and outer zones more sodium-rich. Similarly, reaction rims of pyroxene can be observed around olivine and rims of hornblende around pyroxene.

Textures of Igneous Rocks

Igneous rocks are classified according to two different classed of information, or categories. The first is according to chemical composition, as apparent from our study of magma and its differentiation into mafic and felsic types. Second is on the basis of the texture of the igneous rock. *Texture,* as the word applies to rocks, relates to the sizes and patterns of the mineral crystals present in the rock. Texture also distinguishes between the crystalline and the noncrystalline (glassy) state of mineral matter.

Gelogists use the term texture with somewhat the same meaning as it has in the classification of fabrics. We say that burlap or canvas has a "*coarse texture*", in contrast to the "*fine texture*" of chiffon. Cloth woven on a loom to produce threads that cross at right angles (warp and woof) contains a texture quite different from that of a knitted fabric. A garment can also be made from a sheet of film plastic that shows no structure. Perhaps this last material can be considered the equivalent of glass in the classification of rock texture.

The size of mineral crystals in a igneous rock depends largely upon the rate of cooling of the magma through the stages crystallization. As a general rule, rapid cooling results in small crystals, slow sooling in large crystals. Extremely sudden cooling will result in formation of a natural glass, which is noncyrtalline.

The rate of cooling depends on where the magma is located as it cools. Large bodies of magma trapped deep beneath the surface cool very slowly because the surrounding rock conducts the heat very slowly. Bodies of rock formed this way belong to the class of *intrusive igneous rocks*, whose mineral crystals are usually large enough to be identified with the unaided eye. Rapid cooling occurs in lava, which belongs to the class of *extrusive igneous rocks.* Lava forms thin layers that lose heat rapidly to the atmosphere or to overlying ocean water. Thus lava usually has mineral crystals too small to identify with the unaided eye, or it may solidify as a glass.

Among the crystalline igneous rocks, texture falls into two classes: (1) *Phaneritic texture* consists of crystals large enough to be seen with the unaided eye or with the help of small hand lens. *Aphanitic texture* consists of crystals too small to be distinguished as individual particles without the aid of a microscope.

The phaneritic igneous rocks have crystal grains ranging in diameter from 0.05 mm to over 10 mm. An accepted grade scale is as follows:

Fine-grained	0.05-1mm
Medium-grained	1-5mm
Coarse-grained	5-10mm
Pegmatite texture over	10 mm

Particles under 0.05 mm fall into the aphanitic texture class. Pegmatite texture consists of crystals that are often several centimeters long and in rare cases may be as long as a few meters.

Though it can be seen with the naked eye, the crystalline fabric of the phaneritic rocks is best studied under a specialized microscope in which very thin slices of the rock are examined under polarized light which makes possible mineral identification based upon distinctive optical properties. For the most part, external crystal forms are lacking or only poorly developed. On the the hand, evidences of cleavage show up well as linear markings within the grains.

Where crystals in the rock are all within the same size range, the texture is described as *equigranular.* Where a few large crystals, called *phenocrysts,* are embedded in a matrix, or *groundmass,* of smaller crystals, we have *porphyritic texture;* the rock is designated as a *porphyry* in addition to its proper name . The groundmass may consist of crystals ranging in size from fine-grained to coarse-grained, or it may consist of a glass.

Extrusive igneous rocks have distinctive textures resulting from the rapid expansion of volatile gases are confining pressure is reduced and cooling occurs. The specimen of volcanic *scoria* shown in Figure is full cavities formed by gas bubbles, and is said to have *scoriaceous texture.* Because the cavities go by the name of *vesicles,* an alternative adjective for this texture is *vesicular texture.* An extreme case of scoriaceous texture is seen in *pumice*, formed of magma frothed by expanding gases into a glassy rock of such low density that it easily floats on water. Pieces of pumice are used as abrasive blocks, while powdered pumice serves as an abrasive cleaning powder. In contrast, the volcanic glass also pictured in Figure is dense and free of such cavities. Notice is conchoidal fracture.

IDENTIFICATION OF IGENOUS ROCKS

Texture and mineral composition are the most useful properties for inferring the origin of igneous rocks and are the basis for classification and identification. Although there are hundreds of names used for igneous rocks, most of these represent variations of the relatively few major groups. In a widely used simple scheme, there are ten groups of crystalline igneous rocks: granite, granodiorite, diorite, gabbro, peridotite, rhyolite, dacite, andesite, basalt, and ultramafic extrusives.

In order to identify rocks in each of these groups, it is necessary to recognize texture and a few of the mineral constituents as they appear in the rock itself. To better identify the more common minerals, hold the rock in strong light and turn it back and forth so that you can see reflections from cleavage planes and crystal faces. Quartz can be recognized by its glassy appearance and mostly irregular reflecting surface. Feldspars show cleavage faces, may be white, gray, or pink, and often have rectangular outlines. One can often identify the feldspar as plagioclase by thin parallel striations that develop on one cleavage face. Orthoclase feldspar lacks these striations. Ferromagnesian are black or green. Among ferromagnesium, hornblende is more shiny and elongated than augite, and biotite may be distinguished by its smooth gleaming cleavage surfaces.

Rocks of the granitic clan

The light-colored igneous rocks are, as we have already noted, derived from high-silica magmas. When such magmas crystallize, they yield a high proportion of orthoclase feldspar and quartz. Granite is a familiar representative of this group and is recognized by its light color, phaneritic texture, and the presence of about 25 per cent quartz grains along with larger quantities of potassium feldspar (orthoclase) and sodium-plagioclase. Muscovite and biotite are present, as are small quantities of hornblende. *Granite*, of course, is well known to most of us because it has been used for centuries in the construction of buildings, statues, and monuments. It is not, however, the most abundant granitic rock. *Granodiorite*, somewhat less siliceous granitic rock, is more abundant. The sierra Neveda batholith is composed largely of granodiorite. The fine-grained equivalent of granodiorite is *dacite*. The more finely crystalline but compositional equivalent of granite is *rhyolite*. Actually, the basic aphanitic texture of rhyolite may range into the glassy condition. Many rhyolites tend to be porphyritic, with small phenocrysts of orthoclase, sodic plagioclase, quartz, and mica. Some appear to be welded tuffs. In color, rhyolites tend to be white, light gray, pink, or orange.

Rocks of the dioritic clan

Igneous rocks of the diorite clan include diorite itself and its aphanitic equivalent known as andesite. Diorite is a coarse-to fine-grained phaneritic rock containing less silica than granite or granodiorite but more than gabbro. Thus, in the gradations of composition across the rock chart, it is an intermediate rock type. The most abundant minerals are plagioclases, and these are compositionally in the mid range and contain both calcium and sodium. Quartz and orthoclase are very rare or absent in diorites. Among the ferromagnesian constituents, hornblende ocurs in amounts about equal to plagioclase, and biotite mica is a common accessory mineral. The color of diorite is controlled by its compositional makeup of nearly equal amounts of black ferromagnesians and grayish plagioclase. Thus, it tends to be rather drab gray or greenish gray in color.

The somber color of diorite prevails also in *andesite*- its aphanitic equivalent. Andesites, which were first identified in the summit volcanoes of the Andes Mountains of South America, are mostly found along the more mountainous continental borders and island arcs that surround the Pacific Ocean. In fact, geologists determine the true edge of the Pacific Basin by plotting a line, on the oceanic side of which rocks are principally basalt and on the continental side andsite. Geologists refer to this demarcation as the *andesite line*.

A member of the palgioclase family known as andesine is the most abundant mineral constituent of andesite. It is a mineral that contains nearly equal proportions of calcium and sodium. Dark minerals such as biotite, hornblende, and pyroxene are also prevalent in andesites. Andesites

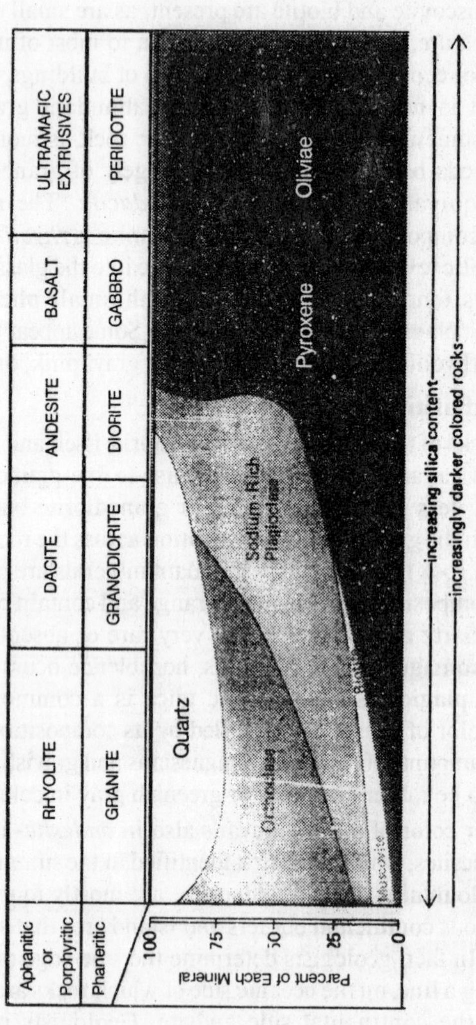

Fig.1.3. Diagram illustrating the mineralogic composition and texture of eight common igenous rocks. In order to ascertain the composition of a rock, estimate the percentages of each mineral beneath its name by reference to the percentage scale.

are intermediate between basalts and rhyolites in composition and also intermediate in relative abundance on the earth's surface.

Rocks of the gabbro clan

In *gabbro*, the chief mineral is labradorite plagioclase, which is darker and more calcium-rich than the plagioclase found in diorite. The typical ferromagnesian constituents are pyroxenes and olivine. Gabbros are typically coarsely crystalline plutonic rocks. One variety called anorthosite is composed mostly of intergrown calcium-rich plagioclase crystals. Anorthosite is characteristic of the lighter-colored crustal areas of the moon. Varieties of gabbro are frequently polished and used as ornamental stone because of their rich dark hue and the iridescent play of colors reflected by the plagioclase crystals.

Basalt is the aphanitic equivalent of gabbro and is the most abundant extrusive igneous rock. Basalts are mostly black or very dark gray and therefore darker than andesites. In thin section, they are found to contain myriads of elongate lathlike crystals of calcic plagioclase interspersed with pyroxene and olivine. Biotite and hornblende, which are common minerals in andesite, are sparse or absent in basalt.

The ultramafic clan

Ultramafic rocks are characterized by having a high density (3.3 g/cm^3), low percentage of silica (45 percent), and a major mineral composition of pyroxenes and olivine. *Peridotite*, in fact, is an ultramafic rock composed of 70 to 90 per cent olivine, while *pyroxenite* is almost entirely an intergrowth of pyroxene crystals. The ultramafic rocks are not common near or on the surface of the earth. They are occasionally encountered in the lower parts of magmatic bodies where dense ferromagnesian minerals accumulated by fractional crystallization and gravity settling. At several locations around the world, peridotites have pushed their way upward from great depths and penetrated near-surface rocks. Geologists are keenly interested in these peridotites, for they may represent samples of the earth's mantle.

Although peridotites contain a high percentage of olivine, they also contain 10 to 30 per cent pyroxene. When the olivine content in an ultramafic rock exceeds 90 per cent, the rock is called a *dunite*.

KINDS OF INTRUSIVE ROCKS BODIES

Bodies of intrusive igenous rocks that have solidified from magmas located deep within the crust are called *plutons*. The shape, size, and relations of plutons to surrounding rock is quite varied. Some represent injections of once molten rock parallel to preexisting strata. Such plutons are said to be *concordant*. In contrast, a pluton that cuts across layering is spoken of as *dicordant*.

Tabular plutons: sills and dikes

A tabular body of rocks is one shaped like a book or board, that is, having small thickness relative to its length and width. There are several kinds of tabular plutons. The concordant ones, which have been injected along bedding planes of sediment or between older lava flows, include *sills* and *lopoliths*. Sills may be either horizontal or tilted depending on the attitude of the enclosing beds. They range in thickness from only a centimeter to hundreds of meters. The well known Palisades of the Hudson River owe their distinctive appearance to columnar jointing in the exposed edge of the 300 meter-thick Palisades sill.

Because both sills and lava flows are sheetlike and parallel to adjacent beds, the distinction between a flow that has been buried by later strata and a sill can be difficult to make. There are, however, a few characteristics that are useful in distinguishing between the two features. Flows bake only the stratum beneath them, may fill the cracks only of the underlying bed, and in their upper portions may contain vesicles (small cavities made by gas bubbles in the lava). In contrast, sills bake the stratum above as well as the one below, penetrate cracks in both underlying and overlying beds, and rarely have vesicular borders.

Lopoliths are tabular pluton in which the roof and floor sag downward so as to give the overall shape of a bowl. Examples of these large-scale structures occur in the Bushveld Igneous complex of South Africa, as well as in the region around Duluth, Minnesota. The Duluth lopolith is estimated to have a diameter of 250 km. and thickness of 15 km. Lopoliths are composed of coarsely crystalline igneous rocks, as is to be expected in deeply buried bodies that have cooled slowly.

Dikes are tabular bodies that are *discordant* in that they cut across preexisting rock layers. Dikes may be many kilometers long and range in thickness from paper-thin to tens of meters. Also, a dike may thin out or alternately pinch and expand along its breadth. Many dikes branch and cross one another so as to form a complex system called a *dike swarm.* They also occur in circular patterns called *ring dikes.* Ring dikes are thought to develop when lava rises into concentric fractures created around an area where overlying rocks sink into a magma chamber below. Although dikes may be composed of nearly any kind of igneous rock, most are basaltic in composition and were derived from magmas of low viscosity.

Batholiths

In many areas of former intrusive igneous activity, great discordant nontabular masses of intrusive rock occur. The largest of such bodies form the cores of great mountain ranges. They are known as batholiths. Among the better known examples are the Idaho Batholith, the Coast Range Batholith of British Columbia, and the Sierra Nevada Batholith of California. Each of these immense bodies of igneous rock actually represents the coalescence of several smaller intrusions of granites and granodiorites. Granitic rocks of this kind form the bulk of most of the world's batholiths.

To be termed a *batholith*, the intrusive body must have an areal extent greater than 100 km^2. In shape, they may be irregular or roughly cylindric. It is difficult to determine the depth to the base of existing batholiths, for at no place on earth is the bottom of batholith exposed for study. However, investigations based on gravity measurements and earthquake data suggest that batholiths begin to form at depth of about 30 km. As intrusive masses, batholiths were once deeply covered by pre-existing rocks. We see batholithic rocks at the surface of the earth today only because great thicknesses of covering rocks have been removed by erosion. Batholiths are usually located in present or former mountainous belts, and such regions are subject to frequent episodes of uplift, which in turn greatly increase the rates of erosion.

Batholiths intrude into *country rock* (pre-existing rock) in a variety of ways. In some places there is evidence that the melt has been forcefully injected. Elsewhere, the heat of the magma appears to have been sufficient to melt surrounding country rock so that the magma melted its way upward. Such a process would, of course, change the composition of the magma. *Stoping*, a process by which magma moves upward as blocks of country rock are wedged loose and fall into the magma chamber, provides another mechanism for batholiths to work their way upward. The upward migration of magma may also be aided by density differences. Magma that is less dense than the enclosing rock to rise bouyantly toward the surface.

As the magma makes it way upward, pieces of the enclosing country rock may spall off and fall into the melt. Some of these fragments may melt and be assimilated by the magma. Included fragments of unmelted country rock are called *xenoliths*, meaning "stranger rocks". Xenoliths also occur in lavas when pieces of rock are torn from the sides of volcanic vents and fissures during eruptions.

Laccoliths are massive concordant plutons that have a mushroom shape. Like sills, they are formed by magma that has been injected into bedding planes. However, unlike sills, they dome-up the overlying rock layers. Some laccoliths represent bulges on the surface of a sill, whereas others are self-contained structures fed by a vent from an underlying magma. Most laccoliths have a granitic composition. Surface exposures of laccoliths can be found in the Henry, LaSal, and Abajo Mountains of Southeastern Utah.

Chapter 2

VOLCANISM

The most apparent and spectacular manifestations of extrusive igneous activity are seen in volcanoes. Nearly everyone would recognize a volcano if he or she saw one, yet they are not easily defined. A *volcano* is a vent in the earth's crust through which molten rock, steam, gas, and ash are expelled. The fragments expelled and the solidified molten rock usually form a mound or peak around the vent. For geologists, volcanoes are dynamic, usually accessible, natural laboratories where they can obtain valuable information about the earth's interior and the way in which igneous melts solidify to form rocks.

Volcanic activity has been an important process on this planet throughout the long span of geologic time. In the earliest stages of the earth's history, volcanoes contributed their products to form parts of the earth's crust. The gases and vapors emitted by the blistering array of primordial volcanoes provided the substance of an earlier atmosphere and of the oceans. Fortunately, volcanic eruptions are probably less frequent today, as compared with those early times, yet eruptions do still occur on nearly all continents, as well as on the floors of the oceans. We view some of these eruptions on television and are able to witness in safety the devastation they cause. Volcanoes evoke not only awe and fear, but also respect for the enormous forces that operate uneasily beneath the frail crust on which we live. Our planet is not a great lifeless blob of cold rock making an annual trip around the sun. It is constantly changing and vibrant with igneous activity. During 1979 alone, the Scientific Event Alert Network at the Smithsonian Institute in Washington, D.C., provided daily observations of eruptions in Japan, Guatemala, the Aleutians, and Mount St. Helens.

THE ERUPTION PROCESS AND ITS PRODUCTS

All volcanic eruptions are rooted in a two-step process that precedes the eruptions. The first step is the melting of rock masses tens of kilometers below the earth's surface to produce *magma,* which is molten rock containing dissolved water and other gases. The second step is the movement of this magma toward the earth's surface. The first step determines the initial temperature and composition of the magma; the second step controls the nature and timing of eruption. Let us consider the material that is produced . Then we will examine the main stages in the volcanic process. Some general sources that may be consulted for amplification include: MacDonald (1972), Sheets and Grayson (1979), and Tazieff an Sabroux (1983).

We will use names designating four types of magma, which can be distinguished on the basis of their content (weight-percent) of silica (SiO_2): (1) basaltless than 50 percent silica; (2) andesite-52 to 55 percent silica; (3) dacite-60 to 65 percent silica; and (4) rhyolite-more than 70 percent silica. These magmas and the rocks formed from them are not generally defined on this criterion alone, but this will suffice for the purposes of this chapter.

Magmas are very hot liquids; temperatures range from as low as 600°C to 1250°C. These magmas differ greatly in the ease with which they will flow and in the ease with which the dissolved gases can escape from them. In general, basalt magma, which is relatively low in silica, flows most easily and is therefore said to have the lowest *viscosity.* Rhyolite magma, which is silica rich, flows less easily and has the highest viscosity. These viscosity difference are important in controlling the physical form that eruptions take. For example, a low-viscosity magma may be erupted in lava fountains and lava flows, whereas a high-viscosity magma rarely displays these forms of eruption.

The gases dissolved in magma are especially important in determining the physical behavior of the magma as it nears the surface and is erupted. It appears that andesitic, dacitic, and rhyolitic magmas generally contain much higher concentrations of dissolved gases than basaltic magma. In general, water constitutes more than half of the total dissolved gases .

The composition of the magma erupted at a particular volcano or fissure is determined by the nature of the rock being melted, by the depth at which melting takes place, and by processes that take place as the magma interacts with other rocks and fluids. Studies of the rocks erupted at many different volcanoes show that magma has been generated for thousands or millions of years at sites deep beneath these volcanoes. In oceanic settings like Hawaii or Iceland, the magma, which is typically basalt, is generated within the upper mantle of the earth. In subduction zone settings like the Aleutians or the Cascades of the northwestern United States, andesitdcites, and rhyolites may be generated by the partial melting of

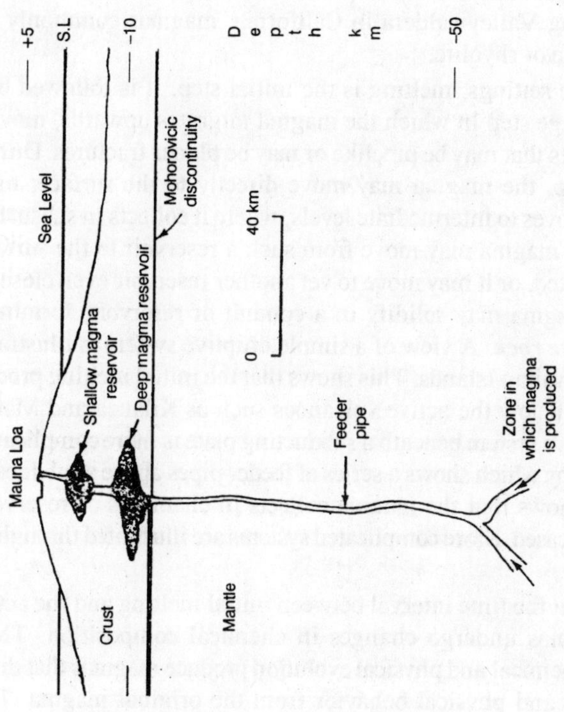

Fig. 2.1. Diagram showing magma source, feeder channel, and magma reservoirs at two levels beneath Mauna Loa volcano, Hawaii.

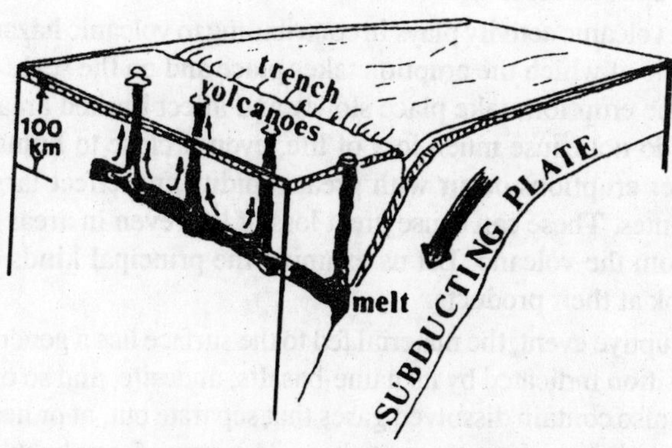

Fig. 2.2. Magmatic feeder pipes above a subducting plate.

crustal rocks overlying the mantle. In continental settings away from subduction zones, such as those represented by Valles Caldera in New Mexica, or Long Valley caldera in California, magmas commonly are silica-rich dacite or rhyolite.

In all these settings, melting is the initial step. It is followed by a second multistage step in which the magma migrates upwards, moving through conduits that may be pipelike or may be planar fractures. During this second step, the magma may move directly to the surface; more commonly it moves to intermediate levels, where it collects in subsurface reservoirs. The magma may move from such a reservoir to the surface, where it is erupted, or it may move to yet another reservoir even closer to the surface. Magma may solidify in a conduit or reservoir, forming a body of *intrusive rock.* A view of a simple eruptive system is illustrated here for the Hawaiian Islands. This shows that the initial melting process takes place far below the active volcanoes such as Kilauea and Mauna Loa. The eruptive system beneath a subducting plate is more complicated, as is suggested by which shows a series of feeder pipes above a subducting plate. It also shows that the magma collects in chambers or reservoirs before being released. More complicated systems are illustrated throughout the chapter.

Throughout the time interval between initial melting and the actual eruption, magmas undergo changes in chemical composition. These proecesses of chemical and physical evolution produce magmas that differ in composition and physical behavior from the original magma. This evolution commonly is reflected in the sequential eruption of different kinds of magma from a single volcano. This sequence also leads to changes in the kinds of eruptions observed over time.

The role that volcanic activity plays in contributing to volcanic hazard depends on the rate at which the eruption takes place and on the scale of the eruption. Some eruptions take place slowly and affect limited areas. These eruptions do not cause much loss of life, even if close to human settlements. Other eruptions occur with great rapidity and effect large areas within minutes. These can cause great loss of life, even in areas at some distance from the volcano. Let us examine the principal kinds of eruptions and look at their products.

During an eruptive event, the material fed to the surface has a general chemical composition indicated by its name-basalts, andesite, and so on. The magma may also contain dissolved gases that separate out, at or near the surface of the earth, as a separate vapor phase. This vapor forms bubbles with in the magma. Thus, at the moment of eruption, the material emitted is a mixture of molten magma, gases, and fragments of solid rock. The character of the eruption depends on the relative abundances of these materials, on the total supply available, and on the geologic setting.

Erupted material that consists largely of molten rock is called *lava.* Highly fluid lava may be erupted in fountains, such as those displayed at Kilauea on the island of Hawaii or in Icelandic volcanoes. These fountains are sites at which gases escape from the magma. The lava may also flow across the surface, forming *lava flows.* Highly viscous lavas may form short and stubby flows that pile up on one another in the crater of the volcano, forming *domes.* The less viscous lavas form flows that may extend many kilometers from the source. Lava ordinarily moves about as fast as a person can walk. On steep slopes, however, lava can move much faster. When activity stops, each flow remains on the surface, forming a deposit that represents a net addition to the landscape.

Where an eruption is driven by the expansion of gases dissolved in the magma or by superheated ground water flash-boiling into steam, eruptions take on a different character. These eruptions are highly explosive. If the expanding water vapor comes from ground water in the pores of the rock of which the volcano is made, the eruption is called a *phreatic eruption.* During these explosive eruptions, hot fragmental material is ejected from the volcano. The same material may be ejected during less explosive eruptions as well. Two general terms are used interchangeably for this fragmental material: *pyroclastic material* and *tephra.* Tephra will be the term generally used here.

When fragmental material is ejected, it consists of blebs of still molten magma and crystalline rock fragments. The molten magma blebs quickly chill into glass. The crystalline rock fragments consist of older rocks torn from the walls of feeder pipes and the upper part of the volcano. These fragments range in size from blocks much larger than a loaf of bread down to particles that are only fractions of a millimeter in diameter. Some of the larger pieces have streamlined forms and are sometimes called *bombs.* The smaller particles are called *lapillae, ash,* and *dust.* Much of the finer material is produced when the expanding gas bubbles explode the hot glassy material within which they are at first contained. We see evidence of this process in the rocks called *pumice* and *vesicular basalt,* which contain closely spaced spherical and tubular cavities surrounded by glassy rock. In these rocks the bubbles were growing but not so rapidly or forcibly that they could shatter the surrounding rock. Where this kind of bubble growth occurs more forcibly, the enclosing rock is shattered to form pyroclastic material.

Tephra may be erupted vertically, rising in great clouds above active volcanoes. This airborne tephra may then drift downwind and settle out in deposits that are thickest closest to the source. However, during some typed of eruptions, fragmental material follows as path down the slopes of a volcano, remaining close to the ground as it moves. Many different names are used to describe these eruptions and the material driven out and deposited by them. Some of the terms used to describe the eruptive activity include *lateral blast, directed blast, pyroclastic flows and surges,* and *nuees ardentes*. In all instances the moving is hot, contains entrained gases, and moves very rapidly. This kinds of activity is the source of the worst volcanic hazard.

A geologic record of volcanic activity in any region exists in the form of lava flows, ash falls, cinder cones, and tephra deposits. The landscape may also provide a record of the centers and fissures from which these eruptions have been generated. On mid ocean islands like Hawaii, these centers are represented by volcanic craters and by fissures that open on the flanks of the volcanoes. In other settings, such as Mono Lake in California, the relatively flat terrain may be dotted with small cinder cones. Some volcanic areas are also marked by large circular depressions called *calderas.* Such structures mark the sites at which a very large volume of lava has been erupted in very short period of time. This sudden expulsion of so much magma leads to the collapse of a circular rock mass to form the depression we call the *caldera.*

In regions such as the active subduction zones around the rim of the Pacific, the volcanic record is extremely complicated. It is dominated by great stratovolcanoes built up of interleaved lava flows and tephra. The rocks in these volcanoes are dominantly andesites and dacites, but basalts and rhyolites may also be present. Within regions of older subduction-zone activity, there are also thick and areally extensive deposits of dacite or rhyolite that formed entirely from fragmental material discharged in fast moving ash flows. Some of the largest of these are associated with giant calderas, and they represent the material erupted from the reservoir beneath the site of the calderas.

These are the basic forms that eruptive activity can take. These forms will become more familiar through a consideration of the case histories. These case histories are presented for a very specific purpose: To show clearly the contribution of the different forms of eruption to volcanic hazard.

LAVA TYPES AND THEIR PROPERTIES

Magma reaching the earth's surface as molten lava gives rise to a wide variety of igneous phenomena with external forms as many and varied as the internal structures and textures. To a large extent this great variety reflects the chemical and physical properties of the liquid lava. (The word "lava" is used for both the liquid magma and the solid rock formed when the magma cools.)

We have already named and described the kinds of extrusive igneous rocks. Generally speaking, each extrusive rock is similar in composition to a particular intrusive type, and these range from felsic to mafic, with extreme types-the syenite group and the ultramafic group-forming the ends of a continuous series. Lavas are classified in a similar manner, but with minor differences in the groups recognized. A threefold classification of lava types is as follow:

Parent magma type	*Class of lava*	*Kind of extrusive rock*
Felsic	Acidic(Silicic)	Rhyolite
Intermediate	Intermediate	Andesite
Mafic	Basic	Basalt

According to this classification, *acidic lavas (silicic lavas)* contain 70% or more of silica (SiO_2); *intermediate lavas, 50% to 70%; basic,* less than 50%.

Properties associated with lavas are temperature, viscosity, and explosiveness. *Viscosity,* a property of all fluids (including both liquids and gases) , describes the degree to which the fluid resists flowage when subjected to unbalanced forces. Everyday words that described different states of viscosity are "runny" and "tacky". For example, in making caramel, we begin with a mixture of water and dissolved sugar. At low temperature, this liquid is runny-i.e., it has low viscosity. After the mixture is boiled for several minutes and then cooled it thickness and becomes tacky-i.e., it develops high viscosity. Fluids of high viscosity flow sluggishly as compared to fluids of low viscosity in the same situation.

The basic lavas, most commonly of the composition of basalt magma, have high temperature and low viscosity as they emerge from the solid earth. Although direct measurements are few, temperatures of basic (basaltic) magma have been observed in the range of 1100° C to 1200°C. Lava of this type moves rapidly and travels far over comparatively gentle land slopes often spreading into thin sheets before solidifying.

As a general rule, basic magma is not explosive in behavior, and even in large quantities it tends to erupt quietly. Explosiveness is related to the presence of gases under high pressure in the magma. Basic Magma that is low in water content (a "dry" magma) tends not to be explosive because the proportion of volatiles is small. Besides, the proportion of silicon-oxygen tetrahedra in the magma is smaller than the felsic magma s. As we noted earlier, a linkage of these tetrahedra into groups exists in magma and may be one cause of its greater viscocity in the felsic types.

The acidic lavas, felsic composition, have tempretures in the range from 800 °C to 1000 °C - somewhat lower than for the basic lavas. The viscocity of acidic lava is generally high, so that this lava flows more slowly and congeals closer to itss place of emergence than the basic type. Explosiveness of the acidic lavas is often very great, and it produces some extremely violent types of volcanic eruptions. Lavas of the intermediate class have properties between the basic and acidic types, but they tend to be more closelyakin to the acidic type in physical behavior.

Lava Flows

A tongue or sheet of lavs formed at a particular time and place is called a *lava flow.* Lava may emerge from the localized central vent of a volcano, in which case it travels away from the vent as a narrow tongue following any one of a number of radial paths. Lava (usually of basaltic composition) may also emerge from a long crack, or *fissure,* in the brittle surface rock, and then it flows out as a succession of thin sheets, known as *fissure flows,* covering considerable surface area . In highly fluid basalt flows, liquid lava may be seen exposed in the central zone of the flow and close to the vent , but usually, because of rapid cooling, the surface and margins of a lava flow are encrusted with solid lava.

Lava flows move downhill under the force of gravity to occupy any available valley or topographic depression. Where the solidified crust of a flow forms a strong structural arch, fluid lava beneath may move out to lower levels, leaving a hollow lava tube or tunnel within the flow.

Flow surface may be extremely rough (*aa texture*), where the lava is highly charged with gases and produced a scoriaceous texture. Other basalt flow have smooth, glassy outer surfaces convoluted into billowy and ropy configurations (*pahoehoe texture)*.

Upon solidification, the interiors of many lava flows exhibit the same type of columnar jointing previously mentioned as characteristic of thin sills and dikes . Lavas may flow into the ocean or may erupt from vents or fissures beneath the ocean. Upon cooling, these water-quenched lavas develop a characteristic *pillow structure* and are known as *pillow lavas*

Pyroclastic Materials

Quite different from lava flows as a class of extrusive rock are *pyroclastic materials*, consisting of *pyroclasts-* rocks and mineral fragments blown out from a volcanic vent under pressure of rapidly expanding gases present in the magma. When projected into the air the pyroclastic fragments are either solid or in a plastic state that occurs immediately prior to solidification. Fragments of the country rock are commonly included in pyroclastic masses.

Pyroclasts are classified in terms of the size of the fragments. The largest are huge solid blocks, and the smallest range down in size to the finest dusts. Spindle shaped or spherical masses a few centimeters to 30 cm or more in diameter, known as *volcanic bombs,* result from the congealing of blebs of fluid lava thrown high into the air. Blebs of plastic lava falling close to a small vent may build a small *spatter cone* . Smaller particles of scoriaceous lava, ranging in diameter from 4 to 25 mm, are called *lapilli,* Particles under about 4 mm constitute *volcanic ash* . Ash particles range downward in size to the fine *volcanic dust* which can be transported for thousands of kilometers in the upper atmosphere. Upon microscopic examination, particles of fine ash will be found to take the form of minute *shards* of volcanic glass.

Tephra is a convenient term widely used by geologists to describe collectively all the varieties and sizes of pyroclastic materials. Thus, all extrusive igneous material consists of lava, of tephra, or of a combination of the two.

Pyroclastic Deposits and Rocks

Accumulations of tephra- *pyroclastic deposits-* form a class intermediate between the igneous and the sedimentary rocks. Pyroclasts are transported by or descend through air or water, but this occurs immediately at the time of volcanic eruption, and thus the original impelling force is volcanic.

Volcanic breccia, a crude mixture of large and small pyroclastic that have fallen close to vent, is a form of rock more closely allied to the igneous than to the sedimentary class. Volcanic breccia is also found in volcanic pipes and may include fragments of country rock. Quite different is tuff, volcanic ash that has been transported by winds or water and deposited layers. It may become compacted into a stratified rock sometimes classed as sedimentary.

A unique form of volcanic material is that carried in *ash flows,* consisting of a highly heated mixture of gases and frothed lava. This phenomenon is called *glowing avalanche* (in French, *nuee ardente).* Moving as a dense, cloud like tongue down the slopes of a volcano, the glowing avalanche leaves a fine-textured rock layer resembling tuff but fused into hard layers by the high temperature. This rock is called a *welded tuff.*

Five Notable Eruptions

Civilized humans have lived on this planet for only a few thousand years. During this time, many noteworthy volcanic eruptions have occurred. Nearly all of the recent eruptions and a few of the older ones have been documented and are a part of recorded history. Many of the most ancient accounts of volcanic activity are associated with superstition and mythology. Some, like Plato's story of the eruption of Santorini, contain just enough information to be intriguing. A more objective account of volcanic phenomena was provided by Pliny the Younger during the A.D. 79 eruption of vesuvius. Pliny factual observations, set down in two letters to the Roman historian Tacitus, are considered one of the earliest contributions to the scientific study of volcanoes.

Santorini

The islands of Santoria in the Aegean Sea mark the location of an eruption of particular interest to historians. This eruption, which occurred about 1470 B.C., may have destroyed a highly developed Minoan culture that had spread from Crete. Because the eruption resulted in explosive destruction of most of the island of Santorin, it may very well have given rise to the ancient legends of Atlantis, the "lost continent". The only known account of this event was written by *Plato* in 355 B.C. He described a city called Atlantis that was built on a circular plan about 24 km in diameter. The city was on an island that sank beneath the sea during a war with the Athenians. During this war, wrote Plato, "there occurred portentious earthquakes and floods, and one grievous day and night befell them when the whole body....of warriors was swallowed up by the earth, and the island of Atlantis in like manner was swallowed up by the sea and vanished".

Today, the name Santoria applies to a small group of islands that enclose a nearly circular bay about 10 km in diameter. The islands are remnants of the large volcanic cone that was the probable source for Plato's story, and they bay is a submerged area that formed by collapse of the central part of the volcano. Careful investigations by archaeologists working in this area have revealed a story of volcanic and earthquake activity to rival that of Pompeii. The major eruptions were apparently

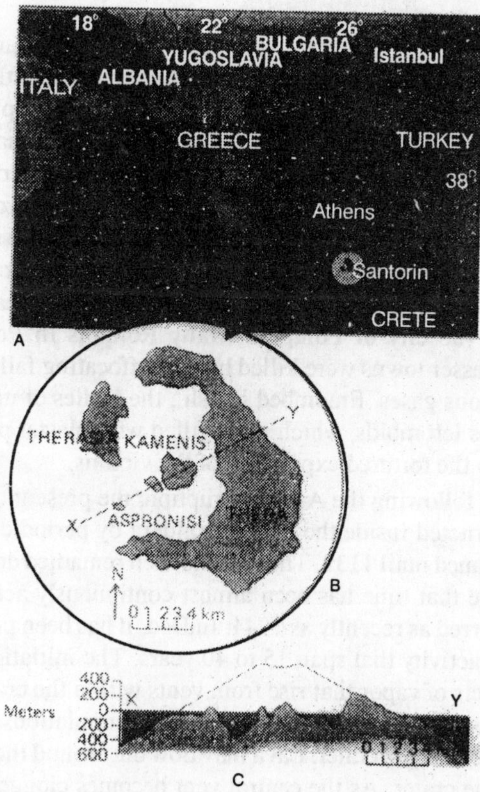

Fig. 2.3. (a) Map of part of the Mediterranean areaz showing the location of the Santorini volcanic complex. (b) Map of the islands of the Santorini complex. (c) Cross-section along line X-Y. Dashed line suggests probable profile of the volcanic cone before its explosive destruction.

preceded by earthquakes. These tremors so terrified the local inhabitants that they gathered their possession and fled to safer ground. This probably accounts for the absence of human skeletons in the excavations of the ruins of the principal town, Akrotira. The eruption itself was of enormous magnitude. Towns and villages were completely buried in ash, and ocean waves generated by associated earthquakes ravaged towns all around Crete. Many believe these catastrophic events contributed to the eventual demise of the Minoan civilization.

Vesuvius

Prior to the year A.D.79, Vesuvius was a cone-shaped mountain with a rounded summit reaching 1200 meters above the shoreline of the Bay of Naples. Fertile vineyards clothed its lower slopes, and the people who lived nearby considered the volcano then known as Monte Somma- to be dead. It was, however, only sleeping. Its awakening was signaled by an increase in earthquakes for several years before the now famous eruption. Then, on August 24th, 79 A.D., Vesuvius blasted away an entire side of Monte Somma, covered the surrounding countryside with a thick gray blanket of ashes and cinders, and formed a hug e caldera. Beneath the blanket of ash lay the city of Pompeii. Many Romans in Pompeii Herculaneum, and lesser towns were killed by the suffocating fall of ash and blasts of poisonous gases. Entombed in ash , the bodies of many of these hapless victims left molds, which when filled with plaster provide casts that show even the tortured expression of the victims.

In the centuries following the A.D. 79 eruption, the present cone of Vesuvius was constructed inside the Somma caldera by periodic bursts of activity that continued until 1139. The volcano then remained dormant until 1631, but since that time has been almost continuously active. A major eruption occurred as recently as 1944. Indeed, it has been possible to discern cycles of activity that span 15 to 40 years. The initiation of a cycle is marked by jets of vapor that rise from vents within the crater. In a second stage, emissions become explosive, and accumulations of ash are built up on the floor of the crater. Lava may flow out around the cones and gradually fill the crater. As the central vent becomes clogged with solid lava, internal pressures build until violent explosions burst the plug and thereby release the pressure. The culminating eruptions are accompanied by a tremendous outpouring of ash, gas, and lava, usually within two or three weeks the pressures are sufficiently relieved and another cycle begins.

Krakatoa

Krakatoa is an island in the Strait of Sunda between Java and Sumatra. It was originally constructed of the materials ejected from several volcanoes that had grown upward from the sea floor. On Sunday, May 20, 1883, Krakatoa came suddenly to life, announcing its awakening with a series of explosive blasts that could be heard by the inhabitants of islands

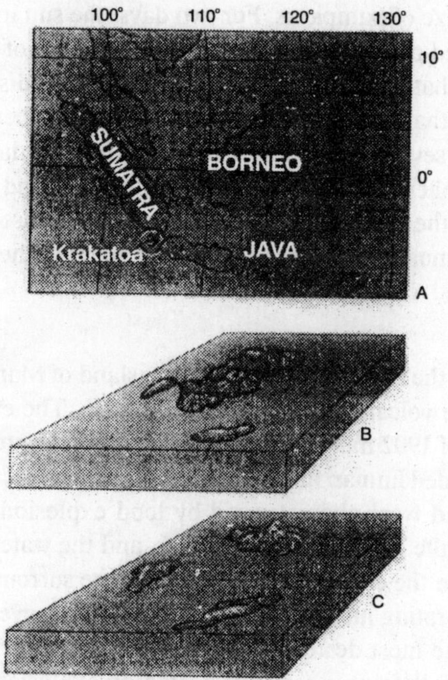

Fig. 2.4. (A) Map showing location of Krakatoa. (B) Appearence of the Krakatoa complex just before the 1883 eruption. (C) Island remnants of the rim of Krakatoa after the 1883 explosive eruption.

nearly 150 km away. On the following day, ships passing through the Sunda Strait could easily see the tall column of steam and ash that rose over 11 km into the atmosphere and showered debris over a radius of 480 km. Activity continued with gradually diminishing intensity until the final week in August. At that time, a series of tremendous explosions shook the islands, and ash began to fall in quantities never before known in human experience. Indeed, the sound of the accompanying barrages was loud enough to wake sleeping people in South Australia, over 3000 km away. In islands far across the Pacific, people ran to vantage points along the beach, thinking they had heard a ship in distress signaling for help by firing its guns. A series of destructive *tsunami* (great oceanic waves triggered by earthquakes) tore through the Sunda Straits, crushing towns and killing over 36,000 people . The cloud of ash over Krakatoa climbed 80 km, and terrified sailors on ships over 40 km away were pelted with volcanic bombs the size of pumpkins, For two days, the sun in that area was completely blotted out by ash and dust. When a vessel of the Royal Dutch Navy covered that about 65 per cent of the island had disappeared. The immense crater that had formed now lay submerged beneath 300 meters of water. For several years following the eruption, dust thrown into the upper atmosphere caused brilliant red sunsets around the earth. By blocking part of the sun's radiation, the dust also caused a slight lowering of mean annual temperatures and irregular weather patterns around the world.

Mount pelee

Ten km north of the city of St. Pierre on the island of Martinique in the west Indies is the volcano known as Mount Pelee. The eruption of Mount Pelee in May of 1902 must surely qualify as one of the great natural catastrophed in recorded human history. Eruptions of the volcano began in the late March and were characterized by loud explosions and ash showers. The rim of the crater broke on May 5, and the water that had been contained within the crater rushed down into the surrounding low coastal areas, incorporating mud and debris and destroying everything in its path. However, the most destructive part of the eruption was yet to come. On may 8 th, following a series of deafening explosions, a great purplish cloud rose from the top of mountain and rolled rapidly down the slopes of mountain, spreading fanlike as it engulfed the town of St. Pierre. Within the next two minute all but two of the inhabitants of the town were killed- presumably by the searing heat. One of the survivors was a murderer imprisoned in the town's dungeon, and the other a shoemaker whose escape seems to defy explanation. In the wake of the hot gases, the entire town was left in flames.

A cloud of incandescent dust, ash, and gases such as that which flowed down the slope of Mount Pelee is known as a *nuee ardente.* (fiery cloud) A nuee ardente may take a high toll in lives whenever it passes through a heavily populated area. The extreme mobility of this fiery cloud is caused by the expanding hot gases, which contain cinders and ash. The solid particles give the cloud the density required to keep it close to the slope. Cooler air, trapped within the front of the hot moving mass, expands and increases the turbulence. It is this storm of turbulence that provides the destructive force of nuee ardente.

The eruption of Mount Pelee did not stop after the destruction of the city. A second nuee ardente swept through the desolated town on May 20. Another eruption killed 2000 people in the small village of Morne Rouge on August 30.

Mount St. Helens

Until recently many mainland Americans preferred to believe that volcanic eruptions were hazardous geologic events that occurred mostly elsewhere. This belief was shattered at 8:31 A.M. on May 18, 1980, when Mount St. Helens in Washington exploded with the energy equivalent of 50 million tons of TNT and a roar that was heard 300 km away from the once scenic mountain. A great turbulent cloud of hot gases, steam, pulverized rock, and ash burst laterally from the north side of the mountain, followed by a vertical column of gas and ash that rose 20,000 meters into the atmosphere, and began to drift slowly toward the east. An estimated 1 km^3 of airborne ash and other rock debris from the explosion blocked out the sun's light and caused automatic street lights to switch on in towns hundreds of kilometers downwind from the rumbling volcano. Turbulent hot masses of gas and ash surged down the mountain sides, flattening millions of trees in scorched irregular rows. Meanwhile, the ash fell like a dismal gray snow, blanketing streets, dangerously burdening the roofs of buildings, choking the engines of vehicles, and covering the leaves of trees and crops . Hot gas and ash from the volcano melted part of St. Helens' snow, and ice cap, and the resulting meltwater mixed with ash and formed mudflows, which surged down the mountain slopes at speeds as great as 80 km per hour. The steaming turbulent mass of debris crashed through the once beautiful valley of the Toutle River and demolished 123 homes in the nearby town of Toutle. People camping or working near the volcano were killed by heat, gases , or burial under the downpour of ash. The May 18th eruption was clearly a major volcanic event. The fact that it was actually rather puny when compared with the famous eruptions of Krakatoa or Santorini was no consolation to the citizens of Washington as they viewed the devastated gray landscape, the hundreds of square kilometers of valuable trees toppled like matchsticks, buried roads, harbors choked with ash-sludge, and smothered fields of wheat.

Mount St. Helens had been dormant since 1857. Its period of rest ended on March 27, 1980, when the peak emitted the first puffs of ash and gas. It seemed a warning signal. Intermittent activity of a relatively mild nature occurred between March 27, 1980, and the massive explosion of May 18. In the wake of the May 18th explosion, there were smaller but nevertheless impressive eruptions of ash. Late in May and in early June, the reddish glow of hot lava was clearly visible to observers on the ground.

The recent activity at Mount St. Helens, and the older eruptions that gave us the volcanic peaks of the Cascades, are surface manifestations of an ongoing collision between two of the earth's crustal plates. One of these is the American Plate, and the other is the small Gorda Plate or Juan de Fuca Plate of the eastern Pacific, which moves eastward on a collision course toward the coasts of Oregon and Washington. The Gorda Plate plunges beneath the coastline, and molten rock generated as the plate moves downward rises to supply the lava of the volcanoes.

Before its recent major eruption, the beautifully symmetric summit of Mount St. Helens stood nearly 3000 meters above sea level. The May 18 th eruption obliterated the upper 400 meters of the peak and also destroyed part of the rock record of earlier eruptions. Fortunately, geologists had previously determined the eruptive history of the volcano. That history was deciphered by careful study of radiocarbon dates obtained from pieces of charred wood enclosed in ash and lava, as well as by careful reconstruction of the super positional order of the layers of volcanic materials. The studies revealed that Mount St. Helens was first active 37,000 years ago. The more recent eruptions can be grouped roughly into four episodes of activity, namely, 2500 to 1600 B.C., 1200 to 800 B.C., 400B.C. to A.D. 400, and A.D. 1300 to middle of the 19th century. During some eruptions the principal products were ash and lava, whereas at other times molten rock too thick to flow freely moved into the crater and piled up over the vents. These glowing viscous masses of lava congealed to form features called *plug domes.* In addition to extrusions of lava and ejections of ash, ancient eruptions were also characterized by the development of mudflows similar to those which have caused so much recent destruction.

When the current cluster of eruptions has ended, how safe will Mount St. Helens be? The history of past activity indicates that those who insist on living and working near the peak do so at risk of property and life. It is interesting that this opinion was expressed five years before the recent catastrophe by U.S. Geological *D. R. Crandell, D. R. Mullineaux,* and *M. Rubin.* In the abstract of their report in *Science* these geologists stated:

Mount St. Helens volcano in southern Washington has erupted many times during the last 4,000 years, usually after brief dormant periods.

This behavior pattern suggests that the volcano... will erupt again with in the next few decades. Potential volcanic hazards of several kinds should be considered in planning for land use near the volcano.

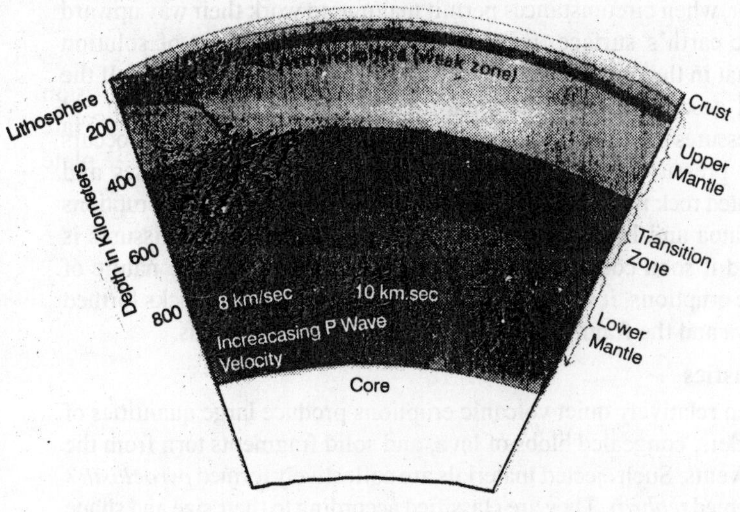

Fig. 2.5. ***Parts of the earth's interior. Boundaries between zones are indicated by changes in the velocity of earthquake waves.***

The Products of Volcanism

Volcanic ash, glass, and rocks are the solidified products of a lavas, which in turn were derived from magma. Depending on the composition of the parent magma, a volcanic eruption may be violently explosive or consist of a relatively quiet outpouring of lava. In general, lavas rich in iron and magnesium tend to flow relatively quietly. Their low silica content makes extensive oxygen-sharing between silica tetrahedra unnecessary. As a result, networks of linked tetrahedra do not form, and individual tetrahedra have great mobility in the melt. The melt has considerable fluidity and flows like honey. In contrast, lavas rich in silica form networks of covalently bonded tetrahedra, which impart high viscosity to the lava. Such lavas are associated with explosive volcanic activity.

In addition to the elements that are involved in the formation of igneous rocks, magmas also contain water and such gases as carbon dioxide, nitrogen, and sulfur dioxide. Water, which may comprise 1 to 9 per cent of the parent melt, expands to 1700 times its former volume when it changes from a liquid to a gas. Pressures resulting from this expansion are sufficient to cause spectacular eruptions. At the great depths where magmas are generated , they tend to hold water and gases in solution. However, when circumstances permit magmas to work their way upward near the earth's surface, water and gases may come out of solution somewhat in the manner of the bubbles in a carbonated soft drink. If the released gases and vapors become trapped as by a congealed plug of lava, pressures may build up underground until a volcanic explosion occurs and the pressures are released. Vast quantities of steam, gases and fragmented rock may be thrown skyward, as was the case during eruptions of Krakatoa and Pelee. The liquid that flows from vents or fissures is lava, and it soon cools into solid rock. Before discussing the nature of volcanic eruptions, it will be useful to describe some of the rocks formed from lava and the fragmented solids ejected during eruptions.

Pyroclastics

Even relatively quiet volcanic eruptions produce large quantities of ash, cinders, congealed blobs of lava, and solid fragments torn from the walls of vents. Such ejected materials are collectively termed *pyroclastics* (also termed *tephra*). They are classified according to their size and shape . *Bombs* for example, are rounded or ellipsoid masses ranging in diameter from only 4 mm to several meters. They frequently display a twisted appearance resulting from the flow of still molten material during ejection. *Blocks* are solid angular pieces of rock greater than 32 mm in diameter. They consist of pieces of the crustal layers beneath the volcano or older lavas broken from the walls of the vent or edge of the crater. Blocks weighing hundreds of tons have been thrown several kilometers during particularly explosive eruptions. In contrast to bombs and blocks, smaller proteoclastics include *lapilli* (Italian meaning little stones), which are mostly the size of gravel, *cinders* (sand size particles of pulverized lava), and *ash*. All of these fragments of volcanic ejecta can be consolidated or lithified to form the so-called pyroclastic rocks. If round in shape, the larger fragments from agglomerates, and if angular, *volcanic breccias*. The rocks from cinders and ash are called *volcanic tuffs*. *Welded tuffs* or *ignimbrites* are developed from ash and cinders that were part of nuee ardente. As noted earlier, a nuee ardente accompanied the eruptions of Mount Pelee. Because of the heat characteristic of nuee ardente, the fine pyroclastics are still hot and soft when they are deposited and are welded together even with only slight compaction. Ignimbrites derived from the pyroclastics of continental volcanoes may attain thicknesses of hundreds of meters and extend over tens of thousands of square kilometers.

Accumulations of volcanic ash have been known to bury entire towns and villages. When mixed with water, cinders can also contribute to the formation mudflows called *lahar*. In tropical areas with heavy seasonal rainfall, ,such as Indonesia and the Philippines, lahars develop on the sides of active volcanoes and may flow downward at velocities of over 80 km per hour, causing death and destruction to everything in their paths. Lahars sometimes form when an eruption blasts up through the rim of a crater lake, expelling a lethal avalanche of boiling water, mud, and boulders.

Glasses

Most volcanic rocks, even though they cool rapidly from lavas, are crystalline solids. However, in such rocks, the individual mineral grains are usually too small to be seen without a microscope. But what about those lavas that have been chilled so quickly that there has not been time for the atoms in the melt to order themselves into the structures necessary to form crystals? The atoms and silica tetrahedra are frozen into the random positions they held in the liquid. The result is a noncrystalline mixture of silicates and silica called glass. The familiar rock *obsidian* and is natural glass which, if it had cooled more slowly, would have developed crystals of feldspar, quartz, and ferromagnesians. Most obsidian is colored black as a result of its content of impurities and its light absorbing properties. Less commonly, impurities such as iron oxide may color obsidian red or brown. It is easily recognized by its glassy appearance and distinctive conchoidal fracture. Over long periods of time, volcanic glasses may experience devitrification.

During devitrification, myriads of tiny crystals develop in the glass, giving it a cloudy or opaque appearance.

Obsidian most commonly forms from lavas that have lost most of their dissolved gases. Like a bottle of beer that has been left open too long, such lavas have gone "flat". However, if the lava still contains abundant gas, bubbles may continue to escape while the melt cools. Such bubbles are preserved in the rock as cavities called *vesicles*. *Pumice* is an extremely vesicular glass. In a very real sense, it is frozen silicate froth. Usually whitish or gray, pumice is light in weight and, because of its many sealed cavities, cab sometimes actually float on water.

FINE-GRAINED VOLCANIC ROCKS

Basalt

By far the most abundant volcanic rock is *basalt*. It underlies the oceans and is the rock from which Iceland and the Hawaiian Islands are constructed. The lavas from which basalts solidify have relatively low viscosity or resistance to flow. As a result, they may flow over great distances before they congeal. The basalt flows of the Columbia plateau, the Deccan Plateau of India, and the maria of the moon cover tens of thousands of square kilometers.

Basalt is a dense dark gray or black rock composed of pyroxene, calcium-rich plagioclase feldspar, and minor amounts of magnetite and olivine. Basaltic lava pours from vents and fissures at temperatures of about 1200° C and becomes solid by the time the lava has cooled to 750° C. Crystallization is relatively rapid, so that a very finely crystalline texture is produced in which individual minerals cannot be discerned with the unaided eye. Thus, the rock is called *aphanitic*. However, one can view the uniformly sized crystals under the miciroscope by preparing a thin section of the rock. With the aid of a diamond saw, a rectangular piece of the basalt is cut and cemented onto a microscope slide. The mounted piece is then ground down until it is so thin that light can be transmitted through it . A cover glass is added to complete the slide, and the myriads of feldspar and pyroxene grains can then be examined with the petrographic microscope.

In order to understand the origin of basalt, it is necessary to refer briefly to a model of the earth's interior that has been formulated by the study of earthquake waves. The model depicts the earth's basaltic crust as a thin zone about 10 km thick and overlying the mantle of denser olivine and pyroxene-rich rocks. The boundary between the crust and the mantle is recognized by an abrupt change in the velocity of earthquake waves as they travel downward into the earth. For many years geologist believed that basaltic lavas originated from the lower part of the basaltic crust. However, several recent lines of evidence suggest that the basaltic lavas may have come from molten pockets of upper mantle material. For example, present-day volcanic activity is closely associated with deep earthquakes that occur within the mantle far beneath crust. It is quite likely that fractures produced by these earthquakes serve as passages for the escape of molten material to the surface. A detailed study of earthquake shocks from particular volcanic eruptions in Hawaii indicates that the erupting lavas were derived from pockets of molten material with in the upper mantle at depths of 65 to 100 km. However, mantle material is denser, richer in iron and magnesium, and more deficient in silica than are oceanic basalts. How then can the melting of mantle material give rise to basaltic rocks that are less dense and contain more silicon? A process that may account for this disparity is partial melting, which was mentioned earlier in the discussion of the origin of intrusive rocks. Partial melting occurs when a rock body (in this case upper mantle rock) is partly melted and the liquid portion allowed to move to another location. The molten fraction, of course, forms from silicate minerals in the parent body that melt at relatively lower temperatures. This melt is usually less dense than the solids from which it was derived and thus tends to separate from the parent mass and work its way toward the surface. In this way melts of basaltic composition separate from denser rocks of the upper mantle and eventually make their way to the surface to form volcanoes.

Many complex and interrelated factors control where in the mantle partial melting may occur or even if it will occur at all. Generally, heat in excess of 1500°C is required, but the precise temperature for melting is also influenced by pressure and the water content of the rock. As pressure increases, the temperature at which particular minerals melt also rises. Thus a rock that would melt at 1000°C near the surface will not melt in deeper zones of higher pressure until it reaches far greater temperatures. Water has an effect opposite to that of pressure, for its presence will allow a rock to start melting at lower temperatures an shallower depths than it would have other wise. Laboratory experiments indicate that the melting of "dry" mantle rock can occur at depths of about 350 km but that the presence of only a little water can cause partial melting and yield basaltic liquid from depths as shallow as 100 km.

The lavas from which basalts are formed consists chemically of about 50 per cent silica (SiO_2), with lesser percentages of oxides of aluminum, iron, calcium, magnesium, sodium, and potassium. Nonbasaltic lavas differ in their silica content, and this difference provides the basis for recognition of such other volcanic rocks as *rhyolite* and *andesite*.

Rhyolite

Rhyolite is gray or pink aphanitic rock derived from a highly siliceous lava. For example, rhyolitic lavas may consist of as much as 75 per cent silica. Quartz, potassium feldspar, sodium plagioclase, and lesser amounts of ferromagnesian minerals occur in rhyolite. Rhyolitic lavas erupt at temperatures of 800° C to 1000° C. Usually they are far more viscous than basaltic lavas and flow very sluggishly, if at all. They are generally associated with the more violent volcanic eruptions.

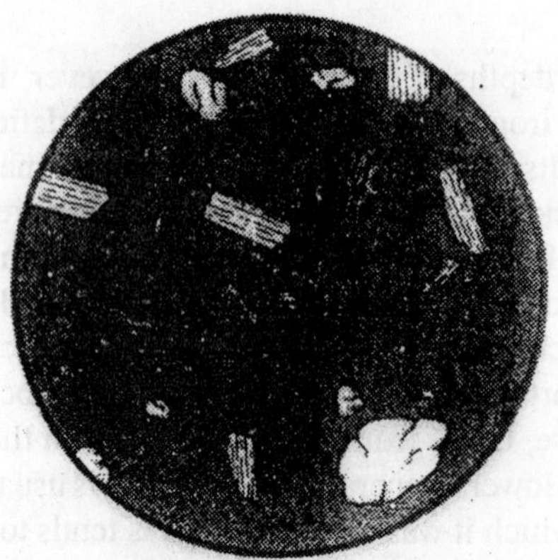

Fig. 2.6. Thin section of rhyolite viewed through a microscope. Clear grains are quartz, elongate grains with parallel lines are orthoclase and sodium-rich plagioclase, and dark grains are biotite. Smaller grains are indistinguishable in the fine groundmass. In hand speciman, this rock would appear to be aphanitic, but under the microscope its "microporphyritic" texture is revealed.

Rhyolites are the products of continental volcanism rather than volcanoes that form on the ocean floor. This suggests that at least some rhyolites are formed by remelting of parts of the silica-rich continental crust. Another theory proposes that rhyolites are formed by the melting of sediments that had been eroded from the continents and deposited along continental margins. Highly silicic sediment, if caught in the vise of converging tectonic plates and melted, could produce magmas of rhyolitic composition.

It may also be possible to produce rhyolitic lavas by fractional crystallization. Imagine a deep reservoir of magma in which olivine and other ferromagnesian minerals have formed early in the cooling period and settled to the bottom of the magma chamber. Early crystallization of these minerals leaves the original liquid changed in composition. The proportion of silica in the melt relative to oxides of iron and magnesium, for example, would be significantly increased. If so, melt might be compositionally suitable for the formation of rhyolite.

Andesite

Andesite is a fine-grained light gray rock intermediate in density and silica content (about 60 percent) between basalt and rhyolite. Andesitic lavas are also intermediate in viscosity and thus form thicker flows than do basaltic lavas. Volcanoes of the andesitic type are common around the edges of continents bordering the Pacific Ocean and are generally more explosive than mid-oceanic volcanoes like those of Hawaii.

Andesitic lavas may originate in more than one way. Some appear to have been formed from originally basaltic magmas by fractional crystallization. Evidence for this mode of origin is provided by Ice land's volcanoes. Iceland is volcanic island formded on oceanic basaltic crust. It has been observed that the longer the quiet period between eruptions of Icelandic volcanoes, the more siliceous is the lava that is extruded. Apparently, longer periods of quiescence provide time for fractional crystallization and settling of ferromagnesian minerals out the residual liquid.

Because andesites are roughly intermediate in composition between rhyolites and basalts, it would appear that at least some andesitic lavas are products of mixing of silica-rich and silica-poor melts. For example, a basaltic magma might work its way into pockets of rhyolitic magma and then blend with the more siliceous liquid. As another possibility, a basaltic magma might engulf, melt, and assimilate surrounding silica-rich rhyolitic rocks. Yet another method for infusing silica into basaltic materials to produce andesite is provided by plate tectonics. In this method, the required amount of silica is derived from the thin layer of oceanic sediment that rests upon the basalt of an oceanic plate as it descends along a subduction zone. As this plate plunges diagonally downward, heat rising from the asthenosphere and generated by friction melts masses of basalts and sediment to produce fluids of andesitic composition. These melts then rise buoyantly and erupt to form the large volumes of andesite frequently found adjacent to subduction zones.

Volcanic Eruption as an Environmental Hazard

Among the great natural environmental hazards to human life and property are several kinds of geologic phenomena. They include volcanic eruptions, earthquakes, seismic sea waves (tsunami), landslides, and floods. Through recorded history volcanic eruptions have been the caused of many disasters in which the toll in human lives has been great and the damage to property high. Volcanoes erupting close to cities have been a particularly serious threat. We offer three examples.

Mount Vesuvius is an active composite volcano situated on the Bay of Naples in southern Italy. Although the city of Naples is not close enough to be directly threatened by lava flows and falls of tephra, explosive activity of Mount Vesuvius can be watched by Neapolitans across the bay. Not so fortunate are a number of town and villages situated on the densly populated lower slopes of the volcanic cone. One of these towns, Torre

Annunziata, had been destroyed by lava flows three times in 900 years before succumbing again in the 1906 eruption of Vesuvius.

Undoubtedly the best publicized of all Vesuvius eruptions occurred in A.D.79, following a long period of inactivity. Severe earthquakes began to occur in A.D. 63 and continued up to the time of the major eruption, which destroyed about half the previous cone and left a large explosion crater. The rim of that former crater persists today, partly encircling the new cone, and is known as Monte Somma. Two small cities were destroyed in the eruption-Pompeii and Herculaneum-but by quite different forms of disaster.

As described in letters written by Pliny the younger, the eruption was first observed as an enormous treelike cloud of dust and gases rising from, the volcano summit. There followed a rain of ash, lapilli, and bombs, as well as large fragments of pumice. The fall of tephra continued for more than two days, during which darkness prevailed through the daytime hours. Pompeii was gradually buried under a layer of ash and pumice that totaled 5 to 8 m in thickness. Although roofs collapsed under the weight of the ash, walls and contents of the buildings survived and are remarkably well preserved to this day. Herculaneum, on the other hand, suffered destruction by a great tongue of (a mudflow) consisting of volcanic ash mixed with water from torrential rains that fell upon the upper slopes of the cone throughout the eruption. Little of the city remained intact under the impact and burial by the flowing mud. Since that time, Vesuvius has undergone many other violent eruptions, the latest in 1944.

Our second example of explosive violence comes from the Island of Martinique in the West Indies. Here, Mount Pelee, a composite volcano built of acidic lava, lies only a short distance from the port city of St. Pierre. The cone rises to a summit elevation of about 1200m. On may 8,1902, following several days of muffled explosion that sent up ash from the crater, four deafening blasts took place. These were followed by the rise of an enormous black cloud from the crater; another black cloud shot horizontally outward, then moved down the mountain slopes with great speed, headed directly for the city. A surviving eyewitness aboard a ship in the harbor described the arrival of the glowing cloud of ash and gases that in an instant reduced all buildings to burning rubble . Of the nearly 40,000 persons believed to be present in the city at the time, only two survived. One was a prisoner in an underground dungeon. A similar glowing avalanche from Mount Pelee, was photographed about seven months after the destruction of St. Pierre.

Out third example is from Heimaey, a small island off the coast of

Iceland. The Island consists largely of a basaltic volcano, apparently dormant for the past several thousand years, and its lava flows. The fishing village of Vestmannaeyjar, with its fine harbor, had a population of over 5000 persons. On January 23, 1973 a fissure located about 1 km from the center of the town began to erupt tephra. Quickly a cinder cone grew up, reaching a height of 100m within two days. Basaltic lava then began to emerge from the fissure and formed a flow which advanced toward the town. Strong winds carried the particles of lapilli and ash over the town, where it began to accumulate in a thick layer on roofs and streets. Gradually, houses nearest the center of eruption became buried in tephra, although efforts were made to remove the layer as it accumulated.

Within six hours of the start of the eruption most of the inhabitants had been evacuated from the island, along with the entire fishing fleet. There remained only a work force of 500 to fight against the advancing lava flow threatening to destroy the town and fill the harbor. With the advice of Icelandic geologists, a plan was formulated to try and stop the forward motion of the lava flow. Powerful pumps were brought in and cold seawater was sprayed directly on the from of the lava. At the peak of the operation 47 pumps were in action. Altogether, over 5 million metric tons of water were sprayed on the flow.

Apparently, the chilling of the lava margin was effective in creating a barrier to the movement of the more fluid lava behind it, for the advance was finally halted, though lava continued to flow from the volcano to the sea in direction away from the town.

Five months and five days after it started, the eruption was officially declared over. The addition of new flows to the harbor shoreline improved the degree of protection from the open sea. The area of the island was increased by about 20% by new flows. Damaged buildings were dug out, and most were repaired and reoccupied. Some of the tephra was used to extend the runways of the island's airport.

Predicting volcanic eruptions

It has been estimated that over a quarter of a million people have lost their lives as a result of recorded volcanic eruptions. Today, even more than in centuries past, heavily populated areas surround some volcanoes. What can be done to warn nearby populations of impending eruptions, and how may some of the effects of volcanism be ameliorated?

There is no reliable way of knowing whether long-inactive volcanoes are extinct or simply dormant. However, methods have been developed that can be used to predict eruptions of volcanoes that are considered still active. Careful monitoring of volcanoes for such warning signals as preliminary minor eruptions, increase in ground temperatures,earthquakes, change in magnetic properties caused by heating of rocks at depth, tilting of the ground, and the appearance of new hot springs and fumaroles can be useful in foretelling the coming of a major eruption. The primary instrument used to detect the multiple minor earthquakes that precede many eruptions is the seismograph. This instrument consists of a weight suspended from a spring. Because of its inertia, the weight remains fixed in space as the container vibrates with the ground, and the movements are translated into electrical impulses and recorded.. The U.S. Geological Survey has seismometer stations on 16 volcanoes in North and South America and Iceland. One or more *tiltmeters* supplement the seismometers at these stations. A tiltmeter is a highly sensitive bubble-type level with associated electronic devices. It records changes in slope of as little as 1 cm in 10 km. The upward movement of magma before an eruption often causes a slight swelling of the overlying ground surface, and this change is readily detected by the tiltmeter. Both seismometers and tiltmeters are automatic devices that report their activity by radio through the Earth Resources Technology Satellite (ERTS) to a designated monitoring center.

Even with such sophisticated devices as seismometers and earthquakes counters, the problem of predicting the precise time of a volcanic eruption is not solved. For example, six days elapsed between the occurrence of earthquakes and the 1973 eruption of Fuego volcano in Guatemala, whereas earthquakes near Paricutin began two weeks before the eruptions.

Although there is no entirely effective way to halt an impending volcanic eruption, there are certain measures that can be taken to guard against destruction caused by lava flows, mudflows, explosive debris, and tsunami. Simply knowing that lava and mudflows move down valleys should suggest that a topographic analysis would be useful in selecting sites for buildings and towns. For eruptions along coastlines, lava flows can somtimes be slowed by spraying with cold ocean water. This method proved useful during the 1973 eruption of *Helgafell* in Iceland.

In all volcano-prone regions, construction and building codes should be formulated and enforced in the location and design of structures. Where pyroclastic accumulation are likely to be heavy, roofs on buildings should be steeply pitched as is done in areas of heavy snows. If crater lakes exist, which, if breached, might trigger mudflows, then tunnels should be installed to siphon off the dangerous waters. Whenever possible, known active volcanoes should be set aside as national parks, so as to limit the growth of towns around their perimeters. It is evident that as populations continue to expand, volcanoes will become potentially even more hazardous. Most of us are fully aware that such hazards are an ongoing concern for peoples living in Hawaii or Alaska but overlook the danger to the increasing numbers of people living close to volcanoes like Mount St. Helens or Mt. Hood in the northwestern United States. Few geologist would be willing to state that presently inactive volcanoes of the Cascades are extinct. However, By monitoring and planning, anxiety and the can be reduced. Such particularly necessary for such United States cities such as Tacoma and Seattle.

Benefits from Volcanoes

Although volcanoes have dealt people some severe blows, they are not without their benefits. They have provided many areas with the raw materials for exceptionally fertile soils. Volcanoes provide more of the earth's most spectacular scenery and have built inhabitable land areas such as Aleutians, Hawaiian Island, and Iceland. The magmas that feed volcanic eruptions are capable of producing steam that can be used to drive electric turbines. There are, for example, several geothermal power plants now in operation that generate electricity from underground waters that have been heated by volcanic processes. These include The Geysers fields in northern California, the Larderello field in northern Itally, the Valle Caldera field near Los Alamos, New Mexico, two Japanes sites, and an area near *Wairaki* in New Zealand. The homes of more than 50,000 persons in Reykjavik, Iceland, are heated with this natural resource. In the future, geologic exploration and drilling are likely to provide many more sources of this kind of geothermal power.

Chapter 3

Earthquakes and Earth Structure

Prelude. In this age of artificial satellites and spacecraft, our attention is often directed toward the remarkable discoveries resulting from the exploration of outer space. We tend to forget that there is still much to learn about the "inner space" of our own planet. This is particularly true of that part of the earth that lies beneath the crust. Our deepest wells penetrate only about ten of the 6300 km that separate us from the center of the planet. Basaltic lavas sometimes provide a glimpse of materials that originated 50 to 60 km below the surface, and some diamond-bearing kimberlites mayhave risen from depths of 200 km. For the most part, however, our knowledge of the earth's insides has been indirectly inferred from the study of earthquake waves (seismic waves). In this chapter, we shal examine the cause and effects of earthquakes and review what they tell us about the hidden interior of our planet.

When the Earth Shakes

Ours is a living dynamic planet. Each year this fact is emphasized for us by over a million earthquakes that occur worldwide. At least 50 of these cause loss of life and significant damage to property. A fewer number of giant earthquakes each year are terrifying catastrophes. The lives lost from earthquakes over the past 500 years number in the millions and far exceed the loss of lives from volcanic eruptions. What happens during an earthquake ? What does it feel like to be in one ? Perhaps the best way to answer these questions is to describe the nightmarish events of a few noteworthy earthquakes.

The Good Friday Earthquake, Alaska, 1964

It was about 5:36 in the afternoon on March 27 in Anchorage, Alaska. Except for a few snowflakes that floated down from partly cloudy skies, the weather had been pleasant, and there was a general mood of geniality as Alaskans looked forward to their Easter holiday and the coming of spring. A housewife was preparing dinner while her two children played in the neighborhood park across the street. Robert B. Atwood, editor of the Anchorage *Daily Times,* was relaxing at home by improving his skill at playing the trumpet. In a real estate office nearby, a new resident of the city was preparing to purchase a home in a tract called Turnagain Heights. Moments later the newcomer and the other unsuspecting citizens of Anchorage were jarred by the strongest earthquake recorded in North America during historic time. In the home of the young housewife, dishes rattled and walls began to sway at awkward angles. Terrified, she rushed out of the thouse to retrieve her two children, but fell headlong into a crack that had unexpectedly opened in the loose sliding soil. She was certain she would lose her life in the next moment, but the floor of the trench heaved upward so that her children and a neighbor were able to bring her to safety.

Across twon, Robert Atwood ran outside his shaking house and watched in panic as his driveway and yard broke into large dizzily sliding blocks. He tried to leap from block to block, but a fissure opened beneath him, and he tumbled downward. Sand and clay rained down upon him. He tried to free himself, but found his right arm anchored in the sand. Suddenly he realized that his hand still clutched the trumpet he had been playing moments before. He released his hold on the instrument and scrambled out of the ditch. Not far away, the customer for a new home in Turnagain Heights stared in disbelief as he watched the new house he was about to purchase slide down the hillside and splinter into a mass of ruin.

The Good Friday earthquake was not centered in Anchorage but rather about 130 km southeast of the city beneath the firgid waters of Prince William Sound. Other cities, such as Valdez and Seward, were also damaged, although not as severely. The greater damage at Anchorage can be attributed to the fact that the city is built on a thick blanket of loose glacial sediment—gravel, sand, and clay. These unstable materials are weakly held together by frozen water. Beneath the glacial deposits, one finds a thick bed of weak plastic clay known to geologists as the Bootlegger Cove Clay. When the tremendous shaking began, the Bootlegger Cove Clay began to flow downward toward Cook Inlet, causing great cracks and landslides int eh overlying glacial material. Indeed, most of the damage to Anchorage was either directly or indirectly due to slumps, slides, and settling of the ground.

The New Madrid, Missouri Earthquake of 1811-12

We are accustomed to hearing about earthquakes in places like California, Alaska, Japan, Peru, and Iran. An earthquake seems an improbable event for persons living in the low-lying stable heartlands of

Fig. 3.1. New Madrid, Missouri, region in which the 1811 to 1812 earthquakes occured. Movement within a recently discovered fault zone in northeastn Arkansas may have caused these historic earthquakes. The fault zone had not been discovered earlier because it is deeply buried by sediments of the Mississippi Valley. U.S. Geological survey geologists discovered the fault zone by studing artificially induced seismic waves.

continents. Such regions, however, are not immune from earthquakes. In the 53 days between December 16, 1811, and February 7, 1812, this fact was powerfully demonstrated to Indians and settlers living in the area that surrounds the village of New Madrid, near the southeastern tip of Missouri. During the period of the distrubance, nearly 2000 earthquakes were counted, many of which were probably greater than the quakes that destroyed San Francisco in 1906. Fortunately, the area was only sparsely populated, but for the relatively few inhabitants of New Mardrid county, the events were an extended nightmare. As the earth heaved and swayed, cabins collapsed on their occupants, stout trees snapped in two, and great chasms, mostly parallel to the river, opened and belched forth fountains of sand, water, and sulphurous fumes. Upheaval of broad dome-like mounds temporarily dmmed the Mississippi, and the backed-up water produced the effect of the river seeming to flow backwads for a time. The surging floods carried logs, furniture, and boats upstream and deposited much of the debris in the tree tops. As the shocks and noisy rumblings continued, Indians and settlers alike fled the area for parts unknown. Ground subsidence accompanying the earthquake converted fertile forests into deep bogs and formed swamps in a zone from Cape Girardeau, Missouri, 190 miles southward into Arkansas. Until subsequently reclaimed by the construction of drainage canals and levees, the area was appropriately dubbed "Swampeast Missouri." Other areas also experienced the sinking of long narrow strips of land, which then promptly filled with water. In Tennessee, one of these troughs became the 20-mile-long and seven mile-wide Reelfoot Lake.

The shocks from the New Madrid earthquake were felt from New Orleans to Chicago and from the east to west coasts of the United States. Indian legend and geologic structures in the area indicate that other earthquakes had occurred prior to 1811. Even within the present decade, citizens of Cairo, Illinois, Memphis, Tennessee, and St. Louis are occasionally jolted into remembering that earthquakes can occur int he so-called stable interior of the U.S.A. They are, however, much less frequent in the midcontinental region than along the continent's western margin, which is a lithospheric plate boundary. Nevertheless, there is no cause for complacency, for a major earthquake is predicted for the New Madrid region by the turn of the century. Because of the increased population, the destruction and loss of lives would be far greater than in 1811.

The 1906 San Francisco Earthquake

The most infamous of American earthquakes struck San Francisco at about 12 minutes past 5 on the morning of April 18, 1906.

Citizens awoke in stark terror amid the awful roar of collapsing buildings and clanging of jostled church bells. For many, crushed by collapsing roofs and masonry that crashed through ceilings, their conscious moments were brief. Those who managed to make their way out into the open and away from falling objects recalled that the earthquake, which had begun with relatively small movement, in creased to a jarring crescendo at the end of about 40 seconds. The shocks abruptly stopped for a few moments and then struck again even more violently for about a half minute. This main shock was then followed by smaller earthquakes, termed aftershocks. Although the destruction to buildings by shaking was extensive, the main damage came from fire, as gas from broken gas mains

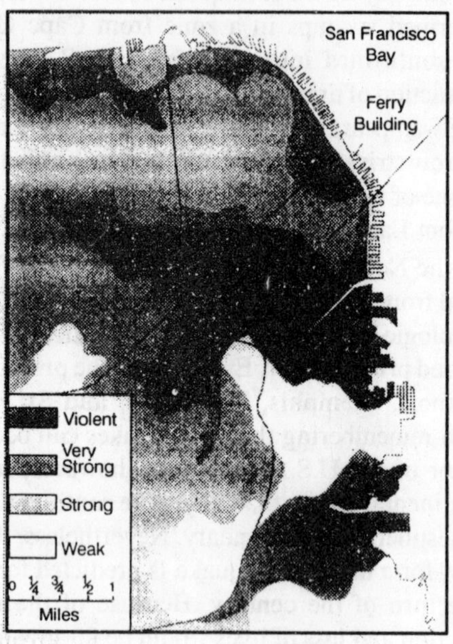

Fig. 3.2. Distribution of the damage due to the 1906 San Francisco earthquake. Land recovered from the bay, reclaimed and filled swampland, river bottoms, and the other areas of thick unconsolidated soil experienced the most damge. Buildings on bedrock experienced relatively little damage.

was ignited. Water lines were snapped by the earth movements, and firemen could not effectively battle the conflagration that raged through the city. For three days, however, firemen and volunteers worked with wet mops, dynamite, and shovels until they had finally put out the fires. Slowly, the thousands who had fled the city returned. It was then apparent that the parts of the city that had experienced the greatest destruction from the earthquake itself had been built on losse soil used to fill ravines and swampy areas. Even today, parts of San Francisco (and other cities) are built on loose materials dumped along the coastline to extend the land into the sea. Such areas are in maximal danger from earthquakes.

The cause of the San Francisco earthquake was sudden movement along the notorious San Andreas Fault. This great scar in the earth's crust can be traced nearly 1000 km from Cape Mendocino to the Gulf of California. The San Andreas Fault, along with adjoining networks of faults, is responsible for most of the earthquakes felt in California. The damage to San Francisco (as well as San Jose, Santa Rosa, and Stanford University) during the 1906 quake was primarily the result of horizontal displacement along the San Andreas Fault. The amount of horizontal movement varied from place to place up to a maximum of 6.5 meters, most of which occurred as the oceanward side of the fault was jolted northwestward.

We know the slowly moving tectonic plates that compose the earth's outer shell. Where such plates slip past one another, faulting can be expected. The San Andreas fault is one such plate margin. It marks the boundary between the North American and Pacific Plates. The Pacific Plate carries a splinter of North America with it as it creeps northwestward at a rate of about 7.5 cm a year (relative to the main body of the continent). Thus, if movement continues for the next 20 million years, Los Angeles will have traveled past San Francisco and have continued to a point far to the north of that city. Californians are well aware that movement along the San Andreas is neither continuous nor smooth. The masses of rock on either side of the San Andreas and other faults tend to lock and then slip suddenly releasing die stress that has accumulated and sending severe jolts throughout the land.

The Cause of Earthquakes

Stress, strain, and rupture

Children of the wanyamwasi tribe of Africa learn from their elders that the earth is a great disc supported on one side by a lofty mountain and on the other by an amorous giant. The giant's lovely wife stands beside him holding up the sky. Occasionally, the giant gets the notion to hug his wife, thereby causing the momentarily neglected earth to totter. Thus a romantic impulse, say the Wanyamwasi, can cause an earthquake.

The Wanyamwasi legend is only one expression of the centuries-old search by peoples of every culture for the cause of earthquakes. Today, of course, most people would say earthquakes result when rocks break or there are sudden movements along "locked segments of faults." But what determines when a rock will break or rupture? Are the forces that break rocks applied instantaneously or gradually over a long period of time? How does a rock resist the forces that tend to break or distort it?

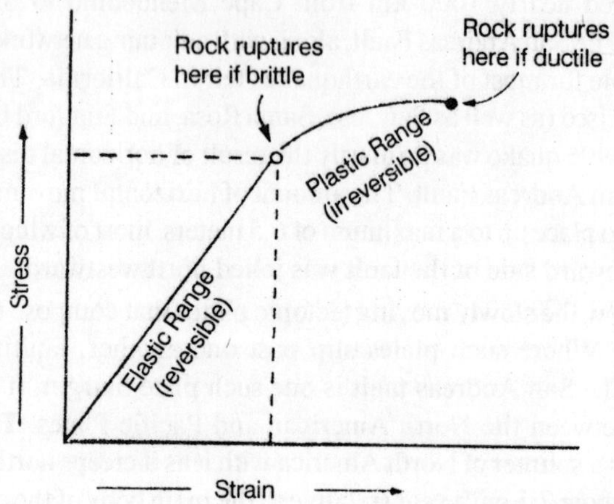

Fig,3.3. Graph of stress vs. strin on hypothetical earth materials.

In regions where earthquakes occur, rocks are being subjected to enormous stress. *Stress* can be defined as a deformational force applied over a specific area of a body of rock so as either to compress it (compressional stress), pull it apart (tensional stress), or cause one part to move past another (shear). The effect of stress on a rock mass is to cause *strain*, which is a measure of the amount a body is deformed by stress. Strain involves an actual change in shape or volume of the rock that has experienced stress. Rocks have the ability to withstand certain amounts of stress without breaking, or distorting, and this ability is a measure of their *strength*. Thus strength can be considered the stress level at which the rock either ruptures or deforms.

The way rocks behave when subjected to stress is illustrated. Initially, while the stress is just beginning to build up, the rock may adapt by deforming elastically. Elastic deformation means that if the stress were removed, the rock mass would recover its original shape. In the region of the graph where elastic deformation occurs, the amount of strain produced is directly proportional to the amount of stress applied. As the stress is increased, a point called the *elastic limit* is reached. Beyond the elastic limit, the rock does not recover its original shape after removal of the stress but rather experiences permanent distortion. The leveling off of the curve indicates that small increases in stress beyond the elastic limit will now cause relatively greater deformation. Finally, the rock will no longer be able to adapt to the stress directed against it, and it will break. In brittle rocks, breakage occurs almost at the elastic limit, whereas in ductile rocks considerable plastic deformation may occur prior to breaking or rupture. At the moment the rock breaks, it *rebounds* into positions that relieve the stresses. This movement generates the shocks we recognize as earthquakes.

Elastic rebound

The mechanism involved in *elastic rebound* was originally described by the Calfornian geologist *H.F. Reid*, who based his model on surveys obtained for land adjacent to the San Andreas fault both before and after the 1906 earthquake. In some ways elastic rebound resembles what happens when one slowly bends a wodden yardstick. The energy applied to bending the stick is stored within it as the wood responds to the stress by bending elastically. When the elastic limit of the wood is finally exceeded, it breaks and the splintered ends whip violently back and forth. (In some instances, of course, the wood may not break but experience permanent deformation, as rocks sometimes do.)

Block A shows a tract of land that has a fault, but there has been no movement along that fault for some time. A road and dike have been constructed across the fault and provide convenient landmarks for measuring displacement. Gradually, stress begins to build up along the fault, and the rocks adapt by bending slightly (Block B). For a while, because of friction or cementation, the opposite sides of the fault remain locked together. They may begin to bend by amounts measurable with instruments called strain gauges. Eventually, so much stress has accumulated that repture occurs (Block C), and the rocks are moved violently in opposite directions. The sudden jolt is like a giant hammer blow to the earth and starts a series of vibrations or earthquake waves, which travel outward in all directions. These vibrations are the earthquakes we feel underfoot or detect with instruments. The release of stress at one place may cause rupture at other places along a large fault so that earthquake activity may continue for days or weeks following the main shock. A preexisting fault is not always a requirement for an earthquake. Stresses may build up in unfaulted rocks, and earthquakes may be generated with initial faulting. Most earthquakes, however, do occur along preexisting faults. Deep earthquakes may result from sporadic slippage in rocks that are simultaneously undergoing plastic deformation.

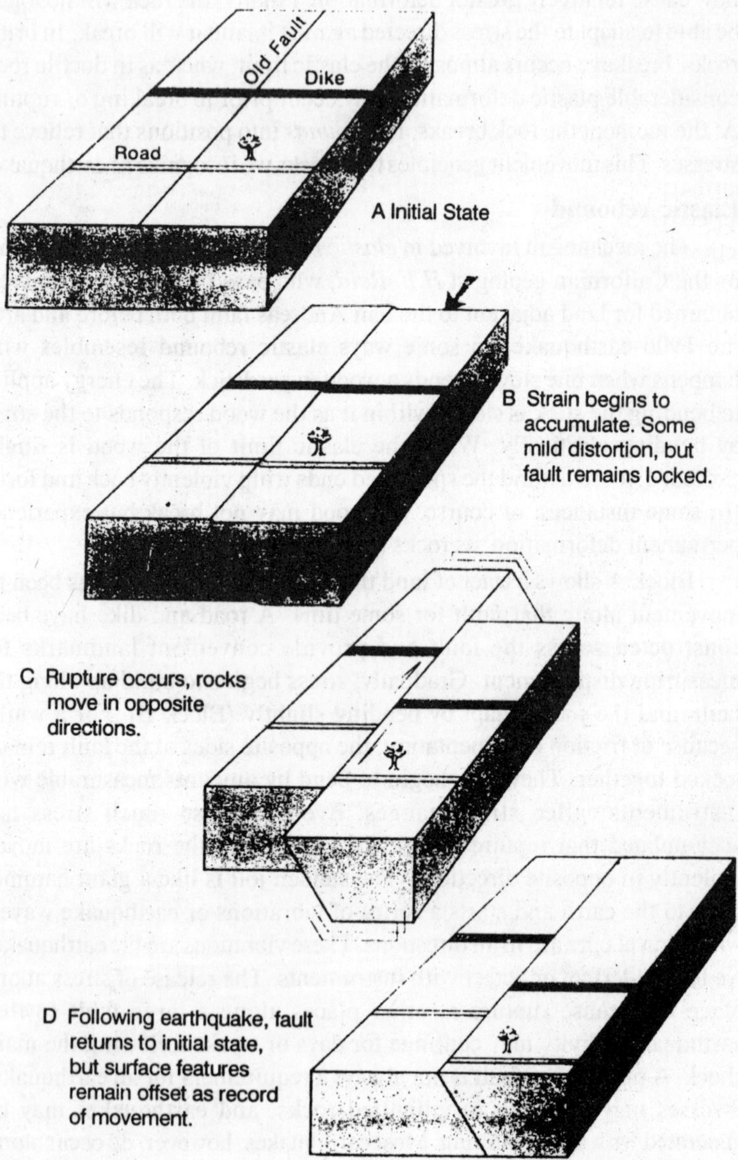

Fig,3.4. Model of the elastic rebound mechanism for earthquake.

EARTHQUAKE DISTRIBUTION AND TECTONICS

If one examines a map showing the location of earthquake epicenters, it is readily apparent that earthquakes do not occur randomly around the globe. Rather, earthquake epicenters tend to be con- centrated along relatively narrow zones. In fact, 80 per cent of the total earthquake energy for the earth is released in the zones that border the Pacific Ocean. A second set of zones extends from southern Europe through Turkey, Iran, northern India and on toward Burma, and accounts for nearly another 15 per cent of earthquake energy. Clearly, there is some sort of disruptive activity along these great earthquake trends. According to the concepts of plate tectonics, which will be examined in detail in the next chapter, the zones of high seismicity are believed to delineate the margins of great moving plates of lithosphere. The plates collide, pull apart, or slide past neighboring plates, and these interactions along plate margins generate the stress in crustal rocks that causes earthquakes.

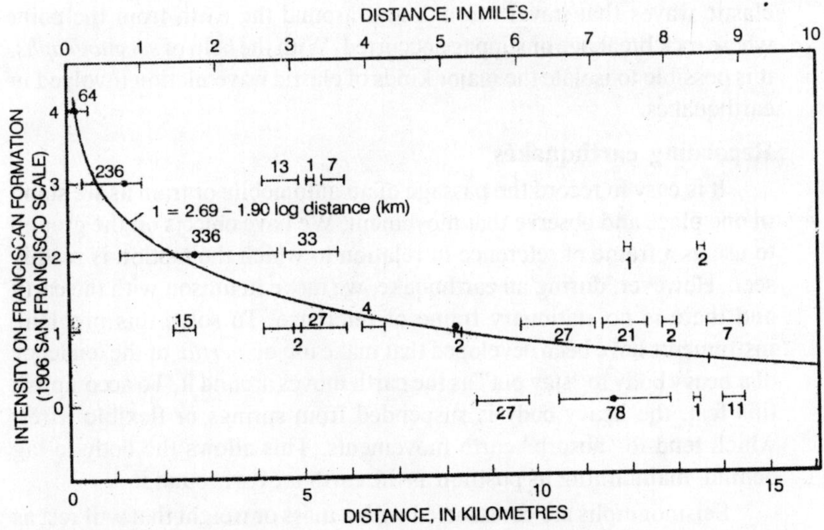

Fig. 3.5. World distribution of earthquakes occuring at depths of 0 to 700 km. Notice the major earthquake belt that encircles the pacific and another that extends eastward from the Mediterranean toward the Himalayas and East Indies. The mid-oceanic ridges are also the site of many earthquakes.

A lesser number of earthquakes occur within the central regions of lithospheric plates. These earthquakes tend to be of lower magnitude, although occasionally an event as large as the New Madrid earthquake may occur. The cause of intraplate earthquakes is not well understood. Many seem to be the result of the erosional removal of vast quantities of surface materials. Without the weighty overburden, segments of continental crust may rise bouyantly and generate stresses in the surrounding rocks. Old faults may be reactivated by this motion, and formerly stable rock masses ruptured. Geologists also speculate that some intraplate earthquakes may represent the early warnings of the breaking apart of continents.

Seismographs and Earthquake Waves

Anyone who has gone through the harrowing experience of a major earthquake will recall sensing the confusion of side-to-side and up-and-down blows and vibrations. However, it is difficult to differentiate particular kinds of movements within the jumble of jerks and jolts. Actually, the various movements are manifestations of different kinds of elastic waves that travel through and around the earth from the point where rock breakage or slippage occurred. With the help of *seismographs*, it is possible to isolate the major kinds of elastic wave motion involved in earthquakes.

Recording earthquakes

It is easy to record the passage of an automobile or train as we stand in one place and observe that movement. We have objects on the ground to use as a frame of reference in relation to which the motion is readily seen. However, during an earthquake, we move in unison with the earth and there is no stationary frame of reference. To solve this problem, instruments have been developed that make use of *inertia,* or the tendency of a heavy body to "stay put" as the earth moves around it. To accomplish this feat, the heavy body is suspended from springs or flexible wires, which tend to "absorb" earth movements. This allows the body to lag behind, maintaining its position as the earth moves around it.

Seismographs are constructed with a mass or weight that will rest as independently of earth motion as possible. This has been achieved in several ways. For recording vertical movements, the seismograph contains a weight suspended by springs from an overhead support. Horizontal movements are recorded by seismographs containing a horizontal pendulum having a weight on a rigid arm supported by a wire. The pendulum is freely attached to a socket joint from the supporting column.

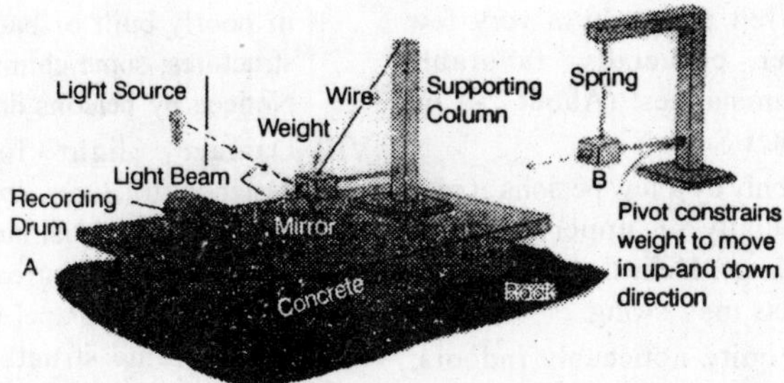

Fig. 3.6. *(A) Sketch of a seismograph that is recording horizental earth motion. A light spot on the boom moves across photographic paper on the recording drum as the boom oscillates. By reorienting the drum and modifying apparatus as shown B, verticle ground motion may be recorded.*

In either type of seismograph, the weight tends to remain at rest while the support vibrates with the earth. The difference in motion can then be recorded and measured in many different ways. One simple device employs a delicate pen atteched to the weight. The pen traces a continuous line on a revolving drum that is itself fixed to the supporting framework of the instrument. The drum turns as a clock so that the arrival times of a vibration can be determined. Of course, the actual seismographs placed in earthquake monitoring stations are far more complex than the simple instruments. Rather than a pen for recording, tiny rays of light are beamed onto photographic paper. The ray of light is reflected off a series of mirrors to amplify even very small motions of the ground. Other devices serve to dampen the natural swinging motion of the pendulum and filter out unrelated background motions. To analyze all movements of earthquakes fully, at least three seismographs must be in simultaneous operation.

Earthquake intensity and magnitude

Soon after an earthquake has been reported, people want to know something about its intensity. Therefore, attempts have been made to formulate standard scales of intensity and magnitude. *Magnitude* is a term that is used to describe the amount of energy released by an earthquake, whereas *intensity* measures the effect of the earthquake on structures and people at a particular place. Intensity scales are qualitative. They record the observable effects of earthquakes as ranging from slight tremors detected by only a few people (ranked 1 on a scale of 1 to XII) to total destruction (XII on the intensity scale). (A widely used standard for judging earthquake intensity is the modified *Mercalli Scale* provided in Table).

Table 3.1. Modified Mercalli Scale of earthquake intensity*

I. Not felt except by a very few under especially favorable circumstances. (About 2-3 on Richter Scale.)

II. Felt only by a few persons at rest, especially on upper floors of buildings. Delicately suspended objects may swing.

III. Felt quite noticeably indoors, especially on upper floors, but many people do not recognize it as an earthquake. Standing motor cars may rock slightly. Vibration like that from passing truck.

IV. During the day felt indoors by many, outdoors by few. At night some awakened. Dishes, windows, doors disturbed; walls make creaking sound. Sensation like heavy truck striking building. Standing motor cars rocked noticeably.

V. Felt by nearly everyone; many awakened. Some dishes, windows, etc., broken; a few instances of cracked plaster; unstable objects overturned. Disturbances of trees, poles, and other tall objects sometimes noticed. Pendulum clocks may stop.

VI. Felt by all, many frightened and run outdoors. Some heavy furniture moved; a few instances of fallen plaster or damaged chimneys. Damage slight. (About 5 to 6 on Richter Scale.)

VII. Everybody runs outdoors. Damage negligible in buildings of good design and construction; slight to moderate in wellbuilt ordinary structures; considerable in poorly built or badly designed structures; some chimneys broken. Noticed by persons driving cars.

VIII. Damage slight in specially designed structures; considerable in ordinary substantial buildings, with partial collapse; great in poorly built structures. Panel walls thrown out of frame structures. Fall of chimneys, factory stacks, columns, monuments, walls. Heavy furniture over-turned. Sand and mud ejected in small amounts. Changes in well-water levels. Disturbs persons driving motor cars.

IX. Damage considerable in specially designed structures; well-designed frame structures thrown out of plumb; great in substantial buildings, with partial collapse. Buildings shifted off foundations. Ground cracked conspicuously. Underground pipes broken.

X. Some well-built wooden structures destroyed; most masonry and frame structures destroyed with foundations; ground badly cracked. Rails bent. Land-slides considerable from river banks and steep slopes. Shifted sand and mud. Water splashed over banks.

XI. Few, if any, masonry structures remain standing. Bridges destroyed. Broad fissures in ground. Underground pipelines completely out of service. Earth slumps and land slips in soft ground. Rails bent greatly.

XII. Damage total. Waves seen on ground surfaces. Lines of sight and level distorted. Objects thrown upward into the air. (About 8 on Richter Scale.)

Intensity values can he plotted on maps by drawing lines called *isoseismal lines*, which connect points of equal earthquake intensity. Such maps are useful in delineating areas in which the effects of earthquakes were similar. Intensity scales, however, have rather obvious limitations. They cannot be used in uninhabited areas because there would be no structures subjected to earthquake damage. Also, the intensity assigned to an area is likely to be influenced by the psychology of the inhabitants, the quality of construction, and local soil stability.

In an attempt to remedy the problems associated with qualitative scales, *C.F. Richter* devised a system that measures the magnitude of an earthquake' in terms of the motion recorded by a seismographs of certain specifications at a standard distance (100 km) from the earthquake source. Calculations permit one to determine the equivalent responses of other seismographs at any distance. In this quantitative scale, one measures the seismic wave amplitude released by the shock rather than the intensity or degree of destructiveness. The Richter Scale has a logarithmic basis, so that an increase in one whole number corresponds to an earthquake 10 times stronger than one indicated by the next lower number. This translates into an approximate 30-fold increase in theamount of energy released. Thus, magnitude 7 represents ground motion of about 10 times that of magnitude 6 and 31.7 times as much energy released. A magnitude-7 earthquake would represent 100 times the ground motion and 900 times the energy released of the magnitude-5 earthquake.

The 8.5 magnitude of the 1964 Alaskan earthquake was the greatest ever recorded in North America. An earthquake rated 2.5 on the Richter Scale would hardly be noticed, but one of magnitude 4.5 may cause local damage. An earthquake with magnitude greater than 8.9 has never been recorded, and this suggests that there is a limit to which rocks can accumulate strain energy before they break or slip.

Seismic waves

From the study of *seismograms* (the records of seismographs), geologists have recognized that earthquakes move through the earth as waves. Although there are several different kinds of waves, the three that are of most importance are *primary*, *secondary*, and surface waves. They are defined by describing the motion of a "particle" of rock that lies in the path of the wave.

Primary waves. *Primary waves* take their name from the fact that they are the speediest of the three kinds of earthquake waves and therefore the first to arrive at a seismograph station after there has been an

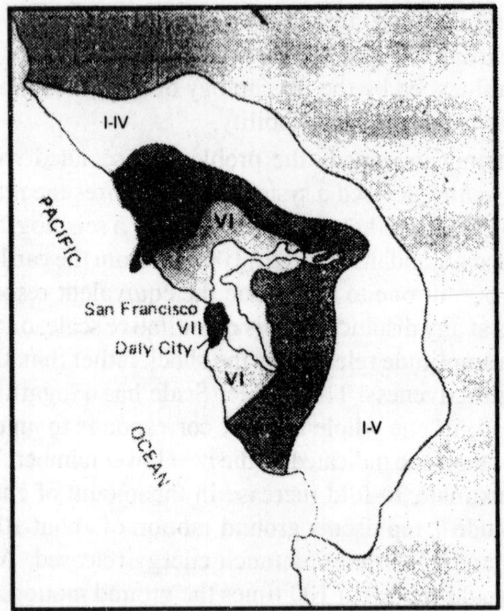

Fig. 3.7. Isoseismal map prepared by the U.S. Coast and geodetic following the 1957 Daly City, California, earthquake. A maximum intensity of VII was observed.

earthquake. They travel through the upper crust of the earth at speeds of 4 to 5 km per second. Near the base of the crust they speed along at 6 or 7 km per second. In these primary waves (also called *P-waves* for brevity), pulses of energy are transmitted in such a way that the movement of rock particles is parallel to the direction of propagation of the wave itself. Thus, a given particle of rock set in motion during an earthquake is driven into its neighbor and bounces back. The neighbor strikes the next particle and rebounds, and subsequent particles continue the motion. The result is a series of alternate compressions and expansions that speed away from the source of shock. Thus P-waves are similar to sound waves in that they are *longitudinal* and travel by compression and rarefaction. It is an accordian-like "push-pull" movement that can be transmitted through solids, liquids, and gases. Of course, the speed of P-wave transmission will differ in materials of different density and elastic properties. They tend to die out with increasing distance from the earthquake source and will echo or reflect off rock masses of differing physical properites.

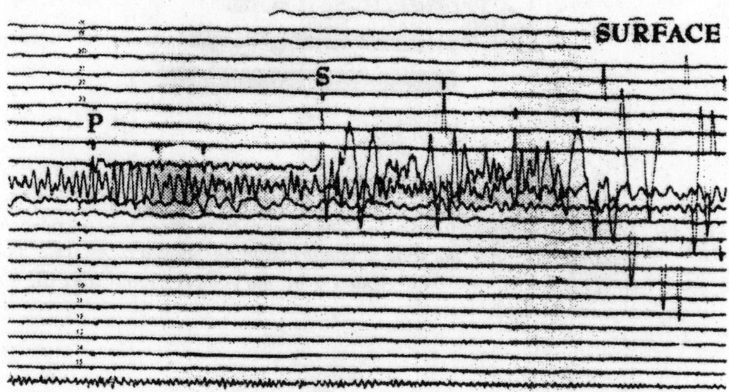

Fig. 3.8. Record of a magnitude 6 earthquake that occurred in Turkey, March 28, 1964, and was recorded by the vertical component seismograph located in northwestern Canada. Time increases from left to right. Small tick marks present 1-minute intervals. P means primary waves, S indicates secondary waves. Notice that the first S-waves arrive about 10 minutes after the arrivsl of first P-waves.

Secondary waves. Another part of the energy released at an earthquake source is carried away by slower-moving waves called *secondary waves*. These waves are also called *shear, transverse or S-waves.* They travel 1 or 2 km per second slower than do P-waves. The movement of rock particles in secondary waves is at right angles to the direction of propagation of the energy. A demonstration of this type of wave is easily managed by tying a length of rope to a hook and then shaking the free end. A series of undulations will develop in the rope and move toward the hook-that is, in the direction of propagation. Any given particle or point along the rope, however, will move up and down in a direction perpendicular to the direction of propagation. It is because of their more complex motion that S-waves travel slower than P-waves. They are the second group of oscillations to appear on the seismogram. Unlike P-waves, secondary waves will not pass through liquids or gases.

Both P- and S-waves are sometimes also termed *body waves* because they are able to penetrate deep into the interior or body of our planet. Body waves travel faster in rocks of greater elasticity, and their speeds

Fig. 3.9. Movement of primary wave. In 1, the compression has moved the particles closer together at A, In 2, the zone of compression has moved to A_1. In 3, the zone of compression has moved to A_2 and a second compressional zone (B) has moved in from the left.

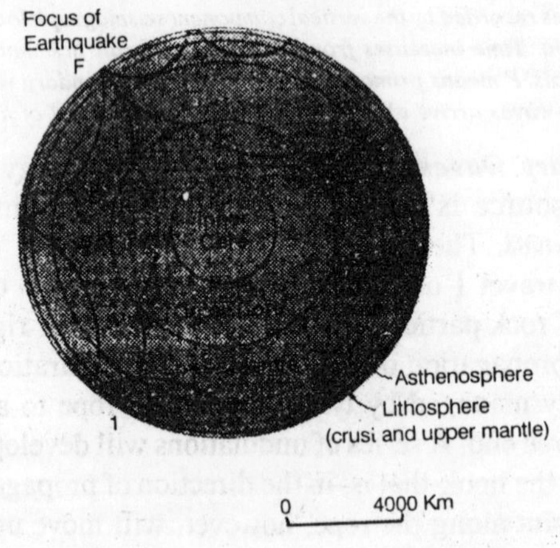

Fig. 3.10. Cross-section of the earth showing paths of some earthquake waves. P-waves. P-waves that penetrate to the core are sharply refracted as shown in path from F to 1. S-waves end at the core, although thay may be converted to P-waves, traverse the core, and emerge in the mantle again as P-and S-waves. Both P- and S-waves may also be reflected back into the earth again at the surface.

therefore increase steadily as they move downward into more elastic zones of the earth's interior and then decrease as they begin to make their ascent toward the earth's surface. The change in velocity that occurs as body waves invade rocks of different elasticity results in a bending or refraction of the wave. The many small refractions cause the body waves to assume a curved travel path through the earth.

Not only are body waves subjected to refraction, but they may also be partially reflected off the surface of a dense rock layer in much the same way as light is reflected off a polished surface. Many factors influence the behavior of body waves. An increase in the temperature of rocks through which body waves are traveling will cause a decrease in velocity, whereas an increase in confining pressure will cause a corresponding increase in wave velocity. As mentioned earlier, in a fluid where no rigidity exists, S-waves cannot propagate, and P-waves are markedly slowed.

Surface waves. Surface waves are large-motion waves that travel through the outer crust of the earth. Their pattern of movement resembles that of waves caused when a pebble is tossed into the center of a pond. They develop whenever P- or S- waves disturb the surface of the earth as they emerge from the interior. There are actually several different types of motion in surface waves. *Rayleigh surface waves,* for example, have an elliptical motion that is opposite in direction to that of propagation, whereas *Love surface waves* vibrate horizontally and perpendicular to wave propagation. Surface waves are the last to arrive at a seismograph station. They are usually the primary cause of the destruction that can result from earthquakes affecting densely populated areas. This destruction results because surface waves are channeled through the thin outer region of the earth, and their energy is less rapidly dissipated into the large volumes of rock traversed by body waves. Indeed, surface waves may

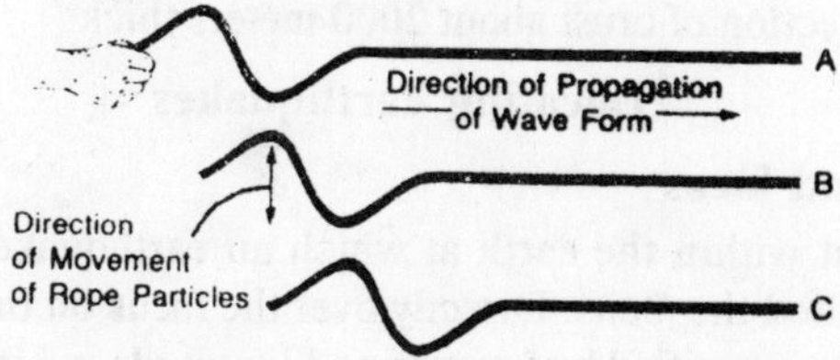

Fig. 3.11. Analogy of propagation of S-waves by displacement of a rope. In rocks, as in this rope, particle movement is at right angles to the direction of propagation of the wave. A,B, and C show the displacement of the crest from left to right at succesive increments of time.

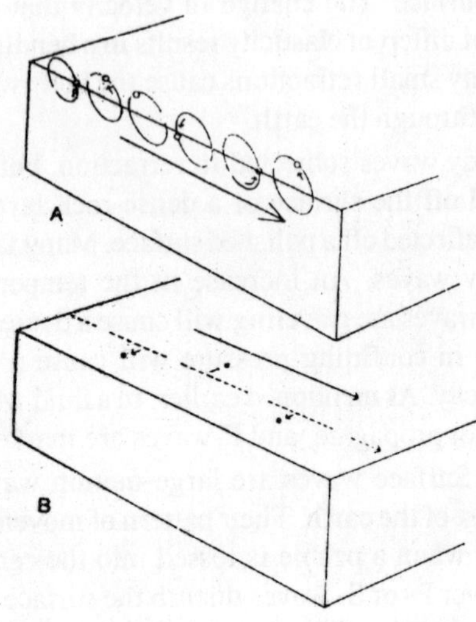

Fig. 3.12. (A) Elliptical particle motion in Rayleigh surface waves (ground surface shown without displacement). (B) Particle motion in love wave is in horizental plane and perpandicular to direction of wave propagation.

circle the earth several times before friction causes them to fade. As is the case with ordinary water waves, the motion of surface waves diminishes with depth. It has been demonstrated that the total depth to which surface wave motion can exist is about equal to the distance between two surface wave crests. Thus, surface waves that are 2000 meters from crest to crest will shake a section of crust about 2000 meters thick.

Locating earthquakes

Epicenter and focus

The point within the earth at which an earthquake disturbance is initiated is called the *focus*. Directly over the focus on the surface of the earth is a point, specified by latitude and longitude, which is termed the *epicenter*. The depth to the focus may vary from nearly zero to more than 600 km. If the depth of focus is less than about 8 km, the earthquake is usually not felt at any appreciable distances from the epicenter. Deep-focus earthquakes, however, are detected at great distances from their epicenters. Seismologists have developed a classification of earthquakes

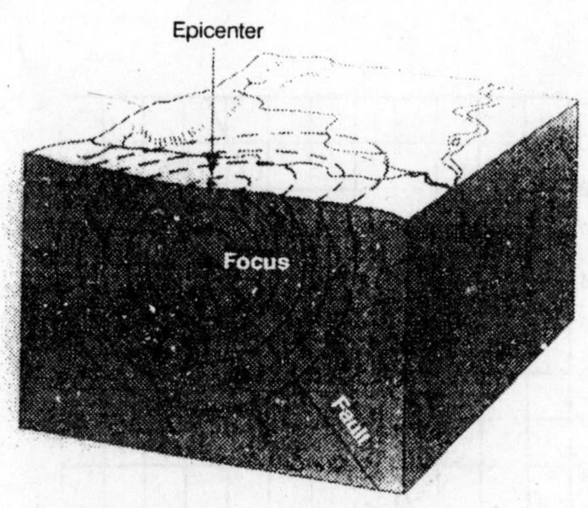

Fig. 3.13. The relation between the focus and epicenter of an earthquake. The focus is the point of intial movement and the epicenter is the point on the surface directly above the focus. The location of an earthquake is usually described by the geographic position of its epicenter and by its focal depth.

according to their depth of focus. A *shallow-focus* earthquake has its focus at a depth between 0 and 70 km. Foci that lie between 71 and 300 km *define intermediate-focus* earthquakes, while *deep-focus* earthquakes have a focal depth greater than 300 km. Earthquakes originating at depths greater than 700 km rarely occur because the rocks at such depths are relatively plastic and do not accumulate strain.

Distance to the epicenter

As a first step in determining the location of the source of an earthquake, one must find the distance between the recording station and the epicenter. The study of seismograms provides the key to determining this distance. Typically, the record of an earthquake can be divided into three major parts. The record begins with relatively simple oscillations produced by the arrival of primary waves. These smaller-scale tracings are followed abruptly by waves of somewhat greater amplitude representing incoming secondary waves. The surface waves come along last and produce the largest and most complex patterns of all. How might the pattern of seismic traces be used to find the distance to the epicenter? The answer to that question was provided in the early 1900s by *John Milne*, the founder of modern seismology. *Milne* discovered that the time

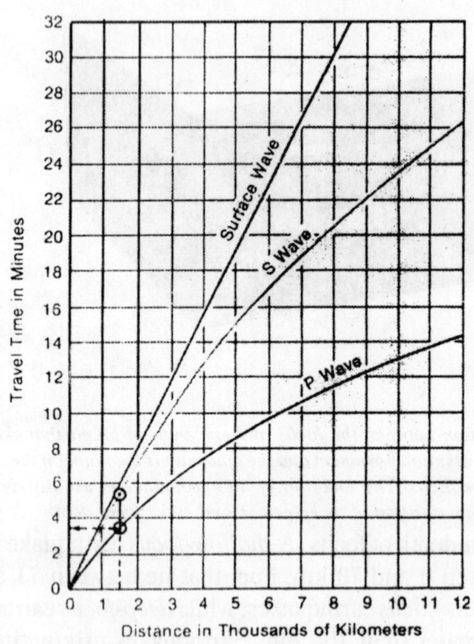

Fig. 3.14. Time-distance graph.

separation on a seismogram between the starting points of the P- and S-waves is greater for a distant earthquake than for one located nearby. For example, the time that elapses between the arrival of the P- and the arrival of an S-wave (sometimes termed the "S minus P interval") for a focus 500 km away is about 30 seconds. For a focus located 1000 km away, 100 seconds would separate the arrival times of P- and S-waves. Thus, the time interval between the arrival of P- and S-waves is different for every distance between the earthquake center and the seismograph. The situation is comparable to a phenomenon we have all experienced when we see lightning in the sky but hear the clap of thunder a moment or two later. The time that elapses between seeing the lightning and hearing the thunder would be greater at greater distances from the location of the lightning bolt.

Geophysicists have determined how rapidly seismic waves travel by observation of earthquakes whose source locations and times of occurrence are well known. The information obtained from these observations is used to construct *time-distance graphs* that can then be employed in locating earthquake epicenters. Assume that a seismograph records the arrival of a P- wave at 8:00 A.M. and the arrival of the S-wave 2 minutes later. On the edge of a piece of paper, the P minus S interval of 2 minutes can be marked off by using the time-travel scale on the left side of the time-distance chart. This interval can then be vertically fitted into just the right size space between the P- and S-wave curve. Then, by reading down onto the horizontal scale, one can ascertain that the earthquake was 1500 km away from the seismograph station. A line extended horizontally from the point where the 2-minute mark touches the P-wave curve to the left edge of the graph indicated that the P-wave required 3 minutes and 15 seconds to reach the seismograph. Thus, the time of the actual shock at the focus occurred 3 minutes and 15 seconds before 8:00 A.M. Newspapers might now announce the time of occurrence of the earthquake and its distance, but precisely where did it occur?

Direction to epicenter

To find the precise location of the epicenter, distance determinations from three or more seismograph sta- tions are needed. On a map, the location of each seismograph station is plotted. A circle is drawn around the location that has the radius of the seismograph-to-epicenter distance. The earthquake must have occurred somewhere on that circle. Communications from two or more other stations are used as the basis for plotting similar circles, and the point where three circles intersect locates the epicenter. Large earthquakes are recorded at hundreds of different earthquake stations. Therefore, there are an abundance of measurements to use in checking the validity of the epicenter's location.

Seismic Waves and the Earth's Interior

The division of inner space

Most of what we know about the earth's deep interior is derived from the interpretation of countless seismograms documenting recent and past earthquakes around the globe. From such studies, geophysicists have found evidence of the gradual change in rock properties with depth as well as the relatively abrupt boundaries between major internal zones. Boundaries where seismic waves experience an abrupt change in velocity or, direction are called *discontinuities*. Two widely known breaks of this

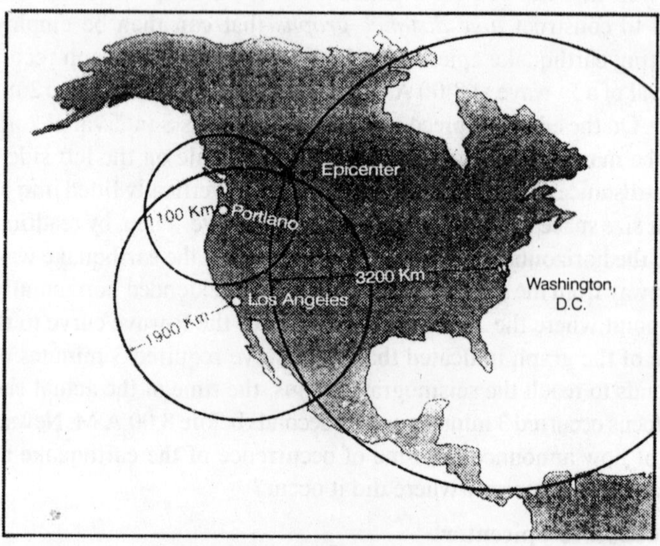

Fig. 3.15. Method used for locating the epicenter of an earthquake. The distance to the epicenter from seismograph stations in Washington D.C.,Los Angles, and Portland was first determined from the P minus S time interval. This distance is used as the radius to draw circles around each station in order to find the intersection of all three. The epicenter was determined to be near Saskatoon, Saskatcheqwan, Canada.

kind are named, after their discoverers, the Mohorovicic and Gutenberg discontinuities.

The discontinuity discovered by Mohorovicic (pronounced Mo-ho-ro-vitch-ick) was based on his observation that two sets of P- and S-waves were re-corded by seismographs located within 800 km of the epicenter of an earthquake having a focus within 40 km of the earth's surface. From their travel times, Mohorovicic determined that one set of these waves had traveled directly from the focus to the recording station. The second set arrived at the station some- what later. He concluded that the second set arrived late because they had been refracted on entering and leaving an internal zone having different composition and physical properties than rocks of the crust. The base of the crust, or *Mohorovicic discontinuity*, had been discovered. It lies at about 30 to 40 km below the surface of the continents and at lesser depths beneath the ocean floors. Beneath the crust lies the mantle.

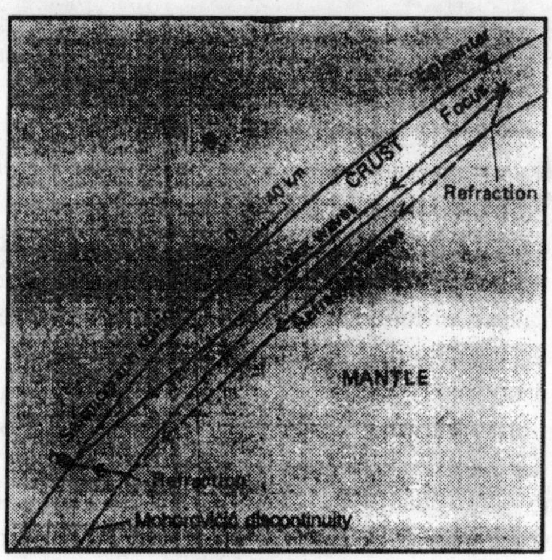

Fig. 3.16. Mohorovicic's conclusion about the location of the base of the earth's crust was based on this interpretation of the travel paths of early and latearriving seismic body waves.

The *Gutenberg discontinuity* is located nearly halfway to the center of the earth at a depth of 2900 km. Its location is marked by an abrupt decrease in P-wave velocities and the disappearance of S-waves. The Gutenberg discontinuity marks the outer boundary of the earth's core.

The core

Inferences from body waves. For many years before the development of modern seismology, geologists correctly inferred that the earth had a very dense central core. Such an interpretation was indicated by the overall density of the earth as compared with the relatively low density of surface rocks. As noted above, the precise boundary of the core was determined by the study of earthquake waves. Seismology has also provided a means for discerning subdivisions of the core and deciphering some of its physical

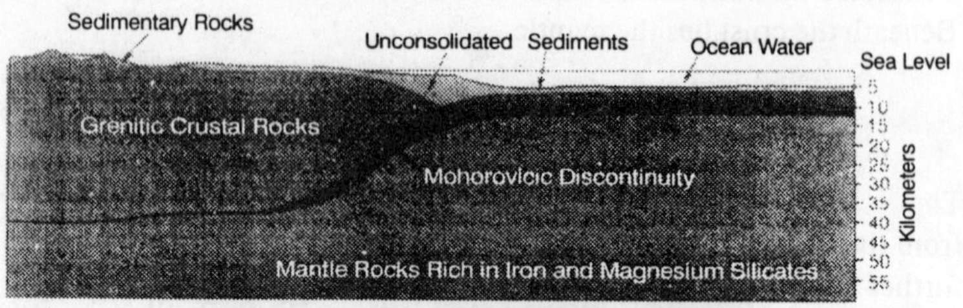

Fig. 3.17. Generalized cross-section of a segment of the earth's crust showing location of the Mohorovicic discontinuity.

properties. For example, at a depth of 2900 km (the core boundary) the S-waves meet an impenetrable barrier, while at the same time P-wave velocity is drastically reduced from about 13.6 km/second to 8.1 km/second. Earlier, we noted that S-waves are unable to travel through fluids. (Fluids cannot sustain shear.) Thus, if they were to enter a fluid region of the earth's interior, they would be absorbed there and would not be able to continue. Geophysicists believe this is what happens to S-waves as they enter the outer part of the core. As a result, the secondary waves generated on one side of the earth fail to appear at seismograph stations on the opposite side, and this observation is the principal evidence for an outer core that behaves as a fluid. The outer core barrier to S-waves results

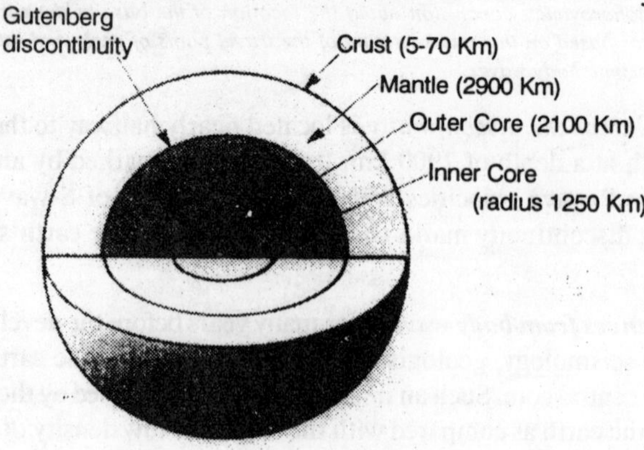

Fig. 3.18. The interior of the earth. The crust appears as a line at this scale.

in an *S-wave shadow zone* on the side of the earth opposite an earthquake. Within the *shadow zone*, which begins 105 degrees from the earthquake focus, S- waves do not appear.

Unlike S-waves, primary waves are able to pass through liquids. They are, however, abruptly slowed and sharply refracted as they enter a fluid medium. Therefore, as primary seismic waves encounter the molten outer core of the earth, their velocity is checked and they are refracted downward. The result is a *P-wave shadow zone* that extends from about 105^0 to 143^0 from the focus. Beyond 143° P- waves are so tardy in their arrival as to further validate the inference that they have passed through a liquid medium. At the upper boundary of the core, P-waves are also reflected back toward the earth's surface. Such P-wave echos are clearly observed on seismograms.

The radius of the core is about 3500 km. The inner core is solid and has a radius of about 1220 km, which makes this inner core slightly larger than the moon. A transition zone approximately 500 km thick surrounds the inner core. Most geologists believe that the inner core has the same composition as the outer core and that it can only exist as a solid because of the enormous pressure at the center of the earth.

Evidence for the existence of a solid inner core is derived from the study of hundreds of seismograms produced over several years. These studies showed that weak late-arriving primary waves were somehow penetrating to stations that were within the P-wave shadow zone. Geophysicists recognized that this could be explained by assuming the inner core behaved seismically as if it were solid.

Core composition. The earth has an overall density of 5.5 g/cm^3, yet the average density of rocks at the surface is less than 3.0 g/cm^3. This indicates that materials of high density must exist in the deep interior of the planet in order to achieve the 5.5 g/cm^3 overall density. Calculations indicate that the rocks of the mantle have a density of about 4.5 g /cm^3 and that the average density of the core is about 10.7g/cm^3. Under the extreme pressure conditions that exist in the region of the core, iron mixed with nickel would very likely have the required high density. In fact, laboratory experiments suggest that a highly pressurized iron- nickel alloy might be too dense and that minor amounts of such elements such as silicon, sulfur, or oxygen may also be present to "lighten" the core material.

Support for the theory that the core is composed of iron (85 per cent) with lesser amounts of nickel has come from the study of meteorites. A large number of these samples of solar system materials are iron meteorites that consist of metallic iron alloyed with a small percentage of nickel.

Some geologists believe that iron meteorites may very well be fragments from the core of a shattered planet. Their abundance in our solar system suggests that the existence of an iron-nickel core for the earth is plausible.

There is another kind of evidence for the earth's having a metallic core. Anyone who understands the functioning of an ordinary compass is aware that the earth has a magnetic field. The planet itself behaves as if there were a great bar magnet embedded within it at a small angle to its rotational axis. Geophysicists believe that the earth's magnetic field may, in some way, be associated with electric currents. This interpretation is favored by the discovery, over 60 years ago, that a magnetic field is produced by an electric current flowing through a wire. The silicate rocks of the lithosphere and mantle are not good conductors, however, and therefore unlikely materials for the development of electromagnetism. In contrast, iron is an excellent conductor. If scientists are correct in the inference made from density considerations and study of meteorites that the core is mostly iron, then the magnetic field lends credence to that inference.

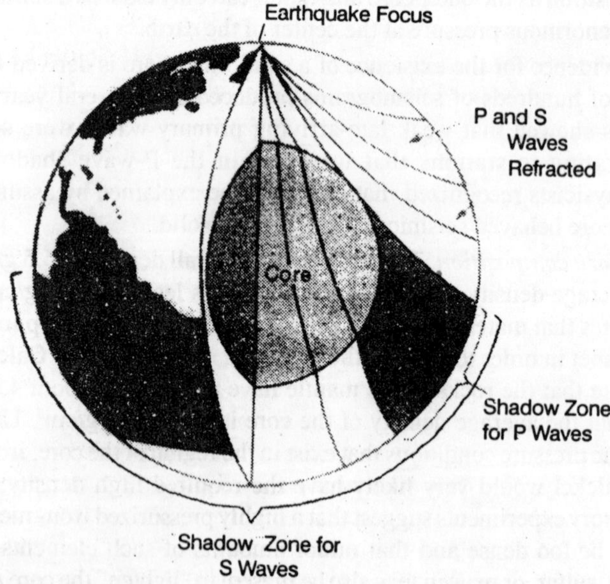

Fig. 3.19. Refraction od seismic body waves. The S-wave shadow zone is believed to be the result of absorption of S-waves in the liquid outer core. When the P-wave enters the liquid enter the liquid outer core, it slows and is bent downward, giving rise to the P-wave shadow zone within which neither P-nor S-waves are received,.

The origin of the core

How does the existence of a dense metallic core relate to theories on the origin of the earth? A currently favored theory would have the earth and other planets created from the atoms, molecules, and particles circulating within a turbulent cosmic dust cloud. According to this concept, the earth would have acquired most of its materials while relatively cool, and its various elements would have been mixed and dispersed from its surface to its center. How, then, did layering develop? The answer that comes immediately to mind is that after the earth had accumulated most of its matter, it became partially or entirely molten. Somewhat like a great blast furnace, much of the excess iron and nickel percolated downward to form the core. Remaining iron and other metals combined with silicon and oxygen and separated into the overlying less dense mantle. Still lighter components may have separated out of the mantle to form an uppermost crustal layer. Geologists do not insist on complete melting for this differentiation of materials into layers. Under conditions of high pressure and temperature, elements might have migrated to their appropriate levels by the slow diffusion of ions through solid materials. Indeed, it would be difficult to account for the present abundance of volatile elements on earth if it had melted completely, for under such circumstances these materials would be driven off. Even for partial melting and solid diffusion to have occurred, however, heat would have been required. That heat may have been supplied in various ways. Certainly, the decay of radioactive elements must have been an important thermal source. In addition, heat was probably supplied by the kinetic energy of debris still showering the photo-planet, from gravitational compression, from solar radiation, and even from tidal friction generated by the nearby moon.

The mantle

Materials of the mantle. As was the case with the earth's core, our understanding of the composition and structure of the mantle is based on indirect evidence. As inferred from seismic data, the mantle's average density is about 4.5 g /cm^3, and it is believed to have a stony, rather than metallic, composition. Oxygen and silicon probably predominate and are accompanied by iron and magnesium as the most abundant metallic ions. The iron- and magnesium-rich rock *peridotite* approximates fairly well the kind of material inferred for the mantle. A peridotitic rock not only would be appropriate for the mantle's drensity but also is similar in composition to stony meteorites as well as rocks that are thought to have reached the earth's surface from the upper part of the mantle itself. Such suspected mantle rocks are indeed rare. They are rich in olivine and pyroxenes and contain small amounts of certain minerals, including diamonds, that can form only under pressures greater than those characteristic of the crust.

Layers of the mantle. The mantle is not merely a thick homogeneous layer surrounding the core but is itself composed of several concentric layers that can be detected by studying earthquake data. In note that within the mantle there are three zones of rapid increase in wave velocity. These sudden increases cannot be explained as simply the result of pressure increases with depth. Such increases would be too gradual to cause seismic wave velocity to increase so abruptly. There must, therefore, be some change in the physical nature of the material. One of the zones is encountered at about 400 km and is taken to mark the base of the *upper mantle*. Beneath the upper mantle is the *transition zone*, which extends downward to about 650 km. The *lower mantle* lies beneath the transition zone and above the core.

Fig. 3.20. Generalized graph of average P-wave velocities vs. depth in the upper 1000 km. of the mantle, showing two zones of velocity increase at A and B.

The composition of the lower mantle is difficult to infer. A plausible guess that is supported by seis- mic evidence is that it consists mostly of silicates and oxides of magnesium and iron. In the high-temperature and high-pressure environment of the lower mantle, iron, magnesium, silicon, and oxygen atoms are rearranged into denser and more compact crystals. For example, near the earth's surface, olivine and pyroxene are relatively stable minerals. However, in the high-temperature and high-pressure environment below a depth of about 400 km, olivine is likely to be converted to minerals whose atoms are more closely packed. Similar dense crystals have been formed from olivine in high-pressure laboratory experiments. Rocks composed of such dense minerals would be capable of causing the increase in seismic velocities that characterize the mantle.

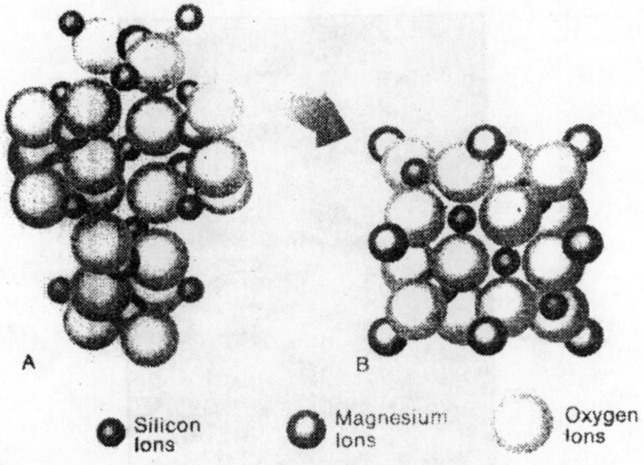

Fig. 3.21. High and low pressure forms of the mineral olivine. At shallow depths in the mentle, olivine is stable in the form shown in (A) this is the form of olivine found at the earth's surface). When the pressure reaches a criticle value corresponding to a depth of about 400 km, the molecule collapses into a more dense form (B) in which oxygen ions are more closely packed.

The upper mantle is of particular importance because its evolution and internal movements affect the geology of the crust. The most remarkable feature of the upper mantle is the *low-velocity zone*. As suggested by its name, this is a region in which there is a decrease in the speed of S- and P-waves. The low-velocity zone occupies an upper region of the much larger *asthenosphere*. Directly beneath the asthenosphere lies the *mesosphere*. This zone of the upper mantle is composed of rocks that are again sufficiently strong and rigid to cause an increase in P-wave velocity.

Geophysicists believe the seismic waves are slowed in the asthenosphere, not because of a decrease in density, but rather because they enter a region that is in the state of a crystalline-liquid mixture. In such a "hot slush," perhaps 1 to 10 per cent of the material would consist of pockets and droplets of molten silicates. This interpretation is strengthened by the observation that in certain regions of the asthenosphere, S-waves are absorbed as if by large bodies of magma. If this interpretation of the physical state of the asthenosphere is correct, then it is capable of considerable motion and flow. Such a slippery mobile layer would enhance movement in the overlying lithosphere.

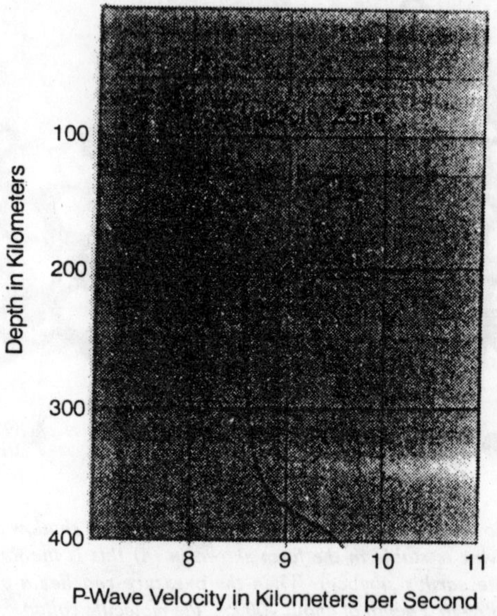

Fig. 3.22. Profile of P-wave velocity for part of the upper mantle showing low-velocity zone.

The Crust of the Earth

The crust of the earth is seismically defined as all of the solid earth above the Mohorovicic discontinuity. It is the thin rocky veneer that constitutes the continents and the floors of the oceans. The crust is not a homogeneous shell in which low places were filled with water to make oceans and higher places make continents. Rather, there are two distinct kinds of crust, which, because of their distinctive compositions and physical properties, determine the very existence of separate continents and ocean basins.

The oceanic crust

Beneath the varied topography of the ocean floors lies an oceanic crust that is approximately 5 to 12 km thick and has an average density of about 3.0 g/cm. Three layers of this oceanic crust can be recognized. On the upper surface is a thin layer of unconsolidated sediment that rests on the irregular surface of the igneous basement layer. The second layer consists of basalts that had been extruded underwater. The nature of the deepest layer of oceanic crust is not clear. Many suspect that it is metamorphosed basaltic mantle material that has become somewhat less dense by chemically combining with sea water. In the oceanic crust, we find a concentration of such common elements as iron, magnesium, and calcium. They are included in the plagioclase feldspars, amphiboles, and pyroxenes of basalts. The upper mantle is the ultimate source for the lavas that formed the oceanic crust. It is likely that magmatic fractionation provided basaltic magmas from an upper mantle source having a composition approximated by three parts olivine to one part basalt.

The continental crust

Properties of the continental crust. At the boundaries of the ocean basins, the Mohorovicic discontinuity plunges sharply beneath the thicker continental crust. Depth to the Moho beneath the continents averages about 35 km, although it may be considerably deeper or shallower in particular regions. The continental crust is not only thicker than its oceanic counterpart but also less dense, averaging about 2.7 g/cm^3. As a result, continents "float" higher on the denser mantle than the adjacent oceanic crustal segments. Somewhat like great stony icebergs, the roots of continents extend downward into the mantle.

The concept of light crustal rocks "floating" on denser mantle rocks was given the name *isostacy* in the previous chapter. Were it not for isostacy, mountain ranges would gradually subside, for there are no rocks having sufficient strength to bear the heavy load of mountain ranges. Thus, mountains are not supported by the strength of the crust but rather are in a state of flotational equilibrium with denser underlying rocks.

Although the continental crust is referred to as being "granitic," it is really composed of a variety of rocks that approximate granite in composition. Igneous continental rocks are richer in silicon and potassium and poorer in iron, magnesium, and calcium than igneous oceanic rocks. Also, extensive regions of the continents are blanketed by sedimentary rocks. On the average, continental sedimentary sequences rarely exceed a few kilometers in thickness, except in narrow deeply subsiding tracts, where they may accumulate to thicknesses in excess of 15 km.

Origin of the continental crust. One of the major questions relating to the history of the earth is how the lighter granitic masses that constitute the continents developed. Many geologists believe the development of the crust involved a series of events that began about 4 billion years ago with upwellings of lava derived from the partially molten upper mantle. This initial crust of lava was then subjected to repeated episodes of remelting, during which time lighter components were separated out and distributed near the earth's surface. Wherever uplands existed, as along volcanic island arcs, the solidified lavas were subjected to erosion and the ordinary processes of oxidation, carbonation and hydration that accompany chemical weathering. The products of this weathering and erosion were the earth's earliest sediments, which were then altered by rising hot gases and silica-rich solutions from below. Recycling and melting of this well- cooked and now lighter mix of earth materials led ultimately to the rocks of granitic character that formed the nuclei of continents. The new continents might then have provided a source for additional sediment that would have collected along continental margins. Subsequently, these sediments also might have been metamorphosed and melted during orogenic events, so that successive bands of granitic crust would have become welded or "accreted" onto the initial continental nuclei.

Proponents of this theory for the origin of continents support their views with the observation that compressional mountain ranges tend to be located, as if accreted, along the margins of the stable granitic core of the continents. Those opposed to the concept have geochemical questions. In conversion of the weathered products of basalt into granite, what happens to the excess iron and magnesium? Also, one needs additions of potassium and sodium to make granite. These elements are rare in sediments that have formed from basalts. Thus, the problem of the origin of the continents will continue to be examined in the decade ahead.

Exploring the crust with explosion seismology. We have seen how the study of seismic waves generated by earthquakes has been of the utmost importance in providing an interpretation of the deep internal zones of the earth. A geophysicist interested in the crust, however, need not wait for the usually unpredictable occurrence of a natural earthquake in order to obtain information. On land, explosions of dynamite detonated in shallow drill holes, and at sea, explosions emanating from electrical devices hauled along behind research vessels, can provide seismic data at any time. As is true for earthquake seismic waves, the velocity of artificially induced seismic waves increases with. depth. This is because the rigidity of crustal rocks generally becomes greater with depth as a consequence of increases in confining pressure and changes in rock composition.

When a charge of dynamite is exploded in a drill hole, seismic waves penetrate into the crust to a depth that depends on the size of the original charge. For most work, the charge is sufficient to send seismic waves to a depth of about 150 km. As the waves travel out from the point of the

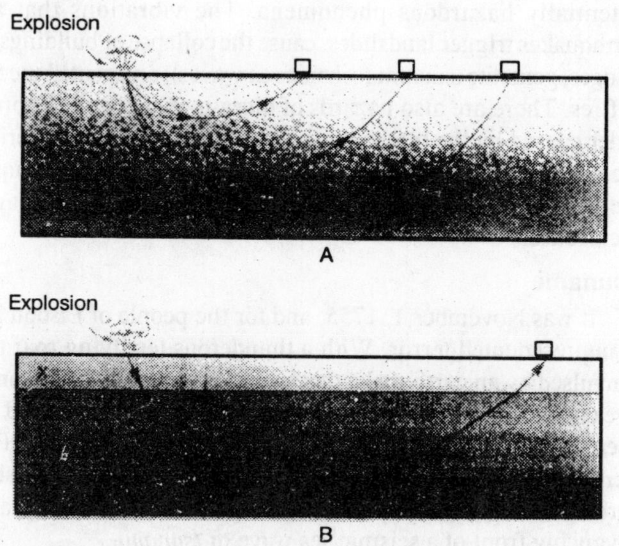

Fig. 3.23. The refraction or bending of seismic waves as they travel through rocks of increasing rigidity. In (A) the area is underline by a nonstratified rock column that gradually increases in rigidity with depth. As a result, wave paths are smoothly curved. Area (B) is underline by three layers, each of which has a uniform rigidity but is more rigid than the overlying layer. Seismic waves are sharply refracted at the xy boundry. The wave encountering layer z at a certain critical angle travels along that boundary and is then refracted back toward the surface.

explosion, they are bent or refracted. If the rocks penetrated have gradually increasing rigidity, the path of seismic wave travel will be a rather smooth curve. In the descending part of that curve, the refraction is due to increasing rock rigidity and wave velocity, whereas in the ascending segment bending occurs as a result of decrease in wave velocity as it passes through rocks of decreasing rigidity. If the study area is underlain by layers, each of which has greater rigidity, seismic waves will travel in straight lines through each layer of uniform rigidity but will be abruptly refracted at layer boundaries. These boundaries are at surfaces of strata, and knowledge of their precise location at numerous localities can be exceptionally useful in locating subsurface strata and structures such as faults and folds. Frequently, such structures serve as natural traps for oil and gas.

EARTHQUAKE-RELATED HAZARDS

Hardly anyone would dispute the notion that earthquakes are potentially hazardous phenomena. The vibrations that accompany earthquakes trigger landslides, cause the collapse of buildings, roads, and bridges, generate tsunami (seismic sea waves), and contribute to outbreaks of fires. There are also hazards of disease, panic, and the breakdown of order caused by the interruption of vital services. The severity of any of the hazards depends not only on the magnitude of the earthquake but on the general geology of the areas affected and the time and place of occurrence.

Tsunami

It was November 1, 1755, and for the people of Lisbon it was a day of unprecedented terror. With a thunderous terrifying roar the city was convulsed by an earthquake that was to claim 60,000 lives and demolish five out of every six buildings. Panic-stricken citizens rushed down to the open wharfs in order to avoid failing masonry and fire but within minutes were hurled into oblivion as a 15- meter wall of water smashed into the harbor, destroying everything in its path. That wall of water was the advancing front of a seismic sea wave or *tsunami*.

Tsunami frequently accompany earthquakes that occur near coastlines. For example, the tsunami associated with the Alaskan earthquake was triggered by the sudden movement of the sea floor in Prince William Sound. Seventy miles away from the quake center at the Port of Valdez, onrushing tsunami lifted the steamship Chena 9 meters skyward and then plunged it to the floor of the bay. Miraculously the steamer was then able to right itself. Only three crewmen were killed (one suffered a heart attack and two were crushed by lurching cargo). People on shore were less fortunate, as the initial and then second wave swept them away without trace and reduced the waterfront facilities to a mass of splintered wood and twisted metal.

Although tsunami may be caused by landslides along a coastline and by volcanic eruptions, the majority are generated by earthquakes. Often they develop when segments of the sea floor subside abruptly or are suddenly thrust upward along faults. Waves are generated in the water mass in much the same way as they would be when a water-filled metal tub is struck by a sharp blow. In the open ocean, tsunami are known to travel at speeds in excess of 400km per hour. They are scarcely noticed on the open ocean, however, because the wavelength of the tsunami is increased to as much as 100 km, and the wave height over so broad a distance is not visibly evident. On approaching the shallow zone near a coastline, however, the bottom of the tsunami is retarded by friction. As the wave is slowed in the shallower zone, the enormous volume of water tends to pile up. The result is an increase in wave height to 30 or 40 meters.

Tsunami travel rapidly, but because of the great distances involved, they may require several hours to cross an ocean. Therefore, it is feasible to set up a warning system to alert coastal areas of the possibility of property damage and loss of life from an approaching tsunami. Such a warning system for the Pacific, called the SSWWS (Seismic Sea Wave Warning System), has been developed by the U.S. Coast and Geodetic Survey with the cooperation of several federal agencies and the Armed Forces. A network of seismograph stations alert scientists in Honolulu of the location and magnitude of earthquakes. If the interpretation of these data indicates the possibility of a tsunami, its estimated arrival times at different locations are calculated with the use of tsunami travel time charts, and warnings are issued. Of course, for locations close to the earthquake, there may be insufficient time to provide a warning. It is also difficult to predict the force and destructiveness of a tsunami when it arrives at a particular locality, as these factors are related to the geographic and bathymetric configuration of the coastline, the direction of the approach of the tsunami, and the state of the tides.

Inhabitants of coastal areas that have just experienced an earthquake would be well advised to evacuate to high ground. They should also be informed that the arrival of a tsunami may sometimes be signaled by a temporary withdrawal of the sea along a coastline. Those that foolishly venture out on the vacated sea floor to gather stranded fish may receive a fatal surprise.

Seiches

A seiche (pronounced sash) is a long wave set up in an enclosed body of water like a lake or reservoir or in a partially enclosed bay. Many are caused by tides, winds, or currents, but earthquakes can also cause the pendulum-like oscillation of water that is characteristic of seiches. During the Alaskan earthquake of 1964, a seiche was set up in Kenai Lake that resulted in a maximal rise of lake levels of 9 meters. The bulge of water flooded inland, knocking down large trees and stripping the soil down to bedrock. Most of the earthquake-induced seiches for which there are adequate records did not result in great loss of life or property. Nevertheless, this type of geologic hazard should be evaluated in the planning of housing developments and recreational areas around reservoirs.

Ground displacements

One of the most pervasive misconceptions about the effects of earthquakes is the terrifying notion that bottomless canyons suddenly open in solid rock, swallow up screaming victims, and then close up to crush them. Actually, there have been very few authenticated deaths caused by people failing into fissures. Fissures do sometimes open up in the unconsolidated materials overlying bedrock but not in solid rock. Usually these cracks appear as a result of settling, slumping, or sliding triggered by the much deeper ruptures in solid rock that caused the earthquake. As noted previously, the extreme fracturing at Anchorage in 1964 and San Francisco in 1906 was largely in the surface layer of unconsolidated materials.

Landslides

Earthquake-induced landslides are more dangerous to humans than are the development of cracks in the ground. As an example of the magnitude of this hazard, one need only recall the 1970 catastrophe in Peru that was responsible for burying tens of thousands of villagers in Yungay and Ranrahirca. Another well-known landslide caused by an earthquake occurred near midnight in Madison Canyon, Montana, on August 17, 1959. An earthquake dislodged a great chunk of the mountain above the Madison River, and a chaotic jumble of fragmented rock roared across the valley, blocking the river and burying 19 vacationers at the Rock Creek Campsite under more than 60 meters of debris. The landslide effectively dammed the Madison River, and a lake, appropriately dubbed Earthquake Lake, formed behind the slide. To the east of the slide area stands Hebgen Dam, which holds back the water of Hebgen Lake. As a result of the earthquake, the reservoir was thrown into seiche movement. The first four oscillations sloshed water completely over the top of the dam, and oscillatory motion was still discernable 11 hours later.

Liquefaction

Often during earthquakes, fine-grained water-saturated sediments may lose their former strength and form into a thick mobile mudlike material. The process is called *liquefaction*. The liquefied sediment not only moves about beneath the surface but may also rise through fissures and "erupt" as mud boils and mud "volcanoes." As described earlier, most of the destruction to buildings at Turnagain Heights during the 1964 Alaskan earthquake could be related to the flowage of liquefied soils.

Following a 1964 earthquake near Niigata, Japan, liquefied sediment flowed out from beneath tall buildings, causing many of them to tilt slowly over onto their sides. People trapped on the roof of one building were able to walk down one side of the structure to safety.

Fire

Injury from falling objects, burial in landslides or collapsed buildings, and fire pose the greatest dangers to life during earthquakes. We have already noted the ravages of fire during the San Francisco earthquake. For many years that disaster was referred to as the "Great San Francisco Fire," as if the earthquake itself was of lesser importance. Yet another example of this hazard is provided by the earthquake that devastated the cities of Yokahama and Tokyo in 1923. The quake struck during the noon hour, when midday meals were being prepared. Hundreds of fires broke out almost instantaneously. The panic-stricken citizens of Tokyo crowded into small open areas only to die of the heat and suffocation as the flames from surrounding buildings consumed most of the available oxygen. When the fires were finally extinguished, there were more than 100,000 dead, 40,000 seriously injured, and nearly a half million houses demolished. The Japanese had learned a costly lesson. The rebuilt cities have broad streets to accommodate fire trucks, fire-fighting systems designed to function even during earthquakes, auxiliary water systems, and buildings constructed to resist damage.

DEFENSE AGAINST EARTHQUAKES

If there is an earthquake near your home this year, will you know what to do to lessen the danger to your family and yourself? Is it possible to reduce the hazards of earthquakes? Can anything be done in earthquake-prone areas to lessen the intensity of future earthquakes? Geophysicists and engineers are aggressively examining these questions, and their research holds great promise.

Planning for earthquakes

Every major earthquake stimulates interest in revising building codes, initiating more rigorous zoning rules, and providing for emergency water and power. The newer buildings in earthquake- prone areas of the U.S., Russia, China, and Japan are designed to resist damage from shaking. The effectiveness of these efforts can be judged by comparing the damage from earthquakes that occur in underdeveloped countries with the lesser damage caused by recent earthquakes of the same magnitude that have occurred in Japan and the United States. Even in the world's most modern cities, however, there is no reason for complacency. Many of our most

Table 3.2. Earthquake safety tips.

The following checklist of action to take in the event of an earthquake may be clipped and posted for handy reference.

Before

1. Store emergency supplies: food, water, first aid kit, flashlight and battery-powered radio.
2. Take a practical first aid course.
3. Locate main switches and valves that control the flow of water, gas, and electricity into your house. Know how to operate them.
4. Support community programs that inform the public and emergency personnel about earthquake preparedness.
5. Take action to strengthen or eliminate structures that are not earthquake-resistant.
6. Support "parapet ordinances" that would remove dangerous unreinforced overhangs and cornices from buildings.
7. Support building codes that require earthquake-resistant construction and careful foundation preparation and grading.
8. Support land-use policies that recognize and allow for the potential dangers of active fault zones.
9. Heavy furniture above the fifth floor in tall buildings should be bolted to the floor.
10. Require guard rails across the inside of plate glass windows that extend to the floor.
11. Support basic research into the cause and mechanism of earthquakes and fault movement.

During

1. Don't panic even if you are frightened.
2. If you are indoors, stay there. Get under a desk, table, or doorway.
3. Do not rush outside. Failing debris has caused many deaths.
4. Watch for falling plaster, bricks, and other objects.
5. If you are outside, move away from buildings and power lines; stay in the open.
6. If you are in a moving car, stop as soon as it is safe. Remain in the car.

After

1. Check your family or the people near you for injuries.
2. Inspect your utilities for damage to water, gas, or electrical conduits. If they are damaged, turn them off.
3. Extinguish open flames.
4. Do not use the telephone except to report an emergency.
5. Turn on your battery-powered radio for emergency information.
6. Don't go sightseeing.
7. Stay away from damaged structures; aftershocks can cause the collapse of weakened structures.
8. Stay away from beaches and waterfront areas subject to seismic sea waves (commonly called "tidal waves").

cherished structures were built long before the advent of seismology, and far too many more recently constructed buildings lack the necessary safeguards, either because of costs, public apathy, or ignorance. Zoning plans frequently fail to include considerations of the nature, water content, and strength of the materials upon which construction is planned. In general, solid rock is a much safer foundation material than granular soil or sediment because such loose material tends to magnify seismic wave amplitudes. On some occasions construction is planned directly over active faults.

Clearly, we cannot start anew in designing earthquake-proof cities. We can, however, continuously improve cities and make intelligent decisions regarding new construction. Buildings being erected in earthquake-prone areas should include special supports and braces to provide good horizontal strength so that they can resist the "whip-lash" effect caused by ground shifting laterally beneath them and the side-to-side shaking that occurs during earthquakes. At all levels, the structure should be anchored and bonded so that the parts of the building move as a unit, although with limited flexibility.

The prediction of earthquakes

If it were possible to predict the precise time, size, and place of earthquakes, thousands of lives could be saved by evacuation. Although the prediction of earthquakes within months or days has been reported in China and Japan, such predictions are still rarely possible for most areas. Seismic risk maps developed from compilations of the distribution and intensity of earthquakes cannot be used for prediction but are at least helpful in evaluating seismic risks for purposes of building design and insurance.

Long-term earthquake prediction of a rather vague nature can be made, and such forecasts help to increase the public's awareness of the need for precautions. For example, studies conducted along the San Andreas Fault in California suggest a break will occur within the next two decades. Forces have been building up along the fault since the 1906 earthquake. Calculations suggest there is now enough of this stored energy to propel one side of the fault at least 5 meters—an amount approaching the 6.5 meters of slippage that occurred in 1906.

In order to predict a major earthquake more precisely, scientists must learn to detect and evaluate the often subtle changes that occur in the physical characteristics of the rocks that are experiencing earthquake-induced stress. Sometimes, the rocks respond to the build-up of stress by a series of staccatolike slippages that generate a cluster of preliminary

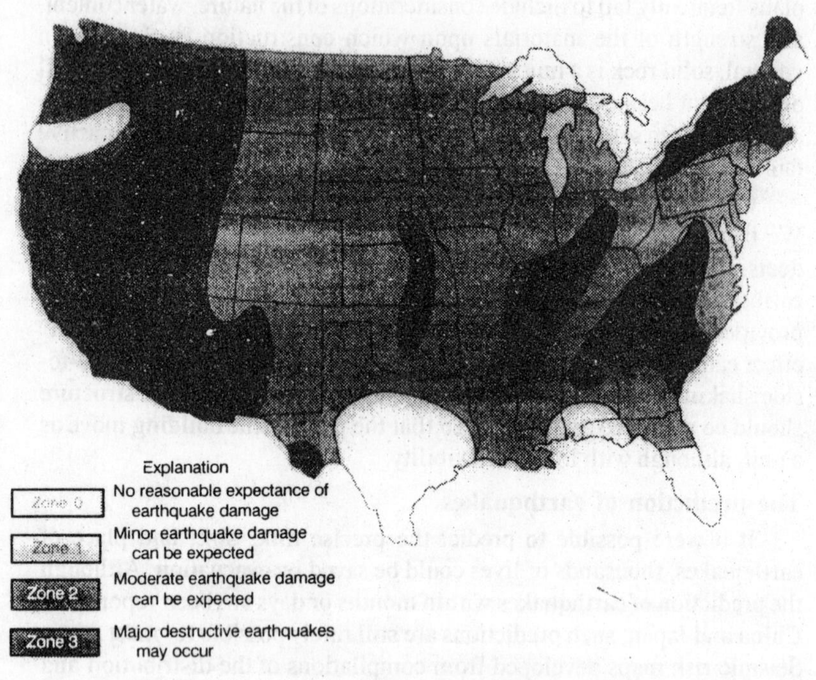

Fig. 3.24. Eathquake risk map of the U.S.

small earthquakes called *foresbocks.* It has been shown that foreshocks have indeed preceded some intense earthquakes. There are, however, other ways that the crust may signal the build-up of stress. Many of these clues are measurable. For example, if parts of the crust are either compressed or stretched, rocks will experience changes in density, water content, and magnetism. They may be tilted, raised, or lowered by amounts that can be measured with the help of sensitive instruments. In the investigations of areas having a high seimic risk, instrument stations are arranged in a network so as to record automatically these crustal changes. The stations in an array contain not only seismographs but tiltmeters, strain gauges, magnetometers, gravity meters, and electrical resistivity devices (for measuring changes in water content). The data are carefully monitored and their importance in predicting earthquakes assessed.

Another promising method for earthquake predictions involves careful analysis of the compressional waves generated when rocks rupture. The velocity of these waves decreases during the warning foreshocks but increases again just prior to the main earthquake. Evidently, the foreshocks create a fracture system in the rock, and the compressional waves are slowed in moving through the suddenly more porous material. Soon after, the voids fill with water, restoring the elasticity to the rock and its ability to transmit seismic waves more rapidly. Study of earthquake records (scismograms) during the 1971 San Fernando earthquake in California revealed that the alternate slowing and speeding up of earthquake waves did precede the major shaking.

Reducing earthquake intensity

Because of the enormity of the forces that cause earthquakes, the very thought of exercising control over them seems absurd. Nevertheless, geologists whose sanity has never been questioned are seriously seeking ways to reduce the intensity of future earthquakes. One method for possibly "defusing" earthquakes came to light in the early 1960s. At that time, water containing chemical waste from the U.S. Army Rocky Mountain Arsenal was being discarded by pumping it down a 3800-meter drill hole into the cracks and joints of an ancient body of deeply buried granite. To the surprise and embarrassment of the Army, it was discovered that the project was causing earthquakes. Furthermore, the frequency of earthquakes correlated closely with the rates at which the fluid was pumped into the granite. Study of the earthquake records indicated the tremors originated from vertical slippages along faults in the granite. The interpretation of the data seemed selfevident. Before pumping the fluid into the granite, the faults had been locked by irregularities in their surfaces and by mineral cement. The injected fluids widened joints and lubricated zones of slippage. The result was to allow movement to relieve minor stress build-up and cause earthquakes.

The Rocky Mountain Arsenal episode suggested to geologists that stress accumulating over a long period of time along a major fault might be relieved gradually (in a series of small shocks) by pumping water into the fault zone. In this way, a major disaster might be averted. It might also be feasible to strengthen the locked segments of a fault by removing water and thereby temporarily prevent an earthquake. These intriguing possibilities were soon to be tested in a controlled experiment at the Rangely oil field in northwestern Colorado. Prior to the experiment, water had been injected into oil-bearing sandstones in the field in an effort to recover residual oil. The practice had caused earthquakes that originated

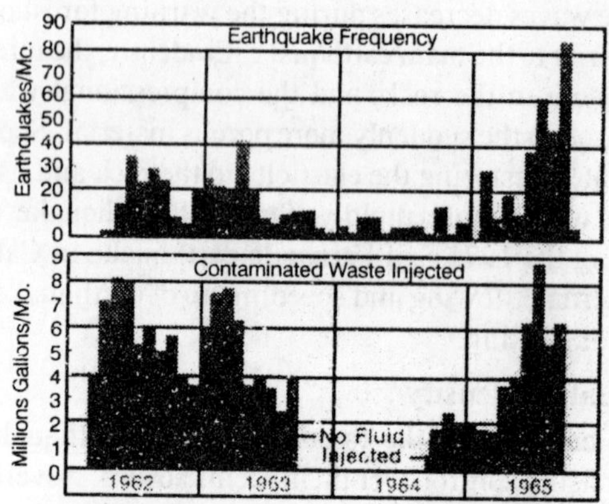

Fig. 3.25. In 1965, geologist David Evans showed this correlation between fluid injected into a waste disposal well at the Rocky Mountain Arsenal and eathquake frequancy.

in a fault that traversed the field at depth. In order to test the relation between water injection and earthquakes fully, a network of seismographs was set up in the field and continuously monitored from 1969 to 1973. During this period, water was alternately pumped into the ground and then withdrawn. The scientists were rewarded with a dramatic correlation. Earthquakes occurred when water was pumped into the subsurface, and earthquakes ceased when the water was pumped out.

The information derived from the Rocky Mountain Arsenal and Rangely studies suggested a scheme for relieving stress along active faults. In theory, deep wells might be drilled several km apart up and down the length of great faults. Next, water might be pumped into the wells in one segment of the fault and withdrawn in the next adjacent segment. The lubricated segment would slip a short distance, but the slippage would be halted in the "dry" section. The process could then be repeated farther along the fault by injecting water in the dry segment and withdrawing water from the next segment farther up the fault line. In this way, stress along the fault could be relieved segment by segment. There might be many small and harmless slippages rather than a disastrous break. The method, however, has not been adequately tested, and it carries with it the risk of generating larger than expected earthquakes.

The Earthquake Source

Earthquakes are generated by a release of stored elastic energy, which is accompanied by the sudden movement of rock masses on opposite sides of a rupture surface cutting through solid rock. These rupture surfaces are called *faults*. The three types of faults are listed here:

1. Strike-slip faults: Displacement of one rock mass past the other is principally in the horizontal direction, parallel with the strike of the fault.
2. Reverse faults: Displacement of one rock mass past the other is principally in the dip direction. The block above the fault moves upwards over the underlying block.
3. Normal faults: Displacement is principally in the dip direction. The block above the fault moves downwards relative to the underlying block .

Fig shows the epicenter and focus for an earthquake originating on a fault that is not vertical, and Fig. shows the epicenter and focus for an earthquake on a vertical fault.

Faulting occurs when the *shear stress* acting along the potential fault plane in solid rock exceeds the *shear strength* of the rock. Thus, the distribution of faulting and of earthquakes is controlled by the processes and conditions responsible for creating local concentrations of *shear stress* in the earth's crust.

Crustal Plates

Most concentrations of shear stress are attributed to the slow movement of the large plates of the earth's crust, movements that take place at rates on the order of centimeters/year (cm/yr). These plates can move away from each other, past one another, or toward one another. Their movement concentrates shear stress at the *boundaries* of the plates; it can also concentrate stress at locations *within* the plates.

The outlines and names of the major crustal plates are shown in Fig. These plates move away from ridges such as the Mid-Atlantic Ridge and Mid- Pacific Ridge. Where two plates move toward one another, they may collide as is illustrated by the collision of India and the Asian continent along the Himalayas. Alternatively, one plate may move under the other in a zone called a *subduction zone*. Subduction zones are important features along the Aleutian Islands and the west coast of South America. In the Aleutian Islands the Pacific Plate moves down under the continental plate represented by Alaska; along the west coast of South America the Nazca plate moves under the South American Plate. Plates also move past one

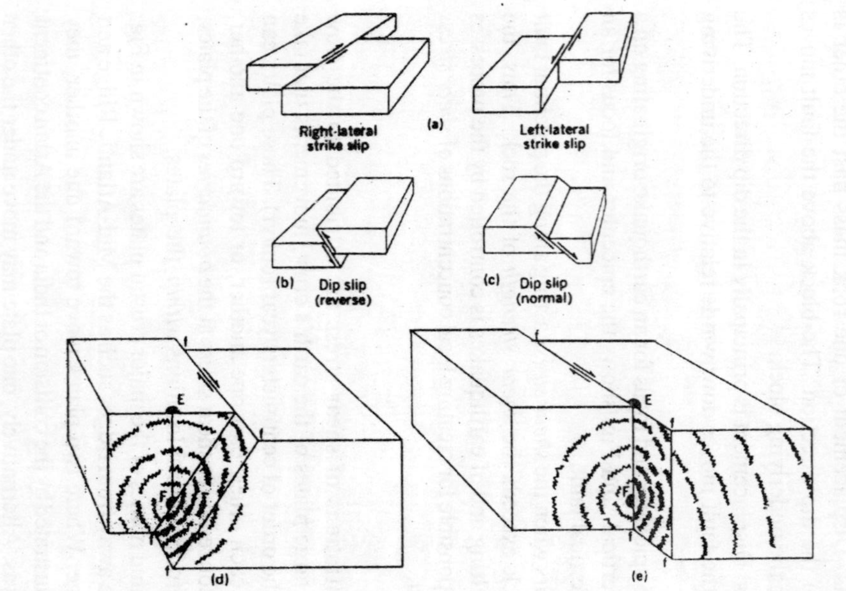

Fig. 3.26. Block diagrams showing sense of movement of bocks on opposite sides of (a) strike-slip fault, (b) reserve fault, (c) normal fault. Diagram (d) and (e) show positions of a possible focus (F) of an earthquake and the corresponding epicenter (E).

another along vertical boundaries that are called *transform faults,* a type of fault illustrated by the San Andreas fault in California.

Many great faults are located along these plate boundaries. Some, like the San Andreas fault, are seen at the earth's surface; other are hidden beneath the surface.

Along some boundaries the dominant form of movement is strike-slip movement, as in California. Along other boundaries, reverse faulting dominates, as in the Aleutians. Reverse and strike-slip faults also occur within plates, and normal faults are important within plates as well, as may be seen in Utah and Nevada. The relationship between earthquakes and the boundaries of these plates may be seen on maps showing the epicenters of moderate-to-large earthquakes occurring in a time interval of a few years. Belts of high earthquake density, marked by closely spaced or overlapping dots, typically lie along the plate boundaries. The greatest earthquake densities are found along the subduction zones and the large transform faults.

Figure also shows that there are clusters of earthquake epicenters well within plates and far from boundaries. Such clusters are conspicuous in the People's Republic of China, in the contiguous Soviet Union, and in a region within the North American Plate centered on New Madrid, Missouri.

This summary provides the large framework that governs fault and earthquake distribution. Before turning to the case histories, it will be helpful to also examine the relationships between plate movement, movement on faults, and earthquake generation as illustrated in a zone along the boundary between the Pacific Plate and the North American Plate, in California.

A Plate-Boundary Fault System

The boundary zone separating the Pacific Plate from the North American Plate is characterized by the presence of a number of large strike-slip faults that divide the earth's crust into large blocks. These blocks move past one another as a result of the movement of the two great plates. The Pacific Plate has been moving northwest past the North American Plate at an average rate of 55 mm/yr for the past 4.5 million years (Atwater and Molnar, 1973), and it continues to do so as confirmed by astronomical observations. From this we infer that the lower parts of these two great plates are moving rather smoothly in opposite directions, each acting like a great conveyor belt carrying the near-surface rocks northwest and southeast. Since the total plate movement is distributed

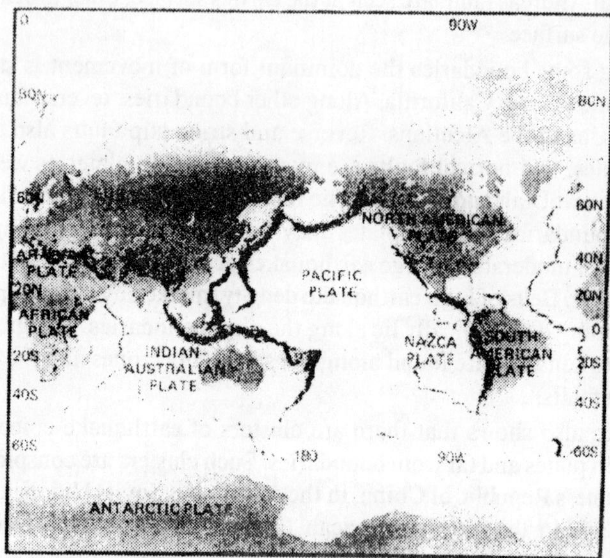

Fig. 3.27. World earthquake map showing relationship between the major plates and earthquake zones.

among the movement of several blocks, the average rate of movement any one block past an adjacent block is less than the 55 mm/yr average for relative movement of the plates. The rates of movement of some of the individual blocks as measured at the surface are shown in Fig..

In some places most of the movement of one block past another takes place during earthquakes. This kind of displacement is called *seismic slip* because it is associated with earthquakes. In other places, most of the movement of one block past another takes place smoothly and continuously. This type of movement is called *aseismic creep.*

Both kinds of movement occur on the three major faults in the San Francisco Bay area-the San Andreas, Calaveras, and Hayward faults. Some important terms and concepts may be illustrated by examining observations made on these faults.

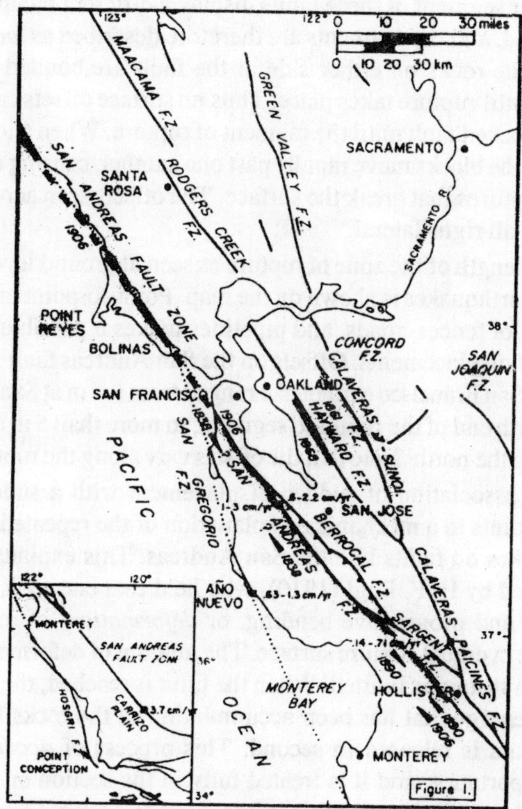

Fig. 3.28. Plate-boundary fault system in the San Francisco Bay area. Zones on which historic rupture has occurred are indicated by shading o by arrows and year. Some historic creep rates are indicated in cm/yr. Inset map shows southen extension of San Andeas fault.

Segments of each of these faults display aseismic creep. These segments are said to be *unlocked* because the rocks on one side of the unlocked segment move slowly past those on the other side. This steady slip progressively displaces structures that cross these unlocked segments. One of the most accessible examples of this is in Hollister, California, where a rectangular street grid is cut by the Calaveras fault. All street crossing this fault are being slowly offset by the movement of the underlying blocks . The offsets shown are called *right-lateral* offset because the block in the back in the background of each photograph has been displaced to the right of the observer.

Other segment of these faults display a different bahavior. No creep is observed, and the segments are therefore described as *locked segments* because the rocks on either side of the fault are bonded firmly to one another until rupture takes place. Thus no surface offsets can be observed across a locked fault until the moment of rupture. When a locked segment ruptures, the blocks move rapidly past one another, causing obvious offsets across ruptures that break the surface. The offsets seen across these three faults are all right-lateral.

The length of the zone of rupture as seen at ground level after several historic earthquakes is shown on the map. Point-to-point measurement of the offset of fences, roads, and pipelines makes it possible to construct a picture of displacements. Offsets on the San Andreas fault resulting from the 1906 San Francisco earthquake ranged from 0.5 m at San Juan Bautista, at the south end of the ruptured segment, to more than 5 m at Point Reyes, 150 km to the north. Note that the offsets vary along the ruptured segment.

The association of sudden displacement with a sudden release of energy points to a mechanical explanation of the repeated occurrence of earthquakes on faults like the San Andreas. This explanation was first formulated by H. F. Reid (1910), who held that energy is stored during the slow and progressive bending, or *deformation,* of rocks in a zone along the eventual rupture surface. The amount of deformation that these rocks can sustain is limited. When the limit is reached, the rocks rupture, and the energy that has been accumulating in the rocks for a period of many years is released in second. This process of *accumulation* is of great importance, and it is treated fully in the section on approaches to earthquake prediction. Further information on each of these concepts will be provided in sections that follow.

In some areas, 90 percent of the houses collapsed. In spite of this, the loss of life was kept relatively low. In one segment of the very heavily damaged area in Haicheng, only 1 of the 3000 residents was injured thanks to complete pre-earthquake evacuation of buildings. In the absence of evacuation, the majority of the 3000 people would have been killed or seriously injured. The importance of prediction was underscored the next year when 650,000 people lost their lives in an earthquake at Tangshen, China.

The Evaluation of Earthquake Hazard

Existing earthquake hazards have been identified in many areas in the United States and have been evaluated by following a systematic procedure described by Hays (1980) and Evernden, Kohler, and Clow (1981):

1. Identify seismic sources.
2. Estimate the probability that large earthquakes will be generated at each source.
3. Estimate the large-scale intensity pattern that might be associated with earthquake activity at each source.
4. Develop detailed local intensity maps and supporting data.
5. Examine the existing distribution of structures of various types. Knowing the expected response of these structures to the predicted instensities, develop maps and supporting data to illustrate expected levels of damage and loss of life and occurrence of injuries.

These steps are reviewed below.

Identifying the Location of Future Earthquakes

Two approaches are used to identify areas in which faulting and future earthquakes can be expected to occur-the *seismologic approach* and the *geologic approach*. These approaches are based on two important principles. The seismologic approach assumes that future earthquakes will occur in those areas where earthquakes have been common in the past. The *geologic approach* assumes that future earthquakes will be most common on faults on which there has been movement in the recent past.

These approaches may appear to be two ways of expressing a single point, but implementing each approach depends on making specific types of observations, one based on instrumental records and the other on the geologic record. Each approach may be employed independently, but they are commonly used in conjunction with one another. Each will be considered separately here.

The *seismologic approach*. Seismologic records of thousands of past earthquakes provide the basis for preparing maps and cross sections showing the distribution of epicenters and hypocenters of past earthquakes. To be readable, these maps and sections show earthquakes activity for limited time interval, or they show epicenter or hypocenter locations for earthquakes within a limited magnitude range.

An epicenter map shows the epicenters of earthquakes in the central United States. If we assume that the future pattern of seismicity will mimic the past pattern, then this map presents a view of the distribution of future seismicity in this region. Maps of this sort serve as raw material for contour maps,that shows the frequency of seismic events in different regions. On such map the areas enclosed by the highest value contour are those in which future earthquake a activity is most probable.

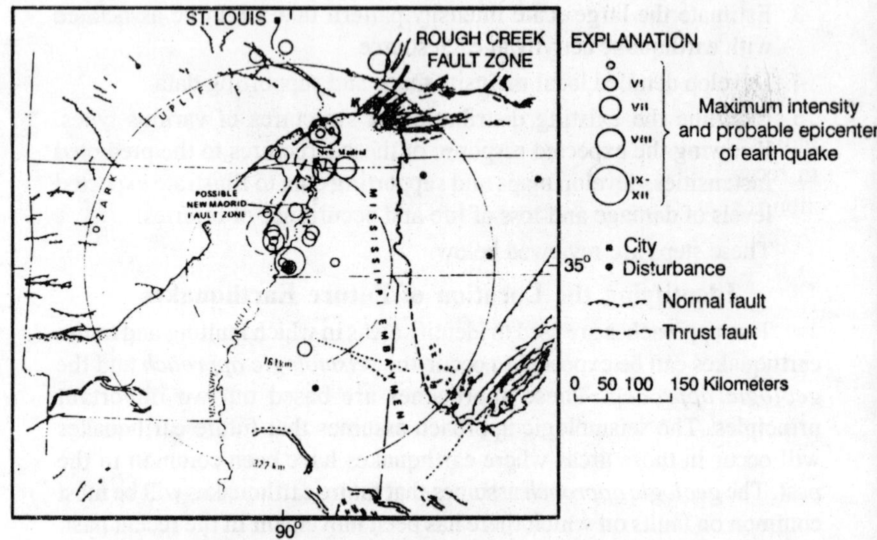

Fig. 3.29. Map of earthquake activity in the Mississippi Valley region of the U.S.

Another seismologic approach is based on the identification of segments of an *active* plate boundary on which no major earthquakes have occurred within a specified time interval, say 30 years. Such segments are called *seismic gaps.* Each such segment is known to have been the site of major earthquakes in the past and is viewed as a segment in which energy is steadily being accumulated and stored. This method does not require that a specific fault be identified at the surface. The technique has been used to make forecasts for the margin of the Pacific Plate along the Aleutian Trench and the Alaskan coast.

This margin is known to have been broken, one segment at a time, during large earthquakes in the historic past, and the entire margin is identified as being active (Sykes et al., 1981). Each major earthquake along this margin has been accompanied by displacement on faults hundreds of kilometers long. These faults have not been mapped at the surface, but their extent has been mapped from the distribution of hypocenters of aftershocks. The hypocenters are believed to lie along the ruptured segment of the fault.

The map of aftershock zones of major earthquakes occurring in Alaska shows several conspicuous gaps in which no earthquake or aftershock activity has been observed for tens of years. Each of these gaps was regarded as one of the most probable locations for a future major earthquake. After these gaps were first identified, a major earthquake occurred in the Yakataga Gap.

Another way of showing this kind of information is on a space-time plot of seismicity for regions in which major earthquakes have occurred in recent years. On such a plot, the time of each earthquake is scaled along the horizontal axis, and the distance of the earthquake epicenter from an arbitrary reference point, called a *pole*, is plotted on the vertical axis. Areas of low seismic activity appear within the pattern of dots. These areas of quiescence may point to the time and place of occurrence of a future large earthquake. This approach was followed by Ohtake, who successfully forecast a 1978 earthquake at Oaxaca, Mexico (Ohtake et al., 1981; see also review by Kanamori, 1981). This approach was successful at Oaxaca, and it is now being employed to identify similar situations along other faults, one of which is the San Andreas fault.

The seismic gap method has been employed worldwide. A record has been compiled showing successful forecasts made by using this method (Nishenko and Mc Cann, 1981). The location of earthquakes forecast around the Pacific is shown in fig., which also shows gaps in which future great earthquakes are expected.

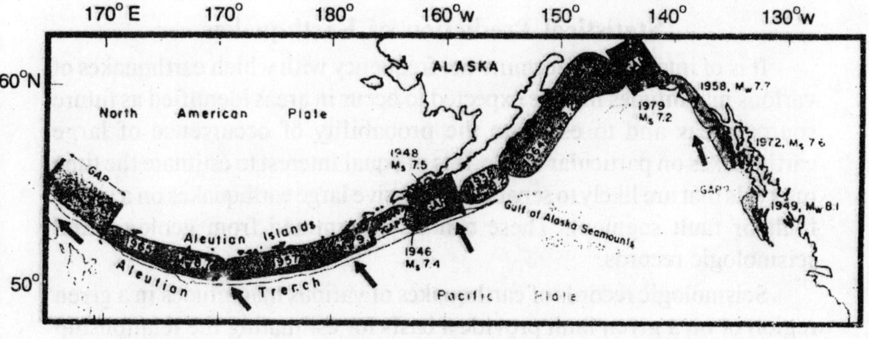

Fig. 3.30. Map of aftershock zones of major earthquake along the Aleutian Tench and Southeasten Alaskan coast.

The *geologic approach*. The second approach provides another way to identify the sites of future earthquakes. It was first described by Allen (1975), who showed that the location of virtually all major California earthquakes between 1912 and 1974 had been or could have been identified on the basis of fault mapping. Allen argued that a study of other less well-known areas might also show the merits of this approach.

As a demonstration of this approach, Allen (1975) showed that the landscape along and on either side of the North Anatolian fault in Turkey displaced physiographic features very similar to those displayed along the San Andreas fault in California. He argued that these features demonstrated a history of repeated movements on the Anatolian fault in the past. He also showed that the Anatolian fault was a guide to the locations of earthquakes. He did this by plotting the epicenters of an extraordinary series of major earthquakes. After an earthquake in 1939, each successive earthquake took place west of the preceding one, and each was separated from its predecessor by periods of from 1 to 13 years.

A strikingly similar relationship is shown for the San Jacinto fault in southern California (Thatcher, Hileman, and Hanks, 1975). Here nine moderate earthquakes having magnitudes between 6 and 7 have been spread along the fault since the firstknown earthquake took place in 1890. In these and other cases, the mapped fault is viewed as the locus of future earthquakes.

Geologically based areal predictions as well as their seismologically based counterparts help to focus attention on zones deserving of special study and concern. These special studies can address the problems of statistical, temporal, and contingent prediction.

Statistical Prediction of Earthquakes

It is of interest to determine the frequency with which earthquakes of various magnitudes may be expected to occur in areas identified as future source areas and to estimate the probability of occurrence of large earthquakes on particular faults. It is of equal interest to estimate the time intervals that are likely to separate successive large earthquakes on a single fault or fault segment. These can be determined from geologic and seismologic records.

Seismologic records of earthquakes of various magnitudes in a given region or on a given fault provide a basis for estimating the relationship between magnitude and frequency. This is illustrated by a record of the occurrence of 10,126 earthquakes that occurred in a 296,000-km2 area in southern California during the period 1934-1962 (Albee and Smith, 1966). The average number of earthquakes that occur in various magnitude ranges

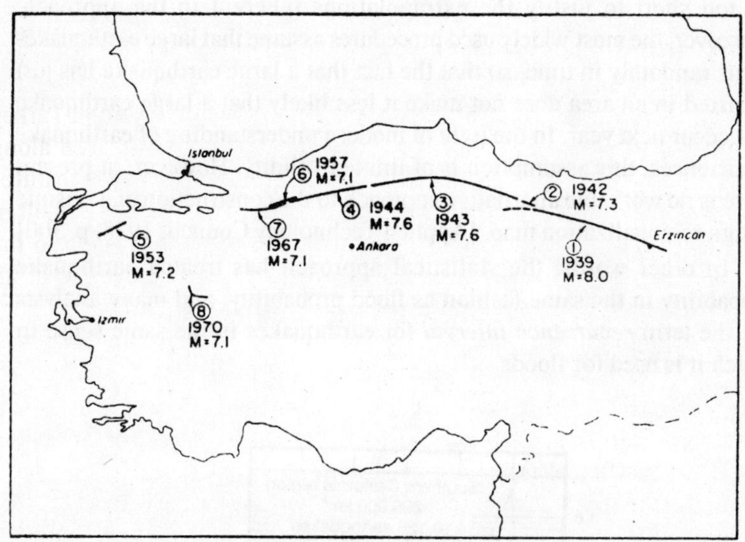

Fig. 3.31. Map of the North Anatolian fault showing epicenters of historic earthquake.

each year per 1000 km2 was determined from this record. These findings are compiled in fig, which shows that the number of earthquakes occurring at any specified magnitude is about eight to ten times greater than the number of earthquakes one unit higher in magnitude.

This provides a basis for estimating the exceedance probabilities for earth- quakes of specified magnitude within the entire region, but it does not help in estimating the probability of an earthquake occurring on a specific fault. A geologic approach has been used to deal with this problem as may be seen from efforts to assign probabilities of large earthquake occurrence on the San Andreas fault and on faults in the Wasatch fault zone in Utah.

Until recently, most statistical predictions were based on instrumental records of seismicity. This is illustrated by the work of Algermissen et al. (1973), which led to the seismic risk map released in 1976 by the Applied Technology Council. All such work leads to estimates of the exceedance probabilities do not vary with time. This has been questioned by some experts, and another Applied Technology Council Report published in 1978 takes note of this in the following statement:

Critics of the seismic risk approach argue that the historical record is far too short to justify the extrapolations inherent in the approach. Moreover, the most widely used procedures assume that large earthquakes occur randomly in time, so that the fact that a large earthquake has just occurred in an area does not make it less likely that a large earthquake will occur next year. In the light of modern understanding of earthquake occurrences, this assumption is of limited validity. However, at present there is no workable alternative approach to the construction of a seismic design regionalization map. [Applied Technology Council, 1978, p. 300]

In other words, the statistical approach has treated earthquake probability in the same fashion as flood probability, and many analysts use the term *recurrence interval* for earthquakes in the same sense in which it is used for floods.

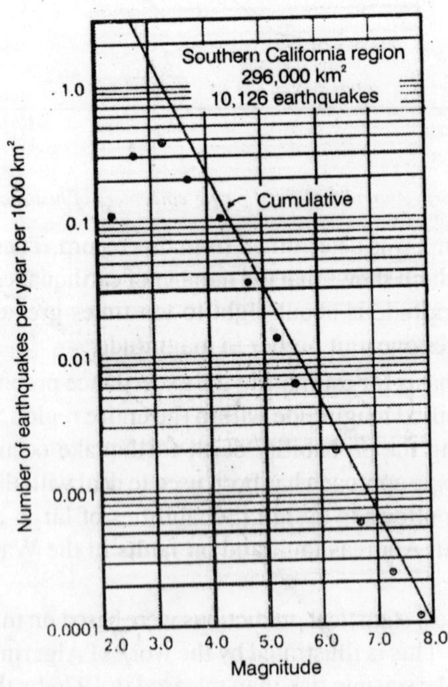

Fig. 3.32. Diagram showing the numberr of earthquakes of varying magnitude that occur per year 1000 km² in southern California.

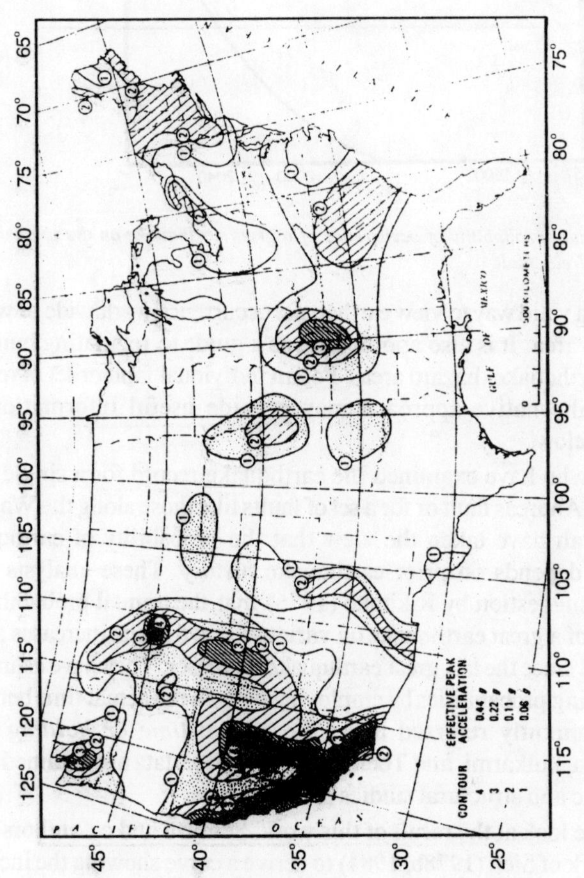

Fig. 3.33. Seismic risk map of the U.S. Contours on the map show the effective peak acceleration expected. This is defined as the acceleration that can be expected at least once in 50 years. It is not the maximum acceleration to be expected.

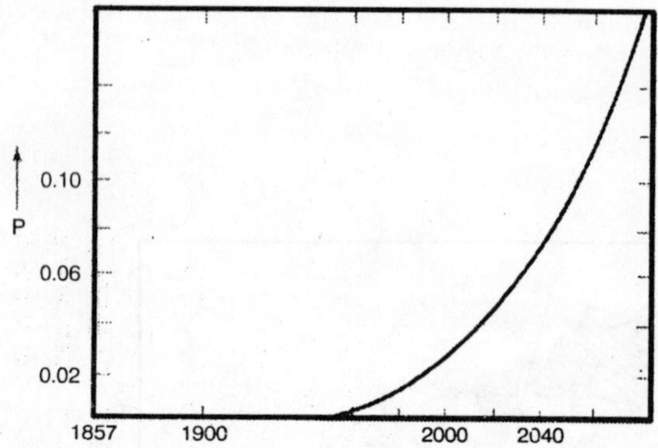

Fig. 3.34. Annual probability of occurrence of a great earthquake on the southern San Andreas fault.

This is a valid way to view earthquake occurrence worldwide or within a very large area. It is also appropriate as a guide to regulating building design in earthquake- hazard areas. For an individual fault or set of related faults, an alternative approach may provide useful information, as discussed below.

Those who have examined the earthquake record for a single fault like the San Andreas fault or for a set of faults like those along the Wasatch Front in Utah have taken the view that the probability of earthquake occurrence depends on prior earthquake history. These analysts have followed a suggestion by Rikitake (1976) that the annual probability of occurrence of a great earthquake on various known faults increases as the time elapsed since the last great earthquake increases. They have estimated these changing probabilities by employing data on the actual time between events, commonly referred to as the *repeat time or holding time* (Patwardhan, kulkarmi, and Tocher, 1980). These data are obtained from stratigraphic and structural studies of fault zones.

Here we look at the result of this work. Schulze and co-authors have used the work of Sieh (1978b, 1984) to derive a curve showing the increase in the annual probability of occurrence of a great earthquake on the south-central segment of the San Andreas fault (Schulze et al., 1981, pp. 1033-38). In 1983, the USGS presented estimates of 0.02 to 0.05 for the then current annual probability of occurrence of great earthquake on the south-central segment of the fault, and it accepted the view that the probability of an earthquake with surficial fault rupture at this site [Pallett Creek] is between 0.2 and 5 percent during 1984 and 7 to 60 percent by the year 2000" (1984,p.7641).

A similar view has been developed for the Wasatch fault system in Utah. Patwardhan, Kulkarni, and Tocher (1980) and Cluff, Patwardhan, and Coppersmith (1980, p. 1473) have argued that the annual probability of the' and damaging earthquake on this system increases with time.

Predicting Earthquake Intensity

The importance of an earthquake to the land-use decision-maker lies in the capacity of an earthquake to do damage and cause harm. The damage or harm results because the shaking of the ground leads to the shaking of structures and geologic materials, which then fail. Because of these failures, every large earthquake in a populated region leaves a record of damage and loss of life. That record is the basis for classifying the effects of the earthquake according to a scale of relative intensity.

We have seen that there are several intensity scales in use , and we have seen intensity maps for the San Fernando and Imperial Valley earthquakes. Now we can examine some of the reasons for the patterns that these maps illustrated.

The basis for observed intensifies. The basis for a particular pattern of earthquake intensity is found in the physics of the earthquake and in the distribution of geologic materials in the affected area.

Each earthquake releases seismic energy that is converted to complex motion of the bedrock, motion that is transmitted in all directions through the bedrock away from the source. In general, the greater the magnitude, the more severe the shaking of the bedrock, and the longer the duration of shaking.

The relationship between the severity of shaking and the distance from the earthquake source is illustrated by examining the variation of intensity on *bedrock* sites according to the perpendicular distance from the fault. This relationship is shown graphically for the San Francisco region and in map form for the 1906 San Francisco and 1811 New Madrid earthquakes.

The graphical representation shows that intensity, as mapped at sites located on bedrock, decreases logarithmically with distance from the epicenter over the distance shown. The intensity at the source is determined by the magnitude of the earthquake. The exact relationship between intensity and distance from the source depends on the nature of the bedrock. This may be seen from the map of the conterminous United States, which shows that the areal extent of a single intensity zone

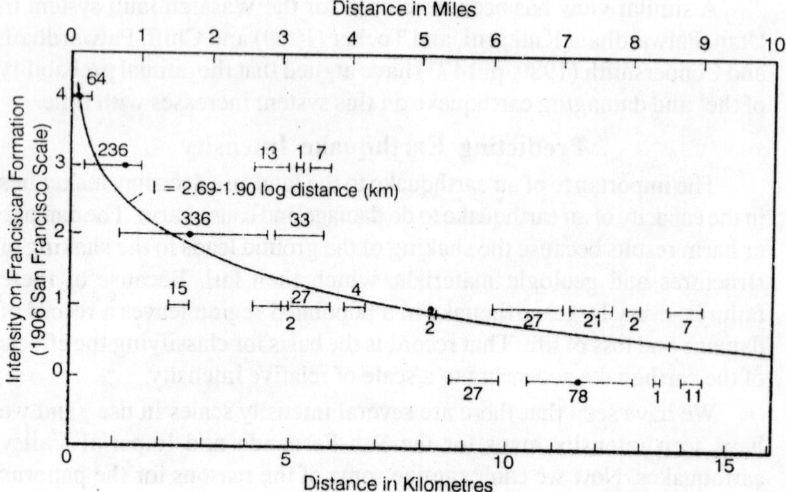

Fig. 3.35. Curves showing the decrease in observed intensity with the increase in perpendicular distance from the San Andrreas fault. The intensities are those observed on bedrock sites.

associated with a magnitude-S earthquake in the eastern United States is much larger than the areal extent of a comparabie zone associated with a magnitude-S earthquake in California. (It is assumed that a magnitude-8 earthquake is possible in the Mississippi Valley because of the occurrence of a great earthquake there in 1812 before instrumental recording had been introduced.) This difference arises because the crystalline rocks that underlie the eastern half of the United States clearly are much more efficient in transmitting seismic shaking'than are the lesswell consolidated rocks that underlie California and the adjacent states.

Earthquake intensity would display a simple pattern in a region where the entire ground surface consisted of bedrock. However, since few developed areas are underlain entirely by bedrock, we can expect earthquake intensity patterns to be complex in direct relation to the complexity of the surficial geology of the region. We turn to this complexity next.

The motion of the ground at a site may be described physically in terms of the peak values of acceleration, velocity, and displacement and

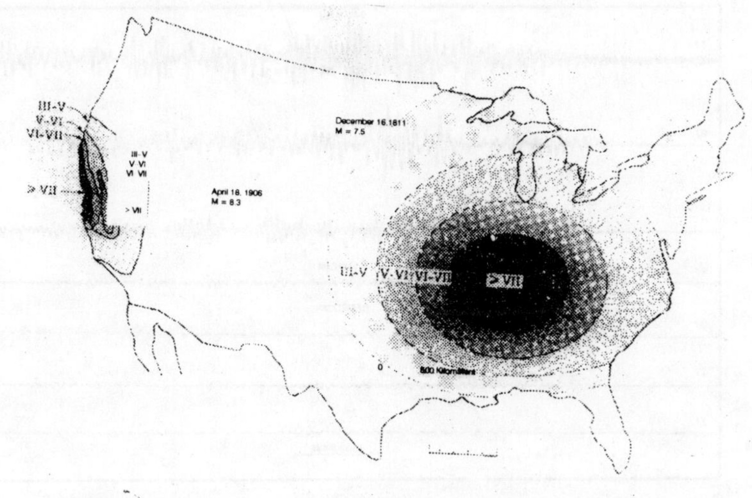

Fig. 3.36. Comparision of areas affected by the 1811 New Madrid earthquake and the 1906 San Francisco earthquake. The larger area occupied by each zone around the new Madrid epicenter results from the greater efficeincy of eastern crustal rocks in transmitting seismic waves.

in terms of the duration of shaking above some threshold amplitude (Page, Blume, and Joyner, 1975, p. 601). These can be determined from seismograms of bedrock shaking at various distances from the source during a particular earthquake.

The potential for damage resulting from this motion depends on these factors and on the frequencies of vibration of the ground. Predicting earthquake intensifies requires that ground motion on different types of surficial material and fill be predicted first. One approach to this problem is to compare seismograms made simultaneously on bedrock and surficial materials.

Recordings of this sort have been made for shaking induced by earthquakes and by nuclear bomb explosions. A comparison of such recordings shows the effect of the surficial materials. Figure shows recordings of the velocity of horizontal ground motion caused at a site in

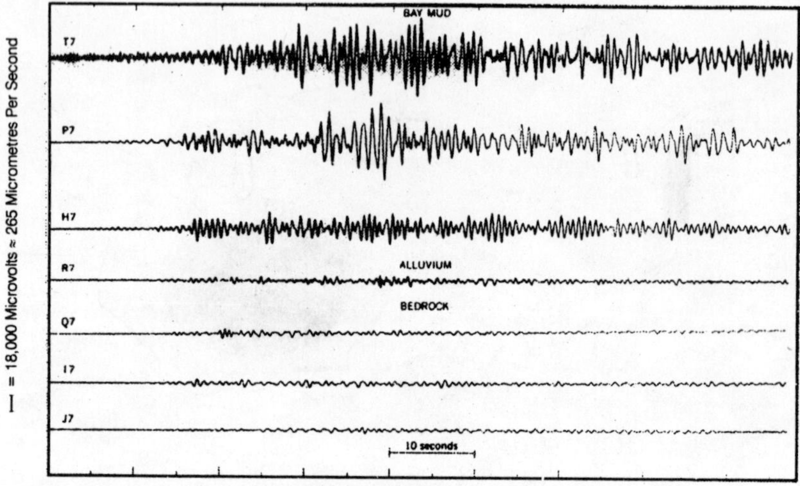

Fig. 3.37. Amplification of horizontal ground motion by bay mud and alluvium in the San Francisco Bay region. Lower three traces show bedrock motion induced by a distance nuclear explosion. Upper three traces show amplification of this motion.

the city of San Francisco by an underground nuclear bomb test 530 km from San Francisco. Note that the velocity of ground motion in the bedrock is small and nearly constant over a 60-second time interval. In contrast, the velocities measured in the overlying alluvium, consisting of water saturated sand, are substantially higher. The velocities in water-saturated bay muds are even higher. These records show instrumental evidence that unconsolidated sediments amplify the input motions provided by the bedrock. Note also that the duration of shaking, as measured by the time interval in which some specified value of velocity is exceeded, is extended in the surficial materials.

The duration of shaking is an extremely important factor as we have seen from Anchorage, Alaska, San Fernando, and the Imperial Valley. At Anchorage, large-scale liquefaction took place after shaking had continued for at least one minute. At San Fernando and the Imperial Valley, it appears that the Olive View Medical Building and the Imperial Valley Services

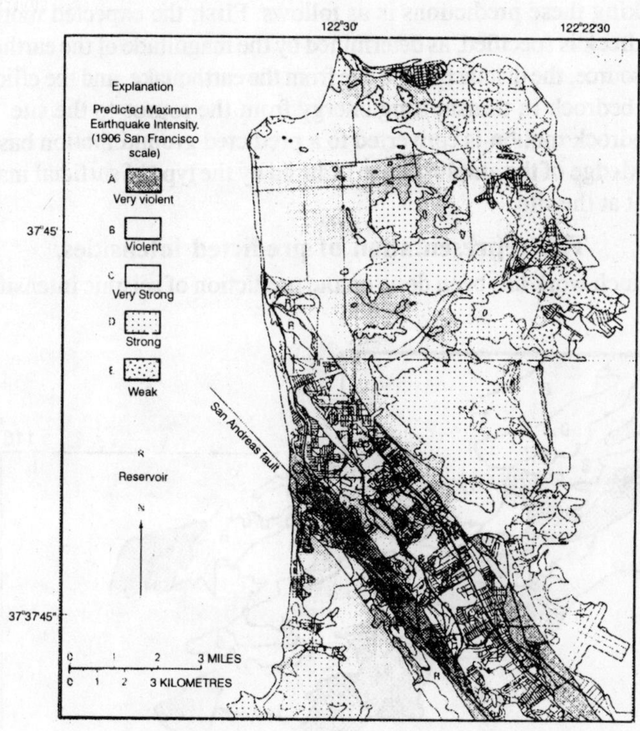

Fig. 3.38. Maximum earthquake intensities predicted for San Francisco assuming a large earthquake on the San Andreas or Hayward faults.

Center remained standing only because strong shaking lasted no more than 12 seconds.

The average duration of shaking on a bedrock site is controlled by magnitude : the larger the magnitude, the greater the duration. Thus, during magnitude- 6 earthquakes, strong shaking may last 10 to 15 seconds, but during a magnitude-8 earthquake, it may last 90 seconds or longer.

These findings provide the necessary foundation for predicting ground motion as influenced by local geologic conditions. The pattern followed in making these predictions is as follows. First, the expected motion of the bedrock is specified, as determined by the magnitude of the earthquake at the source, the distance of the site from the earthquake, and the efficiency of the bedrock in transmitting energy from the source to the site. Then this bedrock motion is converted to a predicted ground motion based on a knowledge of the amplification induced by the type of surficial material present at the site.

The representation of predicted intensities.

Much work has been done on the prediction of seismic intensifies in

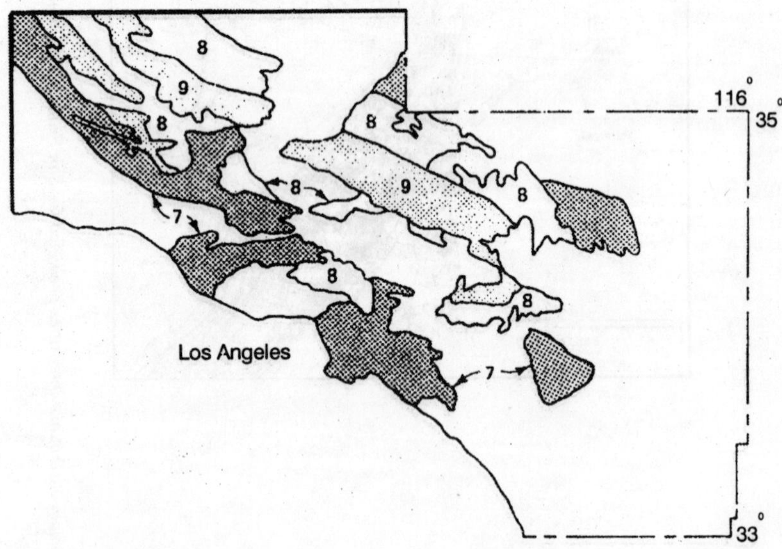

Fig. 3.39. Predicted Rossi-Forel intensities in southern California in the event of a repetition of the 1857 earthquake on the San Andreas fault. Only R-F zones 7, 8, and 9 shown. The fault passes along the center line of R-F zone 9. Note the extensive areas of R-F intensity 8 at a distance from the fault.

the United States and elsewhere. In the United States this work has led to maps drawn on a variety of scales showing the predicted intensifies associated with earthquakes originating at various known sources. Each map represents the expected effects of earthquakes that are known to be possible but that have not yet taken place (see, for example, Evernden, Kohler, and Clow, 1981, and Borcherdt, Gibbs, and Lajoie, 1975).

One of the first of these was published for the San Francisco peninsula. This map showed the maximum earthquake intensifies predicted for San Francisco in the event of a major earthquake on the San Andreas fault or on the Hayward fault. Note that there is a zone of highest intensity (very violent) along the San Andreas fault, and that there is a second such zone 2 km east of the fault at the edge of the San Francisco International Airport. Note also that the area predicted to display the next highest intensity is very large and includes many sites quite distant from the fault.

Another interesting example is provided by Evernden, Kohler, and Clow (1981) for a repeat of the 1857 Fort Tejon earthquake on the southern San Andreas fault. A sample of this map is presented in Fig. Note that the intensity scale used for this map is the Rossi-Forel scale, not the Modified Mercalli scale.

These maps provide the basis for estimating building damages in various zones.

Another anomaly is observed in the form of fluctuation in the amount of the inert gas radon 222 in ground water. This gas is produced continuously by disintegration of uranium 238 (^{238}U) present in the rocks. This gas is itself unstable, having a half-life of 3.8 days. Its concentration in ground water in wells may be measured by radioactivity counting techniques, and the normal level in any well can be established over time. It has been observed that earthquakes are often preceded by a period in which anomalous concentrations of ^{222}Rn are observed in the ground water, as illustrated at Haicheng and in Japan. These radon anomalies are also thought to be the result of dilatancy since the opening up of microcracks could allow radon to diffuse more rapidly toward a given well. The anomalies seem to signal the future occurrence of an earthquake on a time scale of months, but it is not understood why some wells show a rise in the level of 222Rn and others show a decrease. It may be that recognition of the anomaly, whatever its sign (+or -), is sufficient, but efforts continue to determine the explanation for the sign because this may bear on the use of ^{222} Rn as a predictor.

There are many other physical changes that have been studied as possible earthquake precursors; these include changes that appear as gravity or magnetic anomalies or as variations in electrical conductivity in the fault zone. But in addition to all these physical changes, there are effects that are biological, not physical. These biological effects are reported as instances of anomalous animal behavior.

Anomalous behavior of animals

The anomalous behavior of animals prior to large earthquakes has long been reported, but it had not been seriously investigated. In 1974 and 1975, the Chinese may have been encouraged to issue the shortterm prediction of the Haicheng earthquake by a sharp increase in the number of reports of anomalous behavior of animals in the region. These reports were so numerous and seemed to play such a significant part in the Chinese predictions that they were so subsequently studied in some detail by a group of Chinese and American scientific collaborators (Deng et al., 1981).

These investigators compiled reports of 670 incidents of anomalous behavior during the three months prior to the Haicheng earthquake. These

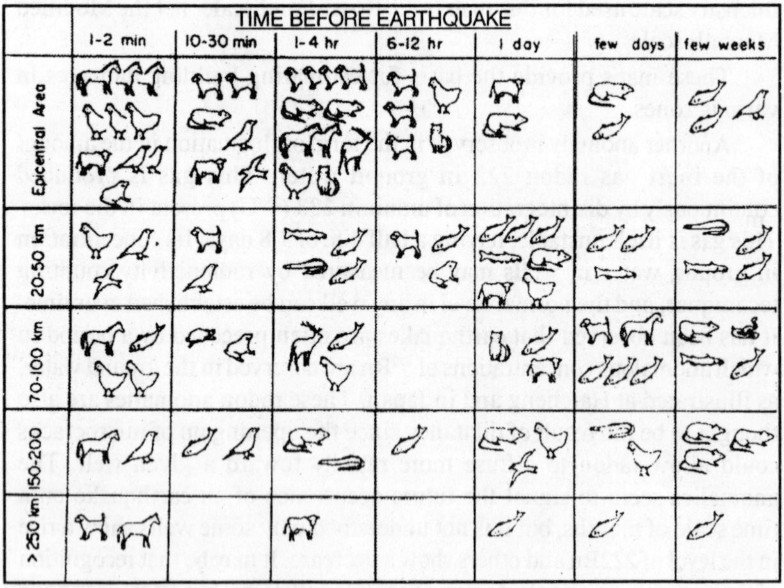

	TIME BEFORE EARTHQUAKE						
	1-2 min	10-30 min	1-4 hr	6-12 hr	1 day	few days	few weeks
Epicentral Area							
20-50 km							
70-100 km							
150-200 km							
> 250 km							

Fig. 3.40. Distribution of animal-behavior incident before the main shock of 36 major earthquake in Europe, Asia, North America, and South America. Symbols indicate reports on : Catfish, eels, other fish frogs, snakes, turtles, sea birds, chickens, other birds, dogs, cats, deer, horse, cows, rats, and mice.

reports ranged from accounts ofbarking dogs and the appearance in homes of apparently dazed groups of mice, to accounts of fish leaping from commercial fish ponds and snakes leaving their holes. Some of these forms of behavior lie within the range of ordinary behavior, but others seem to be quite extraordinary. Of these, the most extraordinary is represented by numerous reports of snakes coming to the ground surface only to freeze, in some instances even before making their way out of their holes. Since temperatures in this part of China average from -10 to -150C in late January and early February, snakes are not normally seen at this time. Such incidents were regarded therefore as extending far beyond the normal range of behavior.

Deng and collaborators (1981) prepared a number of maps showing the geographic distribution of reports of anomalous animal behavior and ground water changes during a series of time intervals prior to the earthquake. They also compared the frequency of reports of anomalous animal behavior with the frequency of reports of ground-water changes. These maps and frequency diagrams were sampled in the section on Haicheng. This examination led to the conclusion that the animals may well have been responding to environmental changes created by physical changes in the region. Fluctuating ground-water levels and ground-water quality may have been sensed by the animals. The animals may also have sensed gases driven from the rocks and small earthquakes not perceptible to humans.

These authors (Deng et al., 1981) note that many of the reports were made by amateur observers already aware of the possibility of the occurrence of an earthquake, so that the reporting was not done under scientifically controlled conditions. But they also note that the reports were so numerous, and some instances of animal behavior so strikingly anomalous, as to suggest that this line of investigation deserves to be pursued carefully.

Buskirk, Frohlich, and Latham (1981) have reviewed research on animal behavior preceding earthquakes. They have found that there is evidence that some animals may be particularly sensitive to detecting geophysical stimuli occurring in earthquake accumulation zones. They have also compiled observations on patterns of animal behavior in an effort to determine what relationships exist between the time interval of anomalous behavior of specific animal species and the occurrence of the earthquake.

Chapter 4

Metamorphic Rocks and the Continental Crust

Rock metamorphism consists of physical and chemical changes in rock in an environment of high temperature, high confining pressure, or intense shearing action, or some combination of two or three of those factors, but without melting. The definition usually excludes chemical changes caused by hydrothermal solutions penetrating rock at shallow depths where pressures are very low. Generally speaking, rock metamorphism occurs under confining pressures of at least 2 kilobars (kb).

Rock metamorphism can result in the formation of new minerals, new rock textures, new rock structures, or a combination of such changes. The formation of new minerals by recrystallization of preexisting minerals is usually the most distinctive and important aspect of metamorphism that affects large masses of rock over wide areas. Crystal lattices are broken down and re-created, using different combinations of the same ions that were present in the earlier minerals. Another aspect of rock metamorphism is the importation of ions and atoms of rock-forming minerals from an outside source, or the export of various substances to an outside region (usually the overlying rock). Geologists refer to this import-export process as *metasomatism*. When it occurs, the rock undergoes corresponding changes in chemical composition. One important example of metasomatism during rock metamorphism is the loss of volatiles-particularly water and carbon dioxide.

The Standad Geologic Time Scale

The early geologists had no way of knowing how many time units would be represented in the completed geologic time scale, nor could they know which fossils would be useful in correlation or which new strata might be discovered at a future time in some distant corner of the globe. Consequently, the time scale grew piecemeal, in an unsystematic manner. Units were named as they were discovered and studied.

Sometimes the name for a unit was borrowed from local geography, from a mountain range in which rocks of a particular age were well exposed, or from an ancient tribe of Welshmen; sometimes the name was suggested by the kind of rocks that predominated.

Divisions in the Geologic Time Scale

The two major divisions in the geologic time scale are termed eons. Approximately seven eighths of all of earth history was expended in the first eon-the Cryptozoic Eon (informally termed "Precambrian"). To a geologist, the biblical phrase "in the beginning" alludes to this long interval of time that began about 4.6 billion years ago.

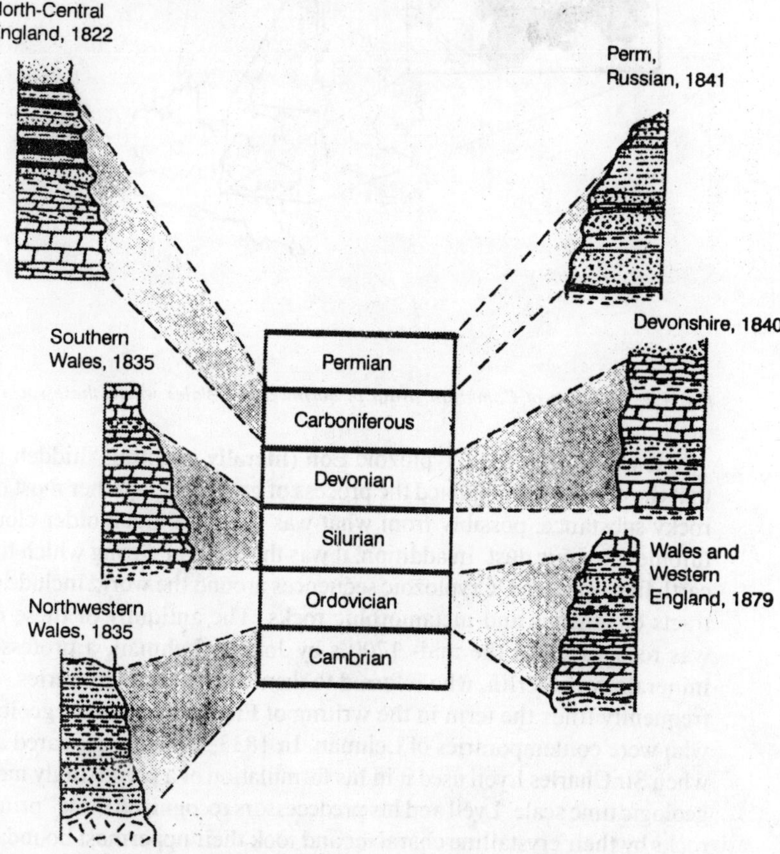

Fig. 4.1. The standard geologic time scale for the Paleogoic and other eras developed without benefit of a grand plan, but rather by the compilation of type section for each of the system.

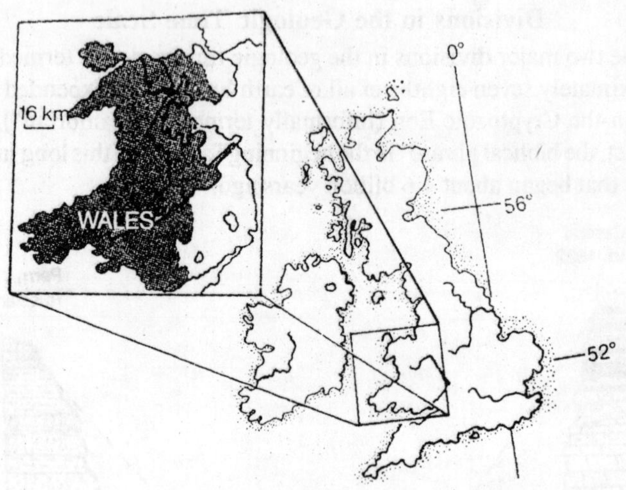

Fig. 4.2. Outcrop of Cambrian strata in northwestern Wales where these rocks were named.

It was during the Cryptozoic Eon (literally meaning "hidden life") that the earth had completed the process of gathering together most of the rocky substance, possibly from what was part of a much older cloud of turbulent cosmic dust. In addition, it was the interval during which life on earth first appeared. Cryptozoic sequences around the world include great tracts of igneous and metamorphic rocks. The antiquity of these rocks was recognized in the mid- 1700's by Johann Lehman, a professor of mineralogy in Berlin, who referred to them as the "primary series." One frequently finds the term in the writing of French and Italian geologists who were contemporaries of Lehman. In 1833, the term appeared again when Sir Charles Lyell used it in his formulation of a surprisingly modern geologic time scale. Lyell and his predecessors recognized these "primary" rocks by their crystalline character and took their uppermost boundary to be an unconformity that separated them from the overlying-and therefore younger-fossiliferous strata.

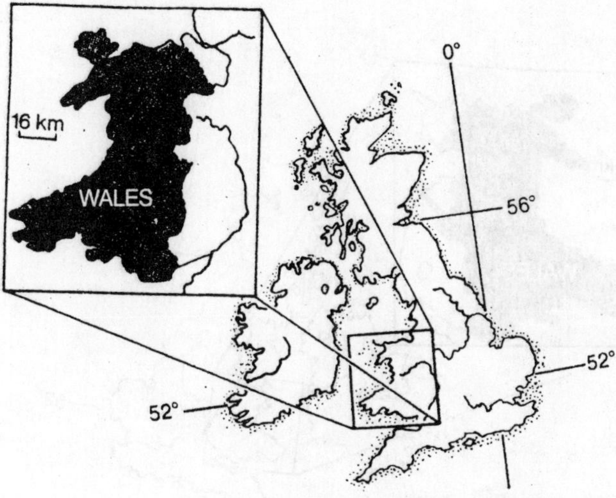

Fig. 4.3. Outcrop of strata of the Silurian Sytem in the classic region of Wales and western England, whee Sir roaderick impey Murchison named them.

All of the remainder of geologic time is included in the second, or *Phanerozoic Eon*. As a result of careful study of superposition accompanied by correlations based on the abundant fossil record of the Phanerozoic, geologists have divided it into three major subdivisions, termed eras. The oldest era is the *Paleozoic*, which we now know lasted about 370 million years. Following the Paleozoic is the *Mesozoic Era*, which continued about 170 million years. The *Cenozoic Era*, in which we are now living, began about 60 million years ago.

The eras are divided into shorter time units called *periods*; periods may in turn be divided into epochs. Eras, periods, epochs, and divisions of epochs, called ages, all represent intangible increments of pure time. They are geologic time units. The rocks formed during a specified interval of time are called time-rock units. For example, strata laid down during a given period compose a *time-rock unit* called a *system*. Each of the geologic systems is recognized largely by its distinctive fauna and flora of fossils.

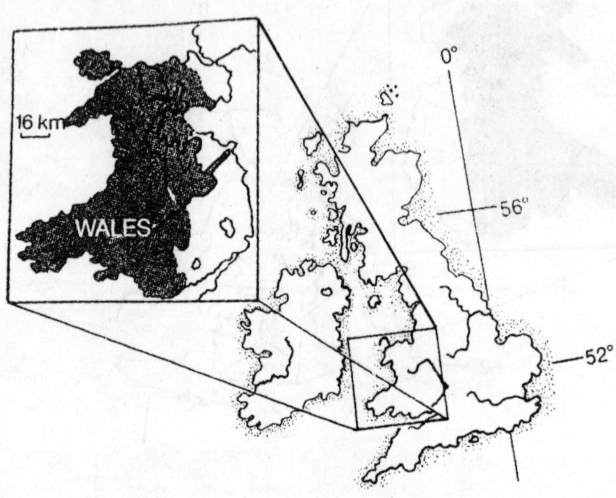

Fig. 4.4. Outcrop pattern of strata of the Ordovician System in the type region of Wales.

The fossils are different in stage of evolution from other fossils in both older and younger systems. Series is the time-rock term used for rocks deposited during an epoch, whereas stage represents the tangible rock record of an age.

Recognition of Time Units

Units of geologic time bear the same names as the time-rock units to which they correspond. Thus, we may speak of the "Jurassic System" or the "Jurassic Period" according to whether we are referring to the rocks themselves or to the time during which they accumulated.

Time terms have come into use as a matter of convenience. Their definition is necessarily dependent upon the existence of tangible time-rock units. The steps leading to the recognition of time- rock units began with the use of superposition in establishing age relationships. Local sections of strata were used by early geologists to recognize beds of successively different age and, thereby, to record successive evolutionary changes in fauna and flora. (The order and nature of these evolutionary changes could be determined because higher layers are successively younger.) Once the faunal and floral succession was deciphered, fossils provided an additional tool for establishing the order of events. They could also be used for correlation, so that strata at one locality could be related to the strata of various other localities. No single place on earth contains a complete sequence of strata from all geologic ages. Hence, correlation to standard sections of many widely distributed local sections was necessary in constructing the geologic time scale. Clearly, the time scale was not conceived as a coherent whole but rather evolved part by part as a result of the individual studies of many earth scientists. Indeed, for some units at the series and stage level, the process continues even today. The fact that the time scale developed in piecemeal fashion is apparent when one reviews its growth and development.

The Cambrian System

The rocks of the Cambrian System take their name from Cambria, the Latin name for Wales. Exposures of strata in Wales provide a standard section with which rocks elsewhere in Europe and on other continents can be correlated. The standard section in Wales is named Cambrian *by definition*. All other sections deposited during the same time as the rocks in Wales are recognized as Cambrian by *comparison* to the standard section.

Adam Sedgwick, a Yorkshire clergyman and professor of geology at Cambridge, named the Cambrian in the 1830's for outcrops of poorly fossiliferous graywackes and dark siltstones sandstones. The area in north Wales that sedgewick studied was noted for its complexity, yet he was able to unravel its geologic history on the basis of spatial relationships and lithology.

The Silurian and Ordovician Systems

At about the same time that Sedgwick was laboring with outcrops that were to become the Cambrian System, another geologist, Sir Rederic lmpey Murchison, had begun studies of fossiliferous strata outcropping in the hills of south Wales. Murchison named these rocks the **Silurian**, taking the name from early inhabitants of western England and Wales know as the *Silures.* In 1835, Murchison and Sedgwick jointly presented a paper, *On the Silurian and Cambrian System, Exhibiting the Order in Which the Older Sedimentary Strata Succeed Each Other in England and Wales.* With this publication, the two geologists introduced the basis of the modern time scale. In the years that followed, a controversy arose between the two men that was to sever their friendship. Because Sedgwick had not described fossils distinctive of the Cambrian, the unit could not be recognized in other countries. Murchison argued, therefore, that the Cambrian was not a valid system. During the 1850's, he maintained that all fossiliferous strata above the "Primary Series" (the old name for Precambrian) and below the Old Red Sandstone (of Devonian age) belonged within the Silurian System. Sedgwick, of course, disagreed, but his opinion that the Cambrian was a valid system did not receive wide support until fossils were described from the upper part of the sequence. The fossils proved to be similar to faunas in Europe and North America. Hence, the Cambrian did meet the test of recognition outside England. Using these fossils as a basis for reinterpretation, the English geologist Charles Lapworth proposed combining the upper part of Sedgwick's Cambrian and the lower part of Murchison's Silurian into a new system. In 1879, he named the system *Ordovician* after the *Ordovices*, an early Celtic tribe. The first three systems of the Paleozoic were now established.

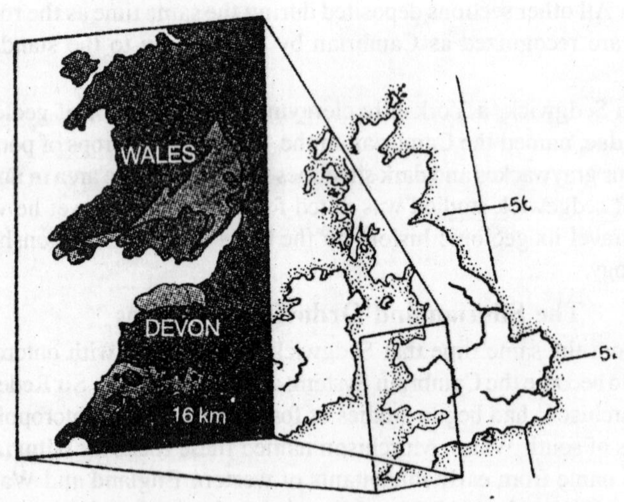

Fig. 4.5. Outcrop of strata of the Devonian System in Wales and southwestern England where these rocks were named.

The Devonian System

The *Devonian System* was proposed for outcrops near Devonshire, England, by Sedgwick and Murchison in 1839 (prior to the years of their bitter debate). They based their proposal on the fact that the rocks in question lay beneath the previously recognized Carboniferous System and contained a fauna that was distinctive and different from that of the underlying Silurian and overlying Carboniferous. In their interpretation of the intermediate nature of the fauna, they were aided by the studies of William Lonsdale, a retired army officer who had become a self-taught specialist on fossil corals. Further evidence that the new unit was a valid one came when Murchison and Sedgwick were able to recognize it in the Rhineland region of Europe. The Devonian rocks of Devonshire were also found to be equivalent to the widely known *Old Red Sandstone* of south Wales.

The Carboniferous System

The term Carboniferous was coined in 1822, by the English geologists William Conybeare and William Phillips to designate strata that included beds of coal in north-central England. Subsequently, it became convenient in Europe and Britain to divide the system into a Lower *Carboniferous and Upper Carboniferous*-the latter containing most of the workable coal seams. Two systems in North America, the *Mississippian* and *Pennsylvanian*, are broadly equivalent to these subdivisions. The American geologist Alexander Winchell formally proposed the name Mississippian in 1870 for the Lower Carboniferous strata that are extensively exposed in the Upper Mississippi River drainage region. In 1891, Henry S. Willams provided the name Pennsylvanian for the Upper Carboniferous System. Although both Pennsylvanian and Mississippian Systems are recognized by most United Stated geologists, neither term has been employed outside North America.

The Permian System

The Permian System takes its name from the small Russian town of Perm on the western side of the Ural Mountains. In 1840 and 1841, Murchison, in company with the French paleontologist Edouard de Verneuil and several Russian companions, travelled extensively across western Russia. To his delight, Murchison found he was able to recognize Silurian, Devonian, and Carboniferous rocks by the fossils they contained. As a result he became even more convinced that groups of fossil organisms succeed one another in a definite and determinable order (this finding is now labeled the *principle of biologic succession*). Murchison established

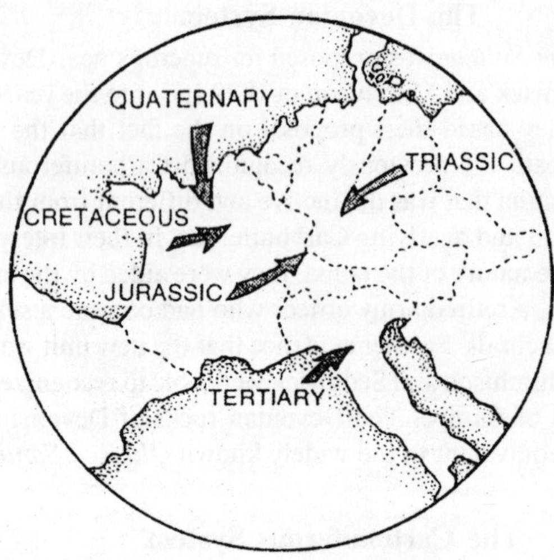

Fig. 4.6. Type areas for the systems of the Mesozoic and Cenozoic.

the new Permian System for rocks that overlay the Carboniferous System and contained fossils similar to those in German strata (the Zechstein beds), which had the same stratgraphic position as the Magnesian Limestone in England. Field studies had previously shown that the Magnesian Limestone rested upon Carboniferous strata. Thus Murchison was able to include the magnesian Limestone within the Permian by correlation. The fossils of the new system appeared distinctly intermediate between those of the Carboniferous below and the Triassic above.

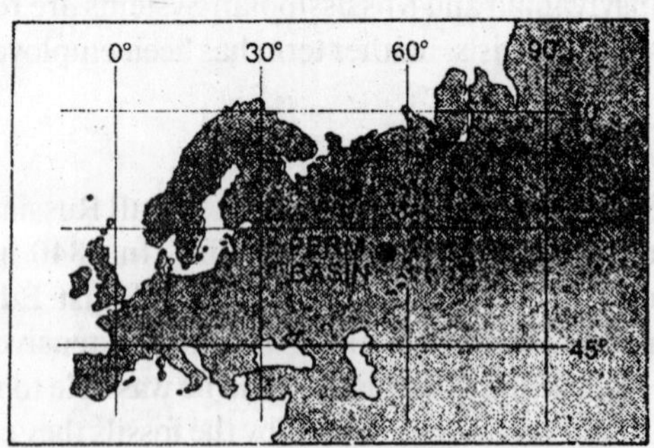

Fig. 4.7. Location of the basin near Perm, where Murchison established the Premian System.

Murchison's establishment of the Permian system provides a fine example of the logic employed by early geologists in putting together the pieces of the standard time scale.

The Triassic System

The influence of British geologists in providing names for the systems of the Paleozoic is by now obvious. However, their presence is not as evident in the development of Mesozoic nomenclature. The Triassic, for example, was applied in 1834 by a German geologist named Frederich von Alberti. The term refers to a threefold division of rocks of this age in Germany. However, because the German strata in the type area are poorly fossiliferous, the standard of reference has been shifted to richly fossiliferous marine strata in the Alps.

The Jurassic System

Another German scientist, Alexander von Humboldt, proposed the term Jurassic for strata of the Jura Mountains between France and Switzerland. However, in 1795 when he used the term, the concept of systems had not been developed. As a result, the Jurassic was redefined as a valid geologic system in 1839 by Leopold von Buch.

The Cretaceous System

During the same year that Conybeare and Phillips were defining the Carboniferous, a Belgian geologist named Omalius d'Halloy proposed the term *Cretaceous* (from the Latin, *Creta*, meaning "chalk") for rock outcrops in France, Belgium, and Holland. Although chalk beds are prevalent in some Cretaceous exposures, the system is actually recognized on the basis of fossils. Indeed, some thick sections of Cretaceous rocks contain no chalks whatsoever.

The Tertiary System

The name Tertiary leads us back to the time when geology was just beginning as a science. Giovanni Arduino suggested a classification with four major divisions: Primary, Secondary, Tertiary, and Quaternary. The Tertiary was derived from his 1759 description of unconsolidated "montes tertiarii" sediments at the foot of the Italian Alps. Later, the Tertiary was more precisely defined, and standard sections for series of the Tertiary were established in France. The *Eocene, Miocene*, and *Pliocene*, for example, were proposed by Charles Lyell in 1832 on the basis of the proportions of species of living marine invertebrates in the fossil fauna. By definition, 3 per cent of the fossil fauna of the Eocene still live, whereas the Miocene contained 17 per cent, and the Pliocene contained 50 to 67 per cent. The term Oligocene was proposed by August von Beyrich in 1854, and the Paleocene was proposed 20 years later by Wilhelm Schimper. Other system names are also used in place of the Tertiary. Some geologists prefer the terms *Paleogene* (for the Paleocene, Eocene, and Oligocene) and *Neogene* (for the Miocene and Pliocene).

The Quaternary System

In 1829, the French geologist Jules Desnoyers proposed the term *Quaternary* for certain sediments and volcanics exposed in northern France. Although these deposits contained few fossils, Desnoyers was convinced on the basis of field studies that they were younger than Tertiary rocks. In the decade following Desnoyer's establishment of the Quaternary, the unit was divided by Charles Lyell into an older *Pleistocene Series,* composed primarily of deposits formed during the glacial ages, and the younger *Recent Series.*

This brief review describing how geologists drew up a table of geologic time clearly shows a lack of any grand and coherent design. These geologic pioneers were influenced by conspicuous changes in assemblages of fossils from one sequence of strata to another. In many places in Europe they found that such changes frequently occurred above and below an unconformity. The success of their methods is apparent from the fact that, by and large, the systems have persisted and found wide use even to the present day.

The Agents of Metamorphism

The three principle agents of metamorphism are heat, pressure, and chemically active fluids. Alone or in combination, these agents operate at various intensities to produce metamorphic rocks having distinctive textures and compositions.

Heat

Heat is a major cause of metamorphism. It can reduce the ability of a rock to withstand deformation, and it causes an increase in the rate of most chemical reactions. The heat for metamorphism may be provided by nearby intrusions of magma. It may be associated with the compression of the crust in regions experiencing mountain-building, or it may be induced by increases in pressure resulting from deep burial. The rate of increase in temperature at increasing depths in the earth is called the *geothermal gradient*. Measurements made in deep mines and wells indicate that the *geothermal gradient* for the crust is about 30° C per km of depth. This rate, however, varies from place to place, and is, not unexpectedly, greater near centres of active volcanism. The geothermal gradient is such that at depths of about 35 km temperatures are high enough to melt rock.

Because particular mineral-forming chemical reactions only occur within a specific range of temperature, heata, influences, the ultimate mineral composition of metamorphic rocks. Also as temperature arises, ions within the atomic lattice of minerals become increasingly agitated. Eventually, they may move to new locations and arrange themselves into structural forms stable under the newer thermal conditions. As an example, consider what might happen to clay minerals in shale strata invaded by a granitic magma. Clay minerals are hydrous aluminum silicates. Heat applied to these minerals from the hot magma would cause a loss of the water contained in the clay and a conversion of clay into a common metamorphic minerals named andalusite. Andalusite is a nonhydrous aluminum silicate having an atomic structure that is stable under the new conditions. The released water in the above example, together with gases such as carbon dioxide, may also participate in the many chemical reactions associated with metamorphism.

As noted in the chapter with igneous geology, if temperatures in a rock mass rise high enough, the melting points of constituent minerals will be exceeded and magma will begin to form. If the melting becomes pervasive, igneous rather than metamorphic rocks will result.

Pressure

The tremendous pressures that exist several kilometers below the earth's surface (about 1000 kg/cm^2 at a depth of 4 km) or that are associated with collisions of tectonic plates can cause profound changes in deeply buried sedimentary rocks, preexisting metamorphic rocks, or igneous rocks. Mineral grains, for example, may recrystallize into new minerals with more tightly packed atomic structure and therefore greater density. Where mineral grains are in contact, the squeezing action may cause melting or solution at the points of contact and precipitation of material along the sides of grains are in contact, the squeezing action may cause melting or solution at the points of contact and precipitation of material along the side of grains that experience less pressure.

Every swimmer knows that as one descends into a body of water, pressure increases with depth because of the progressively greater weight of the column of overlying water. Much of the pressure to which rocks are subjected is similarly caused by the load of overlying rocks. This kind of confining pressure in water is termed *hydrostatic*. When rock rather than water is involved, a more appropriate term is *lithostatic pressure*. Lithostatic pressure is applied nearly equally to all sides of a mass of rock. Like hydrostatic pressure, it increases with depth. In combination with heat from the geothermal gradient, lithostatic pressure causes progressive changes in minerals at progressively increasing depths.

In addition to lithostatic pressure, which affects rocks uniformly, pressure may also be applied to a rock mass along certain preferred directions. Such directional pressure may result in reorientation of grains, the development of tiny shear planes in the rock, and recrystallization. These processes are largely responsible for the development of the lineated and banded textures characteristic of many metamorphic rocks.

Chemically active solutions and gases

In varying amounts, liquids and gases are always present in regions where metamorphism takes places. They play an important role in metamorphism by increasing the efficiency of recrystallization, serving as solvents, and accelerating the rate of chemical reactions. Laboratory experiments have shown that most minerals react so slowly to increases in temperature that metamorphic reactions would require lengthy spans of time to run their course. By adding only a minute amount of water to a laboratory capsule containing the experimental minerals, however, reaction rates are dramatically increased. One reason for this is that ions in a fluid medium can be brought into close proximity with each other and reach appropriate sites in the atomic structure of minerals more readily than in a dry environment. In some instances, water may enter into the composition of newly forming minerals such as mica, amphibole, and chlorite. An example is provided by the reaction below, in which the attractive green mineral serpentine is formed

$$5Mg_2SiO_4 + 4H_2O \longrightarrow 2H_4Mg_3Si_2O_9 + 4MgO + SiO_2$$

(Olivine) (Water) (Serpentine)

(Removed in solution)

The water associated with metamorphic reaction may be derived from several possible sources. Some is water entrapped in parent sedimentary rocks at the time of their deposition. Another source is magma, from which may emanate large quantities of watery liquids and vapors. Smaller amounts of water may be given off by hydrous minerals as they begin to experience the effects of heat and pressure.

In addition to water, the gas carbon dioxide also promotes metamorphism. Carbon dioxide is readily liberated during the heating of limestone. This leaves the remaining oxide of calcium free to combine with silica or other impurities in the limestone. An example of such a reaction involving the liberation of carbon dioxide and the formation of metamorphic mineral known as *wollastonite* is as follows:

$$\underset{\text{(limestone)}}{CaCO_3} + \underset{\text{(quartz)}}{SiO_2} \longrightarrow \underset{\text{(wollastonite)}}{CaSiO_3} + \underset{\text{(Carbon dioxide)}}{CO_2}$$

Other gases containing fluorine as well as hydrofluoric and hydrochloric acids may be important in particular metamorphic environments.

From sediments to sedimentary rock

The most significant factors involved in the origin of sedimentary rocks are *weathering*, which produces sediment, *transportation* and *deposition* of that sediment, and the *lithification* necessary to convert loose particle of sediment into solid rock. Each of these factors may alter the composition or textural features of sediment and thereby provide a variety of different kinds of sedimentary rocks.

Classification of the Metamorphic Rocks

The metamorphic rocks can be broadly grouped into two major classes: cataclastic rocks; recrystallized rocks. The *cataclastic rocks* have experienced mechanical disruption (breaking, crushing) of the original minerals without appreciable chemical change. This process of change can be described as *dynamic metamorphism*. The *recrystallized rocks* have, as the name indicates, undergone a recrystallization of the original minerals. Recrystallization is considered to be a chemical change, because it usually produces minerals of chemical formulas and crystal lattice structures different from the parent minerals.

Within the class of recrystallized rocks we must distinguish two subclasses: contact metamorphic rocks; regional metamorphic rocks. The *contact metamorphic rocks* are formed by recrystallization under high temperature in country rock immediately adjacent to an intruding magma that solidifies into a pluton. The rock is not subjected to tectonic forces (bending and breaking) during the process of change, but new mineral substances emanating from the magma can be added to the country rock (i.e., metasomatism can take place). The *regional metamorphic rocks* undergo recrystallization during the process of being deformed by shearing, often under conditions of high pressure or high temperature, or both, and often to the accompaniment of loss or gain of mineral components by metasomatism. The adjective "regional" refers to the occurrence of this subclass of rocks over large areas and in great crystal thicknesses. The total process is called *dynamothermal metamorphism*.

A third class of rocks, intermediate between metamorphic rocks, is shown in Table. These are rocks characterized by a banded appearance

Table 1.1. Composition of Gases from Internal Earth sources compared with Total Earth Volatiles.

	Volatiles of Earth's hydrosphere and atmosphere	*Gases in hot springs, fumaroles, and geysers*	*Volcanic gases from basaltic lava of Mauna Loa and Kilauea*
Water, H_2O	92.8	99.4	57.8
Total carbon, as CO_2	5.1	0.33	23.5
Sulfur, S_2	0.13	0.03	12.6
Nitrogen, N_2	0.24	0.05	5.7
Argon, Ar	trace	trace	0.3
Chlorine, Cl_2	1.7	0.12	0.1
Fluorine, F_2	trace	0.03	—
Hydrogen, H_2	0.07	0.05	0.04

on an exposed surface, caused by layering. The bands represent alternate layers of igneous rock and metamorphic rock. It is thought that the igneous material penetrated or replaced layers of a preexisting rock of sedimentary origin. Various degrees of transition from metamorphic to igneous rock can be included in this class.

Metamorphic Minerals

Recrystallization under high temperatures produces a distinctive group of metamorphic minerals. Most of these are different from the minerals we have thus far encountered in our study of igneous and sedimentary rocks. On the other hand, some of the same minerals found in the igneous rocks persist or reappear during recrystallization, such as quartz, biotite mica, pyroxene, amphibole, and feldspar. Calcite and dolomite also persist in recrystallized carbonate sedimentary rocks. Metamorphic minerals not encountered in earlier chapters are described in Table. The eleven minerals on this list have been selected because of their importance in the classification and naming of metamorphic rocks and to show a wide range of chemical diversity.

The first three minerals, *kyanite, andalusite*, and *sillimanit*e, are of identical composition. All are aluminosilicates with the formula Al_2SiO_5, but each has a different space lattice structure. They are polymorphs of Al_2SO_5. They form by recrystallization of rock with abundant felsic components, such as quartz and feldspar. It shows that each of these minerals forms under a different combination of pressure and temperature. Andalusite forms under conditions of comparatively low pressure and low temperature; kyanite at high pressure and low temperature; sillimanite at high temperature and moderate pressure. For this reason, the polymorphs can serve as indicators of the environment in which recrystallization took place.

Almandite is one of the *garnet group*-aluminosilicates of magnesium, iron, calcium, or manganese that crystallize in the isometric system. Almandite, the iron garnet, is a red mineral familiar as a semiprecious gemstone. Almandite crystals often grow to diameters of several centimetres in metamorphic rock.

Wollastonite, a silicate of calcium, is usually associated with the metamorphism of limestone. Under high temperatures the following reaction occurs:

$$CaCO_3 + SiO_2 \rightarrow CaSiO_3 + CO_2$$

The carbon dioxide is driven off as a volatile gas-an example of one of the forms of metasomatism.

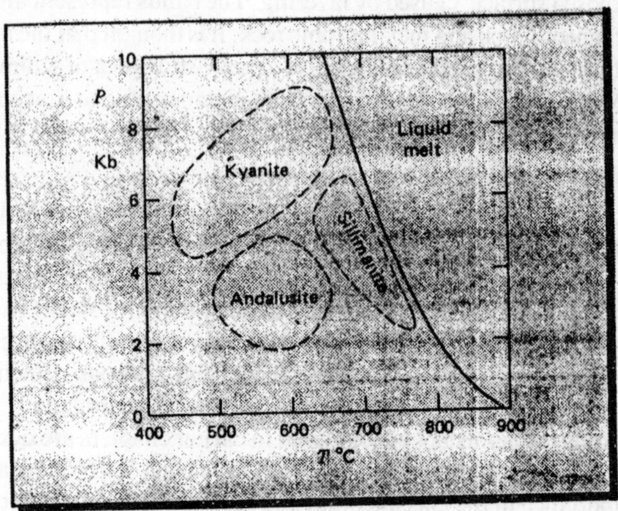

Fig. 4.8. Kyanite, andalusite and sillimanite form in three different ranges of pressure and temperature.

Staurolite, a hydrous aluminosilicate of iron, is formed in a middle range of pressure and temperature. It is a particularly interesting mineral because of its habit of forming as twin crystals penetrating each other at right angles to make a natural cross.

Chlorite, a soft hydrous silicate of iron and magnesium, is similar in some ways to the micas, with sheet structure that forms thin cleavage flakes. Chlorite is associated with metamorphic conditions of comparatively low temperature and is one of the earliestformed of the metamorphic minerals.

Epidote, a hydrous aluminosilicate of calcium and iron, is a green mineral that typically forms in elongate prisms. It is associated with the metamorphism of rocks rich in mafic minerals, such as pyroxene and amphibole, and it is formed in a middle range of temperatures.

Talc is a very soft, scaly mineral, a hydrous silicate of magnesium, and is classed as a clay mineral. Talc occurs in metamorphic rocks that are derived from mafic minerals such as olivine, pyroxene, and amphibole. In massive form as a rock, tale is known as *soapstone*. Because it is immune to action of acids, *soapstone* was once widely used for table tops in chemical laboratories. In powder form, talc has many industrial uses and is perhaps most familiar as talcum powder.

The *serpentine group* consists of two minerals that are hydrous magnesium silicates-antigorite and chrysotile. These minerals are derived from mafic minerals, particularly olivine, pyroxene, and amphibole. Chrysotile is well known as *asbestos*, formed of minute flexible crystals that resemble textile fibers, widely used in fire-resistant industrial products and as an insulator. It is now established that the minute fibers of asbestos cause irreversible lung diseases (asbestosis and lung cancer) in humans.

Graphite, comparatively minor among the metamorphic minerals, illustrates a substance probably derived from hydrocarbon compounds of organic origin that were present in sedimentary rock prior to its metamorphism. In some instances, seams of coal have been converted partly into graphite during metamorphism.

Cataclastic rocks

The cataclastic metamorphic rocks result from mechanical deformation without appreciable chemical change and recrystallization. They form under intense shearing stresses which cause grain fragmentation.

Grains that consist of individual mineral crystals or groups of crystals are crushed and pulverized as they are rotated (turned over and over).

Cataclastic rocks are most commonly produced during the process of faulting. they form a thin layer along the fault plane where strong crushing and grinding action takes place where strong crushing and grinding action takes place. One product of this action is *friction breccia,* a rock consisting of rather large angular fragments in a matrix of small fragments. The largest fragments may measure a meter or more across, while the smallest are a millimeter or smaller in diameter. Where the pulverized rock along a fault plane consists of very small particles-0.01 to 0.1 mm-the rock is called *mylonite*. It is a dense, fine-grained rock often with a streaked or banded appearance, and may outwardly resemble chart. (Chert is a sedimentary form of silica.) Some recrystallization may occur in mylonite, enabling the grains to adapt their shapes so as to fill the entire rock volume.

Contact Metamorphic Rocks

Contact metamorphic rocks form in an environment of high temperature in comparatively shallow crustal locations where confining pressure is not great. The high temperature is provided by intrusive magma, which has entered the country rock to solidify as a pluton, and thus a strong temperature contrast exists between the magma and the country rock. Shearing stress is practically absent under such conditions. The country rock close to the magma body is literally baked, like fired brick or tile, made of mud or clay. The resulting rock is *hornfels*, a word of German origin. The prefix *horn* refers to the hornlike appearance of the rock; the word *fels* means 'rock.' A direct English translation would be close to 'hornstone.' Hornfels has very fine-grained texture because cooling followed rapidly after recrystallization of the parent minerals.

Hornfels forms an *aureole*, which is a metamorphic layer surrounding the magma body. The aureole conforms with the outline of the pluton and may he subdivided into two or more zones of somewhat different mineral content. Where the magma is of granite composition, the aureole contains abundant quartz and potash feldspar. The inner zone may contain wollastonite and andalusite, while the outer zone may have amphibole and mica, which are hydrous minerals.

Texture of Regional Metamorphic Rocks

As regional metamorphism takes place, intense shearing action accompanied by recrystallization brings about new textures and structures. These features give the metamorphic rocks their distinctive appearances.

Consider first the structural changes that take place in a thick mass of black shale, a fine-grained sedimentary rock rich in clay minerals such as kaolinite and illite. Shale shows stratification (bedding) resulting from

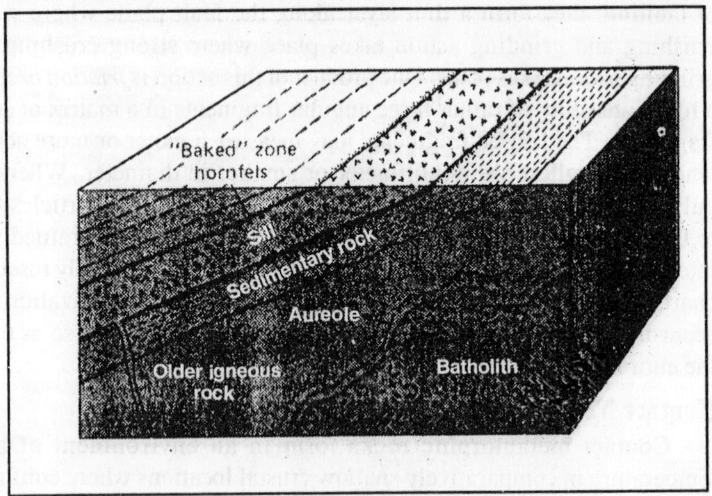

Fig. 4.9. Schematic block diagram of contact metamorphic aureoles adjacent to plutons. At the upper left is a sill of gabbro intruded between shale layers, forming a narrow zone of hornfels. At the lower right is an aureole adjacent to a granite batholite intruding a mass of older igneous rock.

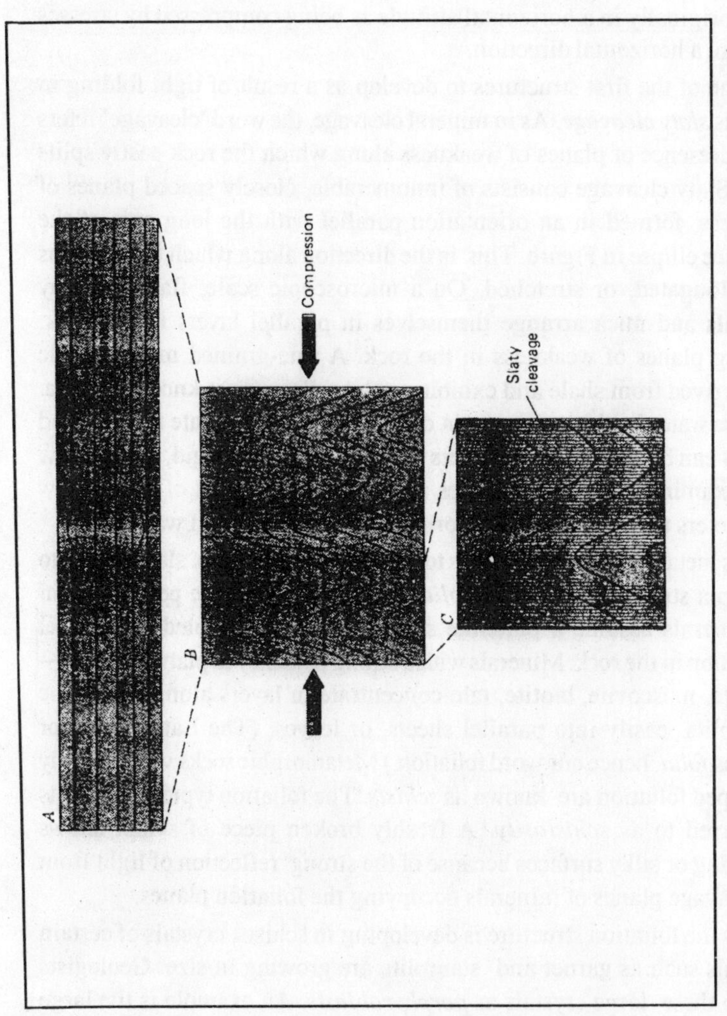

Fig. 4.10. The development of slaty cleavage is associated with shearing within a mass of shale. (A). The original beding is horizontal. (B) Compression causes close folding of shale strata. The reference circle in diagram A is now distorted into an ellipse. C Slaty cleavage forms in planes at right angles to the axis of compression and cuts across the original bedding.

fluctuations in the particle size grades deposited from one layer to the next. Typically, regional metamorphism of shale results in crumpling of the beds into small, tight folds. This tectonic process results from shear stresses that tend to deform a ductile rock mass. We can visualize shale layers originally in a horizontal attitude as being compressed by stresses acting in a horizontal direction.

One of the first structures to develop as a result of tight folding in shales is *slaty cleavage*. As in mineral cleavage, the word 'cleavage' refers to the presence of planes of weakness along which the rock easily splits apart. Slaty cleavage consists of innumerable, closely spaced planes of weakness, formed in an orientation parallel with the long axis of the reference ellipse in Figure. This is the direction along which the rock has been elongated, or stretched. On a microscopic scale, flakes of clay minerals and mica arrange themselves in parallel layers in the rock, forming planes of weakness in the rock. A fine-grained metamorphic rock derived from shale and exhibiting slaty cleavage is known as slate. Because water has been driven out during deformation, slate is dense and hard. It can be split into thin layers that are strong and rigid, as we know from examining roofing shingles made of slate. Layers of slate a few centimeters thick make ideal flooring slabs for patios and walkways.

As metamorphism continues to a more intense phase, slate begins to develop a structure known as *foliation*, in which a large percentage of the minerals assume a platelike shape and are assembled in parallel orientation in the rock. Minerals with a strong tendency to platy cleavage—Chlorite, muscovite, biotite, tale-concentrate in layers along which the rock splits easily into parallel sheets, or leaves. (The Latin word for leaves is *folia*, hence our word foliation.) Metamorphic rocks with strongly developed foliation are known as *schists*. The foliation typical of schists is referred to as *schistosity*. A freshly broken piece of schist shows glistening or silky surfaces because of the strong reflection of light from the cleavage planes of minerals occupying the foliation planes.

As the foliation structure is developing in schists, crystals of certain minerals such as garnet and staurolite are growing in size. Geologists refer to these large crystals as *porphyroblasts*. An example is the large garnet crystal shown in figure..

Another structure found in metamorphic rocks is *lineation*, the presence of mineral grains drawn out into long, thin, pencillike objects, all in parallel alignment. Lineation is associated with massive types of metamorphic rock and does not produce planes of weakness. The elongated mineral grains may have been formed by lengthening as the rock was stretched along one axis, or may have assumed an alignment parallel with the direction of maximum rock stretching.

Another common structure of metamorphic rocks is *banding*, a rough kind of layering in which minerals of different varieties or groups have become segregated into alternate layers. These layers are usually of different shades-light or dark-so that the banding is conspicuous. Metamorphic rock of this description is called gneiss. (The word is also applied to some metamorphic rocks showing lineation, but poor banding.) Within individual bands, the rock is coarsely crystalline and strongly bonded. Orientation of grains parallel with the banding is usually present in the banded gneisses. Weakness may exist between individual bands, so that the rock may tend to break apart in layers and can he said to show coarse foliation.

Porphyroblasts are common in many kinds of banded and lineated gneiss. These large crystals or crystal masses appear on a rock exposure as lumps around which the lineation or foliation is deflected. The lumps thus resemble eyes and the rock is described as *augen* gneiss, from the German word for "eye."

Gneiss is thought to originate in different ways and from different parent rocks. Some banded gneisses are derived from sedimentary rock; others, from igneous rocks. *Granite gneiss* differs little from ordinary granite except that the dark grains of biotite and hornblende show a distinct lineation, as if flowage had slightly affected the granite when it was in a plastic state.

The texture and structure of schists and gneisses show almost infinite variation, and it is not surprising that even a highly trained geologist is often at a loss to reconstruct the history of a particular rock seen in an outcrop. No metamorphic rock can be studied in the environment in which it formed. Moreover, we can see only the final stage in a long series of changes through a changing environment. Detailed laboratory analysis, using sophisticated tools of research, is needed to unravel the mysteries of dynamothermal metamorphic rocks. Chemical analysis of the regional metamorphic rocks sheds a great deal of light on their origin. We therefore turn from metamorphic textures to the assemblages of minerals present in the rock and how they are related to the environment in which metamorphism occurred.

Mineralogical Classification of the Regional Metamorphic Rocks

The regional metamorphic rocks involve large-scale dynamothermal processes. Recrystallization takes place along with wholesale shearing of thick masses of crustal rock. The environments in which these processes act span a wide range of temperatures and pressures. The most important concept relating to these rocks is that they are produced in a well-defined sequence according to increasing temperature and confining pressure. Followed across country, exposures of regional metamorphic rocks show *metamorphic zones*, which reflect the increased temperature that accompanied recrystallization. Geologists found that each zone can be defined by the first appearance of an index mineral, not present in zones of lower temperature. A typical sequence of index minerals is shown in figure; it runs as follows: chlorite, biotite, almandite, staurolite, kyanite, sillimanite. This sequence would result from metamorphism of a large

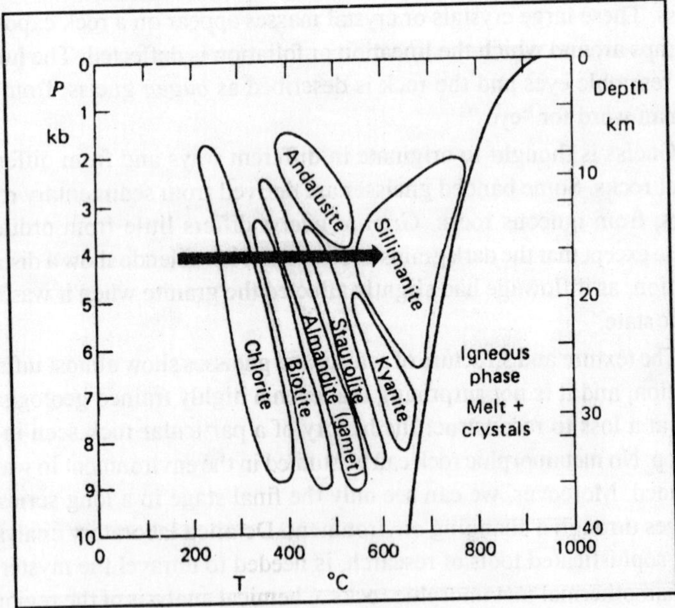

Fig. 4.11. This graph shows how the grade of regional metamorphism are related to pressure and temperature. The arrow shows the typical series of changes from lower to higher grades at a given depth.

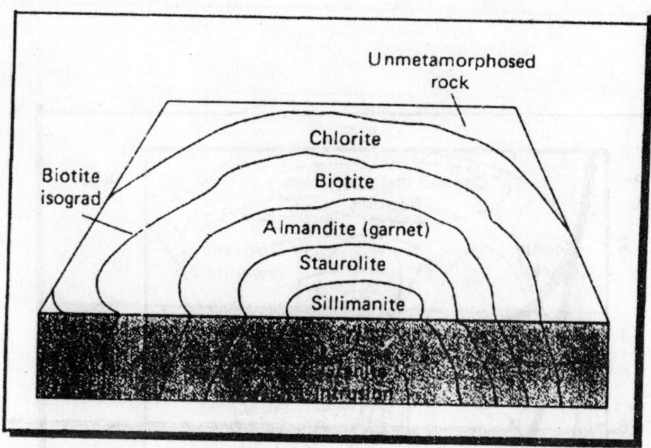

Fig. 4.12. Schematic diagram of isograds of regional metamorphism forming concentric zones around a region of the highest grade of metamorphism. The granite intrusion might represent melting or granitization occuring at a higher temperature.

mass of sedimentary rock made up mostly of shale. The appearance of each mineral can be shown on a map by a line, called an *isograd.*

The metamorphic rock is thus zoned into a succession of *metamorphic grades,* each associated with a particular type of metamorphic rock. figure shows typical sequences of metamorphic rock types in terms of pressure and temperature. The broad arrows suggest the sequence of changes that took place as the rock was subjected to increasing temperature. As metamorphism begins at comparatively low temperature. As metamorphism begins at comparatively low temperatures and pressures, a mass of shale develops new minerals of a group called the *zeolites.* We have not referred to the zeolite minerals previously and mention them only briefly at this point. They are hydrous aluminosilicates of calcium and sodium with a rather large water content, and they are soon destroyed as water is driven out of the changing sedimentary clay minerals.

The rock now enters the first major metamorphic grade, *greenschist,* formed under moderate pressure and fairly low temperature (low-grade metamorphism). Minerals dominant in greenschist are chlorite, muscovite mica, biotite, sodic plagioclase feldspar, and quartz. From this point on, the pressure is assumed to hold about constant, while temperature increases.

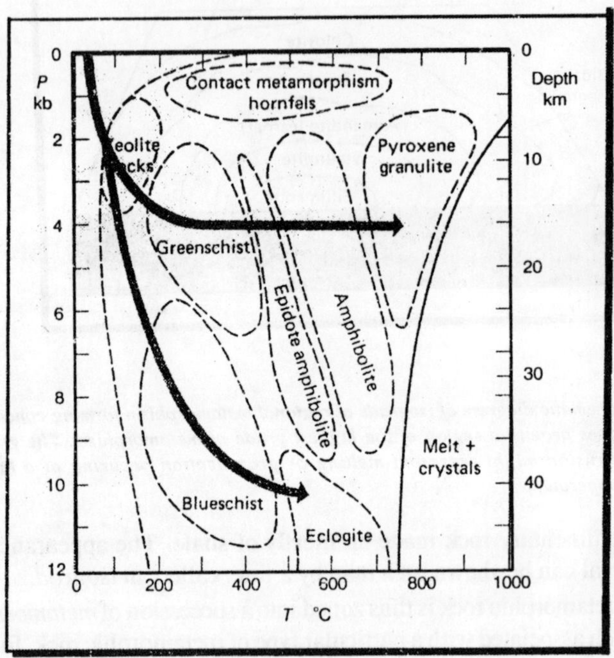

Fig. 4.13. A schematic graph of the major types of metamorphic rocks in relaiton to pressure(depth) and temperature. The arrows show tow possible patterns of evolution in the sequence of regional metamorphic rocks. Contact metamorphism is limited to a shallow zone.

The next higher, or intermediate grade is characterized by a rock called *amphibolite*, named for the presence of hornblende (an amphibole). In some places this grade is preceded by *epidote amphibolite*, characterized by the presence of epidote. Amphibolite may also contain quartz, plagioclase feldspar, almandite garnet, and biotite. The rock composition varies according to the original rock composition, whether felsic or mafic.

At still higher temperature, above about 600 °C, a high-grade metamorphic rock, *pyroxene granulite*, is produced. *Granulite* is a term describing the rock texture, which consists of small mineral grains of more or less equal size, developed through shearing action. Grains of quartz and feldspar show a flattening into platelike shapes. Pyroxene is an important new mineral in the rock, while sillimanite appears as the index mineral. With an increase in temperature above the granulite grade, the melting point of the rock would be reached, and new magma could be produced, yielding an igneous rock.

It is possible for the confining pressure to increase to high levels while temperature remains low. The result is formation of *blueschist*, named for the presence of a blue variety of amphibole (glaucophane).

With an increase in temperature to a middle range (400 °C to 600 °C) and with extremely high pressure (8 to 10 kb or higher), blueschist may become *eclogite*.

Dominant minerals in eclogite are an unusual green pyroxene rich in sodium and calcium and a red-brown variety of garnet rich in magnesium. The rock grains are coarse in texture. The total chemical composition of eclogite is approximately that of gabbro and basalt. Thus, eclogite may be the end product of dynamothermal metamorphism of mafic igneous rocks at very high confining pressures corresponding to great depths.

Two regional metamorphic rocks that show recrystallization with little or no chemical change are marble and quartzite. *Marble* is recrystallized limestone or dolostone, and may also be formed by contact metamorphism. Under moderate shearing stresses, calcite is easily deformed, because the lattice structure permits gliding motions to occur easily within crystals. *Marble* often shows a granular structure such that a freshly broken surface has the appearance of a broken sugar cube. *Quartzite*, formed from quartz sandstone or siltstone, may consist almost entirely of quartz with only minor impurities. It is an extremely hard and durable rock. When struck a hard hammer blow, quartzite shows a conchoidal fracture in which the fracture surface cuts through the quartz grains.

Granitization

Certain gneisses appear to be composed partly of metamorphic rock and partly of igneous rock. These are banded rocks known as *migmatites*. Between bands that appear to be true metamorphic rock, originally of sedimentary origin, are bands of the composition and texture of granite. In some cases, the granite bands may represent magma that forced its way between layers of metamorphic rock. An alternative explanation is that the granitelike layers represent matter imported by slow injection of fluids and the diffusion of ions from a nearby magma body. These imported substances have replaced the original rock, and many of the original constituents have been exported to other locations. Thus, granitelike layers may have been formed by metasomatism.

Conversion of preexisting rock to a granite by metasomatism is called *granitization.* Melting does not occur during granitization, but the end result is much the same as if the affected rock had been melted and recrystallized by cooling to form a plutonic rock. Since we have already stated that large granite plutons are perhaps best explained by wholesale melting of large masses of crustal rock, this means granite may form both by metasomatism and by melting. The process of granitization is obscure and its importance has been strongly debated for many decades as part of the general question of the origin of granite.

Hydrothermal Alteration and Serpentinite

Hydrothermal solutions that rise from intrusive magma bodies in the final stages of cooling. These hot-water solutions consist of volatiles and carry a wide variety of mineral-forming ions in solution. Under favorable conditions, hydro- thermal solutions are capable of altering the mineral composition of large masses of rock, a process known as *hydrothermal alteration*. Because the temperatures and pressures under which hydrothermal alteration occurs are generally low, the process is often excluded from the scope of metamorphism. Hydrothermal solutions adjacent to shallow magma bodies range in temperature from as low as 60 °C to as high as 500 °C. Thus, in terms of temperature alone, the process can fall well within the range found in regional metamorphism. However, the hydrothermal process usually operates at pressures under 1 kb and at depths of only 1 to 3 km. This is much less than the pressure and depth required for regional metamorphism.

Chemical changes brought about by hydrothermal alteration are those in which water combines with the rock-forming minerals to form new hydrous minerals. Perhaps the most important of these minerals is serpentine, $Mg_3Si_2O_5(OH)_4$. It can be formed through the alteration of olivine, $(Mg,Fe)_2SiO_4$, and other mafic silicate minerals rich in magnesium. The resulting rock is called *serpentinite*; the process by which it is formed is *serpentinization*. Serpentinite is a fine-grained, dark green to black rock with massive structure. Bands of lighter-colored minerals fill joint fractures or are deformed into swirling lines (serpentine patterns), giving the rock an ornamental quality similar to that prized in marble.

Geologists are interested in the origin of large bodies of serpentinite exposed in orogenic belts. The rock is generally considered to have been derived from oceanic crust altered in the presence of water. Evidence is now accumulating to show that hydrothermal activity is intense along spreading plate boundaries. Seawater, which is rich in magnesium, penetrates the rifted crust and is highly heated by the underlying rock. Returning to the surface, the heated water alters the mafic minerals of the crustal basalt to form serpentine-rich basalt. Descending seawater is thought to penetrate the crust to depths on the order of 2 to 3 km, but probably no deeper. For serpentinization to occur deeper in the oceanic crust, affecting the entire crust down to the Moho at a depth of 5 to 6 km beneath the ocean floor, a different source of water would he required.

Professor Harry Hess of Princeton University suggested that the lower part of the oceanic crust is formed from rising peridotite rock of the upper mantle. In the axis of the spreading zone, peridotite is altered to serpentinite on a large scale by the addition of water moving upward from the deeper mantle beneath. The serpentinized mantle rock then spreads laterally to form the oceanic crust. This possibility is to some degree credible, because serpentine and peridotite are often found in adjacent masses at the surface in deeply eroded orogenic belts. These rocks may represent parts of the lower oceanic crust and upper mantle that were finally lifted to the surface by overthrust faulting during orogeny. Evidently, serpentinization may be a process that operates under a wide range of environments, including both low and high confining pressures, and with widely different sources of the water required to form the serpentine.

Radioisotopes and Radioactivity

Although we have now covered the full scope of the rock transformation cycle, two basic problems of geology connected with that cycle require detailed attention: (1) What is the source of the internal energy that drives plate motions and provides beat for igneous and metamorphic processes? (2) How do geologists determine the ages of the crustal rocks and of the earth itself? Both questions are answered through an understanding of radioactivity, a fundamental process of nuclear physics.

Element- carbon for example-there exist isotopes. Whereas the atomic number (number of protons in the nucleus) is always the same for a given element, the number of neutrons may vary. Thus, the mass number of a given element differs from one isotope to another. In referring to a given kind of isotope in terms of the composition of its nucleus, physicists use the term *nuclide*. All nuclides with the same atomic number answer to the same element name, but as isotopes of that element, they differ from one another because of differences in mass number.

Protons and neutrons in the atomic nucleus are held together by nuclear forces quite different from any kinds of forces with which we are familiar from every- day experience (e.g., gravitational attraction and electromagnetic forces). The nuclear forces are effective only when protons and neutrons are very close together, as they are in the nucleus of the atom. Some nuclides, with a *stable nucleus* that effectively resists natural forces which might tend to break apart the nucleus, are *stable isotopes*. Other nuclides, with an unstable nucleus whose protons and neutrons are not strongly bound and with excess energy, are *unstable isotopes*.

An unstable isotope will undergo a natural process of nuclear disintegration to be transformed into a stable isotope of a different element. This spontaneous process of nuclear disintegration is called *radioactivity*, a term first applied by a French physicist, Henri Becquerel, who observed in 1896 that uranium emitted a mysterious radiant form of energy capable of leaving a photographic image, even under conditions of total darkness. Isotopes that undergo spontaneous disintegration are called *radioisotopes* or *radionuclides*, and the process is referred to as *radioactive decay*.

Radioactive decay can occur in one of three ways: (1) alpha decay, (2) beta decay, and (3) electron capture. In *alpha decay*, the nucleus emits an *alpha particle*, consisting of two protons and two neutrons. (You will recognize this particle as the nucleus of a helium atom.) As a result of *alpha particle* emission, the mass number is decreased by four; the atomic number by two. The original radioisotope is referred to as the parent isotope, the product of decay is a daughter isotope.

In *beta decay*, the nucleus emits a high-speed electron, whose expulsion has the effect of changing one of the neutrons into a proton. As a result, the atomic number is increased by one but the mass number remains unchanged.

In *electron capture*, one of the protons in the nucleus acquires an electron from one of the electron orbitals. The positive charge of the proton is thus neutralized and the protron becomes a neutron. The atomic number decreases by one, but the mass number remains unchanged.

In viewing radioactive decay as an energy-producing mechanism for geologic processes, we must look at the types of emissions associated with the nuclear changes. In alpha decay, the motion of an alpha particle represents a form of kinetic energy. When they alpha particle is lost, the remaining nucleus is in an excited state and becomes stable only by the emission of a *gamma ray,* which is a high-energy photon. Energy contained in both the alpha particle motion and the gamma ray is produced by a very small reduction in the combined mass of the alpha particle and the remaining nucleus. This mass difference is equated to energy by the Einstein formula:

$$E=mc^2$$

where E is energy

m is mass and

c is the speed of light (300,000 km/sec)

From this equation, we see that an extremely small quanitity of mass converts into a comparatively enormous quantity of energy.

In beta decay, another form of energy, the *beta particle* is produced. It is an electron travelling at high speed, derived from one of the neutrons in the nucleus. In furnishing one electron (one negative unit electrical charge) for the beta particle, the neutron acquires a unit positive charge and becomes a proton. (The neutron also emits a particle called an *antineutrino*, but this is not important in our discussion of energy released by radioactive decay.)

The important point about radioactive decay is that it generates energy which takes the form of heat in the substance surrounding the radioisotope. This form of heat is called *radiogenic heat.* As alpha particles travel outward through the surrounding matter, they lose energy by interacting with electrons in the orbitals of other atoms and by colliding with other atomic nuclei. This lost energy is transformed into heat and raises the temperature of the substance. Both gamma rays and beta particles interact with electrons in the surrounding matter, also causing a buildup of heat. The total quantity of radiogenic heat produced per unit of time can be exactly calculated for a given quantity of a radioisotope.

We can illustrate radioactive decay and heat production by using the important *decay series* in which the parent radioisotope uranium-238 (U^{238}) eventually ends up as a stable isotope of lead, lead-206 (Pb^{206}). In the figure, arrows show the direction of successive changes. Note that each step in the direction of the arrow to the left is alpha decay; each diagonal step downward to the right is beta decay. Uranium-238 decays to produce thorium-234. This is followed by a succession of isotopes of seven different elements, listed along the bottom of the graph. The disintegration process achieves a steady rate, or equilibrium, with time. In the case of the uranium-238-lead-206 series, each gram of uranium produces 0.71 calories of heat per year.

Other important heat-producing decay sequences in the rocks of the earth are those of uranium-235, thorium-232, and potassiurn-40. Uranium-235 produces 4.3 calories of heat per gram per year, thorium- 232 produces 0.20 calorie, and potassium-40 produces only 0.000027 calorie.

Of great importance in both the early history of the earth and the dating of geologic events is a physical law that governs the rate of decay of radioisotopes. Once an equilibrium has been reached in the process of radioactive disintegration, the ratio of decrease in the number of atoms of the parent isotope with each unit of time is a constant.

Take for example, postassium-40, which decays to the stable isotopes calcium-40 and argon-40. We can start at any point in time. Let the number of atoms of potassium-40 at tune zero be designated by unity (1.0). After 1.31 billion years have elapsed, the number of atoms of potassium-40 will have been reduced to half the initial number, designated as 0.5 on the vertical scale. The span of time of 1.31 billion years is designated as the half-life. In a second elapsed span of 1.31 billion years, the number of atoms of potassium-40 will again be halved, reducing the remaining quantity to 0.25 on the vertical scale. Notice that the ratio of reduction is always the same, i.e., one- half. Such a schedule of decrease in quantity with time is known as exponential decay. This schedule applies to all radioactive decay, but the ratio of change, and hence the value of the half-life, is different from one isotope to another.

It should be noted that calcium-40 is produced about 71/3 times more rapidly than argon-40, hence the curve of calcium-40 rises more steeply. We shall refer to the ratios of parent isotopes to daughter isotopes in our discussion of methods of rock dating.

In projecting the production of radiogenic heat back into earliest geologic time, these differences will be highly important. Isotopes with the shorter half-lives were then present in very much larger quantities than today, in contrast with isotopes having extremely long half-lives.

Table 7.3 Half-Lives of Important Radioisotopes (strachler)

Distribution of Radiogenic Heat

Heat flows continuously upward from depths of the earth toward the surface. The increase in temperature with depth, or geothermal gradient, is well known from observations in deep mines and bore holes and has a value of about 3 C^0 per 100 m. The flow of heat because of this thermal gradient averages about 1.4 microcalories (0.0000014 calories) per square centimetre per second. At this rate, the total heat flow in one year is about 50 calories per square centimetres, enough to melt an ice layer 6 mm thick. This quantity of heat is extremely small compared with that received by one square centimeter of the earth's surface from solar radiation. Therefore the earth's heat flow from depth is of no significance in the earth's surface heat balance or in powering the atmospheric and oceanic circulation systems.

The rate of temperature increase with depth falls off very rapidly after the first 200 km or so. The flattening of the temperature curve in the lower mantle and core expresses the very low thermal gradient that is postulated to exist within the deep interior. If the thermal gradient decreases rapidly with depth, a logical interpretation is that the rate of production of radiogenic beat is greatest near the earth's surface and decreases rapidly with depth. It has been concluded that the concentration of radioisotopes is greatest in the rocks of the crust, but falls off rapidly in the mantle rocks and is very small in the lower mantle and core.

Both the concentrations and rates of heat production of the radioisotopes of uranium, thorium, and potassium in each of three classes of rocks. These rates are based upon chemical analyses of samples of igneous rocks collected at the earth's surface. If we project these figures to the assumed corresponding rocks of the crust and mantle, gas shown in figure we see that the most rapid production of radiogenic heat is by felsic (granitic) rocks of the upper zone of the continental crust. The ultramafic mantle rock produces very little heat per unit of weight. It has been estimated that about one-half of all radiogenic heat is produced above a depth of 35 km in the continental crust.

Some support for the conclusion that the iron core of the earth produces almost no radiogenic heat is found in the analysis of iron meteorites. These fragments of matter are thought to represent the disrupted cores of planetary objects of origin similar to the earth, and they show radioactive minerals in only very small quantities.

Early Thermal History of the Earth

Modern hypotheses of the earth's origin, favor the process of accretion of the earth and other planets through the condensation of a hot interstellar cloud of gases and dust as it collision and gravitational attraction. Once formed, solid masses would have grown by the infall of solid bodies of many sizes, perhaps including objects similar to the asteroids of our present-day solar system. It is generally supposed that at the time planetary accretion was largely complete, the earth's interior temperature had not risen to the melting point, although local areas may have become molten from the energy of impacts. Modern thinking is thus along quite different lines from that of early scholars, who postulated that hot nebular gases condensed to the molten state and finally cooled to the solid state.

The discovery of natural radioactivity by Henri Becquerel in 1896, followed by the isolation of radium by Marine and Pierre Curie in 1898, radically altered all scientific thinking about the earth's internal heat John Joly in 1909 applied the new knowledge of radioactivity to recalculations of the earth's thermal history. Moreover, Joly brought forward the underlying principle that radiogenic heat provides the prime energy source for volcanism, igneous intrusion, and deformation of the earth's crust into mountain belts. Today radiogenic heat is usually regarded as the basic source of energy for lithospheric plate motions.

We must first accept as a premise that the earth's supply of radioisotopes was furnished, along with all other elements, at the time the earth was formed. It is most unlikely that the earth, at the time of its formation as a planet about 4.5 billion years ago, contained the same quantity and distribution of radioisotopes that we find today. The obvious reason is that radioactive decay progressively reduces the initial store of radioisotopes. We conclude that the total production of radiogenic heat within the earth was at the maximum level at the time of the earth's formation and has diminished even since. The relative rates of decay of uranium, thorium, and potassium isotopes are not the same, but are well established for each isotope.

A graph in which time is plotted on the horizontal axis starting at an arbitrary zero point at the assumed time of formation of the earth. Total planetary radiogenic heat production per year is given on the vertical scale. Curves have been plotted for the major radioisotopes of uranium, thorium, and potassium individually, while the total production is shown in a separate curve. Note that uranium-235 and potassium-40 have short half-lives in comparison with these of uranium-238 and thorium-232. Referring to the total curve, it is obvious that total radiogenic heat production was vastly greater when the earth was first formed than it is at present, roughly by a factor of six. The implications of such a history are of great consequence.

First, assume that at the time of the earth's formation by accretion the radioisotopes were uniformly distributed throughout the entire earth. (There is no reason to think otherwise.) Silicate minerals and iron were also more or less uniformly mixed. As radlogenic beat accumulated at great depths, the temperature of the solid rock would have been raised to a level close to the melting point. At a certain point in time, which may have been about one billion years after planetary accretion was completed, the melting point of iron would have been exceeded. This event probably occurred first in a depth zone ranging from 400 to 800 km. The silicate minerals remained crystalline, forming a spongy mass through which droplets of molten iron could filter down under the force of gravity. As molten iron accumulated in the central core region, the silicate minerals were gradually displaced upward.

At this point, a new factor would have come into play to raise the earth's internal temperature. As the iron sank toward the earth's center, its potential energy would have been converted into kinetic energy of molecular motion in the form of sensible heat. It seems likely that the additional heating was sufficient to cause melting or partial melting of a large proportion of the entire earth. At various times and places, melted rock would have risen as magma toward the surface, bringing radioisotopes up with it. Minerals containing the radioactive elements are largely of felsic composition and tend to remain in the liquid state at temperatures lower than the mafic minerals. Cooling and crystallization of the mafic minerals would have been accompanied by a sinking of those mineral crystals (which are denser), leaving the less mafic liquid fraction to solidify closer to the earth's surface. Although such a process of differentiation is speculative, it offers a mechanism for the selective removal of the radioisotopes from the inner earth and their eventual concentration near the surface.

So we see that during this great thermal event, the density layering of the earth came into existence, resulting in the concentration of metallic iron in the core, a less dense ultramafic rock mantle above it, and a mafic-felsic crust at the top. During and after the segregation process, the rate of radiogenic heat production was steadily falling. Consequently, along with redistribution of the heat-generating isotopes, the final episodes of deep melting must have become fewer and eventually ceased. Today the earth is thermally stable, in the sense that melting and movement of magma are limited to an extremely shallow layer compared with the earth's total diameter. The inner core and much of the mantle are no longer subject to melting through the accumulation of excess heat.

It is fortunate, indeed, that the chemistry of the radioactive elements is such that they would tend to rise towards the earth's surface throughout its history. If, on the other hand, they had tended to sink and collect near its center, the heat produced by their concentrated activity would have repeatedly melted the earth. Under such conditions, no planetary stability would have been possible throughout geologic history. As we find conditions today, radiogenic heat production in the core is negligible, while the rate of surfaceward flow of heat from the upper mantle and crust closely balances the rate of heat production. Consequently, the mantle remains for the most part at a temperature lower than its melting point. Only in the soft layer of the mantle (the asthenosphere) is melting on a large scale a likely occurrence.

Radiometric Methods of Dating the Earth

Radioactivity

The radioactivity discovered by Henri Becquerel was a consequence of the fact that some elements, such as uranium and thorium, are unstable. Such elements will decay to form other elements or other isotopes of the same element. To understand what is meant by "decay", let us consider what happens to a radioactive element like uranium 238. Uranium 238 has an atomic weight of 238. The "238" represents the sum of the atom's protons and neutrons (each proton and neutron having a "weight" of 1). Uranium has an atomic number (number of protons) of 92. Such atoms with specific atomic number and weight are sometimes termed *nuclides*. Sooner or later (and entirely spontaneously) the uranium 238 atom will fire off a particle from the nucleus called an alpha particle. Alpha particles are positively charged ions of helium. They have an atomic weight of 4 and an atomic number of 2. Thus, when the alpha particle is emitted, the new atom will have an atomic weight of 234 and an atomic number of 90. From the decay of the parent nuclide, uranium 238, the daughter of the nuclide, thorium 234, is obtained. A shorthand equation for this change is written:

$$^{238}_{92}\mathrm{U} \rightarrow {}^{234}_{90}\mathrm{Th} + {}^{4}_{2}\mathrm{He}$$

This change is not, however, the end of the Process, for the nucleus of thorium 234 is not stable. It eventually emits a beta particle (an electron discharged from the nucleus when a neutron splits into a proton and an electron). There is now an extra proton in the nucleus but no loss of atomic weight because electrons are essentially weightless. Thus, from 238 90 Th the daughter element 234 91 Pa (protactinium) is formed. In this case, the atomic number has been increased by one. In other instances, the beta particle may be captured by the nucleus, where it combines with a proton to form a neutron. The loss of the proton would decrease the atomic number by one.

A third kind of emission in the radioactive decay process is called *gamma radiation*. It consists of a form of invisible electromagnetic waves having even shorter wavelengths than do x-rays.

As alpha and beta particles, as well as gamma radiation, move through the surrounding materials, their energy is transformed into increased activity of the electrons in the atoms of the surrounding medium. The result is heat. This radiogenic source of heat was the unknown entity in Lord Kelvin's calculations of the earth's thermal history.

The Clocks in the Rocks (Radiometric Dating)

Nuclear adjustments such as those described previously occur many times before a final, stable daughter element, such as lead, is formed. The rate at which the steps in the process take place is unaffected by changes in temperature, pressure, or the chemical environment, since these do not involve the nucleus. Indeed, one can confidently assume that the rate of decay of long-lived isotopes has not varied since the earth came into existence. Therefore, once a quantity of radioactive nuclides has been incorporated into a growing mineral crystal, that quantity will begin to decay at a steady rate with a definite percentage of the radiogenic atoms

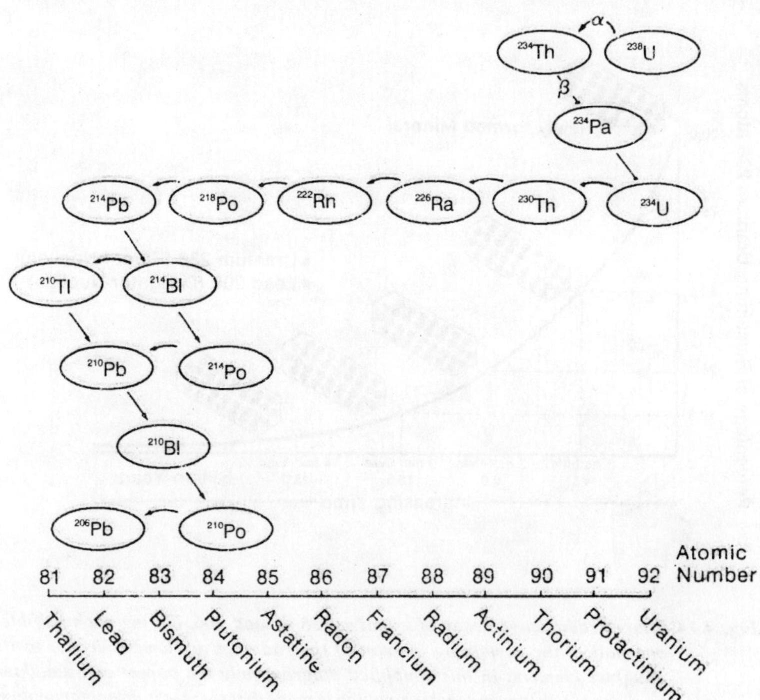

Fig. 4.14. Radioactive decay series of uranium 238 to lead 206.

undergoing decay in each increment of time. Each radioactive element has a particular mode of decay and a unique decay rate. As time passes, the quantity of the parent nuclide diminishes and the amount of daughter atoms increases, thereby indicating how much time has elapsed since the clock began its time-keeping. The "beginning," or "time zero," for any mineral containing radioactive nuclides would be the moment when the radioactive parent atoms became part of a mineral from which daughter elements could not escape. The retention of daughter elements is essential, for they must be counted to determine the original quantity of the parent nuclide.

The determination of the ratio of parent to daughter nuclides is usually accomplished with the use of a mass spectrometer, an analytical instrument capable of separating and measuring the proportions of minute particles according to their mass differences. In the mass spectrometer, samples of elements are vaporized in an evacuated chamber, where they are bombarded by a stream of electrons. This bombardment knocks electrons

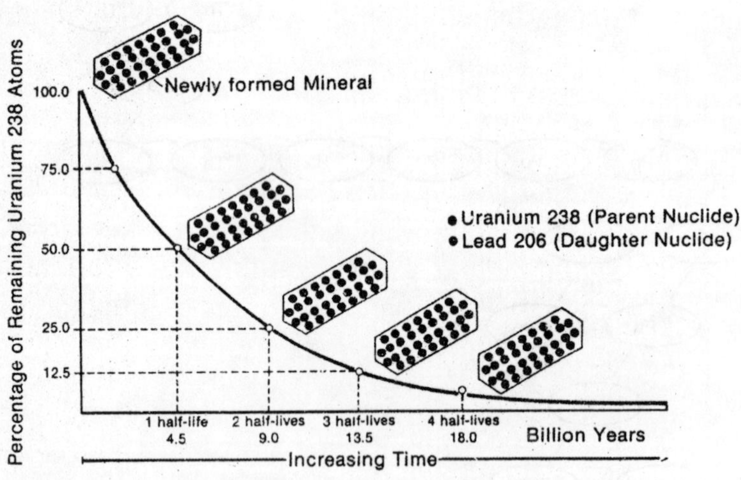

Fig. 4.14. Rate of radioactive decay of uranium 238 to lead 206. During each half-life, one half of the remaining amount of the radioactive element decays to its daughter element. In this simplified diagram only the parent and daughter nuclides are shown and the assumption is made that there was no contamination by daughter nuclides at the time the mineral formed.

off the atoms, leaving them positively charged. A stream of these positively charged ions is deflected as it passes between plates that bear opposite charges of electricity. The degree of deflection is proportional to the masses of the atoms .

Not all radioactive decay are measured by means of a mass spectrometer. In the case of carbon 14, which decay by beta particle emission, the measurement of nuclides is accomplished indirectly by the use of a very sensitive *geiger counter.*

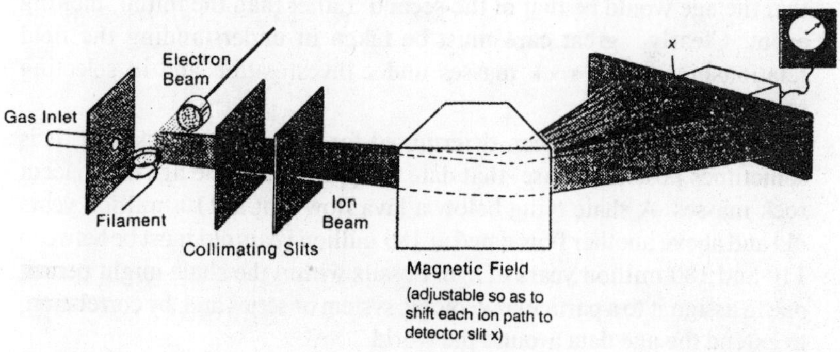

Fig. 4.15. Schematic drawing of a mass spectrometer. In this type of spectrometer the intensity of each ion beam is measured electricity to permit determination of the isotopic abundances required for radiometric dating.

Of the three major families of rocks, the igneous clan lends itself best to radiometric dating. The dates obtained from such rocks indicate the time that a silicate melt containing radioactive elements solidified. In contrast to igneous rocks, sedimentary rocks can only rarely be dated radiometrically. Some dates for sedimentary strata have been obtained from a mineral called *glauconite*, which is believed to form "in place" at the time of deposition. This greenish mineral contains radioactive potassium 40, which decays to argon 40 and can be used in geochronology. Because of possible, losses in the daughter element argon, care must be taken in interpreting dates, however; in most instances, potassium-argon dates derived from glauconite are considered minimal ages for the enclosing strata. As for classic sedimentary rocks that contain radioactive elements in their detrital mineral grains, the ages obtained refer to the parent rock that was eroded and is older than the sedimentary layer.

Dates obtained from metamorphic rocks may also require special care in interpretation. The age of a particular mineral may record the time the rock first formed or any one of a number of subsequent metamorphic recrystallizations.

There are many other problems that can affect the validity of a radiometric age. If some of the daughter products are removed from the sample by weathering or leaching, its age would be under- estimated. If the element being analysed was a gas, some of that gas (as with argon in glauconite) might have diffused out of the rock. The heat accompanying burial or mountain building might enhance such losses. There is also the possibility that at a later time older rocks may be partially remelted so that the age would be that of the second, rather than the initial, melting event. Clearly, great care must be taken in understanding the field relationships of the rock masses under investigation and in selecting samples.

Once an age has been determined for a particular rock unit, it is sometimes possible to use that date to approximate the age of adjacent rock masses. A shale tying below a lava flow that is 110 million years old and above another flow dated at 180 million years old must be between 110 and 180 million years of age. Fossils within the shale might permit one to assign it to a particular geologic system or series and, by correlation, to extend the age data around the world.

Half-Life

There is no way that one can predict with certainty the moment of disintegration for any individual radioactive atom in a mineral. We do know that it would take an infinitely long time for all of the atoms in a quantity of radioactive elements to be entirely transformed to stable daughter products. Experimenters have also shown that the decline in the number of atoms is rapid in the early stages but becomes progressively slower in the later stages. One can statistically forecast what percentage of a large population of atoms will decay in a certain amount of time.

Because of these features of radioactivity, it is convenient to consider the number of years needed for half of the original quantity of atoms to decay. This span of years is termed the half-life. Thus, at the end of the years constituting one half- life, one half of the original quantity of radioactive element still has not undergone decay. After another half-life, one half of what was left is halved, so that one fourth of the original quantity remains. After a third half-life, only one eighth would remain, and so on.

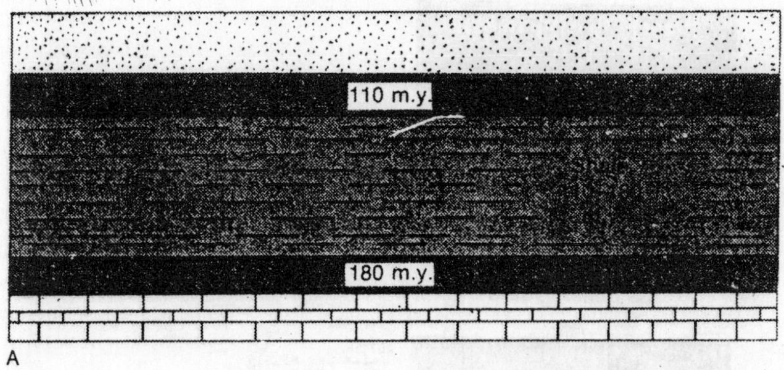

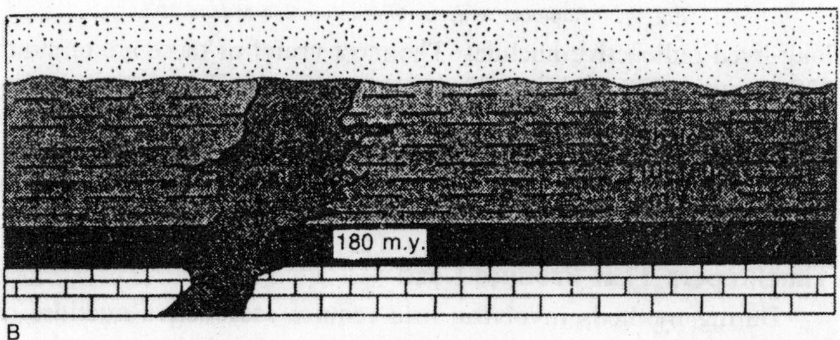

Fig. 4.16. Igenous rocks that have provided absolute radiogenic ages can often be used to date sedimentary layers. In A, the shale is bracketed by two lava flows. In B, the shale lies above the older flow and is intruded by a younger igneous body.

Every radioactive nuclide has its own unique half-life. (Uranium 235, for example, has a half-life of 704 million years. Thus, if a sample contains 50 per cent of the original amount of uranium 235 and 50 per cent of its daughter product, lead 207, then that sample is 704 million years old. If the analyses indicate 25 per cent of uranium 235 and 75 per cent of lead 207, two half-lives would have elapsed, and the sample would be 1408 million years old.

The Principal Geologic Timekeepers

At one time, there were many more radioactive nuclides present on earth than there are now. Many of these had short half-lives and have long since decayed to undetectable quantities. Fortunately, for those interested in dating the earth's most ancient rocks, there remain a few

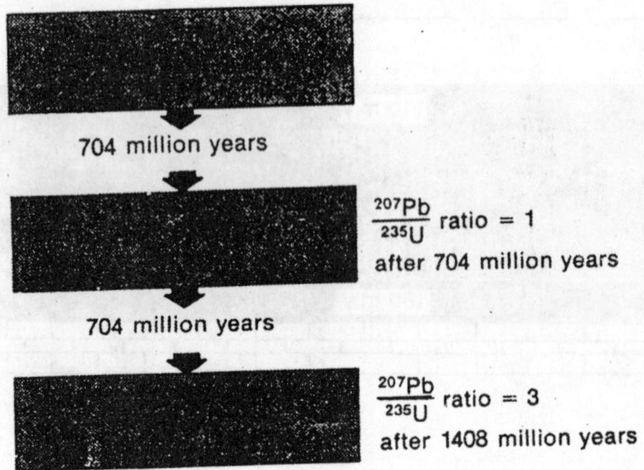

Fig. 4.17. Radioactive decay of uranium 235 to lead 207.

long-lived radioactive nuclides. The most useful of these are uranium 238, uranium 235, rubidium 87, and potassium 40. There are also a few short-lived radioactive elements that are used for dating more recent events. Carbon 14 is an example of such a short-lived isotope. There are also short-lived nuclides that represent segments of a uranium or thorium decay series.

Timekeepers That Produce Lead

Dating methods involving lead require radioactive nuclides of uranium or thorium that were incorporated into the earth's crust when it congealed. To determine the age of a sample of mineral or rock, one must know the original quantity of parent nucildes as well as the quantity remaining at the present time. The original number of parent atoms should be equal to the sum of the present quantity of parent atoms and daughter atoms. This raises the question of whether or not some of the lead may not have already been in the mineral and, if not detected, cause its radiometric age to exceed its true age. Lead 204, which is never produced by decay, provides a means of detecting original lead. All common lead contains a mixture of four lead isotopes. In most minerals used for dating, the proportions of the lead isotopes are nearly constant, so that lead 204 can be used to calculate the quantities of original lead 206 and lead 207. These quantities can then be subtracted from the total to give the amount due to radioactivity.

As we have seen, different isotopes decay at different rates. Geochronologists take advantage of this fact by simultaneously analysing two or three isotope pairs as a means to crosscheck ages and detect errors. For example, if the $^{235}U/^{207}Pb$ radiometric ages and the $^{238}U/^{206}Pb$ ages agree, then they are said to be *concordant*; there then exists a high probability that the radiometric age is valid. (Uranium-lead ages that vary widely are said to be *discordant*. However, even the best of concordant dates do not agree perfectly but are expected to vary within reasonable limits. (Inavoidable losses or gains of isotopes by interactions with surrounding solutions or from the beat accompanying geologic processes are the usual causes for variance. Radiometric ages should be considered reasonable approximations of true age.

Radiometric ages that depend upon uranium/lead ratios may also be checked against ages derived from lead 207 to lead 206. Because the half-life of uranium 235 is much less that the half-life of uranium 238, the ratio of lead 207 (produced by the decay of uranium 235) to lead 206 will change regularly with age and can be used as a radioactive timekeeper.

The Potassium-Argon Method

Potassium and argon are another radioactive pair widely used for dating rocks. By means of *electron capture* (causing a proton to be transformed into a neutron), about 11 per cent of the potassium 40 in a mineral decays to argon 40, which may then be retained within the parent mineral. The remaining potassium 40 decays to calcium 40 (by emission of a beta particle from a neutron, thereby transforming it into a proton). The decay of potassium 40 to calcium 40 is not for obtaining radiometric ages, because radiogenic calcium cannot be distinguished from original calcium in a rock. Thus, geochronologists concentrate their efforts on the 11 per cent of potassium 40 atoms that decay to argon. One advantage of using argon is that it is inert-that is, it does not combine chemically with other elements. Argon 40 found in a mineral is very likely to have originated there following the decay of adjacent potassium 40 atoms in the mineral.

Another advantage to the potassium scheme for dating rocks is that potassium 40 is an abundant constituent of many common minerals, including micas, feldspars, and hornblendes. However, like all radiometric methods *potassium- argon dating* is not without its limitations. A sample will yield a valid age only if none of the argon has leaked out of the mineral being analyzed. Leakage may indeed occur if the rock has experienced temperatures above about 125°C. In specific localities, the ages of rocks dated by this method reflect the last episode of heating rather than the time of origin of the rock itself. A less serious problem is mechanical entrapment of atmospheric argon in flowing lavas.

The half-life of potassium 40 is 1251 million years. If the ratio of potassium 40 to argon 40 is found to be 1 to 1, then the age of the sample is 1251 million years. If the ratio is 3 to 1, then yet another half-life has elapsed, and the rock would have a radiogenic age of two half-lives, or 2502 million years.

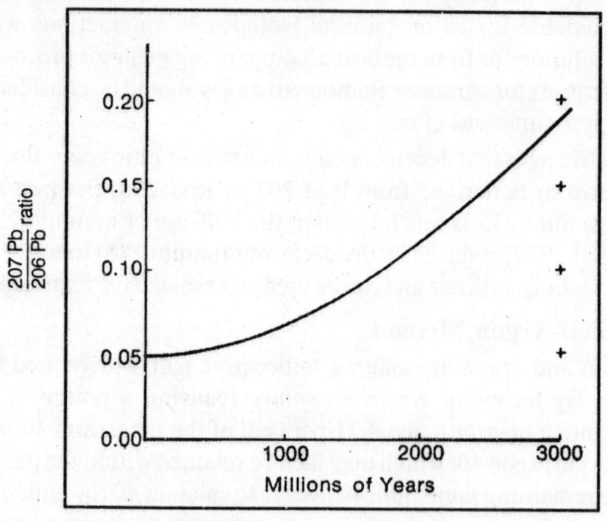

Fig. 4.18. Graph showing how the ratio of lead 207 to lead 206 can be used as a measure of age.

Potassium-argon is widely used in deciphering various types of geologic problems. Geologists are now using the method in studies relating to sea floor movements. For many years, scientists have been curious about the alignment of the major Hawaiian Islands and the adjacent seamounts. With the advent of the theory of sea floor spreading, scientists developed the concept that these volcanic islands were built over a relatively fixed "hot spot" deep in the upper mantle. Conduits from the "hot spot" brought lavas up to the sea floor, where eruptions periodically occurred. Volcanoes that developed over the "hot spot" were then conveyed along by sea floor movement, and new volcanoes were produced over the vacated position. Geologists reasoned that if this process had taken place in the Hawaiian Islands, then potassium-argon radiometric ages should change in sequence along the island-seamount chain. The

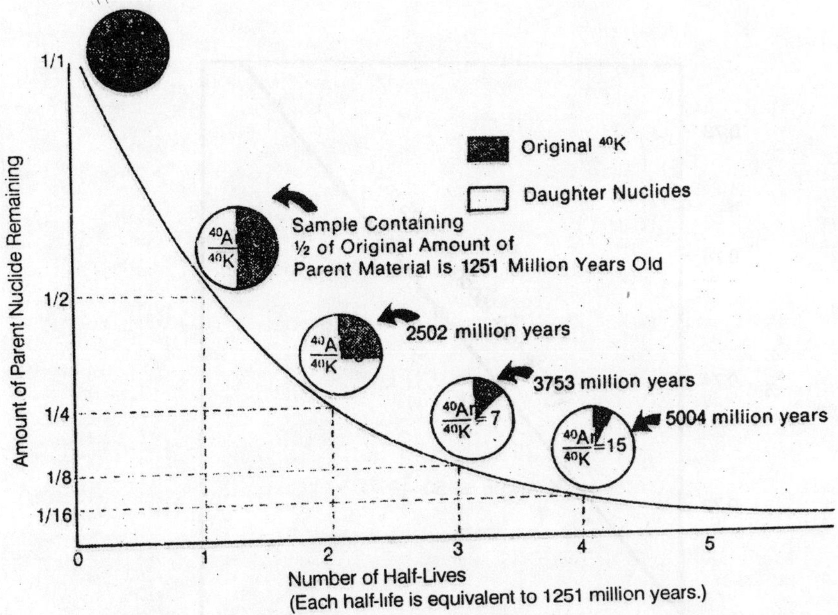

Fig. 4.19. Decay curve for potassium 40.

dates do indeed support the theory, and they even suggest that the direction of movement changed from a more northerly trend to northwesterly trend about 40 million years ago.

The Rubidium-Strontium Method

The dating method based on the disintegration by beta decay of rubidium 87 to strontium 87 can sometimes be used as a check on potassium- argon dates, because rubidium and potassium are often found in the same minerals. The rubidiumstrontium scheme has a further advantage in that the strontium daughter nuclide is not diffused by relatively mild heating events, as is the case with argon.

In the rubidium-strontium method, a number of samples are collected from the rock body to be dated. With the aid of the mass spectrometer, the amounts of radioactive rubidium 87, its daughter product strontium 87, and strontium 86 are calculated for each sample. Strontium 86 is an isotope not derived from radioactive decay. A graph is then prepared in which the ^{87}Rb/^{86} Sr ratio in each sample is plotted against the ^{87}Rb/^{86} Sr

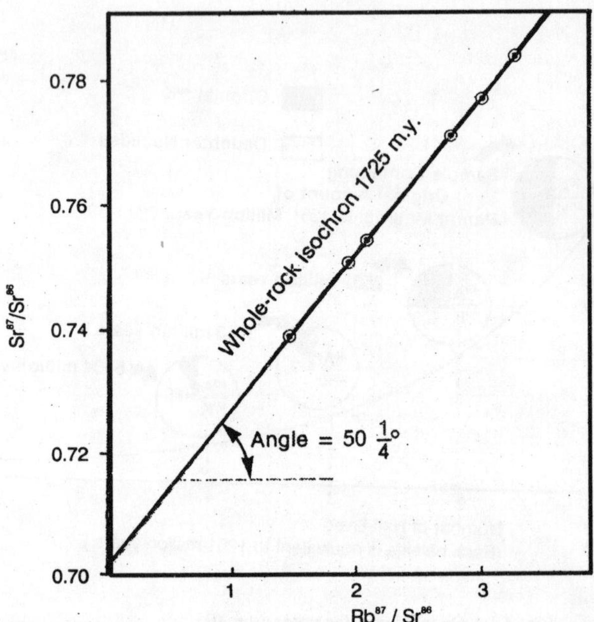

Fig. 4.20. Whole-rock rubidium-strontium isochron for a set of samples of a Precambrian granite body exposed near Sudbury, Ontario.

ratio. From the points on the graph, a straight line is constructed that is termed an isochron. The slope of the isochron results from the fact that, with the passage of time, there is continuous decay of rubidium 87, which causes the rubidium 87/strontium 86 ratio to decrease. Conversely, the strontium 87/strontium 86 ratio increases as strontium 87 is produced by the decay of rubidium 87. The older the rocks being investigated, the more the original isotope ratios will have been changed, and the greater will be the inclination of the isochron. The slope of the isochron permits a computation of the age of the rock.

The rubidium-strontium and potassium-argon methods need not always depend upon the collection of discrete mineral grains containing the required isotopes. Sometimes the rock under investigation is so finely crystalline and the critical minerals so tiny and dispersed that it is difficult or impossible to obtain a suitable collection of minerals. In such instances, large samples of the entire rock may be used for age determination. This method is called *whole-rock analysis*. It is useful not only for fine-grained rocks but also for rocks in which the yield of useful isotopes from mineral separates is too low for analysis. Whole-rock analysis has also been useful in determining the age of rocks that have been so severely metamorphosed that the potassium-argon or rubidium-strontium radiometric clocks of individual minerals have been reset. In such cases, the age obtained from the minerals would be that of the episode of metamorphism, not the total age of the rock itself. The required isotopes and their decay products, however, may have merely moved to nearby locations within the same rock body, and therefore analyses of large chunks of the whole rock may provide valid radiometric age determinations.

The Carbon 14 Method

Techniques for age determination based on content of radiocarbon were first devised by W. F. Libby and his associates at the University of Chicago in 1947. It has become an indispensable aid to archaeologic research and frequently is useful in deciphering the very recent events in geologic history. Because of the short half-life of carbon 14-a mere 5730 years-organic substances older than about 40,000 years no longer contain carbon 14 in measurable amounts.

Unlike uranium 238 and rubidium 87, carbon 14 is created continuously in the earth's upper atmosphere. The story of its origin begins with cosmic rays, which are extremely high-energy particles (mostly protons) that bombard the earth continuously. Such particles strike atoms in the upper atmosphere and split their nuclei into smaller particles, among which are neutrons. Carbon 14 is formed when a neutron strikes an atom of nitrogen 14. As a result of the collision, the nitrogen atom emits a proton and becomes carbon 14. Radioactive carbon is being created by this process at the rate of about two atoms per second for every square centimetre of the earth's surface. The newly created carbon 14 combines quickly with oxygen to form CO_2, which is then distributed by wind and water currents around the globe. It soon finds its way into photosynthetic plants, because they utilize carbon dioxide from the atmosphere to build tissues. Plants containing carbon 14 are ingested by animals, and the isotope becomes a part of their tissues as well.

Eventually, carbon 14 decays back to nitrogen 14 by emission of a beta particle. A plant removing CO_2 from the atmosphere should receive a share of carbon 14 proportional to that in the atmosphere. A state of equilibrium is reached in which the gain in newly produced carbon 14 is

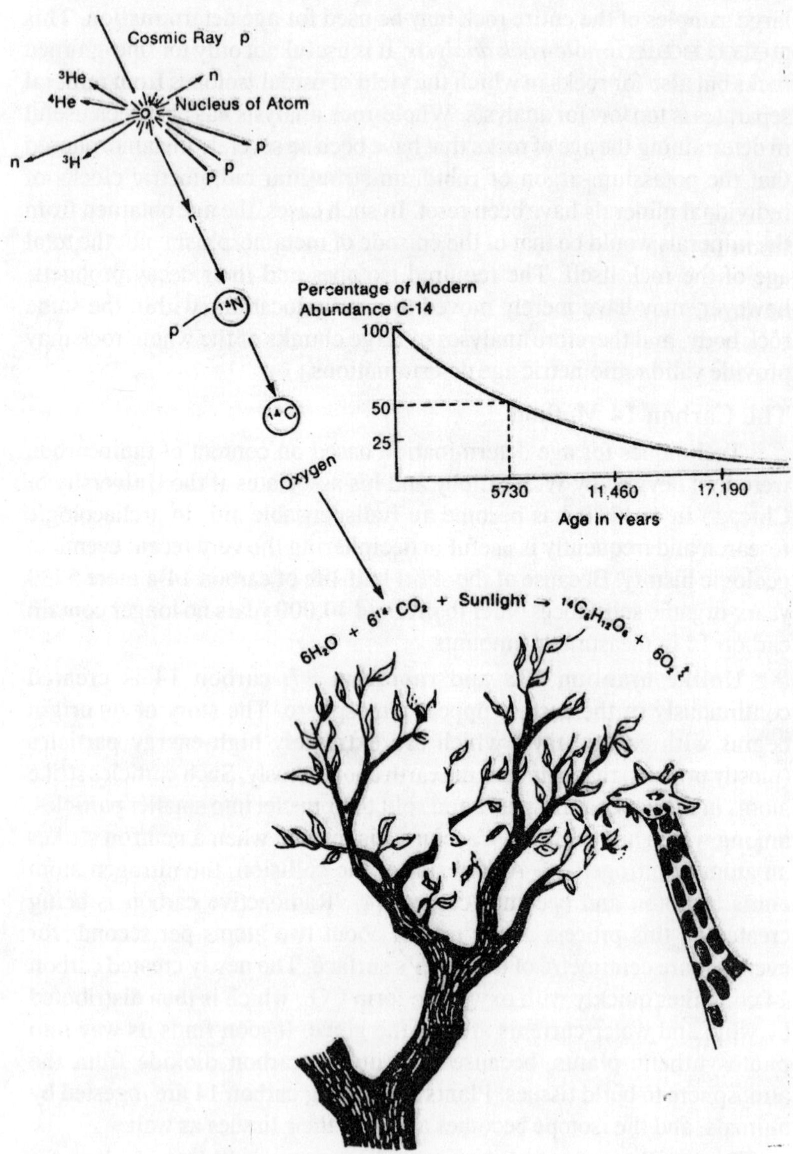

Fig. 4.21. Carbon 14 is formed from nitrogen in the atmosphere. It combines withoxygen to form radioactive carbon dioxide and is then incorporated into all living things.

balanced by the decay loss. The rate of production of carbon 14 has varied somewhat over the past several thousand years. As a result, corrections in age calculations must be made. Such corrections are derived from analyses of standards such as wood samples, whose exact age is known.

The age of some ancient bit of organic material is not determined from the ratio of parent to daughter nuclides, as is done with previously discussed dating schemes. Rather, the age is estimated from the ratio of carbon 14 to all other carbon in the sample. After an animal or plant dies, there can be no further replacement of carbon from atmospheric CO_2, and the amount of carbon 14 already present in the once living organism begins to diminish in accordance with the rate of carbon 14 decay. Thus, if the carbon 14 fraction of the total carbon in a piece of pine tree buried in volcanic ash were found to be about 25 per cent of the quantity in living pines, then the age of the wood (and the volcanic activity) would be two half- lives, or 11,460 years. To allow for unavoidable error, the age of the wood might be expressed as 11,460 +_ 250 years.

The carbon 14 technique has considerable value to geologists studying the most recent events of the Pleistocene ice age. Prior to the development of the method, the age of sediments deposited by the last advance of continental glaciers was surmised to be about 25,000 years. Radiocarbon dates of a layer of peat beneath the glacial sediments provided an age of only 11,400 years. The method has also been found useful in dating the geologically recent uppermost layer of sediment on the sea floors. For the deeper and older marine sediments, however, the thorium method described further on is employed.

Methods Involving Thorium 230

The past 2 decades of intensive exploration of the sea floor has prompted the development of yet other dating methods that are especially useful for oceanic sediments too old to be dated with carbon 14. These new techniques utilize isotopes that are produced in the intermediary stages of the uranium decay series. Scientists who developed these methods recognized that most of the uranium brought to the oceans by streams remains in solution. While in solution it decays, eventually producing thorium 230. The thorium isotope is precipitated and becomes a component of ocean floor sediments. Thorium 230 itself decays with a half- life of 75,000 years. Because lower levels of the sediment have been undergoing decay longer, geochronologists are able to detect the expected decrease in quantity of thorium 230 at greater depths in a cored column of sediment. The thorium 230 concentration of each measured

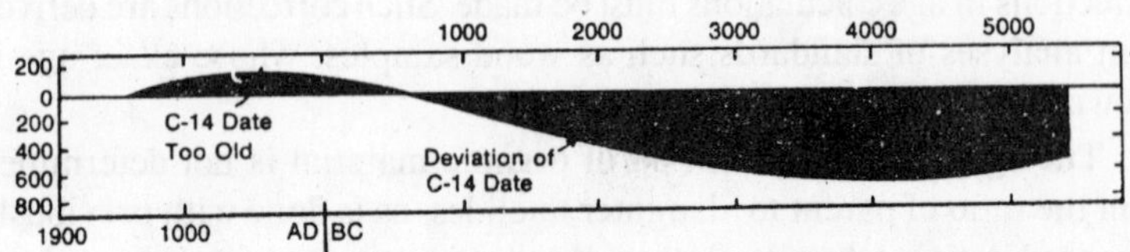

Fig. 4.22. Deviation of carbon 14 ages from true ages from the present back to about 5000BC. Data are obtained from analysis of bristle cone pines from the western U.S. Calculation of ^{14}C deviations are based on half-life of 5,730 years.

interval is compared to the quantity in the surface layer, and a time scale relating age to quantity of remaining parent nuclides is then formulated.

Deep sea sediments can also be dated by means of a procedure based upon thorium and protactinium. Thorium 230 has a half-life of 75,000 years and is in the decay series from uranium 238. Protactinium 231 has a half-life of only 34,300 years and is in the line of descent from uranium 235. Both parent nuclides are precipitated in the same proportions, but because of their different rates of decay, the ratio of the two changes regularly with time. Thus, the greater the differences in the quantity of undecayed parent isotopes, the older the sediment.

Nuclear Fission Track Timekeepers

Nuclear particle fission tracks were discovered about 20 years ago when scientists using the electron microscope were able to examine the areas around presumed locations of radioactive particles that were embedded in mica. Closer examination showed that the tracks were really small tunnels-like bullet holes—that were produced when high-energy particles of the nucleus of uranium were fired off in the course of *spontaneous fission* (spontaneous fragmentation of an atom into two or more lighter atoms and nuclear particles). The particles speed through the orderly rows of atoms in the crystal, tearing away electrons from atoms located along the path of trajectory and rendering them positively charged. Their mutual repulsion produces the track. The tracks are only a few atoms in width and are impossible to see without an electron microscope. Therefore, the sample is immersed for a short period of time in a suitable solution (acid or alkali), which rushes up into the tubes, enlarging the track tunnel so that it can be seen with an ordinary microscope.

The natural rate of track production by uranium atoms is very slow and occurs at a constant rate. For this reason, the tracks can be used to determine the number of years that have elapsed since the uranium-bearing mineral solidified. One first determines the number of uranium atoms that have already disintegrated. This number is obtained with the aid of the microscope by counting the etched tracks. Next, one must find the original number of uranium atoms. This quantity can be determined by bombarding the sample with neutrons in a reactor and thereby causing the remaining uranium to undergo fission. A second count of tracks reveals the original quantity of uranium. Finally, one must know the spontaneous fission decay rate for uranium 238. This information is determined by counting the tracks in a piece of uranium-bearing synthetic glass of known date of manufacture.

Fission track dating is of particular interest to geochronologists because it can potentially be used to date specimens only a few centuries old as well as to date rocks billions of years in age. The method helps to date the period between about 40,000 and 1 million years ago-a period for which neither carbon 14 nor potassium-argon methods are suitable. As with all radiometric techniques, however, there can be problems. If rocks have been subjected to high temperatures, tracks may heal and fade away.

The Age of the Earth

Anyone interested in the total age of the earth must decide what event constitutes its "birth." Most geologists assume "year 1" commenced as soon as the earth had collected most of its present mass and had developed a solid crust. (Unfortunately, rocks that date from those earliest years have not been found on earth. They have long since been altered and converted to other rocks by various geologic processes. The oldest rocks on earth that have been dated thus far include 3.4-billion- year-old granites from the Barberton Mountain Land of South Africa, 3.7-billion-year-old granites of southwestern Greenland, and metamorphic rocks of about the same age from Minnesota. These dates permit us to say the planet is at least about 3.7 billion years old.

Meteorites, which many consider to be remnants of a disrupted planet that originally formed at about the same time as the earth, have provided uranium-lead and rubidium-strontium ages of about 4.6 billion years. From such data, and from estimates of how long it would take to produce the quantities of various lead isotopes now found on the earth, geochronologists feel that the 4.6-billion-year age for the earth can be accepted with confidence. Substantiating evidence for this conclusion comes from returned moon rocks. The ages of these rocks range from 3.3 to about 4.6 billion years. The older age determinations are derived from rocks collected on the lunar highland, which may represent the original lunar crust. Certainly, the moons and planets of our solar system originated as a result of the same cosmic processes and at about the same time.

Chapter 5

The Oldest Rocks

Beneath the Cambrian

When eighteenth century geologists first began to diagram local columns of strata, they frequently found a "basement complex" of igneous and metamorphic rocks beneath the lowest sedimentary layers. Such names as the "Primitive" or "Primary" were applied to these jumbled and often complex rock bodies. In 1835, the geologist *Adam Sedgwick,* while mapping in North Wales, used the name "Cambrian" for the strata lying above the basement rocks. Subsequently, geologists commonly referred to the underlying rocks simply as *Precambrian.* The term *Cryptozic* ("hidden life") was later applied to the Precambrian time interval, whereas the companion term *Phanerozoic* ("obvious life") was retained for all of subsequent geologic time.

Although early geologists correctly recognized that the Cryptozoic probably lasted several times longer than all the rest of geologic time, they gave rocks of this period only scant attention. Because older Cryptozoic rocks bore few if any fossils and were so contorted and intricately intruded, they were generally thought to be undecipherable. Nevertheless, Precambrian rocks form the very cores of the continents. They are also enormously important source rocks for iron and other metals. For these reasons, it was inevitable that a few intrepid geologists would devote their lives to deciphering the relationships of the tangled masses of schists, slates, and granites.

One of these pioneers of Precambrian geology was *Sir William Logan* of the Canadian Geological Survey. In the middle 1800's, Logan was able to associate groups of Precambrian rocks according to their superpositional and cross-cutting relationships. As a further aid, Logan speculated that those rocks that had suffered the most metamorphism were probably the oldest. Modern geologic investigations clearly show that Logan frequently erred in attempting to correlate degree of metamorphism with age. Older rocks may escape metamorphism, and younger ones may be radically metamorphosed. Nevertheless, in southeastern Canada, where Logan mapped, one could find an older terrain of gneissic rocks as well as younger sequences of less altered metamorphic and sedimentary rocks. For this reason, it seemed reasonable to think of Precambrian time as divisible into an older *Archean Era* and a younger *Proterozoic Era.* More recent work based on absolute dating techniques

Table 5.1. Some Chronologic and time-rock terms used in Precambrian Historical Geology

TIME IN BILLIONS OF YEARS			CANADIAN CLASSIFICATION	INTERNATIONAL CLASSIFICATION*	MAJOR NORTH AMERICAN OROGENIES
0.57	CRYPTOZOIC	PROTEROZOIC	Hadrynian	Proterozoic III	Grenvillian (1.2-.9 b.y.)
1.0					
1.5			Helikian	Proterozoic II	Elsonian (1.37 b.y.)
					Hudsonian (1.73 b.y.)
2.0			Aphebian	Proterozoic I	
2.5					Kenoran (2.48 b.y.)
3.0			ARCHAEAN	ARCHEAN	
3.5					

* *Provisional recommendation of the Subcommission on Precambrian Stratigraphy of the International Union of Geological Sciences.*

that were not available to Logan and his contemporaries has shown that one can continue to use these two terms in a very general way.

Today, geologists around the world agree that the only truly reliable basis for chronologic correlation of unfossiliferous Precambrian masses is through isotopic dating techniques. Only after the ages of rocks in a particular region are known can those rocks and the events they record be placed in the proper chapter of Precambrian history. The hundreds of dates already obtained include rocks that are about 3980 million years old, although most near-surface outcrops were formed less than 3600 million years ago.

Precambrian Shields

Distribution of Outcrops

Although Precambrian exposures are common place in cores of mountain ranges and canyons of plateaus, the most obvious and largest areas of Precambrian rocks are the erosionally stripped, regionally upwarped, geologically stable regions of the continents. Such regions are called *Precambrian shields* because of their broadly convex shape (reminiscent of a Greco-Roman shield). Shield rocks are exposed over only about 20 per cent of the earth's land surface, yet they represent about 75 per cent of the observable time span accounted for by crustal rocks. Every continent has one or more Precambrian shields bordered by Phanerozoic mobile belts. North America, for example, has the great Canadian Shield, which covers over 3 million square miles. Even where covered by younger layers, shield rocks poke through the cover at structural domes, as in the Ozarks and the Black Hills. Because of the great difficulty in making intercontinental correlations of Precambrian rocks, the terms and groupings used vary for each of the continents. However, as progress continues to be made in establishing the synchrony of outcrops, a standard body of terminology will probably emerge.

Overview of Shield History

Detailed geologic mapping of the Scandinavian and Canadian Shields during the 1930's provided a more complete understanding of Precambrian history. Although the events in any particular shield might differ from those in another, generalities emerged that were applicable to all shields. Radiometric dates for particular outcroppings began to accumulate; they gave geologists their best tool for correlating and deciphering field relationships. The improved data generated new ideas about the way shields developed. One hypothesis for shield growth suggests that at first a few primary continental nuclei might have differentiated from the mantle.

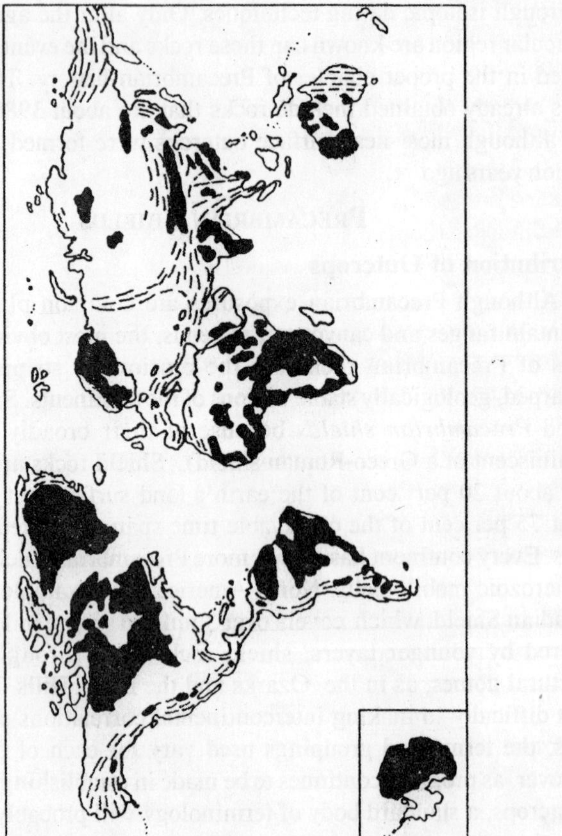

Fig. 5.1. Major areas of exposed Precambrian rocks.

Linear geosynclinal tracts might next have developed along the edges of these nuclei, experienced depositional and then orogenic phases, and ultimately become welded onto the continental nuclei. Erosion would next begin to wear away the crumpled sediments and volcanies and, aided by occasional uplifts, would strip the highlands down to the intensely metamorphosed and intruded roots of the old mountains. After repeated episodes of uplift and erosion, these once deeply buried stumps of mountains would come into gravitational balance with underlying rocks. They would become stable segments or provinces of the shield. One or more new geosynclines might then develop along the margins of the previously formed tract, and the continent (and shield) would grow by accretion of yet another marginal belt.

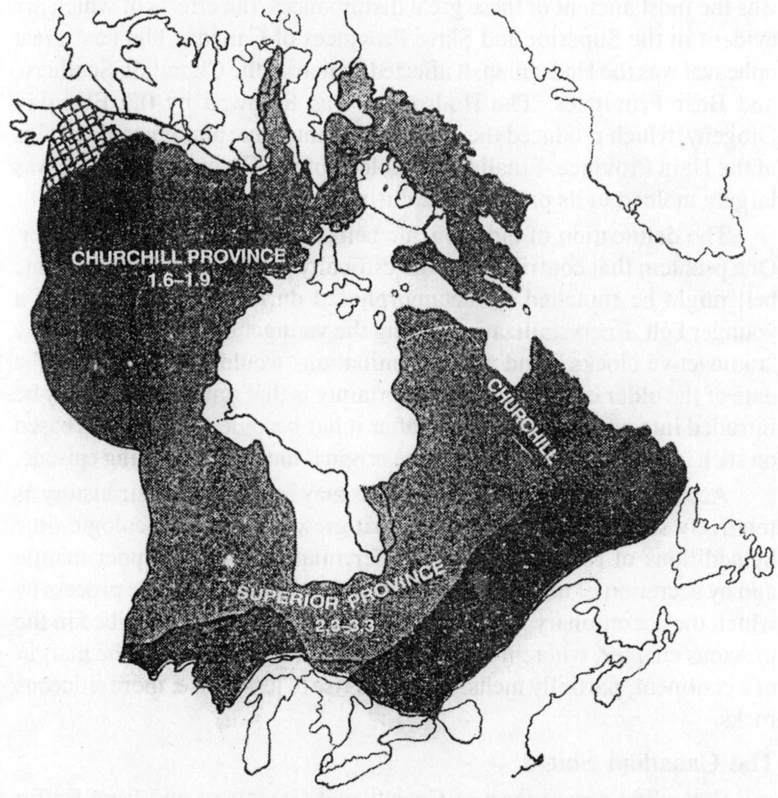

Fig. 5.2. Tectonic provinces of the Canadian Shield.

What is the evidence for this view of shield history ? When locations of dated Precambrian rocks are plotted on a map one finds that rocks of about the same age tend to occupy distinct belts. Each belt or Precambrian province is inferred to represent an ancient orogenic belt in which rocks were crystallized during metamorphism and granitic intrusion. Uranium-bearing minerals formed at the time of orogeny provide the materials for age determinations.

When the ages of North American shield rocks are plotted on a graph according to frequency of occurrence, they show peaks of metamorphism and intrusion at 2.5, 1.7, 1.4, and 1.0 billion years ago. This suggests that there were four major orogenic episodes that occurred at different times and places in this region of North America. As indicated in the Kenoran was the most ancient of these great disturbances, the effects of which are evident in the Superior and Slave Provinces of Canada. The next great upheaval was the Hudsonian. It affected primarily the Churchill, Southern, and Bear Provinces. The Hudsonian was followed by the Elsonian Orogeny, which produced the complex metamorphic and igneous terrains of the Nain Province. Finally, the geology of the Grenville Province was largely molded to its present state during the Grenville Orogeny.

The delineation of old orogenic belts is not at all a simple matter. One problem that contributes to the difficulty is that an ancient orogenic belt might be remelted or metamorphosed during the orogenesis of a younger belt. Recrystallization during the younger event might reset the "radioactive clocks," and age determinations would no longer give the date of the older event. Another uncertainty is that igneous rocks may be intruded into an ancient belt long after it has become stable. Dates based on such intrusions would not date the original mountain-building episode.

According to modern views, shields may have begun their history as relatively small continental blocks that grew throughout geologic time by additions of rocks chemically differentiated from the upper mantle and by accretion of new material at or near their margins. The process by which the accretionary growth occurs might be like that described in the previous chapter, wherein oceanic crust is subducted beneath the margin of a continent, partially melts, and gives rise to less dense, more siliceous rocks.

The Canadian Shield

Extending across most of Canada and Greenland and from Baffin Island southward to Minnesota is the great Canadian Shield. This great expanse of Precambrian rocks is mostly a low-lying land of conifers, muskeg, and tundra. The shield is bordered by the Appalachian fold belt on the east and the Rocky Mountains on the west. It extends southward beneath the central United States, where deep bore holes have permitted geologists to map its surface and extent. To the north, the shield is bounded by the Franklinian fold belt of the Arctic.

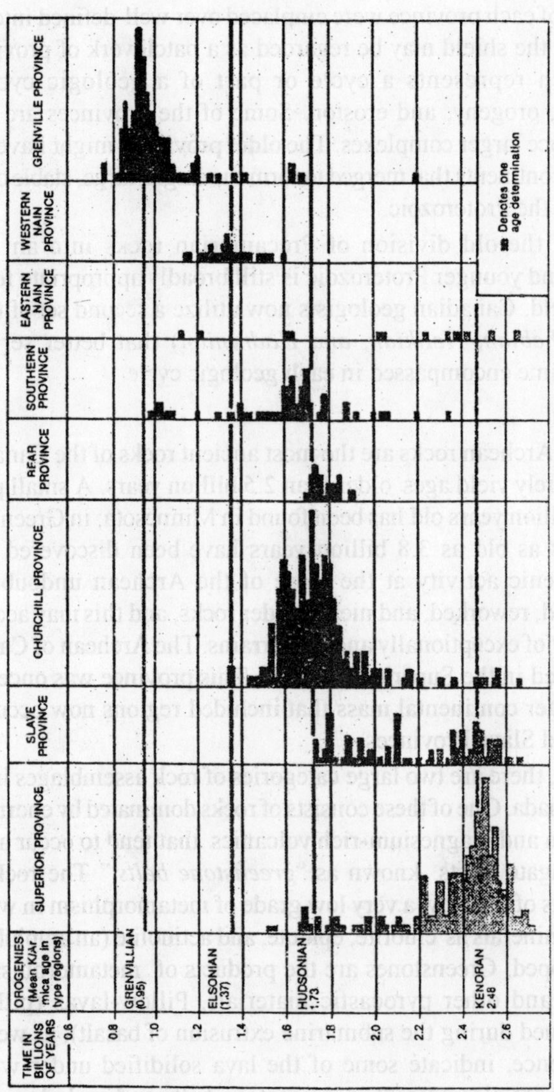

Fig. 5.3 Histograms showing numbers of K-Ar, Rb-Sr, and derived mean K-Ar ages of orogenies in the Canadian Shield. Each province has a cluster of dates that indicate major orogenic episodes.

As a result of field work that began in the midnineteenth century, it became evident that the Canadian Shield could be divided into a number of structural provinces, each recognized by characteristic structural patterns, lithologic assemblages, mineralization, and geologic age. Subsequent isotopic dating, mainly by potassium-argon methods, indicated that the rocks of each province were emplaced over well-defined intervals of time. Thus, the shield may be regarded as a patchwork of provinces, each of which represents a cycle or part of a geologic cycle of sedimentation, orogeny, and erosion. Some of the provinces are mere remnants of once larger complexes. The older provinces might have been growing protocontinents that merged to form the single, large, stable craton characterizing the Proterozoic.

Although the old division of Precambrian rocks into an older Archaeozoic and younger Proterozoic is still broadly appropriate for the Canadian Shield, Canadian geologists now utilize a second set of terms (*Archean, Aphebian, Helikian, and Hadrynian*) that better serve to delineate the time encompassed in each geologic cycle.

The Archean

Although Archean rocks are the most ancient rocks of the Canadian Shield, they rarely yield ages older than 2.5 billion years. A small patch of rocks 3.6 billion years old has been found in Minnesota; in Greenland, Archean rocks as old as 3.8 billion years have been discovered. The Kenoran orogenic activity at the close of the Archean undoubtedly metamorphosed, reworked, and melted older rocks, and this may account for the sparsity of exceptionally ancient terrains. The Archean of Canada is best developed in the Superior Province. This province was once part of a much larger continental mass that included regions now occupied by the Nain and Slave Provinces.

In general, there are two large categories of rock assemblages in the Archean of Canada. One of these consists of rocks dominated by enormous amounts of iron and magnesium-rich volcanics that tend to occur along numerous elongate tracts known as "*greenstone belts.*" The rocks of greenstone belts often show a very low grade of metamorphism in which such greenish minerals as chlorite, epidote, and actinolite (an amphibole) are well developed. Greenstones are the products of metamorphism of basaltic lavas and other pyrocastic materials. Pillow-lavas (pillowy structures formed during the submarine extrusion of basalt), as well as chemical evidence, indicate some of the lava solidified under water. Metasediments are also present in greenstone belts and include poorly sorted clastic rocks that suggest rapid deposition in unstable basins. Iron-rich cherts, thought to have derived their silica from volcanic ash, are also prevalent. The combination of pillow-lava and other volcanics, graywackes, and chart beds has led geologists to interpret greenstone belts as remnants of elongate volcanic troughs. Perhaps these arcs were developed parallel to terrains of crystalline granitic rocks, because the conglomerates of the greenstone belts do contain pebbles of granite. Greenstone belts show intricate and complicated patterns of folding and can be traced over several hundred kilometres. They appear to be "supracrustal" features developed on older Archean basement rocks.

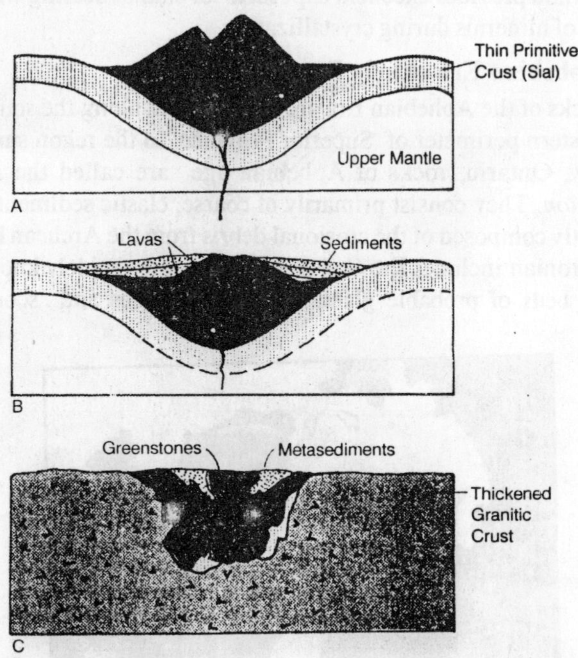

Fig. 5.4. Model for the origin of Precambrian green-stone belts. (A) Development of downwarps on an unstabel thin primitive crust and accumulation of lavas. (B) Erosion of volcanic fill (and adjacent granitic areas) produces sediment accumulations. (C) Massive invasion by younger granitic melts obliterates primitive crust, but the deep accumulations of lava in the elongate troughs are preservedand metamorphosed to form the greenstone belts.

The second large category of Archean rocks consists primarily of granites and gneisses that occur in the broader areas between greenstone belts. Most of these granitic terrains are products of widespread igneous intrusive activities associated with the *Kenoran Orogeny*. The Laurentian and Algoman granites of the Superior Province are representatives of this Archean assemblage.

Following the Kenoran Orogeny near the end of the Archean, the Superior and Slave Provinces were extensively invaded by swarms of basaltic dikes and sills. The arm of the Superior Province that extends into Wyoming and Montana experienced the intrusion of a 5-km thick sheet of chromite-bearing gabbroic rocks that composes part of the Stillwater Complex. The layer has since been dated to an almost vertical position and provides excellent exposures for studies dealing with gravity settling of minerals during crystallization.

The Aphebian Era (Early Proterozoic)

Rocks of the Aphebian Era are best exposed along the southern and northeastern perimeter of Superior Province. In the regon surrounding Sudbury, Ontario, rocks of Aphebian age are called the *Huronian Succession*. They consist primarily of coarse, clastic sediments that are frequently composed of the erosional debris from the Archean basement. The Huronian includes the *Gowgonda Formation*, widely known for its boulder beds of probable glacial origin. Scratches and scour marks,

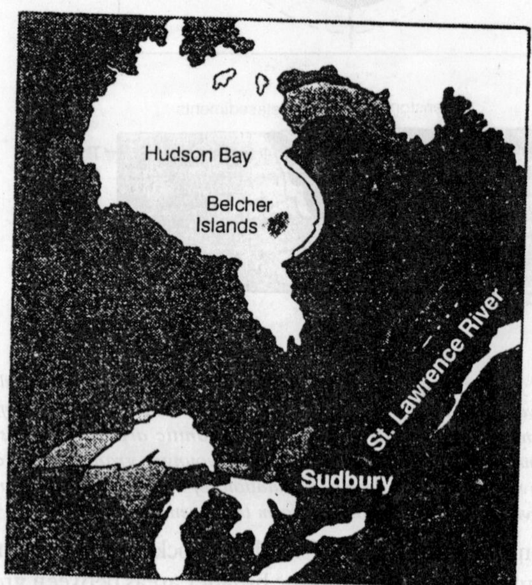

Fig. 5.5. Principal outcrop regions for rocks of the Early Proterozoic, or "Aphebian Era".

presumably produced by glaciers, are found on the surfaces of igneous rocks that lie below the conglomerates.

Aphebian rocks surrounding the western shores of Lake Superior constitute the *"Animikean System"*. This group is world-famous for the bonanza iron ores it contains. The ores are in the form of hematite (Fe_2O_3) and indicate that by about 1.9 billion years ago free oxygen had begun to accumulate in the atmosphere and to combine with dissolved iron, forming iron oxide. The formation of this compound also implies an abundance of photosynthetic organisms in the world's oceans to generate the oxygen that has oxidized the iron. In the Thunder Bay District of Ontario, the Animikean includes the Gunflint Formation, which contains fossil remains of early forms of life.

South of Lake Superior, the Aphebian section thickens and becomes more severely folded. In this region, shallow-water sandstones, carbonates, and slates constitute the lower part of the section and are overlain by siliceous iron beds, slates, graywackes, and basaltic volcanics.

Another interesting tract of outcropping Aphebian rocks can be found along the northeastern border of the Superior Province. The succession in this far northern region bears a resemblance to the classic model of a geosyncline. Sedimentation occurred within two parallel troughs. The western tract accumulated quartz sandstones and carbonates and appears to have been miogeosynclinal. Pillow-lavas are prevalent in the eastern tract as well as other volcanics, cherts, and graywackes. The rocks of this "eugeosynclinal" area have been severely folded and metamorphosed.

Aphebian orogenic activity continued sporadically in various parts of Superior Province until general province stability was achieved about 1.4 billion years ago. A large central craton was then well established, and subsequent orogenic belts tended to develop around its borders.

The Helikian Era

Among the rocks deposited or emplaced during the Helikian Era were those of the Keweenawan succession. These layers rest upon either the crystalline basement or the Animikian strata and extend from the Lake Superior region southward beneath a cover of Phanerozoic rocks for hundreds of kilometers. Keweenawan rocks consist of clean quartz sandstones and conglomerates as well as basaltic volcanics. Keweenawan lava flows are well known for their content of native copper. Holes, originally formed as gas bubbles in the solidifying rock, provide the voids in which the metal was deposited.

The Keweenawan lavas accumulated to thickness of over 10,000 meters. Even so, much of the supply of mafic magma was not tapped but remained beneath the surface, where it crystallized to form the 12,000-meter thick and 160-km long mass of the Duluth Gabbro. Basalts, as we have seen, are rock types more characteristic of oceanic areas. When such large quantities of mafic materials come to the surface within the stable parts of continental areas, the cause may be the breaking apart of the continent. The place where the break occurs is characterized by a system of tensional faults that form a rift zone. Along the rift zone the mafic magma may rise toward the surface to form Keweenawan-like accumulations. Evidence from gravity and magnetic surveys, as well as samples from deep drill holes, indicates that the rift zones associated with Keweenawan volcanism extended from Lake Superior southward into the United States. It has been suggested that the rift along which Keweenawan lavas were extruded may possibly have joined with two other arms of a triple-rift system having its junction at the southern margin of ancestral North America. Faulting and volcanism along the Keweenawan and adjoining rifts may have been associated with an early separation of Gondwanaland about 1.15 billion years ago.

The Grenville Province is composed of rocks that can also be included in the Helikian. This Late Proterozoic province has an exposed tract east of the Superior Province. Under a cover of Phanerozoic rocks, it can be traced southwestward almost to Mexico. Because the Girenville parallels the Appalachian Belt closely, parts of it have been obliterated by Paleozoic orogenic events in the eastern United States. Typically, Grenville surface rocks consist of highly metamorphosed carbonates and quartz sandstones that have been severely deformed and extensively invaded by intrusive rocks during the Grenvillian Orogeny. Grenvillian deformation produced an impressive mountain range along the eastern margin of the continent. Paleomagnetic studies suggest that this great compressional orogenic episode was the result of a collision with another continent. Indeed, the eastward movement of the Grenville tract to the collision zone may have caused some of the crustal tension to the west that resulted in the Keweenawan rifts. Clearly, the earth's tectonic plates were actively shifting about during the Late Proterozoic.

The Hadrynian Era

The final segment of Precambrian time has been named the Hadrynian. It is represented in North American by sedimentary rocks and some volcanics that were deposited in the geosynclines that rimmed the continent and were deformed in Paleozoic orogenic events. Rocks of the Hadrynian Era range in age from about 600 to 900 million years old. Of particular interest is the occurrence of unsorted boulder beds considered

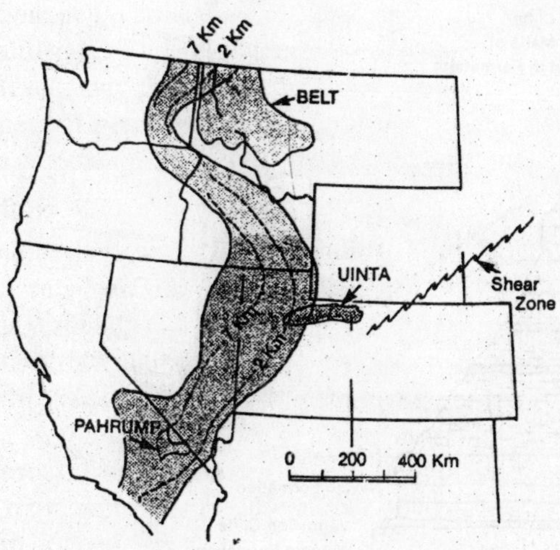

Fig. 5.6. Elements of western United States Precambrian geologic history. Giray are represents the Cordilleran miogeosyncline with generalized isopachs for late Precambrian to early Cambrian continental shelf sediments. Orange patterns are Belt, Uinta, and Pahrump sequences, 0.85 to 1.4 billion year old.

by many geologists to be glacial deposits. In North America, they have been described in Utah, Nevada, Western Canada, Alaska, and Greenland. If these conglomerates are indeed tillites, they indicate a second major Precambrian continental glaciation about 700 million years ago.

Precambrian Rocks South of the Canadian Shield

Although outcrops are not as extensive as in Canada, Precambrian rocks also occur south and west of the Canadian Shield. Particularly impressive successions are exposed in the Rocky Mountains and Colorado Plateau regions. These rocks have had a complex history that began over 2.5 billion years ago with the evolution of an Archean terrain composed of strongly deformed and metamorphosed granitic rocks. Largely on the basis of the study of remnant patches of volcanic rocks and greenstones in Wyoming, it appears likely that this old Archean mass collided with one or more island arc terrains about 1.7 or 1.8 billion years ago. The line of collision is believed to be marked by a shear zone in southern Wyoming

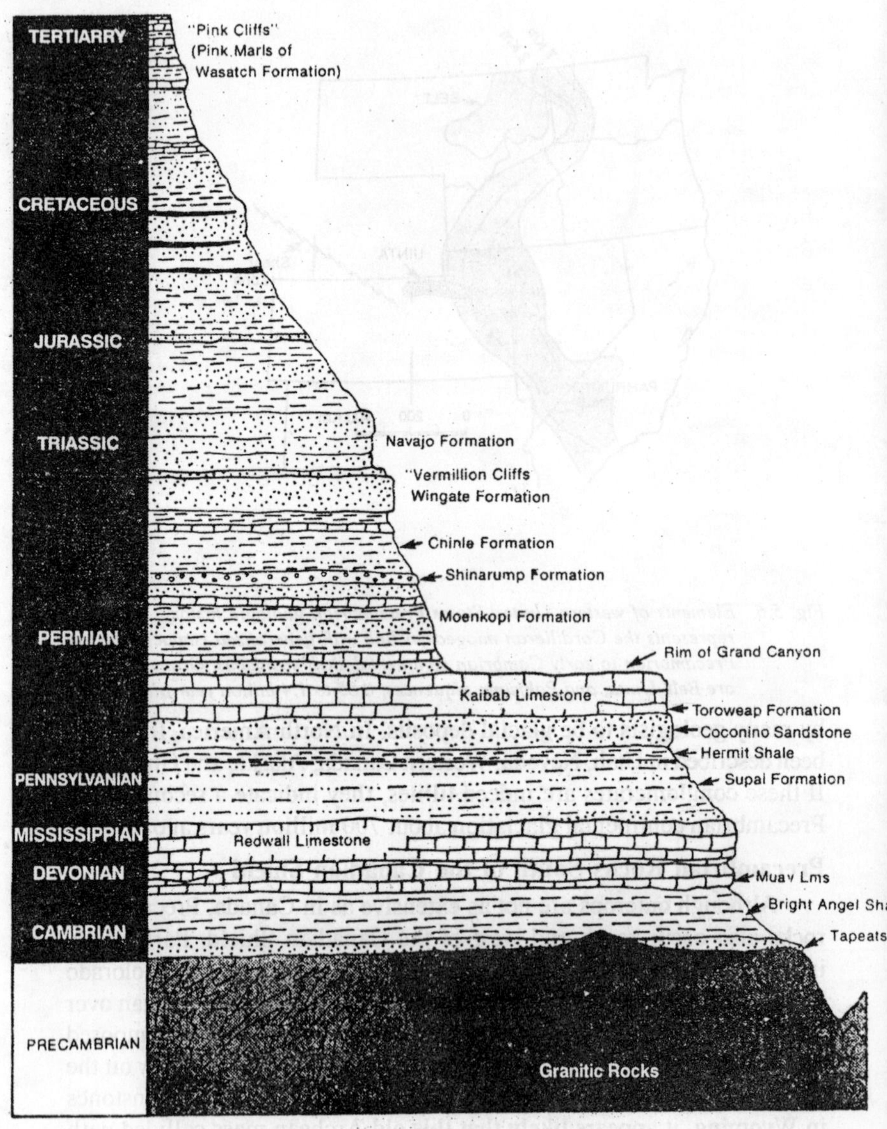

Fig. 5.7. Generalized statigraphic section for the western part of the Colorado Pleateau.

characterized by severely crushed and brecciated rocks. The next event was a widespread episode of rift development about 0.85 to 1.4 billion years ago. Large fault-controlled depressions were formed in which thick sequences of Late Precambrian sediments accumulated. They include the Uinta Series of central Utah, the Pahrump Group of southeastern California, and the Belt Supergroup of Montana, Idaho, and British Columbia. Because of the scenic features with which they are associated, the Belt rocks are of particular interest. In places these rocks are over 12,000 meters thick. Especially impressive are the massive cliff-forming limestones that can be viewed at Waterton Lakes and Glacier National Park . Although exceptionally thick, the Belt rocks display features such as ripple marks and algal structures that indicate they were deposited in relatively shallow water.

The last event in the Late Precambrian history of the western United States was the development of a north-south trending geosyncline. At this time the North American plate was moving away from a spreading center located somewhere to the west, and the geosyncline marked the continent's trailing edge. The continental shelf was the site of the miogeosyncline. A westward thickening wedge of latest Precambrian and Cambrian sediments was deposited on this shelf. The distribution of these sediments was not at all affected by the fault-controlled basins of the earlier episode of deposition.

Precambrian rocks of the Grand Canyon region consist of two distinct units. The lower and older unit is the Vishnu Schist, and the upper unit is the Grand Canyon Series. The Vishnu is a complex body of metamorphosed sediments and gneisses that have been intensely folded and invaded by granites. The granitic intrusions that cut into the Vishnu (and correlative rocks of the southwestern United States) were emplaced 1300 to 1400 million years ago as part of a deformational event named the *Mazatzal Orogeny.*

A splendid example of an angular unconformity occurs at the contact between the Vishnu Schist and the overlying Grand Canyon Series. The latter unit is Late Proterozoic in age and is itself unconformably overlain by Paleozoic rocks.

The Baltic Shield

Precambrian rocks are found in many of Europe's mountain ranges. However, the most extensive exposures form the surface of the Baltic Shield. The northwestern edge of the shield is bounded by an Early Paleozoic orogenic belt. To the southeast, the shield is covered by layered sedimentary rocks that were deposited after the Precambrian. Scandinavian

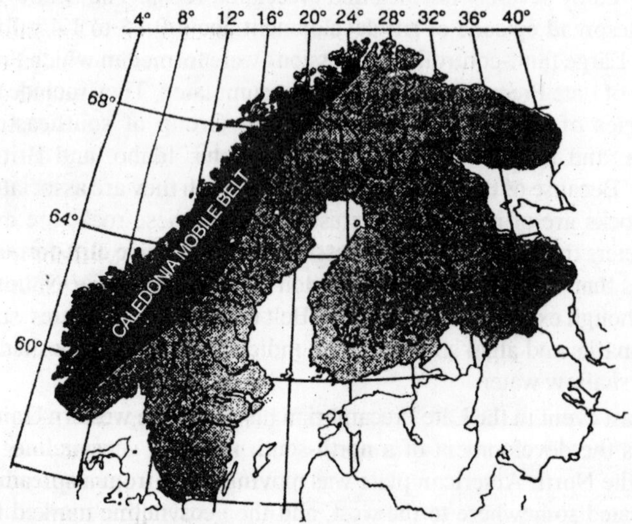

Fig. 5.8. Region over which Precambrian rocks outcrop in the Battic Shield. Early Paleozoic rocks deposited in the Caledonian Geosyncline are shown.

geologists have recognized four great episodes in the Precambrian history of the shield. Each of these episodes involved the accumulation of great thicknesses of sediments and volcanics that were subsequently subjected to severe compression, metamorphism, and massive intrusion by granitic masses. The rocks representing the two oldest episodes are mostly schists and gneisses that were once sandstones and vol canies. Conglomerates, ripplemarked quartz sandstones, dolostones, greenstones, slates, and iron ores characterize the third cycle. The topmost Precambrian rocks managed to escape severe metamorphism. These youngest shield rocks consist of lavas and sandstones that were later intruded by granite.

The Angaran Shield

The Angaran Shield is more difficult to study than either the Canadian or the Baltic Shield. These Precambrian rocks are not exposed over a vast region. Rather, they are revealed as small, exposed patches that elsewhere are covered by younger sedimentary rocks of the great Siberian Platform. Covered or not, however, the shield is important as the very nucleus of Asia. To the east and south of this region lay the mobile belts that were later to be fashioned into the Ural and Himalayan Mountains. Not unlike the Precambrian of other shields, the Angaran has an older complex of

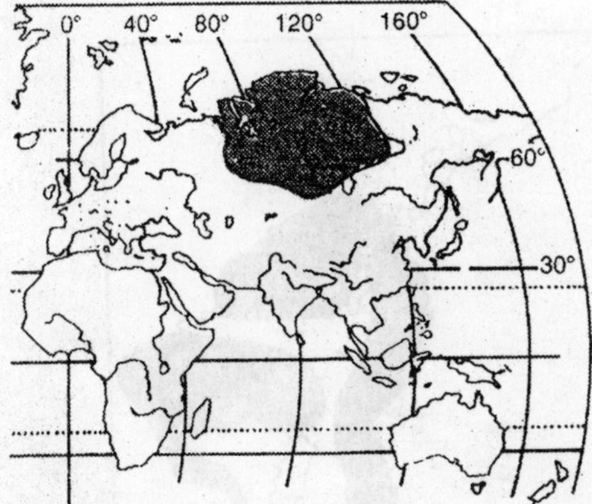

Fig. 5.9. The Angaran Shield. Precambrian rocks ove most of this vast egion are covered by Phanerozoic strata.

gneisses, schists, and granites that provides evidence of a long and complicated history. There is also a younger sequence of sedimentary rocks, volcanics, and granitic intrusives that dates from about 1600 millions years ago. Russian geologists have named these rocks *Rhiphaean*. They include the sandstones and limestones of Precambrian shallow seas. Many of the limestones include moundike growths called *stromatolite*. Such structures were produced by algae and formed impressive reef structures along coastal areas.

The Shields of South America

The number three seems to characterize the Precambrian geology of South America. These are *three* shields: the Guianan, the Brazilian, and the Patagonian also, the Precambrian rocks of South America are usually grouped into *three* divisions: Early, Middle, and Late Precambrian. As might be expected, gneisses and schists form the oldest sequence. The Middle Precambrian consists, in large part, of metamorphosed sediments, volcanics, and intrusions that appear to be the product of geosynclinal evolution Metamorphic effects are less profound in the Late Precambrian. Slates and phyllites are still in evidence, however, along with quartzites, conglomerates, volcanic flows, and ash beds. Because of a covering of younger sediments over parts of the shields, as well as the dense forests that cover many regions, the Precambrian rocks of South America are still not as well known as those of the relatively barren shields of Canada and Scandinavia.

Fig. 5.10. Regions of exposed Precambrian rocks in South America.

Africa

Precambrian rocks outcrop over half the surface of Africa and elsewhere lie beneath a veneer of Paleozoic and Mesozoic rocks. Indeed, Africa appears to be basically a vast platform of abutting shield segments. It is mostly a very stable continent but has along its eastern edge the remarkable faulting and fracturing that has produced the African rift valleys. Africa's Precambrian rocks are renowned for their treasure of minerals; exploration for gold, diamonds, copper, uranium, chromium, and cobalt has resulted in improved understanding of the continent's very complex geology.

The long Precambrian history of Africa can be divided into an early, middle, and late phase. The Early Precambrian encompasses events that occurred prior to about 2600 million years ago. Its record consists of some of the oldest rocks in Africa. In the Barberton Mountain land of South Africa, metasedimentary rocks have been radiometrically dated at 3.0 to 3.6 billion years old. One pebble from a conglomerate yielded an astonishing age of 4.1 billion years. In Transvaal and Rhodesia, the Early

Precambrian includes 17,000 meters of dense, basic volcanic rocks that appear to be immersed in a "sea" of granite. Geologists speculate that these volcanics were extruded at a time when the crust was very thin and the upper mantle beneath it was extremely hot and possibly even molten. The volcanic fireworks and crustal jarring that accompanied the extrusions must have been spectacular.

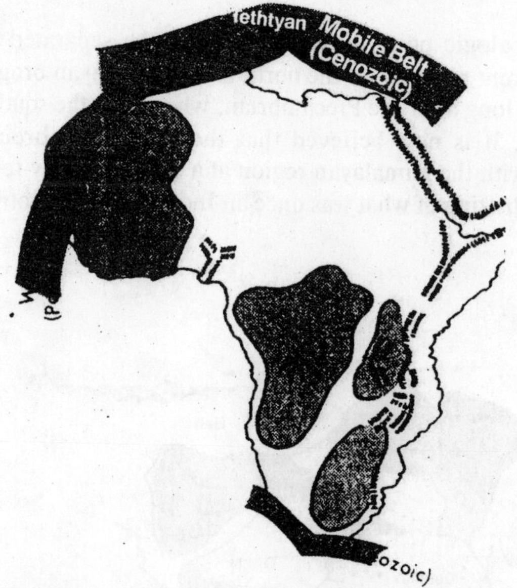

Fig. 5.11. Four large Precambrian cratonic segments formed in Africa by middle Precambrian time.

More extensive than the basalts in Africa are the massive intrusions of old granites that were emplaced between 2.6 and 3.1 billion years ago. These constitute the "crystalline basement" of South Africa. A great unconformity separates these batholithic masses from younger sequences of the Middle Precambrian.

The African Middle Precambrian probably began about 2.6 billion years ago and ended 1.1 to 1.8 billion years ago. By this time, four stable segments of the evolving African crust had been formed. One large segment now constitutes much of the west African bulge, two large elements were established in central Africa, and one was formed in South Africa. Quartzites, shales, conglomerates, and lavas characterize the rocks of the Middle Precambrian. Except for occasional volcanic eruptions, it was a quieter time than the Early Precambrian had been. The crustal segments were relatively stable.

The Late Precambrian of Africa is characterized by the deposition of sedimentary rocks and by widespread orogenies in the regions that bordered the old crustal segments. Strips of metamorphosed granitic crust formed between the segments and welded them into a unified shield. The orogenic activity continued until about 400 million years ago and resulted in the continent's taking on its present-day outlines.

India

From a geologic point of view, India can be separated into two distinctly different regions. To the north is the Himalayan orogenic belt that developed long after the Precambrian, whereas to the south lies the Indian Shield. It is now believed that the shield was brought into juxtaposition with the Himalayan region at a comparatively recent date by northward drifting of what was once an Indian "island continent."

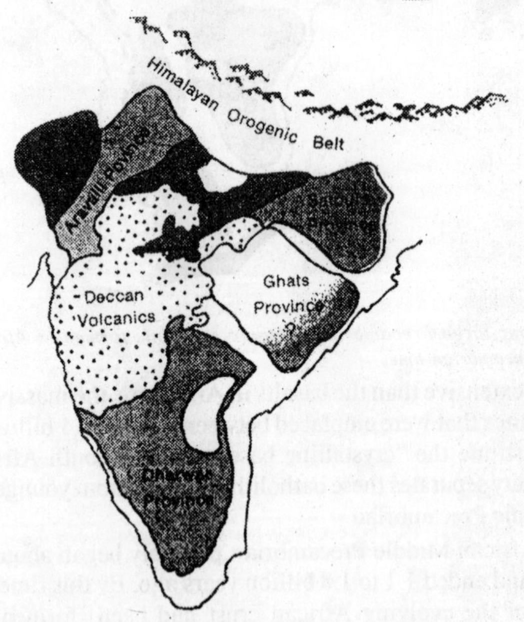

Fig. 5.12. Precambrian geologic segments of India.

As is the case in North America, geologists have been able to recognize a number of separate provinces within the Indian Shield that can be distinguished by the approximate dates at which they had experienced orogeny and by their unique structural characteristics. Altogether, there are five of these provinces. The oldest is the Dharwar Province, which contains rocks 2.4 or more billion years old and probably acted as a nucleus around which other provinces became attached. The granites, gneisses, and volcanics of the Dharwar are exposed along the eastern side of the Indian peninsula. Northeastward lies the 1.6-billion-year-old Ghats Province, which is composed of generally similar rocks. Over 500,000 sq km of the Indian peninsula southwest of Delhi are covered by Late Cretaceous and Early Cenozoic basalts. These flood basalts blanket large areas of the shield. At their northeastern edge, geologists have found evidence of a third province, the Satpura. The Satpura probably stabilized about 1000 million years ago. Northwest of the Satpura Province is the Aravalli Province, which experienced its culminating orogenies about 750 million years ago. The fifth province contains stratified shales, sandstones, and limestones that rest unconformably on older rocks. They are called the Vindhyan Group and are considered Late Precambrian by the Geological Survey of India. However, part of the Upper Vindhyan strata may be Cambrian in age. These uppermost beds are of particular interest, because they contain small, disklike structures that may be fossils of multicellular animals.

Australia

Structurally, Australia is composed of mobile belts along the eastern third of the continent and a vast Precambrian shield that occupies most of the central and western parts of the continent. As is the case with many other shields, the Precambrian surface is partially covered by younger layered sedimentary rocks. One especially interesting feature of the Australian Precambrian is the presence of a thick sequence of relatively unaltered sedimentary rocks that span a time interval of over 1.5 billion years. Such rocks permit more direct comparisons with modern sedimentational processes and provide valuable insights into paleoclimatic conditions.

Although more complicated classifications have been proposed, it is nevertheless possible to divide the Precambrian of Australia into an Archean region and a Proterozoic region. The Archean is reserved for igneous and metamorphic rocks over 2.5 billion years old. At least two great cataclysms of mountain building seem to be represented in these Archean rocks. The Proterozoic rests upon the worn roots of the Archean mountains. It consists of three great systems of quartzitic sandstones, basaltic laval flows, and siliceous rocks. The youngest of these rocks, called the Adelaidean, has two notable features. At a location in Edicara

Hills, the Adelaidean contains fossils of primitive multicellular organisms. It also contains rocks that were probably deposited by continental glaciers.

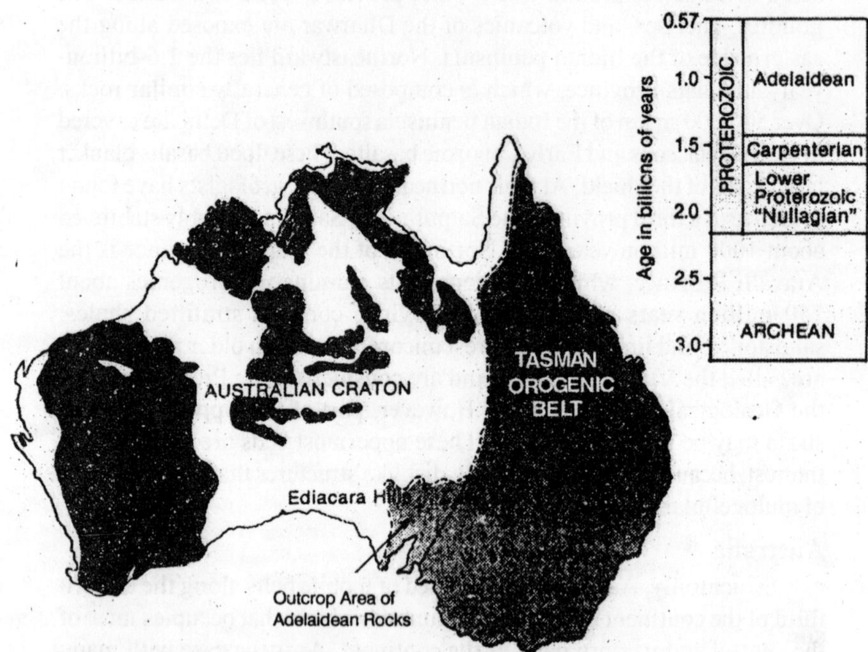

Fig. 5.13. Central and western Australia consists of a vast cratonic region composed of Precambrian rocks exposed as large patches wherever the cover of mostly horizontal Phanerozoic rocks is absent. The eastern third of the continent contains folded Paleozoic strata of the Tasman Orogenic Belt. Inset indicates Australian precambrian time classification.

Antarctica

Beneath the frozen surface of Antarctica lies a Precambrian shield that was poorly understood until the advent of modern techniques for geophysical exploration. Over the past 3 decades, geologists have had an opportunity to examine the bedrock exposed around the edges of the glacier and in mountain ranges that pierce the ice cover. Most of the rounded eastern half of Antarctica consists of Precambrian shield. The oldest rocks, sometimes referred to as the Archean, occupy the most extreme eastern edge. Rocks of the Proterozoic occupy the remainder of the shield.

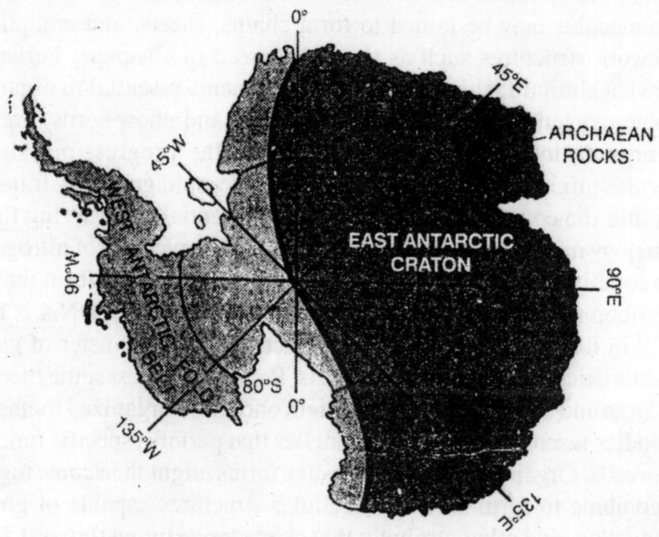

Fig. 5.14. Antarctica has Archean rocks exposed along its eastern margin and Phanerozoic fold belts acros most of the western one third of the continent.

Most of the western part of Antarctica consists of fold belts of Late Cretaceous and younger age. These mountainous tracts show a marked similarity to the Andean mobile belt of South America.

The Begining of Life

The splendid diversity of life today, and as it is recorded in the Phanerozoic fossil record, is primarily the result of billions of years of chemical and biologic evolution that occurred during the Precambrian. There are few clues to the events that led to the first organism. Hypotheses are based on our understanding of modern biology and on our most rational inferences about the nature of the planet 3 or 4 billion years ago. A coherent story of the stages involved in the origin of life has emerged. However, it is a decidedly theoretic story and should not be viewed as undisputed fact.

From Simple to Complex

Systematic progressions from simple to complex structures are a manifest characteristic of both living and nonliving systems. Awareness of such progressions has strongly influenced the development of theories on the evolution of life. Subatomic particles like neutrons, protons, and electrons are built into atoms. Atoms in turn combine to form molecules; and molecules may be joined to form chains, sheets, and complicated framework structures such as those discussed in Chapter . Perhaps in somewhat similar fashion, the atoms of elements essential to organisms (carbon, oxygen, hydrogen, nitrogen, sulfur, and phosphorus) are built into organic molecules. At some stage in the progression, simpler molecules might have added components that would gradually transform them into the complex organic molecules essential to all living things. An analogy might be the manner in which small molecules of nitrogenous bases combine with sugar and phosphorous compounds to form the large deoxyribonucleic (DNA) molecule. In living organisms, DNA is found chiefly in the nucleus of the cell. It functions in the transfer of genetic characteristics and in protein synthesis. Perhaps, suggest some theorists, such large and complex molecules might once have organized themselves into bodies resembling certain organelles that perform specific functions within cells. Organelles or organelle-like forms might then come together and combine to form simple unicellular structures capable of growth, reproduction, and other attributes that characterize living things. Could a progression even remotely similar to this have actually occurred in the early years of the Precambrian? An unequivocal answer is not yet possible, but at least newly available evidence indicates that such a progression toward life is feasible.

Preliminary Considerations

The oldest fossil evidence for life is found in rocks that are 3.2 billion years old. To produce these simple organisms, life must have originated before that time. If our theory for the evolution of the atmosphere is valid, then the earliest organisms developed on a planet deficient in free oxygen. They were *anaerobic* and did not require oxygen for respiration. The environment in which they lived lacked a protective atmospheric shield of ozone, which is derived from oxygen and which absorbs ultraviolet radiation from the sun. Perhaps early life escaped the lethal ultraviolet rays by developing beneath protective ledges of rock or at deeper water levels. Some biologists insist that in the late stages of chemical evolution, ultraviolet radiation may not have been a hindrance at all but rather served to impel the molecules to interact and to produce the more complex structures that were precursors to true organisms.

Prior to 1828, most geologists believed that all organic molecules were products of living organisms. However, in that year, the German chemist *Frederich Wohler* accidentally discovered that by heating the inorganic compound now called ammonium cyanate, he could produce crystals of urea. Urea, an essential component of urine, is a decidedly organic compound. In the 3 decades that followed, other chemists succeeded in producing several other simple organic substances. Scientists began to favor the view that life may have ultimately arisen from inorganic materials. This view continued to be held for a long period even before experimenters found the means to detect the small quantities of complex organic molecules synthesized in their experiments from inorganic substances. It was not until the late 1960's that biochemists were able to create and detect complex protein molecules.

The elements necessary to produce organic compounds are carbon, oxygen, hydrogen, nitrogen, phosphorus, and sulfur. These elements are also the main components of a living cell. They are among the most abundant elements in the solar system. Clearly, the elementary materials for the development of life were present on the primitive earth. What had to be accomplished was the utilization of those materials in the enormously intricate fabrication of a living cell.

Reduced to a fundamental definition, life can be viewed as a system with four basic components. The first of these is *proteins*. Proteins are essentially strings of comparatively simple organic molecules called *amino acids*. Proteins act as building materials and as compounds that assist in chemical reactions within the organism. The second of the basic components is *nucleic acids*, such as DNA, mentioned earlier, and ribonucleic acid (RNA). *Organic phosphorous compounds* provide a third component of life. They serve to transform light or chemical fuel into the energy required for cell activities. The fourth essential for life is some sort of container, such as a *cell membrane*. The enclosing membrane provides a relatively isolated chemical system within the cell and keeps the various components in close proximity so that they may interact.

From the previous description, it is apparent that amino acids have an important role in the development of the larger and more complex molecules. They are the building blocks of proteins. Two environmental circumstances in the early years of earth history may have been important in the natural synthesis of amino acids. Prior to the accumulation of the ozone layer in the earth's upper atmosphere, ultraviolet rays bathed the earth's surface. As demonstrated in experiments, ultraviolet radiation is capable of separating the atoms in mixtures of water, ammonia, and hydrocarbons and of recombining those atoms into amino acids. A second form of energy capable of accomplishing this feat is electrical discharge in the form of lightning. Either together or separately, lightning and ultraviolet radiation may have stimulated the production of amino acids in the air, in tidal pools, in the upper levels of the oceans, and wherever suitable environmental conditions existed.

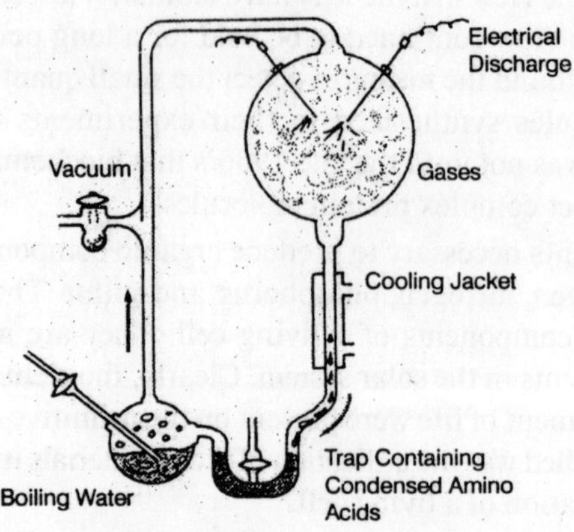

Fig. 5.15. Diagram of the apparatus used by S.Miller in experiments of prebiotic synthesis. The mixture of gases (methane, hydrogen, and ammonia) are circulated through the apparatus together with water vapor by boiling water in a flask. The mixture is subjected to an electrical dischage in a second flask and is condensed by a cooling jacket.

Test Tube Amino Acids and a Step Beyond

As noted earlier, scientists in the mid-nineteenth century had succeeded in manufacturing some relatively simple organic compounds in the laboratory. However, it was not until 1953 that the laboratory synthesis of amino acids and molecules of roughly similar complexity was announced. *Stanley Miller*, at the suggestion of *Harold Urey*, performed the now famous experiment. He infused an atmosphere at that time thought to be like that of the earth's earliest atmosphere into an apparatus similar to the one. It was a methane, ammonia, hydrogen, and water vapor atmosphere. As the mixture was circulated through the glass tubes, sparks of electricity (simulated lightning) were discharged into the mixture. At the end of only 8 days, the condensed water in the apparatus had become turbid and deep red. Analysis of the crimson liquid showed that it contained a bonanza of amino acids as well as somewhat more complicated organic compounds that enter into the composition of all living things. In additional experimenus by other biochemists, it was shown that similar organic compounds could also be produced from gases (carbon dioxide, nitrogen, and water vapor) of the preoxygenic atmosphere. The main requirement for the success of the experiments seemed to be the lack, or near absence, of free oxygen. To the experimenters, it now seemed almost inevitable that amino acids would have developed in the earth's prelife environment. Because amino acids are relatively stable, they probably increased gradually to levels of abundance that would enhance their abilities to join together into more complex molecules.

In order to come together and form protein- like molecules, amino acids must lose water. This loss can be accomplished by heating concentrations of amino acids to temperatures of at least 140°C. Volcanic activity on the primitive crust would be capable of providing such temperatures. However, the biochemist *S. W. Fox* discovered that the reaction also occurred at temperatures as low as 70°C if phosphoric acid was present. *Fox* and his coworkers were able to produce protein-like chains from a mixture of 18 common amino acids. He termed these structures *proteinoids* and reasoned that billions of years ago they were the transitional structures leading to true proteins. This is not extravagant conjecture, for *Fox* was able to find proteinoids similar to those he created in his laboratory among the lavas and cinders adjacent to the vents of Hawaiian volcanoes. Apparently, amino acids formed in the volcanic vapors and were combined into proteinoids by the heat of escaping gases.

Hot aqueous solutions of proteinoids will, on cooling, form into tiny spheres that show many characteristics common to living cells. These *microspheres*, as they are called, have a filmlike outer wall; are capable of osmotic swelling and shrinking; exhibit budding, as do yeast organisms; and can be observed to divide into "daughter" microspheres. They occasionally aggregate linearly to form filaments, as in some bacteria, and they exhibit a streaming movement of internal particles similar to that observed in living cells.

Although complete long-chain nucleic acids have not yet been experimentally produced under prelife conditions, short stretches of ordered sequences of nucleic acid components have now been produced in the laboratory. Indeed, in 1976, *Har Gobind Khurana* and his associates at the Massachusetts Institute of Technology announced that they had made a functioning artificial gene-one of thousands in the DNA spiral molecule of the bacterium *Escherichia coli*.

Speculations about Earliest Life

There are several good reasons to believe that the earliest organisms originated in the sea. The sea contains the salts needed for health and growth. The waters of the oceans serve as universal solvents capable of dissolving a great variety of organic compounds, and currents in the oceans ceaselessly circulate and mix these compounds. Such constant motion would have favored frequent collisions of the vital molecules and would thereby have increased the probability of their combining into larger bodies. One can imagine the larger bodies adding components, increasing in complexity, and ascending in a thousand infinitesimally small steps from nonliving to transitional things of a biologic netherworld to the first living organisms. Such a sequence could not occur in an environment like that which exists today. Oxygen and present-day microbial predators would destroy the delicate structures. However, life originated before there were organisms to cause decay and before there was sufficient free oxygen to be troublesome.

Largely from our knowledge of paleontology and biology, it is believed that the first living things were microscopic in size and were unicellular. It is likely that these earliest forms of life would not have evolved a means of manufacturing their own food but rather assimilated small aggregates of organic molecules that were also present in the surrounding medium. Some, undoubtedly, would have consumed even their developing contemporaries. Today, organisms with this type of nutritional mechanism are termed heterotrophs. The food gathered by the ancestral heterotrophs was externally digested by excreted enzymes before being converted to the energy required for vital function. In the absence of free oxygen, there was only one way to accomplish this conversion-by *fermentation*. There are many variations of the fermentation process. The most familiar reaction involves the fermentation of sugar by yeast. It is a process by which organisms are able to disassemble organic molecules, rearrange their parts, and derive energy for life functions. A very simple reaction may be written as follows:

$$C_6H_{12}O_6 \rightarrow 2\,CO_2 + 2\,C_2H_5OH + \text{Energy}$$

Glucose → Carbon Dioxide + Alcohol

Animal cells are also able to ferment sugar in a reaction that yields lactic acid rather than alcohol.

Sooner or later, the original fermentation organisms were to experience difficult times. By con- suming the organic compounds of their environment, they would eventually have created a food shortage; this scarcity, in turn, might have caused selective pressures for evolutionary change. At some point prior to the depletion of the food supply, organisms evolved the ability to synthesize their needs from simple inorganic substances. These were the first autotrophic organisms. Unlike the heterotrophs, *autotrophs* were able to manufacture their own food. The organisms that had developed this remarkable ability saved themselves from starvation. Their evolution proceeded in diverse directions. Some manufactured their food from carbon dioxide and hydrogen sulfide and were the probable ancestors of today's sulfur bacteria. Others employed the life scheme of modern nitrifying bacteria by using ammonia as a source of energy and matter.

However, more significant than either of these kinds of autotrophs were the *photoautotrophs*, which were capable of carrying on photosynthesis. Their gift to life was the unique capability of dissociating carbon dioxide into carbon and free oxygen. The carbon was combined with other elements to permit growth, and the oxygen escaped to prepare the environment for the next important step in the evolution of primitive organisms. In simplified form, the reaction for photosynthesis can be written as follows:

$$6\,CO_2 + 6\,H_2O \xrightarrow{\text{Sunlight}} 6\,C_6H_{12}O_6 + 6\,O_2$$

With the multiplication of the photoautotrophs, billions upon billions of tiny living oxygen generators began to change the primeval anoxygenic atmosphere to an oxygenic one. Fortunately, the change was probably gradual, for if oxygen had accumulated too rapidly, it would have been lethal to developing early microorganisms. Some sort of oxygen acceptors were needed to act as safety valves and prevent too rapid a buildup of the gas. Iron in rocks of the continental crust provided suitable oxygen acceptors. Eventually, organisms evolved oxygen-mediating enzymes that permitted them to cope with the new atmosphere.

After the surficial iron on the earth's surface had combined with its capacity of oxygen, the gas began to accumulate in the atmosphere and hydrosphere. Solar radiation acted upon atmospheric oxygen to convert part of it to ozone, and ozone in turn formed an effective shield against harmful ultraviolet radiation. Still-primitive and vulnerable life was thereby protected and could expand into environments that formerly had not been able to harbor life. The stage was set for the appearance of aerobic organisms.

Aerobic organisms use oxygen to convert their food into energy. The reaction, which can be considered a form of cold combustion, provides far more energy in relation to food consumed than does the fermentation reaction. This surplus of energy was an important factor in the evolution of more complex forms of life.

Prokaryotes, Eukaryotes, and Symbiosis

There is no unequivocal evidence to date the transition from chemical or prebiotic evolution to organic evolution. The most accurate statement that can be made in this regard is that the transition occurred at some time prior to 3.2 billion years ago. In rocks of that age, paleontologists have discovered the earliest fossil evidence of life. These oldest fossils belong to a category of organisms called *prokaryotes* and are represented today by bacteria and blue-green algae. Primitive organisms such as these lack definite internal organell es and do not have a membrane-bound nucleus in which genetic material is neatly arranged into discrete chromosomes. Modern prokaryotes do possess cell walls, and most are able to move about. The blue-green algae and some bacteria are prokaryotes capable of photosynthesis.

Prokaryotes are asexual and thereby restricted in the level of variability they can attain. In sexual reproduction, there is a union of gametes (egg and sperm) to form the nucleus of a single cell, the *zygote*. The formation of the zygote results in recombination of the parental chromosomes and leads to a multitude of gene combinations among the gametes that give rise to the next generation. In the asexually reproducing prokaryotes, in contrast, a cell divides from the parent and becomes an independent individual containing the identical chromosome complement of the parent cell. Unless mutation intervenes, the number and kinds of chromosomes in individuals produced by asexual reproduction are exactly

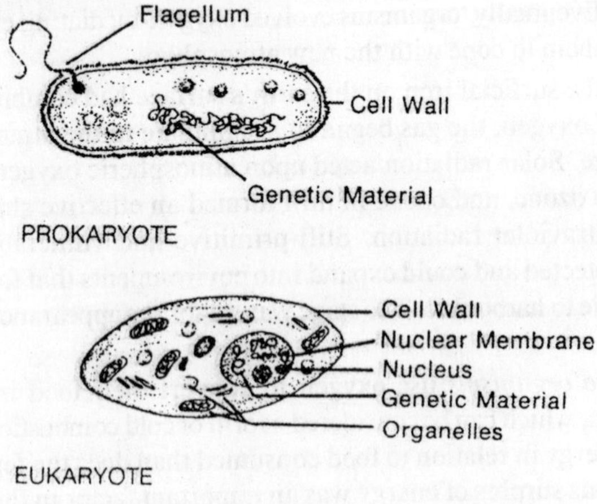

Fig. 5.16. Diffeence between a eukayote and a prokayote.

the same as those in the parent. Thus, the possibilities for variation are more limited than in sexually reproducing organisms. It is probably for this reason that prokaryotes have shown little evolutionary change through over 2 billion years of earth history. Nevertheless, such organisms represent an important early step in the history of primordial life.

Evolution proceeded from the prokaryotes to organisms with a definite nuclear wall, well-defined chromosomes, and the capacity for sexual reproduction. These more advanced forms were *eukaryotes*. Unlike prokaryotes, eukaryotes contain organelles such as chloroplasts (which convert sunlight into energy) and mitochondria (which metabolize carbohydrates and fatty acids to carbon dioxide and water, releasing energy-rich phosphate compounds in the process). Biologists believe that the organelles in eukaryotic cells were once independent microorganisms that entered other cells and then established symbiotic relationships with the primary cell. For example, an anaerobic, heterotrophic prokaryote like a fermentative bacterium might have engulfed a respiratory prokaryote and thereby would have an internal consumer of the oxygen that might otherwise threaten its existence. A nonmotile organism might acquire mobility by forming a symbiotic association with a whiplike organism like a spirochete. The resulting cell would appear to have a flagellum for locomotion. Natural selection would clearly favor such advantageous symbiotic relationships.

The Fossil Record for the Precambrian

Problems in Interpreting the Early Precambrian Fossil Record

Paleontologists seeking traces of the earth's earliest organisms are confronted with rather formidable problems. They must determine not only if a given microstructure is of biologic origin but also if it is truly contemporaneous with the enclosing sediment. The possibility of contamination by microorganisms coming into the rock postdepositionally must be recognized. In cases where chemical traces of life are detected, investigators must evaluate whether the compounds might have leaked into the rocks long after they were deposited or might have formed after deposition by more recent bacterial activity. There are also hazards associated with dating the presumably fossiliferous strata. Rather than directly dating the fossil-bearing formation, investigators often determine its age by correlation and superpositional relationships to rocks dated by radiometric methods.

Fossils Older than 2 Billion Years

The most ancient rocks that contain fossil microorganisms outcrop in South Africa and belong to the Precambrian Onverwacht Series. Onverwacht sediments are somewhat older than 3.2 billion years and are very likely the oldest little-altered sedimentary rocks on earth. Thus, the probability of finding significantly older fossils is remote. The microfossils of the Onverwacht consist of spheroidal and cup-shaped carbonaceous alga-like bodies. They not only are morphologically similar to some living forms of primitive algae but also are closely associated with filamentous structures that contain carbon compounds of biogenic origin.

Approximately 10,000 meters above the Onverwacht beds is another formation that has achieved fame because of its content of primitive fossils. Its name, somehow reminiscent of another story of genesis, is the *Fig Tree Formation*. The Fig Tree rocks consist of variously colored cherts, slates, ironstones, and tough sandstones. By means of radioactive isotopes, the formation has been dated as 3.1 billion years old. In 1967, samples of the Fig Tree Formation were studied by Harvard University paleobotanist, *Elso S. Barghoorn*, and his former graduate student, J. William Schopf. With the use of the electron microscope, these scientists were able to find a number of tiny, double-walled, rod-shaped structures that had a striking resemblance to modern bacteria. Barghoorn and Schopf named their find *Eobacterium isolatum*-the "isolated dawn bacteria." In their search for larger fossils, the scientists prepared thin sections of the chert and examined these with the optical microscope. The examination disclosed numerous spheroidal bodies very similar to certain blue-green algae. Because the samples were collected near the town of Barberton, Barghoorn and Schopf named the fossils *Archaeosphaeroides barbertonensis*. The filaments of organic matter and hydrocarbons of organic derivation found in the Fig Tree Formation (and later in the older Onverwacht rocks) confirmed the existence of a primitive but vigorous flora of microscopic life in the Early Precambrian.

The presence of photosynthetic organisms among the Fig Tree fossils has not yet been positively established. Like the Onverwacht rocks, the Fig Tree chert is black and rich in carbon. Biochemists have analyzed the carbonaceous materials extracted from these rocks and have detected organic compounds normally formed during the alteration of a particular component of chlorophyll called the porphyrin-magnesium complex. However, vanadium-porphyrin complexes also result from geochemical alteration of chlorophyll, and these have not yet been detected in the Fig Tree rocks. Two other organic compounds, phytane and pristane, are also regarded as breakdown products of chlorophyll. Both of these substances were detected in the extracts. However, this evidence has been judged inconclusive because some nonphotosynthetic microorganisms may also be capable of producing phytane and pristane.

Additional evidence for the existence of photosynthetic organisms in the Early Precambrian is provided by structures called stromatolites. Stromatolites are distinctly laminated accumulations of calcium carbonate having rounded, cabbage-like, branching or frondose shapes. Today, the metabolic activities of certain marine colonial blue-green algae result in the formation of similar structures. The fine particles of calcium carbonate settle between the minute filaments of the matlike algal colonies and are temporarily bound within a film of gelatinous organic matter. Successive additional layers result in the laminations. The stromatolites are thought to have had a similar origin, particularly because of the discovery of concentrations of filamentous and spherical blue-green algae in the laminations of Precambrian stromatolites.

Near Bulawayo in southern Rhodesia, stromatolites have been found in limestone that is 2.7 billion years old. The carbon 12 /carbon 13 ratio in the Bulawayo rocks suggests the occurrence of biologic fixation of carbon dioxide by photosynthetic organisms. Of equal importance is that it suggests biologically generated atmospheric oxygen was present about 2.7 billion years ago.

Although stromatolites are found in the Early Precambrian, they do not become common until Middle Precambrian. Late Precambrian stromatolites are sufficiently widespread and abundant to serve as guide fossils. They have formed extensive reeflike structures in Precambrian limestones. In the United States, the most notable of these stromatolitic structures occurs in rocks of the Belt series. They are exceptionally well exposed in Belt strata of Glacier National Park . The photosynthetic activity of stromatolite microorganisms was probably important in causing the precipitation of the calcium carbonate that formed the thick layers of Belt limestone.

Modern stromatolites grow in the intertidal zone with their tops at the high-water mark. In this regard, it is interesting to note that some Late Precambrian stromatolites were approximately 6 meters in height. If these forms were also restricted to the intertidal zone, then Precambrian tides must have been considerably higher than they are today. Such high tides would indicate that the moon was closer to the earth during the Precambrian. More recent stromatolites are not as tall, suggesting the distance between the earth and the moon has been increasing, causing a corresponding decrease in tidal amplitude. It was noted that the length of the day on earth has been increasing. Conservation of angular momentum would indeed require a slowing down of the earth's rotation as the moon increased its distance from the planet. Thus, stromatolite studies are in accord with astronomic observations.

The Gunflint Flora

Extending eastward from Thunder Bay in the northern portion of Lake Superior are outcrops of a rock unit called the *Gunflint Chert.*

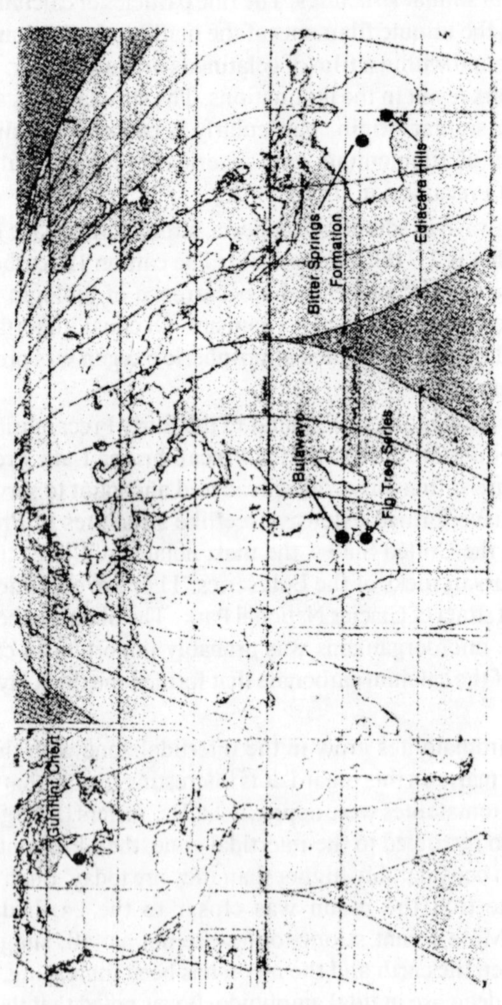

Fig. 5.17. Location of some of the better known fossil-bearing Precambrian formations.

Radiometric age determinations indicate that the formation is approximately 1.9 billion years old. It contains a varied and abundant flora of the so- called thread bacteria and nostocalean blue-green algae. Unbranched filamentous forms, some of which are septate, have been given the name *Gunflintia*. More finely septate forms, such as *Animikiea*, are remarkably similar in appearance to such living algae as *Oscillatoria* and *Lyngbya*. Other Gunflint fossils, such as Eoastrion (the "dawn star"), resemble living iron- and magnesium-reducing bacteria. *Kakabekia* and *Eosphaera* are so different from any known microorganism that their classification is uncertain. That these and other Gunflint and stromatolitic organisms were actively producing oxygen and thereby altering the composition of the atmosphere does seem certain. Not only do they resemble living photosynthetic organisms but also their host rock contains phytane and pristane-organic compounds regarded as the breakdown products of chlorophyll.

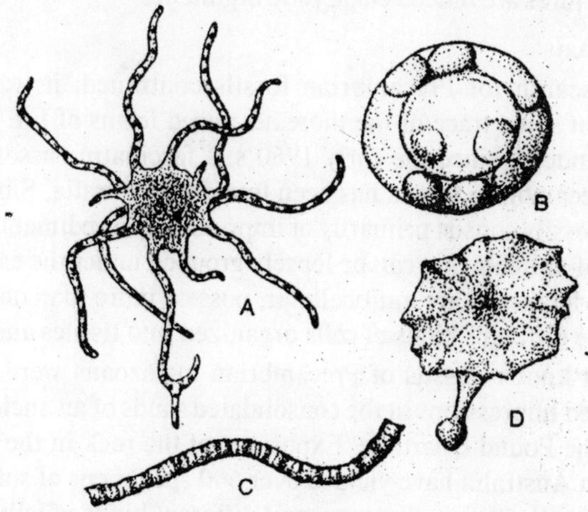

Fig. 5.18. Eoastrion (A), Eosphaera (B), Animikiea (C) and Kakabekia (D) from the Gunflint Cherts. All specimens are drawn to the same scale. Eosphaera is about 30 microns in diameter.

One of the major events in biologic evolution was undoubtedly the origin of the eukaryotic cell, with its enclosed nucleus for the storage and transmission of genetic information. Although the potential for sexual reproduction provided by eukaryotes enormously increased the possibilities for evolutionary change, the fossil record for earliest eukaryotic organisms is ambiguous. This is not surprising, since the first eukaryotes probably were simple microscopic unicellular organisms that in the altered fossil state would be difficult to distinguish from prokaryotes. At the present time, one group of paleobotanists suggests that eukaryotes were present about 0.9 billion years ago. These scientists support their view with microfossils found in the Bitter Springs Formation of central Australia. In addition to a prokaryote assemblage of fossils, the cherts of the Bitter Springs yielded several forms that are the size of eukaryotes and have ghostly internal structures that might be the remnants of nuclei or organelles of eukaryote green algae. If these are indeed the structures they appear to be, then the passage from prokaryotic to eukaryotic life with its capacity for sexual reproduction and genetic variability had been accomplished at least as long ago as 0.9 billion years. However, the identification of some unicellular organisms in the Bitter Springs as eukaryotic is currently being challenged by those who doubt that the internal structures are indeed eukaryotic organelles.

Dawn Animals

As the search for Precambrian fossils continued, it was almost inevitable that some trace of the more advanced forms of life would be discovered. Indeed, since the early 1960's, a fascinating assortment of advanced Precambrian fossils has been found in Australia, Siberia, and Africa. The fossils consist primarily of impressions in sedimentary rocks of the types of animals that can be loosely grouped under the category of *metazoans*. Metazoans are multicellular, possess more than one kind of cell, and have different kinds of cells organized into tissues and organs.

The best known fossils of Precambrian metazoans were found as well-preserved impressions in the consolidated sands of an ancient beach now called the Pound Quartzite. Exposures of the rock in the Ediacara Hills of south Australia have yielded over 600 specimens of soft- bodied animals. The collection includes several different kinds of jellyfish, soft corals resembling the modern "sea pen," polychaete worms, echinoderms, arthropod-like animals, and a number of unique forms whose precise biologic affinity is uncertain. There are also large numbers of tracks and burrows made by the members of this nearshore community. As nearly as can be determined, the "Ediacara fauna," as it is known, is around 650 to 700 million years old. Its importance lies in the glimpse it provides of the ancestors to the vast array of invertebrates that were to populate the seas in subsequent geologic time.

Another occurrence of Late Precambrian metazoan fossils that is rather similar in preservation to the Ediacara forms was discovered in the rocks of the Conception Group of Southeastern Newfoundland. The fossils at that site occur as hundreds of imprints on ripple-marked surfaces of graywackes. They include leaf-shaped animals that resemble sea pen corals, lobate forms that appear to be jellyfish, and other probable coelenterates with either branching or spindle shapes.

The sudden appearance of the diverse Ediacara and Conception Group fossils, and the apparent absence of any fossils or even traces of animal life in rocks older than 700 million years, suggests that metazoans expanded abruptly near the end of the Precambrian. According to *Berkner* and *Marshall* (1964), their rapid expansion may very well correlate with the accumulation of sufficient free oxygen to permit oxidative metabolism in organisms. On the other hand, the Ediacara life may have evolved more gradually from earlier small and naked forms that were essentially incapable of leaving a fossil record. Perhaps, as suggested by *A. G. Fischer* (1965), the ancestral metazoans lived in "oxygen oases" in which marine plants were concentrated. After the atmospheric oxygen content had reached about 1 per cent of the present level, these as-yet-undiscovered animals would have been free to leave their oases and spread widely in the seas. According to this view, the evolutionary development of metazoans may not have been abrupt, but their dispersal may have been rapid after suitable conditions became prevalent.

The Fig Tree, Gunflint, and Pound Formations represent only brief and isolated glimpses of the progress of biologic evolution during an almost incomprehensible span of more than 3 billion years. Unlike the fossil record, life is a continuous progression. Other exposures of Precambrian rocks will continue to be scrutinized in the years ahead to find the many missing chapters in the history of Precambrian life. Figure depicts the current state of our knowledge.

Aspects of Precambrian climate and Environment

Because so much of the Precambrian rock sequence is either altered or devoid of fossils, interpretations of climate and environment are more difficult than in the rocks of younger eras. This is especially true for the oldest Precambrian rocks. As noted previously, the earth's early atmosphere and hydrosphere were largely devoid of free oxygen. Then about 2 billion years ago, the atmospheric oxygen began to accumulate because of increased plant activity. One result of the oxygen buildup was the accumulation on land of considerable amounts of ferric iron oxide, which stained terrestrial sediments a rust-red color. Such sedimentary rocks are known as *red beds* and are considered a valid indication of the advent of an oxygenic environment. Of course, the oxygen level probably rose slowly and very likely did not approach 10 per cent of present atmospheric levels of free O_2 until the Cambrian Period.

In general, Precambrian rocks provide evidence for a wide range of climatic conditions, but there is no indication that these climates were especially unique in comparison with those of the Phanerozoic Eras. Thick limestones and dolostones with reeflike algal colonies were deposited along the Precambrian equator, where warm tropical conditions prevailed much as they do today. During the Early Proterozoic, the equator lay close to the northern border of North America. Precambrian evaporite deposits in eastern Canada and in Australia suggest that conditions were periodically rather arid during the Middle Proterozoic. In the middle and low latitudes, climates were more severe, as indicated by consolidated deposits of glacial debris (tillites) and glacially striated basement rocks. The best known of these poorly sorted, thick, boulder-like deposits is the Gowganda Tillite. Its widespread distribution over the southern portion of the Canadian shield indicates the presence of continental, rather than mountain, glaciers. In deed, geologic mapping suggests that the ice sheet was probably more than 1500 km in diameter and covered most of central Canada. The Gowganda Formation has been dated by radiometric methods as about 2.3 billion years old. Striations on the rock surfaces beneath the tillites suggest that the ice moved toward the Precambrian North Pole, which was located near lat. 22°N, long. 97°W at the time. These Precambrian glaciers ground their way northward into the Arctic Ocean from the Canadian and Baltic Shields.

The Gowganda tillites, although impressive, are not the only evidence of glaciation during the Precambrian. In southern Africa, the Chuos Tillite attains thicknesses of over 450 meters and has been recognized across an expanse of over 30,000 sq km. Tillites of Late Proterozoic age have been found on all continents except Australia, although they are not necessarily synchronous. The ample evidence of Precambrian glaciation around the world clearly indicates that the recent Pleistocene ice age was not at all a unique event in the earth's geologic history.

The Mineral Wealth of the Precambrian

Precambrian rocks contain a host of metal ores that have been of inestimable economic importance. Major sources of iron, nickel, gold, silver, chromium, and uranium are derived from Precambrian rocks. Iron is most notable of these ores in term of tonnages that have been mined. The world's largest group of iron are localities is in the Canadian Shield. Of these, the most famous are the sedimentary ores of the Lake Superior region. The ore deposits were formed in local areas where the iron-bearing sedimentary rocks were altered and enriched by removal of nonmetallic constituents. Other major sources of Precambrian iron occur in Sweden, the Ukraine, South Africa, and South America.

About half of the world's gold is mined from Precambrian quartz conglomerates near Johannesburg, South Africa. A Precambrian gabbro intrusion at Sudbury, Ontario, provides 70 per cent of the world's nickel. Uranium of Precambrian age is mined in largest quantities in Ontario and South Africa. Enormous amounts of copper were once recovered from Proterozoic rocks along the Keweenaw Peninsula of Lake Superior; however, today the ores are almost exhausted. These abandoned mines provide mute testimony to the fact that every mineral deposit is exhaustible and irreplaceable.

Chapter 6

Sedimentary Rocks

Sedimentary Rocks and Their Forms of Occurrence

Rocks are geological bodies composed of mineral aggregates in a certain composition and formed by various geological processes within the crust or on its surface. They may consist of one mineral (monomineralic rocks). Minerals that constitute more than 5 per cent of a rock are called rock-forming, while those present as a slight admixtue (less than 5 percent) are called accessory.

All rocks are divided into three main types according to their origin (genesis): viz., igneous, sedimentary, and metamorphic.

Igneous rocks are formed during the cooling and hardening of magma melts within the Earth or on the surface.

Sedimentary rocks are formed through the destruction of previously formed rocks on the Earth's surface dnd subsequent accumulation and transformation of the products of that destruction. Atmospheric agents, the hydrosphere, and the organic world are involved in their formation.

Metamorphic rocks are formed from igneous and sedimentary rocks that have been affected by high temperatures and pressures, and chemically active substances within the Earth.

Igneous rocks constitute 95 per cent of the total mass of the rocks composing the crust. Sedimentary and metamorphic rocks constitute the remaining 5 per cent.

Rocks als differ from one another in texture, fabric, and forms of occurrence in the crust, as well as in mineral composition and origin.

The *texture* of rocks is governed by the size, shape, and character of accretion of the mineral grains composing them.

The *fabric* or rocks is governed by the mutural spatial arrangement of the mineral grains composing it and the character of the in-filling of the rock's volume.

FROM SEDIMENT TO SEDIMENTARY ROCK

The most significant factors involved in the origin of sedimentary rocks are *weathering*, which produces sediment, *transportation* and *deposition* of that sediment, and the *liquification* necessary to convert loose particles of sediment into solid rock. Each of these factors may alter the composition or textural features of sediment and thereby provide a varity of different kinds of sedimentary rocks.

SEDIMENT TRANSPORT AND DEPOSITION

Once, weathering products have been formed from preexisting rocks, the next stage in the sequence of events leading to sedimentary rock is the removal and transport of those products. Many denudational agencies, including running water, moving ice, and wind, assist in this removal. The wind is an effective agent in picking up and blowing away the smaller and lighter particles. Glacial ice can move very large pieces of rock and carry an immense load of coarse sediment. Streams are also exceptionally effective in carrying not only solid particles of sediment but invisible dissolved salts as well. Ultimately, sediment-laden streams flow into lakes or the sea and their load of sediment is deposited. It may form sandy beaches, silty floodplains, and sometimes muddy boggy areas of estuaries and deltas.

The solid particles carried by wind or water will be deposited whenever there is insufficient energy to carry them further. For example, if the velocity of dust-laden wind abates, there will be insufficient energy to carry particles of given size, and those particles will be dropped. Similarly, if a stream's velocity is checked, as when entering a standing body of water, the stream also loses energy and is unable to carry the material formerly carried at the higher velocity.

A reduction in a stream's velocity does not, of course, affect the dissolved materials as it does suspended solid particles. Material carried in solution is deposited by a process called *precipitation*, in which dissolved material is changed to a solid and separated from the liquid in which it was formerly dissolved. For example, calcium carbonate, the principal substance in the widespread sedimentary rock known as limestone, may be precipitated from water that contains calcium in solution as indicated below :

$$Ca^{2+} + 2HCO_3^- \rightleftharpoons CaCO_3 + H_2O + CO_2$$

Ca^{2+} +	$2HCO_3^-$ ⇌	$CaCO_3$ +	H_2O +	CO_2
(Dissolved Calcium ions)	(Dissolved bicarbonate ions)	Calcium carbonate	Water	Carbon dioxide

The bicarbonic ions that participate in the above reaction can be derived from ionization of carbonic acid. As indicated by the arrows, the reaction is reversible. If carbon dioxide is removed from sea water, the reaction will proceed toward the right, and calcium carbonate will be precipitated. If, however, carbon dioxide is added to sea water, then the amount of carbonic acid in the water would build, and the reaction would proceed to the left. This would result in a chemical environment not conducive to calcium carbonate precipitation, and one in which existing calcium carbonate might begin to dissolve. As is evident here, the precipitation of calcium carbonate is a complex and delicate process in nature. It is influenced by organisms that utilize of liberate carbon dioxide, by processes that alter the acidity or alkalinity of the water, by the presence of organic compounds, and by ions of sulfur, phosphorus, and magnesium that may be present.

Lithification

Many changes take place in sediment after it has been deposited. Mineral grains may be dissolved away, some may grow by additions of new mineral matter, and the shapes of particles may be distorted by compaction. The result of some of these changes is to convert sediment into sedimentary rock. The conversion process is called *lithification*. *Cementation, compaction,* and *crystallization* are the principal means by which unconsolidated sediment is lithified.

Cementation involves the precipitation of minerals in the pore spaces between larger particles of sediment. The precipitated mineral, which

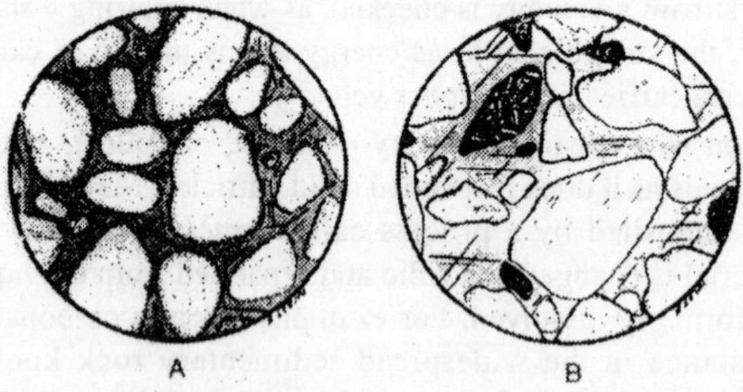

Fig. 6.1. Two common types of cement in sedistones. (A) Quartz sandstone composed of well-sorted rounded quartz grains tightly cemented by quartz(SiO_2) outgrowths. (B) Sandstone composed of quartz, feldspar, and rock fragments cemented by coarse sparry calcite. Both are drawing of thin sections as viewed under the microscope. Diameter of each area is 1.0 mm.

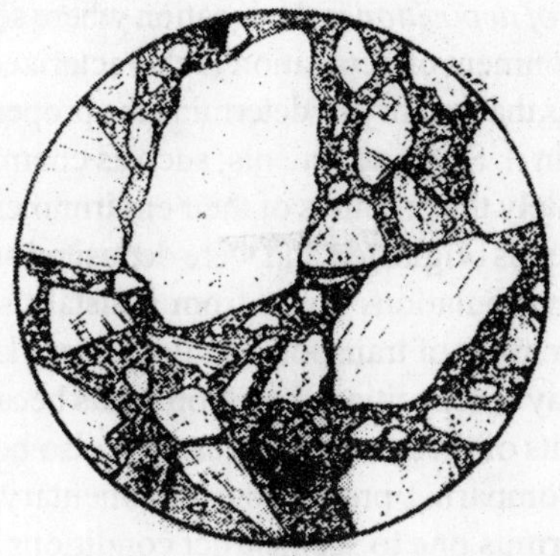

Fig. 6.2. Thin section of sandstone composed of poorly sorted angular grains of quartz(clear), feldspars (thin stripes), rock fragments. This sandstone lacks cement. Spaces between grains are filled with a matrix of clay and slit.

most frequently is either calcium carbonate ($CaCO_3$), silica (SiO2), or ferric iron oxide (Fe_2O_3), is called the *cement*. Cement is added to sediment *after* deposition. It differs from a rock's *matrix*, which consists of clastic particles (often clay) that are deposited at the same time as the larger grains and help to the grains together.

The reduction in pore spaces in a rock as a result of the pressure of overlying rocks or pressures of earth movements is termed *compaction*. During compaction, individual grains are pressed tightly against one another, causing the expulsion of water and rearrangement of particles. The result is often the conversion of loose sediment into hard rock. Compaction is greatest and most important as a lithification process in finer-grained sediments like clay and mud.

Lithification by *crystallization* may begin with an initial chemical precipitate in which the developing crystals grow together to form a crystalline solid. The process of crystallization, however, may also result in a change in the form of grains that have already been deposited. For example, quartz may be precipitated onto rounded quartz grains to form a strong interlocking mosaic of crystals, clay may be converted to a matted aggregate of tiny mica crystals, or calcium carbonate skeletal debris may be reorganized into hard crystalline calcite. The migration of watery solutions through sediment favors crystallization, as does deep burial and consequent increases in temperature and pressure.

Environments of deposition

The *environment of deposition* is the location where sediment in being deposited. Each environment of deposition is characterized by geographic and climatic conditions that modify or determine the properties of sediment that is deposited within it. Some sediments, such as chemical precipitates in water bodies, are solely the products of their environment of deposition. Their component minerals originated and were deposited at the same place. Other sedimentary accumulations come from a distant source and have experienced particular kinds of transport. Geologists are keenly interested in the sediment of today's depositional environments because the features they find in the deposits of these modern areas can also be seen in ancient sedimentary rocks. Comparing present-day sedimentary deposits to old sedimentary rocks permits one to reconstruct conditions in various parts of the earth as they were hundreds of millions of years ago.

The three major environment of deposition are the *marine, continental,* and *transitional environments*. Each contains a number of specific subenvironments. In a very general way, the marine environment may be divided into shallow marine (water depth less than 200 meters) and deep marine (200 to 10,000 meters). As illustrated in, the shallow marine environment extends from the shore to the outer edge of the continental shelves. The kind of sediment deposited in this environment depends on many factors, including climate, parent bedrock, distance from shore, elevation of the adjacent land area, water depth, and the presence or absence of carbonate-secreting organisms. Because of wave turbulence and currents, sediment deposited in the shallow marine environment tends to be coarser than material laid down in the deeper realms of the ocean. Sands, silts, and clays are common. Where there are few continent-derived sediments and the seas are relatively warm, lime muds of biochemical origin may be the predominant sediment. Coral reefs are also characteristic of warm shallow seas.

In the deep marine environment far from the continents, only very fine clay, volcanic ash, and the calcareous or siliceous remains of microscopic organisms settle to the ocean floor. The exceptions are sporadic occurrence of coarser sediments that are carried down continental slopes into the deeper realms of the ocean by dense masses of mud and silt laden water called *turbidity currents.*

The shoreline of a continent is the transitional zone between marine and nonmarine environments. Here one finds the familiar shoreline accumulations of sand or gravel we call beaches. Mud-covered *tidal flats* that are alternately inundated and drained of water by tides are also found here, as are deltas. *Deltas* form when streams enter bodies of standing water, experience an abrupt loss of velocity, and drop their load of sediment. Provided shoreline currents and waves do not remove the deposits faster than they are supplied, the delta will grow seaward. In general, progressively finer sediment will be deposited in progressively finer sediment will be deposited in progressively deeper water as the current provided by the stream diminishes. At the same time, the stream channel is extended over former deposits, periodically chokes in its own debris, and breaks out to form new branches of the delta.

In addition to deltas, the transitional zone in cludes such features as *barrier islands,* which are built parallel to shorelines by wave and current action, and *lagoons*, which are often found between the mainland and a barrier island. *Swamps* are also frequent features of low- lying areas adjacent to the sea.

Continental environments of deposition include river *floodplains*, alluvial fans, lakes, glacial, and eolian environments. The silt, sand, and clay found along the banks, bars, and floodplains of streams are familiar to most of us. In general, stream deposits develop as elongate lenses that are oriented downstream and that grade abruptly from sediment of one particle size to another. In another setting, streamtransported materials may accumulate quickly when a rapidly flowing river emerges from a mountainous area onto a flat plain. The result of the abrupt deposition is an *alluvial fan*. Somewhat quieter deposition occurs in lakes, which are ideal traps for sediment. Silt and clay are common lake sediments, although a variety of sediment is possible, depending on water depth, climate, and the character of the surrounding land areas. The *playa lakes* of arid regions are shallow temporary lakes. Periodically they become dry as a result of evaporation. Perhaps the most dramatic environments of deposition are found in areas having active glaciers. Glaciers have the ability to transport and deposit huge volumes and large fragments of rock detritus. Deposits are characteristically unsorted mixtures of boulders, gravel, sand, and clay. Where such materials have been reworked by glacial meltwater, however, they become less chaotic and resemble stream deposits.

Whereas glaciers can move materials of great size, wind is much more selective in the particle size it can transport. Environments where wind is an important agent of sediment transport and deposition are called *eolian environments*. They are characterized by an abundance of sand and silt, little plant cover, and strong winds. These characteristics typify some desert regions.

The influence of tectonics on sedimentation

One final factor, called tectonics, also has an effect on the characteristics of sedimentary rock formed at a particular location. *Tectonics* refers to the crustal behavior of a part of the earth over a long period of time. For example, a region may be tectonically stable, subsiding, rising gently, or more actively rising to produce mountains and plateaus. Where a source area has recently been compressed and uplifted, an abundance of coarse clastics derived from the rugged upland source area will be supplied to the basin. In the geologic past, such a tectonic setting has resulted in the accumulation of great "clastic wedges" of sediment that thickened and became coarser toward the former mountainous source area. In other tectonic settings of the past, the source area has been stable and topographically more subdued, so that finer particles and dissolved solids became the most abundant components being carried by streams.

The tectonic setting influences not only the size of clastic particles being carried to sites of deposition but also the thickness of the accumulating deposit. For example, if a former marine basin of deposition had been provided with an ample supply of sediment and was experiencing tectonic subsidence, enormous thicknesses of sediments might accumulate. Over a century ago, James Hall, an early New York geologist, recognized that the thick accumulations of shallow-water sedimentary rocks in the Appalachian region required that crustal subsidence accompany deposition. His reasoning was quite straightforward. It was easy to visualize filling a basin that was 12,000 meters deep with 12,000 meters of sediment. However, if the basin was only a few hundred meters deep, the only way to get tens of thousands of meters of sediment into it would be to have subsidence occurring simultaneously with sedimentation.

In a marine basin of deposition that is stable or subsiding very slowly, the surface on which sedimentation is occurring is likely to remain within the zone of wave activity for a long time. Wave action and currents will wear, sort, and distribute the sediment into broad blanket-like layers. If the supply of sediment is small, this type sedimentation will continue indefinitely. Should the supply of sediment become too great for currents and waves to transport, however, the surface of sedimentation would rise above sea level, and deltas would form.

It is possible to view the tectonic frame work of entire continents as well as of particular areas. The principal tectonic elements of a continent are *cratons* and *mobile belts*. The craton consists of the central stable region of continent. Such regions have a generally subdued topography and are composed of ancient igneous and metamorphic rocks that may be either exposed or covered by flat-lying younger sedimentary strata. In contrast to the relative stability of the craton, mobile belts are curving elongate crustal zones of great instability. They are thought to be zones of plate convergence, and are recognized by their high frequency of earthquakes and volcanic eruptions.

Color in Sedimentary Rocks

We have seen that color in igneous rocks can be used to indicate the approximate amount of ferromagnesian minerals. Color in sedimentary rock can also provide useful clues to identification. For example, varieties of chert can be identified as flint if they are gray of black, or as jasper if they are red. Color is also useful in providing clues to the environment of deposition of sedimentary rocks. Of the sedimentary coloring agents, carbon and the oxides and hydroxides of iron are clearly the most important.

Black Coloration

Black and dark gray coloration in sedimentary rocks- especially shales-usually results from the presence of organic carbon compounds and iron sulfides. The occurance of an amount of organic carbon sufficient to result in black colouration implies compiles and abundance of organisms in or near the depositional areas as well as environmental circumstances that kept the remains of those organisms from being completely destroyed by oxidation or bacterial action. These circumstances are present in many marine, lake, and estuarine environments today. In a typical situation, the remains of organisms that lived in or near the depositional basin settle to the bottom and accumulate. In the quiet bottom environment, dissolved oxygen needed by aerobic bacteria to attack and break down organic matter may be lacking. There may also be insufficient oxygen for scavenging bottom-dwellers that might feed on the debris. Thus, organic decay is limited to the slow and incomplete activity of anaerobic bacteria; consequently, in completely decomposed material rich in black carbon tends to accumulate. In such an environment, iron combines with sulfur to form finely divided iron sulfide (FeS_2), which further contributes to the blackish coloration. Such environment of deposition are likely to yield toxic solutions of hydrogen sulfide (H_2S) . The lethal solution rise to poison other organisms and thus contribute to the process of accumulation. Black sediments do not always from in restricted basins. They may develop in relatively open areas, provided the rate of accumulation of organic matter exceeds the ability of the environment to cause its decomposition.

Red coloration

Hues of brown, red, and green are frequently formed in sedimentary rocks as a result of their iron oxide content. Few, if any, sedimentary rocks are free of iron, and less than 0.1 per cent of this metal can color or sediment a deep red. The iron pigments not only are ubiquitous in sediments but also are difficult to remove in most natural solutions.

Iron form two sorts of ions: *ferrous* iron has two positive charges, whereas ferric ion has three positive charges. Thus, iron may form two oxides: FeO (Ferous oxide) and Fe_2O_3 (Ferric oxide). In air, ferrous iron is slowly oxidized to ferric iron. When oxygen is in short supply, ferric iron may be similarly reduced to ferrous iron. Ferric minerals like *hematite* tend to color the rock red, brown, or purple, whereas the ferrous compounds impart hues of gray and green. Hydrous ferric oxide (*Limonite*) is often yellowish in color.

Red Beds

Strata colored in shades of red, brown, or purple by ferric iron are designated red beds by geologists. Oxidizing conditions required for the development of ferric compounds are more typical of nonmarine than marine environments; most red beds are flood plain, alluvial fan, or deltaic deposits. Some, however, are originally reddish sediment carried into the open sea. Electron microscope studies (Walter, 1967), of red beds forming today in Baja, California, indicate that red coloration developed long after the sediment was deposited. After burial, the decay of clastic ferromagnesian minerals released iron that was oxidized by the oxygen in underground water circulating through the pore spaces. Thus, red coloration may be imparted in the subsurface and may be dependent on climate. The interpretations one can draw from red beds should be based to a large degree on the associated rocks and sedimentary structures. Red beds interspersed with evaporite layers indicate warm and arid conditions.

Although red beds are more likely to represent nonmarine than marine deposition, occasionally the reddish strata are interbedded with fossiliferous marine limestones. In such cases, the color may be inherited from red soils of nearby continental areas. Lands located in warm, humid climates often develop such reddish soils. When the soil particles arrive at the marine depositional site, they will retain their red coloration if there is insufficient organic matter present to reduce the ferric iron to the ferrous state. Otherwise, they will be converted to the gray or green coloration of ferrous compounds.

In summary, sedimentary rocks of red coloration may be a product of the source materials, may have developed after burial as a result of a lengthy period of subsurface alteration, or may be the result of subaerial oxidation. Geologists are suspicious of the last possibility, because most modern desert sediments are not red unless composed of materials from nearby outcroppings of older red beds.

Principal Types of Sedimentary Rock

Detrital sedimentary rocks are formed through the accumulation of products of the mechanical destruction of previously existing rocks. They consist of fragments of various rocks and minerals. Depending on the size of the fragments the following types of rock are distinguished: coarsely fragmented, medium fragmented, finely fragmented, and very finely fragmented.

Coarsely fragmented (rudaceous) rocks consist of distinctly visible grains of rocks and minerals, porous or cemented, with particles above one millimetre in size. According to the character and size of the particles and the degree of cementation, friable rocks composed of rounded particles (boulders, cobbles, and pebbles) and angular ones (lumps, chippings, rotten stone) are distinguished. Cemented accumulations of angular fragments are known as breccia, and of rounded ones as conglomerate.

Medium fragmented rocks (arenaceous or sandstones) consist of particles of minerals and rocks between 1.0 and 0.1 millimetre in diameter. Sands and sandstones are divided into coarse-grained (1.0-0.5 mm), medium-grained (0.5-0.25 mm), and fine-grained (0.25-0.1 mm). Arenaceous rocks are also divided into loose (sands) and cemented (sandstones). Depending on the composition of the grains sands may be monomineralic or polymineralic, the former consisting of grains of one mineral and the latter of grains of various minerals. Depending on what mineral is predominant, quartz, micaceous, hornblende, chlorite, feldspar (arkose), glauconite, and other sands are distinguished. Sandstones are classified according to the composition of the minerals forming them, grain size, and the composition of the cement.

Quartz sands and sandstones consist of quartz; feldspars and mica are found as admixtures. The cement is various (siliceous, calcareous, ferruginous, phosphoritic, etc.), and sandstones are classed according to it as siliceous, ferruginous, calcareous, etc. (e.g. a coarse-grained calcareous sandstone). Quartz-glauconite sands and sandstones (greensands) consist predominantly of quartz (60-80 per cent), glauconite (40-20 per cent), and mica (as an admixture), and are a yellowish-green. Ferruginous sands and sand- stones are formed by ferruginous minerals and are brown or a rusty orange. Arkose sands and sandstones are composed of quartz and feldspars formed through the breakdown of intrusive igneous rocks (granites, etc.) and are a rosy brown. Greywackes consist predominantly of fragments of sedimentary, igneous, and metamorphic rocks, and grains of various minerals, and are a greenish brown or greyish green.

Finely fragmented rocks (argillaceous rocks-mudstones or siltstones) consist of particles of 0.1 to 0.01 mm in diameter.

Finely fragmented rocks (dusts or silts) consist of particles 0.1 to 0.01 mm in diameter. Silts include a big group of rocks of continental origin (sandy loam, loamy clay, and loess). Sandy loams contain up to 25 or 30 per cent of fine sandy particles and between 10 and 20 per cent of clay particles, while loamy clay contains 20 to 25 per cent of clay and 10 to 15 per cent of sandy particles. The latter is formed through the action of atmospheric agents, rivers, and glaciers.

Loess is a pale pinkish yellow or yellowish grey uniform rock consisting of particles of quartz and lime 0.05 to 0.01 mm in diameter with an admixture of clay particles. The calcareous formations often have the form of fine irregular concretions (lime nodules or loess dolls). Carbonates form 6 or 7 per cent of the total mass of the rock, quartz 50 to 80 paer cent, and alumina 4 to 20 per cent. Loess is highly porous (up to 55 per cent). It swells rapidly in water and becomes sodden.

Silts cemented by calcareous, siliceous, and other cements are known as shales.

Very finely fragmented (argillaceous) rocks consist of particles finer, than 0.01 mm in diameter. They include clays and mudstones.

Clays consist of particles formed either through the chemical disintegration of bedrock or through its mechanical breakdown. Clay sediments are formed through the depositing of matter from colloidal solutions. Typical clay minerals are kaolinite and montmorillonite. Some clays contain carbonate minerals (marlaceous and calcareous clays), iron pyrites, carbonaceous substances, and bitumen (bituminous clays), gypsum (gypsiferous clays), anhydrite, halite (saliferous clays). Clays are of various colours: reddish brown, yellow, greyish green, and dark grey. Clays readily soften in water. In the dry state they are earthy and grind to a fine powder, when wet they are plastic. Plastic clays consisting of kaolinite, aluminium hydroxides, or micas are called refractory (they do not melt below a temperature of 1700°C). The following clays are distinguished in accordance with their composition: kaolinite, bentonite, and montmorillonite. Clays are also known as meagre (containing a torrigenous admixture of quartz, chalcedony, opal, and ferrous oxides) and rich (without terrigenous admixtures).

Mudstones are dense, indurated clay rocks. When enriched with $CaCO_3$, clays become marls.

Biogenic sedimentary rocks are formed through accumulation of products of organisms' vital activity, mainly of the skeletal remains of marine (and less often freshwater) invertebrates. The following biogenic rocks are distinguished according to their composition: carbonate, siliceous, and caustobioliths. The carbonate rocks include limestones and chalk.

Several types of structural fabric are distinguished among biogenic rocks: (1) biomorphic, in which the rock consists of the whole, unbroken skeletal remains of organisms; (2) biomorphicdetrital, in which the biogenic material is both intact and broken skeletal remains; (3) detrital, when the rock consists only of the fragmented skeletal remains of organisms. The structure of the rock may be massive or layered.

Limestones of biogenic origin are formed from the calcareous shells and internal skeletons of various aquatic animals and plants. They consist of calcite ($CaCO_3$,) and are deposited on the bottom of lakes and seas. In appearance they are massive porous or dense rocks. They readily effervesce when reacting with hydrochloric acid and have a comparatively low hardness. Depending on the predominance of certain kinds of remains in their composition the following limestones are distinguished: foraminiferal (nummulitic, consisting of the shells of nummulites; and fusulinite, consisting of the shells of *Fusus*); coral (consisting of the skeletons of colonial coral polyps); shelly (consisting almost wholly of the shells of various molluscs). Limestones containing an admixture of organic (bituminous) materials are called bituminous. They are dark grey to black in colour and smell of oil when struck or heated. Siliceous limestones are encountered in which some of the $CaCO_3$, has been replaced by SiO_2.

Chalk is a variety of organic limestone consisting mainly of the very fine remains (coccoliths) of calcareous algae (Coccolithophoreae) and is a soft, fine-grained, uniform, usually white, rock that 'boils' vigorously with hydrochloric acid.

Siliceous rocks of organic origin include diatomito and tripoli.

Diatomito is a white cemented or friable rock (diatomaceous earth), consisting mainly of the very fine frustules of diatomic algae (SiO_2nH_2O). It is white in colour. It is very light owing to its microporosity.

Tripoli consists of the very fine opal frustules of diatoms. It is light grey, almost white, in colour, but there are grey and dark grey varieties. It is found both as a friable rock and a compact porous mass. Typical features are its capacity to absorb moisture (avidly sticking to the tongue') and its low density.

Chemical sedimentary rocks are formed through the precipitation of matter from true and colloidal solutions. They are precipitated mainly on the bottom of water basins, but are also deposited by underground waters (stalactites, stalagmites, etc.). Chemical sedimentary rocks formed by precipitation from true solutions have a crystalline texture (coarse, medium, fine, and very fine), while those from colloidal solutions are cryptocrystalline. The rocks are mainly of a layered structure but may also be massive (uniform).

These rocks are divided into several groups: carbonates, silicates, ferruginous, halides, sulphates, allitic, and phosphates.

The *carbonate* group includes limestones (crystalline, aphanitic, oolitic), calc tufa (travertine), dolomite, siderite, and stalagmite or dripstone.

Limestones of chemical origin are formed through the precipitation of calcium carbonate ($CaCO_3$) from aqueous solutions. They have a dense, massive structure of a crystalline or cryptocrystalline texture, and effervesce vigorously with hydrochloric acid. Their colour is white, grey, and where there are admixtures of ferrous salts a pinkish brown. Oolitic limestones consist of concentric, shell-like spheres or ooliths, outwardly resembling peas, cemented together by a calcareous cement. Stalagmite or dripstone is formed through precipitation of $CaCO_3$, from percolating ground waters; its typical forms are the stalactites, stalagmites, and incrustations formed in the karst caverns of limestone massifs. They have a crystalline, sometimes 1 a coarse-grained texture.

Calc tufa (or travertine) is a highly porous, spongy or cellular rock with a fine crystalline texture that is formed where underground waters flow out onto the surface; with liberation of carbon dioxide the surplus dissolved calcium carbonate is precipitated. It often includes the shells of terrestrial organisms, or the imprint of leaves and twigs. The colour is predominantly light, white, grey, yellowish, and pink. Dripstones and calc, tufa react vigorously with hydrochloric acid.

Dolomite is a monomineralic rock consisting of the mineral from which it is named $CaMg(CO_3)_2$. It is formed either through joint precipitation of calcium and magnesium salts and subsequent formation of the mineral dolomite in the sediment or through direct, precipitation of dolomite from the water of brackish lagoons. Some dolomites are formed through metasomatic replacement of limestones by the action of underground magnesian solutions (dolomitisation). Dolomites resemble a dense limestone in appearance but differ from it in their weak reaction in powdered form with hydrochloric acid. They are usually light in colour: yellowish, pink, and brownish shades, depending on the various admixtures, and in particular on the presence of clay minerals.

Silicate rocks of chemical origin include siliceous sinter, a hard, sometimes 'weakly porous rock of various light colours, normally white and yellowish white, that is formed through the precipitation of amorphous alumina (SiO_2nH_2O) from the waters of hot springs. Siliceous sinter includes the sediments of geysers known as geyserite.

Ferruginous rocks include brown iron ore, which is a mixture of iron hydroxide and clay materials. Iron hydroxides (limonite, goethite, etc.) compose 50 per cent of the rocks. They are laid down both in marine basins and in lakes and bogs. Limonite containing more than 30 or 40 per cent of iron is considered iron ore. Oolitic and pisolitic ores are distinguished; the first consist of ferruginous ooliths, the second of nodules and concretions of ferrous minerals. The rocks are a yellow-brown in colour.

Rocks of a typically Chemical originrock salt, consisting of the mineral halite (NaCl), and sylvinite, composed of sylvine (KCl) and halite- are called *haloids*.

Rock salt is a monomineralic, rock, colourless or a milky white in its pure form. Admixtures give it a yellow, brown, or other hue. The texture is medium or coarse crystalline. The rock has a salty taste, dissolves readily in water, and is very Common. Layers of rock salt sometimes alternate with anhydrite and gypsum.

Sylvinite is a less common rock of a white, grey, yellowish, blue, or yellowred colour. Its texture is medium and coarse crystalline. It has a bitter salty taste and dissolves readily in water.

The group of *sulphate* rocks includes the widespread gypsums and anhydrites. They are formed through precipitation of sulphate salts from aqueous solutions in basins with heightened mineralisation of their waters (shallow lakes and lagoons).

Anhydrite is a rock consisting of the mineral anhydrite (CaSO4). It is usually a bluish white. It forms dense finegrained accumulations.

Gypsum is a rock consisting of the mineral of the same name ($CaSO_4 \cdot 2H_2O$). It is generally layered or massive, of a density varying between a micro-grain and coarse-grained texture. The colour is white, light grey, yellowish, pink, and brown. The massive white and pink, fine-grained varieties are called alabaster, the silvery white and pink parallelfibrous variety selenite. Gypsum is readily identified by hardness, being scratchable by the fingernail.

Allitic rocks include laterites and bauxites, which consist mainly of aluminium and iron hydroxides.

Laterite is a rock formed through the weathering of alumosilicate igneous rocks in regions with a hot, humid climate. The rock is hard and friable, often porous, frequently with an oolitic structure. The colour varies-white, grey, pink, etc. In origin laterites are similar to residual clays because they are the residual products of the weathering of igneous rocks rich in alumina.

Bauxite is a rock similar to laterite. It frequently has a pisolitic or oolitic, texture but is a little more uniform. Bauxites are divided by origin into residual (laterite) and sedimentary (redeposited). In the main they are friable, earthy, or harder masses of a greyish white, yellowish brown, brownish red colour.

Phosphate rocks include such common ones as phosphorites (rock phosphate). They are formed in seas and on continents (in lakes, bogs, etc.) and are sedimentary rocks (sands, clays, etc.), heavily enriched with phosphate minerals. The colour of phosphorites is grey and dark grey with violet or brown tinges. Bedded and nodular phosphorites are distinguished. Bedded ones are dense uniform, dark rocks consisting of fine grains (0.01 to 1.0 mm) of weakly crystallised phosphate (apatite) cemented by a phosphate or phosphato-carbonate (siliceous) cement. Pebble phosphates are sandy argillaceous or argillaceous carbonate rocks containing either fine grains of phosphorite (0.1-0.4 mm) or larger phosphorite concretions (0.5 to 5 or 6 mm), composed of phosphate substances mixed with clay or carbonate material.

Sedimentary rocks of mixed origin are complex in structure and contain detrital, biogenic, and chemical material in various proportions. They include calcareous sandstones, marls, siliceous clays, etc.

Calcareous sandstones consist of carbonate material of an organic or chemical origin and detrital sandy material. There are transitional varieties between calcareous sandstones and sandy limestones.

Marl is a calcareous clay rock consisting of calcite and clay minerals. It has a fine-grained texture and a layered, loss often massive (uniform) structure. It is generally light in colour or white, but grey, brown, and yellow-brown varieties are met. It 'boils' well with hydrochloric, acid, forming a dirty patch on the surface of the rock caused by the concentration of clay particles on the spot of the reaction. Marl contains from 20 to 80 per cent $CaCO_3$. With a lower content of carbonate material the rock is called calcareous or marly clay, with a higher content of argillaceous limestone. Marls with an 80 per cent content of $CaCO_3$ and not less than 3 per cent MgO are known as cement clay and are used to produce Portland cement.

Opoka or *gaize* is a porous white, grey, or dark grey rock with conchoidal fracture consisting of argillaceous material and alumina or silicon hydroxide (of organic or chemical origin). It is dense, strong, and when struck produces a characteristic ringing tone.

Caustobioliths (combustible organic rocks) are rocks that are rich in organic matter and are the product of the transformation of the remains of plant and animal organisms in the crust.

Unlike other biogenic rocks they do not consist of the mineral remains of organisms (skeletons) but are the result of transformation of their organic tissues. Caustobioliths are solids (peat, brown coal or lignite, coal, oil shales, asphalt), liquid (oil), and gaseous (natural gas). The most common ones are fossil coal, combustible gases, and oil. They are divided into rocks of the coal and bitumen series.

Rocks of the coal series consist of substances that are insoluble in organic solvents and are formed from the residues of plants (either higher plants or algae) and the simplest planktonic organisms. Those formed from higher plants belong to the humic coals, which are the most common rocks of the coal series; the second are sapropolic rocks. Such formations as peat, lignite (brown coal), coal, and anthracite are distinguished among humic coals, depending on the degree of transformation of the organic matter. Peat corresponds to the initial stage of this transformation and is the initial material for subsequent transformation into lignite, bituminous coal, and anthracite. The processes of coalification, i.e. of the transformation of peat into coal and then into anthracite, is controlled by the history of the geological evolution of the sector of the crust concerned and is governed by the depth of burial of the rock and the pressure and temperature at that depth.

Coalification. The formation of coal from peat can he regarded as the diagenesis and katagenesis of sediments represented by an organic, mass. In bog or swamp conditions plant remains sinking to the bottom are partially disintegrated. Their incomplete breakdown is due to a lack or complete absence of oxygen. Anaerobic bacteria play a considerable role.

Ultimately the organic residues accumulating at the bottom of the bog are converted into humus, a dark substance of colloidal nature. Humus constitutes a considerable part of peat. Peat is thus a compacted mass of dead plant residues enriched with carbon. It contains carbon (35 to 59 per cent), hydrogen (6 per cent), oxygen (39 per cent), and nitrogen (2.3 per cent). It is a brown, more or less friable, porous rock.

As layers of peat accumulate to a great thickness they are compacted further and the water squeezed out. The peat is finally consolidated beneath a series of overlying sediments. As the pressure increases water and gases continue to he squeezed out, while the peat itself is enriched with carbon. As a result brown coal is formed in which the plant structure is retained.

Brown coal or lignite contains 70 per cent of carbon. It is a dense, dark brown or black rock with an earthy fracture, and a dull lustre (hardness 1 to 1/2); density-1.1 to 1.3 g/cm^3-depends on the clay and other admixtures that govern its ash content. Occurs in the form of strata and lenses. Brown coals are typical of a number of coalfields in Europe and North America.

Subsequent changes in brown coal through the effect of high pressures and temperatures convert it into coal and anthracite. Bituminous coal contains up to 85 per cent of carbon. The rock is black, dense, with a grainy fracture and dull tarry lustre. Its hardness varies from 1/2 to 21/2, and density from 1.1 to 1.8 g/cm^3. *Anthracite* is generally hard and brittle, with a peculiar lustre, burns without smoke, and has high calorific value. Deposits of high quality anthracite are found quite often (in Donbass, South Wales, and other places).

Coal measures formed in continental lakes and swamps and containing mainly brown coal are called *limnic*; those formed in coastal conditions are called *paralic*.

Rocks of the bituminous series consist .of matter easily dissolved by organic .solvents. They include oil, solid bitumen, and bituminous oil shales.

Oil is a mixture of liquid and gaseous hydrocarbons. In appearance it is a light, oily brown, dark brown, reddish brown, sometimes white liquid. Its density is 0.7 to 1.0 g/cm^3.

Asphalt is a dense, brownish black bituminous substance with a very tarry lustre and conchoidal fracture. It has a strong odour of bitumen. It melts and burns easily. Its density is 1 to 1.2 g/cm^3.

Oil (bituminous) shales are thin layered argillaceous or marly rocks containing up to 60 per cent of bituminous matter. They are of a dark grey or brown colour and give off a strong smell of bitumen when burning. By composition and occurrence they can be classed as rocks of mixed origin.

The most important rock of the bituminous series is oil, which is a very valuable mineral occurring commonly in the sedimentary layer of the crust.

The origin of oil is a very complicated matter and has not yet been fullyexplained. There is no unanimity among scientists on the origin of oil, it must be noted, and there are two hypotheses- the *inorganic and the organic*.

The originator of the inorganic hypothesis, Mendeleev, considered oil to be formed from the gaseous product of magma, which included methane (CH_4). In his view these gases, in rising, filled ,racks and pores in the rocks, where they were converted into hydrocarbons of the petroleum series. Subsequently they migrated further into strata of sedimentary rocks where they filled reservoirs in the form of gas or liquid oil. At present the inorganic, hypothesis has few supporters because it does not explain a number of points connected with the composition and properties of oil, or with its geographical distribution.

Most scientists support the organic hypothesis. Modern views of the origin of oil wore advanced by Gubkin and developed by his pupils. They concluded that oil is formed from organic matter included in the oozes accumulating in depressions of the sea bed. The very small organisms (plankton) living in profusion in the surface waters sink to the bottom when they die, creating an initial sapropelic mass. With a lack of oxygen the initial organic mass is converted into hydrocarbons of the petroleum series occurring in a dispersed state. Thick series of predominantly argillaceous deposits containing a large amount of organic matter in dispersed form are called *oil-source* beds. During the subsidence of sedimentary series they come into conditions of increased pressure and temperature, with the consequence that the hydrocarbons migrate from the very fine subcapillary pores of the argillaceous' deposits to very permeable porous or fractured reservoir rocks, where liquid oil is formed.

The series in which oil or gas is formed through the migration of hydrocarbons to reservoir strata are called oil-and-gas producing. For an oil-source bed to be converted into an oil-producing one two conditions are required: (1) the presence of reservoir strata; (2) the presence in that sector of the crust of descending tectonic movements in the course of which the oil-source series comes into conditions of heightened pressure and temperature.

Carbon forms the basis of all caustobioliths-oil, combustible gases, coal, peat, and oil shales. While there is no doubt about the biogenic origin of peat and coal, and it is easily demonstrated (by the marks of leaves, spores, and pollen), elements had not been found in oil until recently that have been inherited from living matter; in connection with the rise of the new science of palaeobiochemistry, fragments with a very peculiar biogenic molecular structure have been found in the composition of oil that have undoubtedly come down from living matter. The presence of such structures is yet another factor in favour of the organic origin of oil.

The Forms of Occurrences of Sedimentary Rocks

The original form of occurrence of sedimentary formations is the layer or stratum.

A *layer or stratum* is a geological body composed of a uniform sedimentary rock bounded by two more or less parallel bedding surfaces, with a uniform thickness and occupying a considerable area. The name given to the layer generally depends on the composition of the rocks forming it, e.g. a layer of limestones, or bed of sandstone, etc. The lower surface bounding a layer is called the floor and the upper surface the roof. In a series or suite of beds the roof of the underlying stratum is at the same time the floor of the overlying one.

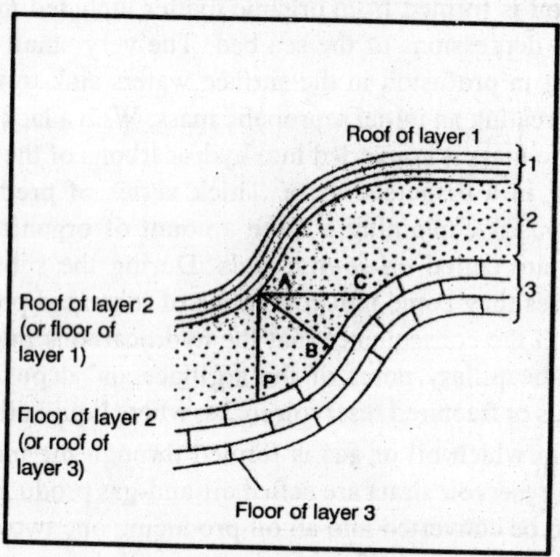

Fig. 6.3. The elements of a bed.

Every bed or stratum is characterised by thickness. True, vertical, and horizontal thicknesses are usually distinguished. True thickness is the shortest distance between the roof and the floor. Vertical thickness is the distance along the vertical from any point in the roof to the floor. Horizontal thickness is the distance along the horizontal from any point in the roof to the floor of a bed.

The thickness of beds maybe relatively constant (sustained) or inconstant (variable). With changes in thickness phenomena of bulging (a marked local increase in thickness) and pinching (marked local thinning of the bed) are observed. Gradual thinning of a bed to its complete disappearance is called petering out. Beds of marine sedimentary series are the most sustained in thickness over large areas. Continental deposits are distinguished by a loss sustained thickness; lens and pocket-like forms of bedding are typical of them.

Apart from the roof, floor, and thickness of a bed its strike and dip are distinguished.

The *strike* is the line of intersection of a bed with the horizontal plane; its position relative to a cardinal point is determined by the azimuth of its bearing.

Dip, i.e. the inclination of a bed to the horizontal plane, is characterised by its direction and the angle it makes with the plane (angle of dip).

The *angle of dip* is the angle between the plane or surface of a bed and the horizontal plane. The direction or azimuth of the dip and the angle of inclination (or dip) are determined by means of a combination compass and clinometer and are measured in degrees. The azimuth of the dip is always perpendicular to the strike of a layer. The strike, dip, and angle of dip are elements of the bedding of a layer that define its position in space.

The Surveyor's Compass and Determination of the Elements of the Bedding of a Layer

To determine the elements of the bedding of a layer (azimuth of the strike, azimuth of the dip, and angle of dip) a combination compass and clinometer is employed. It differs rather from an ordinary compass in the following ways.

1. The compass is usually fixed to a rectangular plate (castiron or plastic in such a way that the 0^0-180^0 diameter, i.e. the north-south direction, is parallel to its length.
2. The divisions on the circle from zero to 360^0 go counterclockwise. The signs for east and west are thus the opposite from the normal compass. This is done so that the value of the azimuth of the strike can be calculated directly from the position of the north-pointing end of the magnetic needle.
3. A clinometer is attached to the compass needle with a half-circle divided from zero to 90^0. The angle of the dip is measured by its position on the half-circle.

The elements of the bedding of a layer are determined in the following way. The direction of its strike is first determined on cleared patch on the bed. For that the long side of the compass is applied to the plane of the

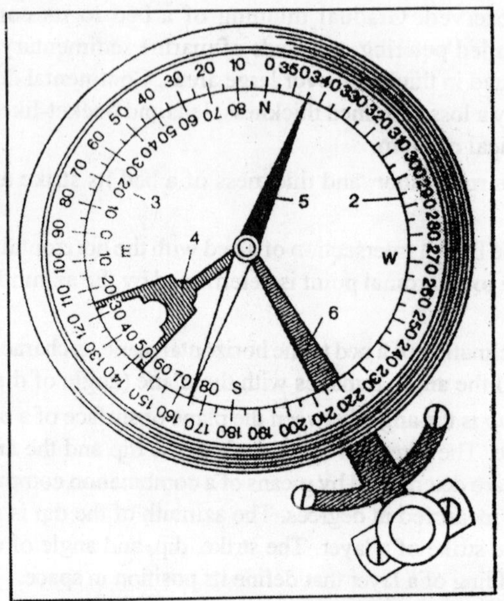

Fig. 6.4. **Combination compass-clinometer : *1—base plate; 2—azimuth circle; 3—semi-circle; 4—clinometer; 5—magnetic needle; 6—locking device.***

bed so that the clinometer registers zero. A line drawn along the long side of the plate indicates the direction of the strike. Having determined the strike, the angle of dip is then measured. To do that the compass is turned so that the clinometer gives a maximum reading. A line parallel to the long side of the compass will then indicate the direction of the dip. In all these cases, it must be noted, the line of the bed's dip is always perpendicular to that of the strike. The angle of dip is often determined immediately (when it is small). To determine the azimuth of a bed's dip, the compass is applied to the strike so that the south end is pressed against the bed and the north end is pointed down the dip. The compass is then brought to the horizontal position. When it has been so fixed the locking device is released and the needle allowed to settle; the azimuth of the dip is read from the graduated circle, (according to the direction of the black, north-seeking end of the pointer).

Knowing the azimuth of the bed's dip there is no need to measure the azimuth of the strike; it is usually calculated from the measured azimuth of the dip by adding or subtracting 90^0; for example, the azimuth of the dip is 300^0 NW, the strike is 210^0 SW, and the angle of dip 45^0.

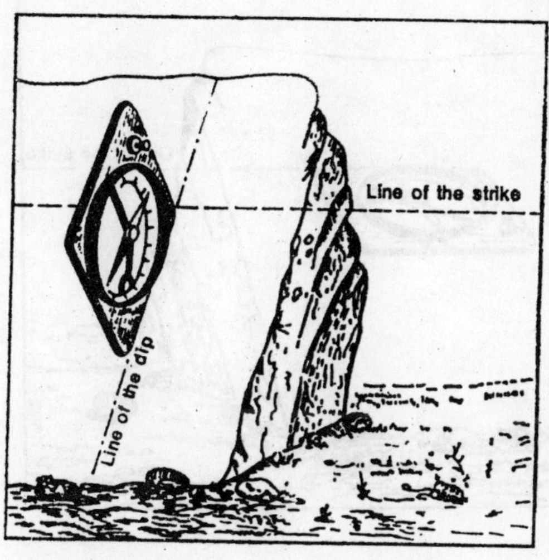

Fig. 6.5. Determination of the dip and angle of dip of a bed.

Fig. 6.6. Determination of the azimuth of bed's dip.

Fig. 6.7. Determination of the azimuth of bed's strike.

If it is necessary to determine the azimuth of the strike by compass, the long side of the latter is applied to the line of the strike, and the azimuth read from the graduated circle. The reverse bearing can be calculated from this reading by adding 180° to the measured azimuth.

The readings obtained for the elements of the bedding of a layer are usually written NE 63° W 48°. Normally the strike and dip are given. When a rock dips vertically, i.e. has an angle of dip of 90°. Only the strike is recorded.

FOLDING AND FAULTS

The main area of the accumulation of sediments is the sea bed. There, on a surface planated by erosion, sediments are deposited in the form of nearly parallel horizontal beds. This original horizontal bedding is undisturbed, but in the course of geological development no one area or another of the original form of the bedding of rocks remains undisturbed, but is disrupted by endogenous processes, mainly by tectonic movements of the crust. Any disturbance of the original bedding of rocks is known as a displacement. They are divided into disjunctive displacements and plicated deformations.

Plicated deformations

Plicated deformations (folds) are disturbances that occur without rupture of the beds' continuity. The following main types of tectonic disturbance are distinguished: monoclines, flexures, and folds.

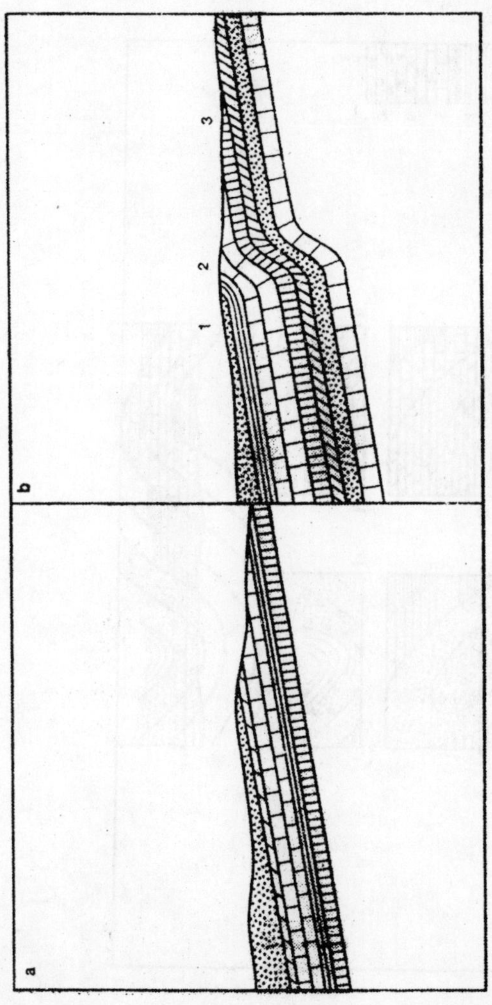

Fig. 6.8. Monocline (a) and flexure (b). Limbs : 1—upper; 2—connecting; 3—lower.

Monoclines are a series of strata uniformly inclined in one direction for a considerable distance.

Flexure is the name given to displacements in the form of an elbow-like bend ,of horizontal and monoclinal beds. They are due to a steep increase in the dip of the beds on a limited sector of a monocline. Upper, lower, and medium or connecting limbs are distinguished. The connecting limb is the part of the series in which the beds have a steep dip and are often thinner.

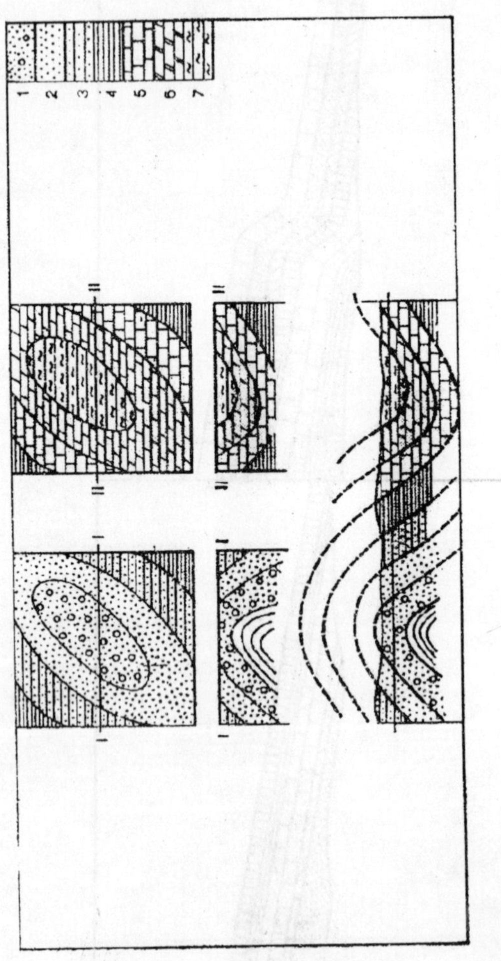

Fig. 6.9. Anticlines and synclines in plan and section. a—anticline; b—syncline; c—parallel; 1—Ordovician; 2—Silurian; 3—Devonian; 4—Carboniferous; 5—Permian; 6—Triassic; 7—Jurassic.

Folds are the main form of plicated deformations. They exist in two main forms: anticlinal and synclinal. *Anticlinal folds* are convex ones in which the beds dip on the opposite sides, while older rocks are located in the central portions than on the limbs. Synclinal folds are concave ones in which the beds dip toward one another and the rocks at the centre are younger than on the limbs.

Folds consisting of both concave (synclinal) and convex (anticlinal) sectors are called parallel or concentric.

Anticlines and synclines have the following elements: limbs, crest, hinge, core, axial plane, axis, width, height, and length of the fold. The limbs are the sides of the fold. The hinge is the line running through the points of maximum bending of any of the beds forming the fold. In a longitudinal vertical section the hinge line is often undulating. The crest is the part of a fold in the area of the hinge where the limbs bend. The crest of an anticline is sometimes called a dome and that of a syncline a saddle. The angle of a fold is the angle between the limbs or the interlimb angle, mentally projected to their intersection. The axial plane is the imaginary plane passing through the hinges of all the beds of the fold. The *axis of a fold* (fold axis) is the line of intersection of the axial plane and the ground surface. The core is the series of rocks lying in the bend, of an anticline or syncline. The width of a fold is the distance between its limbs where they cut the ground surface. When there are several parallel folds the width of a fold is taken as the distance between the axial surfaces of two neighbouring anticlines or synclines. The amplitude of a fold is the vertical distance from the bend of an anticline to the bend of its attendant syncline. The length of a fold is the distance in plan between its extremities. The closing of an anticline is called a pericline. Folds are

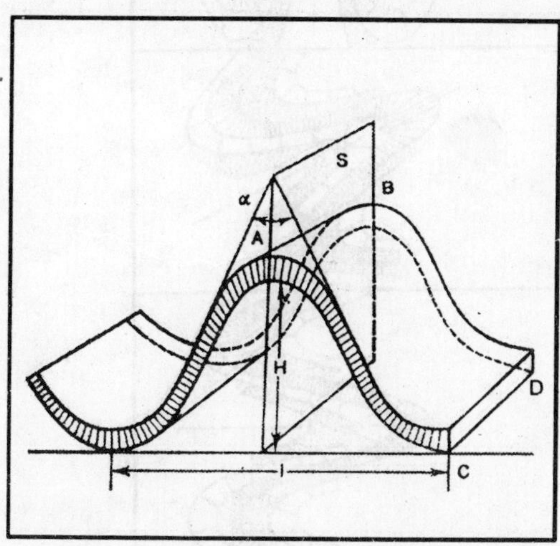

Fig. 6.10. Elements of a solid; ABCD—limb; AB—hinge; α—interlimb angle; S—axial plane; l—length; H—height.

differentiated by a number of attributes and also by their projection in cross-section and plan.

The following types of fold are distinguished *by cross-section from the position of the axial plane and limbs:* upright, inclined (reclined), recumbent, and overturned. An *upright* fold has a vertical axial plane and limbs disposed symmetrically in relation to it. An inclined (reclined) fold

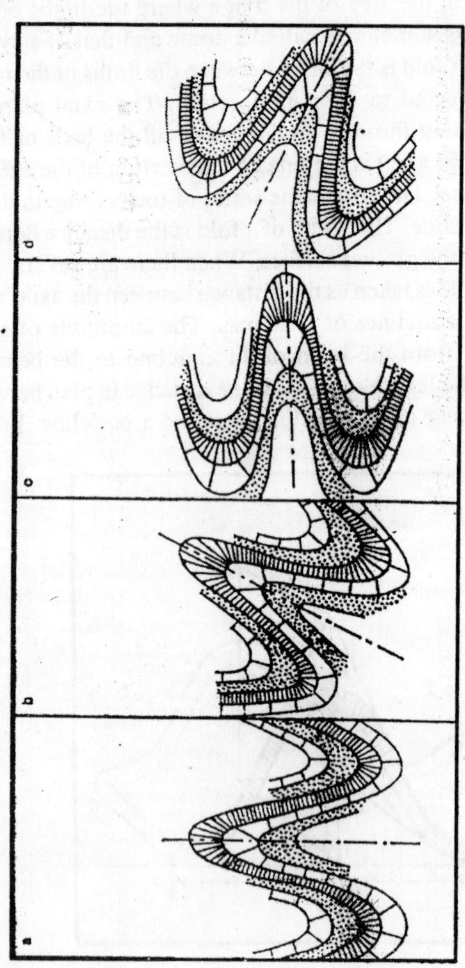

Fig. 6.11. Folds (according to the position of the axial plane and limbs) : a—upright; b—inclimed; c—reci,nemt' d—overturned.

has an inclined axial plane, with the limbs dipping in different directions. The variety of inclined fold in which the limbs dip in the same direction is known as overturned. A *recumbent* fold is one in which the position of the axial plane is close to the horizontal and the limbs are nearly parallel with one another. An inverted fold is one with a subhorizontal axial plane, the limbs closing downward.

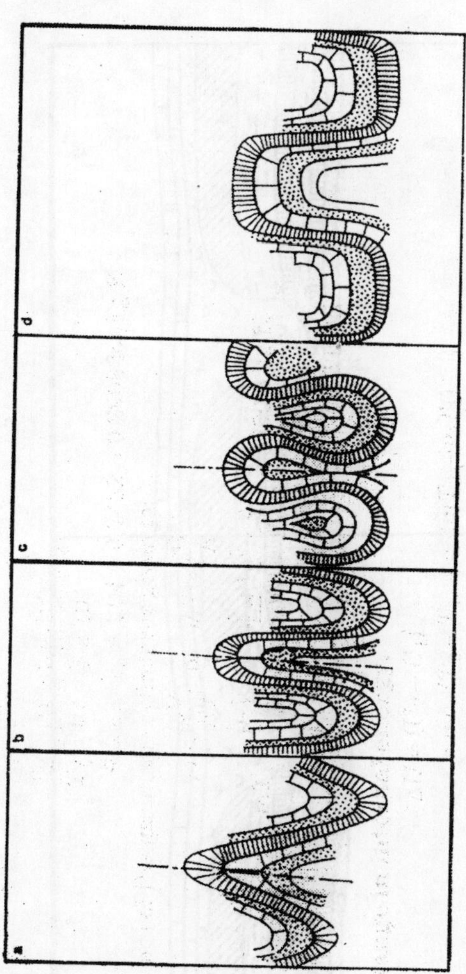

Fig. 6.12. Folds (by character of the disposition of the limbs and shape of the hinge) :a—normal; b—isoclinal; c—fan-shaped; d—box.

Normal (ridge-shaped), isoclinal, fanshaped, and box folds are distinguished according to the position of the limbs and the shape of the hinge in crosssection. In a normal (upright) fold the limbs close at an acute angle and the crest has a narrow, sharp shape. *Isoclinal* folds have a sharp crest and parallel limbs. *Fan-shaped* folds have a wide crest, the limbs are located fan-wise and compress the core. Box folds have a broad crest, and relatively steep, almost vertical limbs.

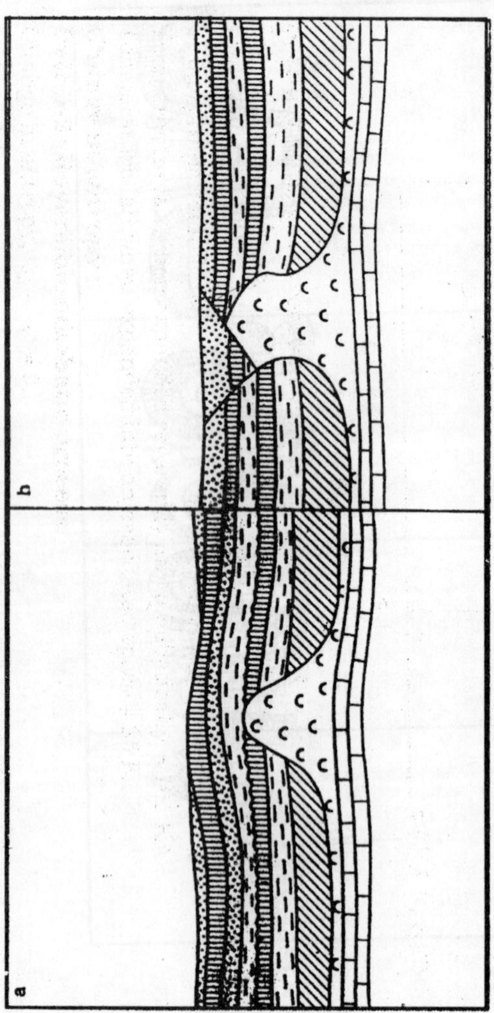

Fig. 6.13. Diapiric fold (salt dome): a—deep-seated; b—piercing.

In plan linear and discontinuous folds are distinguished according to the relation of their length and width. Linear folds are characteristic of geosynclinal regions. Their width may be on a fraction their length, the ratio of length to width being 10 : 1, 20 : 1, or more. In periclinal and centroclinal structures the slope of the beds is gentler than on the limbs. Linear folds are divided in plan into rectilinear, arcuate, branching virgate, imbricated, and sigmoid. One form often gives way to another along the strike.

Interrupted folds are characteristic of platformal areas. In plan they are slightly longer than wide. Among them brachyfolds, arches, domes, and diapirs are distinguished.

Brachyfolds are a type in which the ratio of length to breadth varies from 2: 1 to 5 : 1. They are divided into *brachyanticlines* and *brachysynclines*. A *dome* is a fold in which the ratio of the long axis to the short is 1 : 1 to 2 : 1. In plan they are a circular outline. The negative analogue of a dome is a *trough* or *syncline*. Large anticlines consisting of brachyanticlines and domes are called arches. They may stretch for tons or hundreds of kilometres. The amplitude of an arch-like uplift is often as much as 200 to 300 metres. The dip of the beds on the limbs of the uplift is between 3^0 and 5^0 and on the downwarp up to 1^0.

A special form of dome-like imbricate fold is the *diapir (a dome with an intrusive core)*. The presence of plastic rocks (salt, gypsum, clay, etc.) in the core is typical of them, and also a regular increase in the dip of the beds from the limbs to the core of the fold. When the core consists of salt, the fold is called a salt dome. Diapirs are formed through the intrusion of highly plastic rocks (salt, gypsum, clay) into the country rock. The pressure core of diapiric core may have the form of a lens, stock, mushroom, etc. A dome-like fold is formed in the overlying rocks, and is often complicated by faulting (Fig. 161b). As a consequence of the outflow of plastic rocks from the area of a diapir, a *compensation trough* is formed.

Faults

Faults (or disjunctive fractures) are breaks in the continuity of strata accompanied with a rupture. They take the form of fractures along which there is no displacement of the bed or of jointruptures (fracture zones), with displacement of the beds along the plane of rupture. The plane of the fracture along which there is relative displacement of strata is called a fault. The parts of the rock adjoining the fault plane are called walls. In a dipping fault hanging and foot walls are distinguished; the fault covers the foot wall and lies beneath the hanging wall.

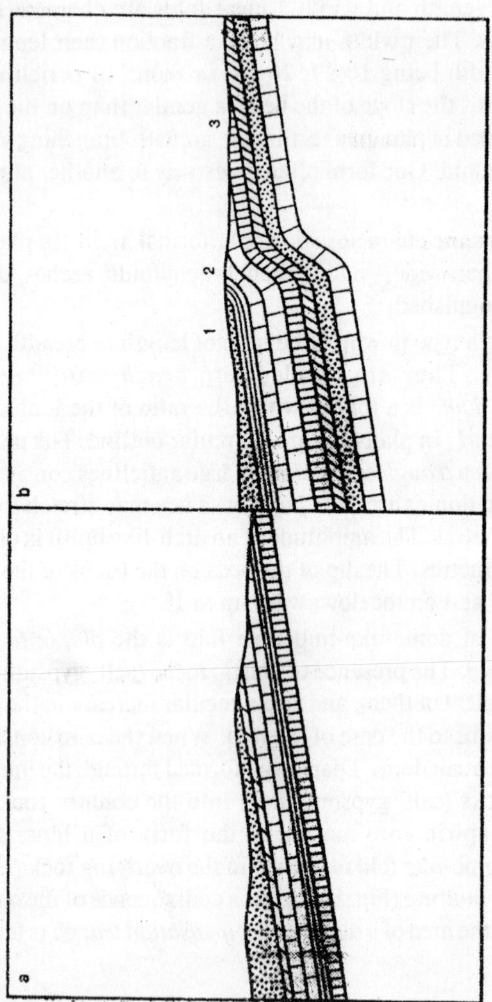

Fig. 6.14. Monocline (a) and flexture (b). Limbs : 1. upper; 2, connecting; 3, lower.

The amount of relative displacement of strata along a fault is called its amplitude. The following types are distinguished: true (oblique) amplitude or the distance along the fault plane between the roof or floor of one and the same bed in the hanging and foot walls; vertical amplitude, or heave, the projection of the true amplitude on the vertical plane; horizontal amplitude or throw, the projection of the true amplitude on the horizontal plane; and stratigraphic amplitude, or the distance along the

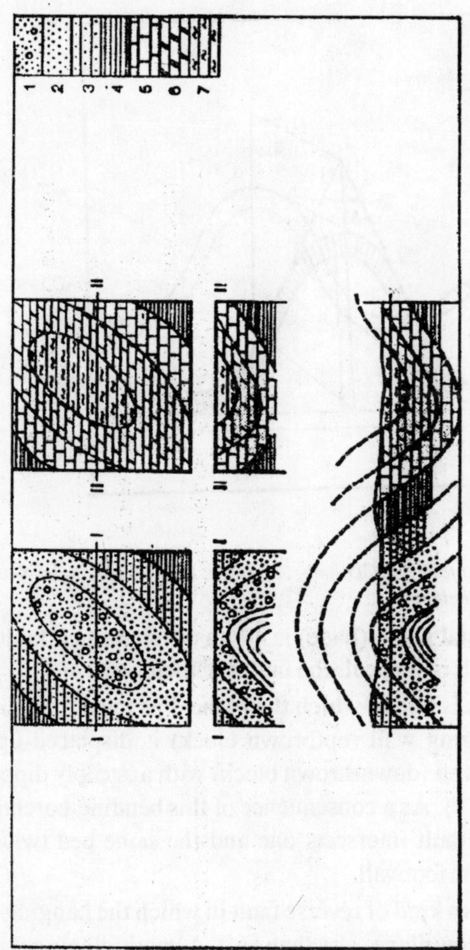

Fig. 6.15. Anticlines and synclines in plan and section. a-anticline; b-syncline; c-parallel; 1-ordovician; 2-Silurian; 3-Devonian; 4-Carboniferous; 5-Permian; 6- Triassic; 7-Jurrassic.

normal between the roof and floor of one and the same bed in the hanging and foot walls.

Faults are distinguished as normal, reverse, thrust, and tear or wrench (transcurrent) faults.

A *normal fault* is one in which the fault plane dips toward the downthrown block, and the hanging (downthrown) wall is displaced downward in relation to the footwall (upthrown block). The angle of the

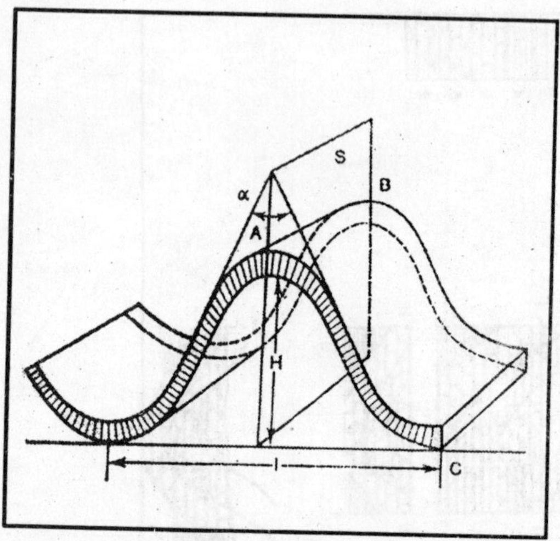

Fig. 6.16. Elements of a fold : ABCD-limb; AB-hinge; α-interlimb angle; S-axial plane; l-length; H-height.

fault in the horizontal plane (hade) is 40^0 to 60^0 in normal faults. When the plane of the fault is vertical, the fault is called *vertical*.

A *reverse fault* is one in which the plane dips toward the upthrown block and the hanging wall (upthrown block) is displaced upward in relation to the footwall (downthrown block) with a ,steeply dipping fault plane (more than 60^0). As a consequence of this bending borehole in the sector of a reverse fault intersects one and the same bed twice, in the hanging wall and the footwall.

A *thrust fault* is a kind of reverse fault in which the hanging wall has moved along a shallow plane (less than 60^0). A gently sloping thrust fault with a large throw and low dip is called a mass overthrust or tectonic sheet. Its horizontal amplitude can be as much as 30 or 40 kilometres.

Tear or wrench faults are fractures whose blocks are predominantly displaced horizontally parallel to the strike of the fault plane. They are frequently combined with normal faults, reverse faults, and thrust faults (strike faults, etc.).

Fractures are usually encountered in groups, forming complex faults (stop faults, grabens, and horsts). *Step faults* are a system of normal faults

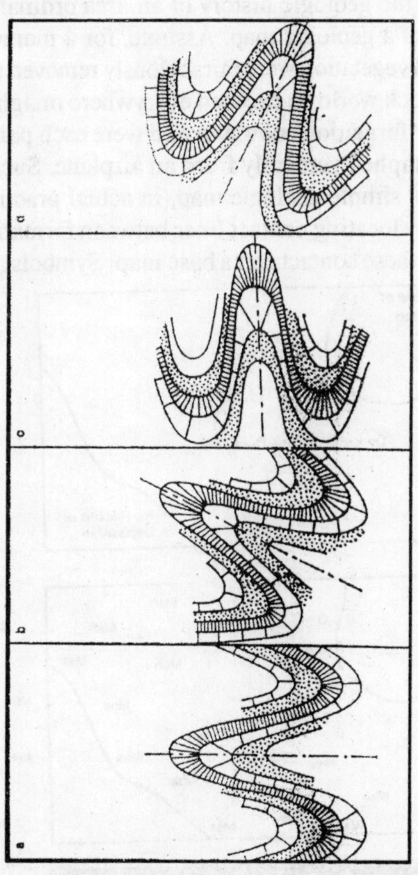

Fig. 6.17. Folds (according to the position of the axial plane and limbs).

in which each successive block is downthrown in relation to the preceding one. A *graben* is a system of stop faults the central part of which is downthrown in relation to elevated peripheral blocks. A *horst* is a system ,of reverse faults the central part of which is elevated in relation to the peripheral downthrown blocks.

Mapping the Past

Geologic Maps

The study of the geologic history of an area ordinarily begins with the construction of a geologic map. Assume, for a moment, that all the loose material and vegetation were miraculously removed from your home state, so that bedrock world be exposed everywhere imagine, further, that the surfaces of the formations now exposed were each painted a different color and photographed vertically from an airplane. Such a photograph would constitute a simple geologic map, in actual practice a geological map is prepared by locating contact lines between formations in the field and then plotting these contacts on a base map. Symbols are added to the

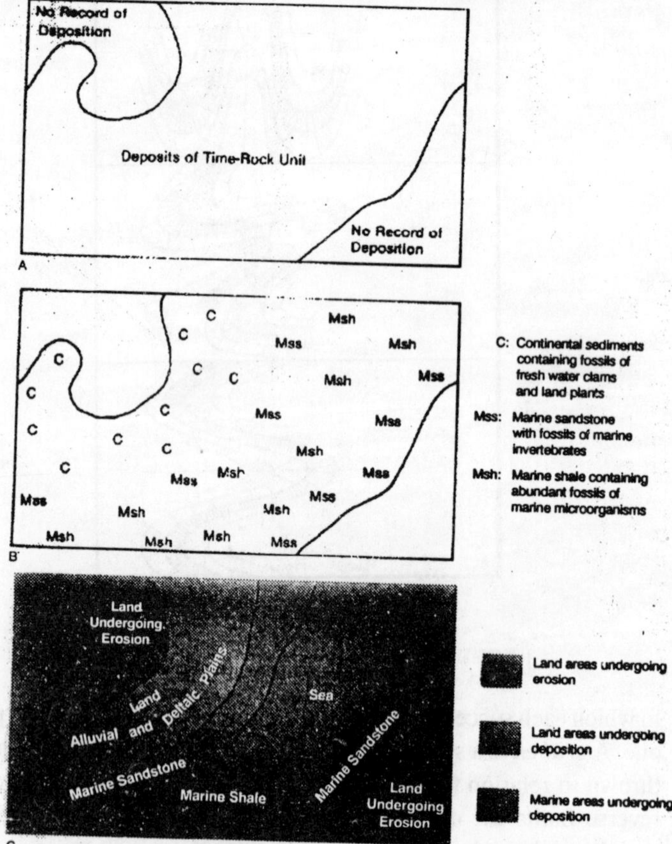

Fig. 6.18. Stages in the construction of a paleogeographic map. (A) Area of occurrence of time-rock unit. (B) Plot of rock types within the time-rock unit.

colored areas to indicate formations and lithologic regions, mineral deposits, and structures such as folds and faults. Once the geologic map is completed, a geologist can tell a good deal about the geologic history of an area. The formations depicted represent sequential pages in the geologic record. From the simple geologic map , the geologist is able to reduce that there was an ancient period of compressional folding, that the folds were subsequently faulted, and that an advance of the sea resulted in deposition of younger sedimentary layers above the more ancient folded strata.

Paleogeographic Maps

A map showing the geography of a region area at some specific time in the geologic past is termed a *plaeogeographic map.* Such maps are really interpretations based on all available paleontologic and geologic data. The majority of such maps show the distribution of ancient lands and seas. Palegeographic maps are at best, of limited accuracy, because as seas advance and retreat endlessly through time, the line drawn at the sea's edge may represent an average of several shorline positions. They are nevertheless useful for showing general geographic conditions within regions or continents. To prepare a paleogeographic map, one would plot all occurrences of rocks of a given time interval on a map and enclose the area of occurrence in boundary lines. Areas of nonoccurrence may be places of no deposition or places where deposites once existed but were subsequently eroded away. Nondeposition appears to be the case in the northwestern corner of , for that area is nicely encircled by sandstones that grade outward to shales. If the time- rock unit thins toward areas of nondeposition, this interpretation would be strengthened.) With the help of fossils, the nature of the sediments- that is, whether marine or nonmarine-is determined and plotted on the map. The final step is to complete the paleogeographic reconstruction.

Isopach Maps

Isopach maps are prepared by geologists in order to illustrate changes in the thickness of a formation or time-rock unit. The lines on an isopach map connect points at which the unit is of the same thickness. On a base map, the geologists plot the thickness of units as they are revealed in drilling or in measured surface sections. Isopach lines are then drawn to conform to the data points as perfectly as possible. Ordinarily, the upper surface of the unit being mapped is used as the datum from which thickness measurements are made. An isopach map may be very useful in determining the size and shape of a depositional basin, the position of

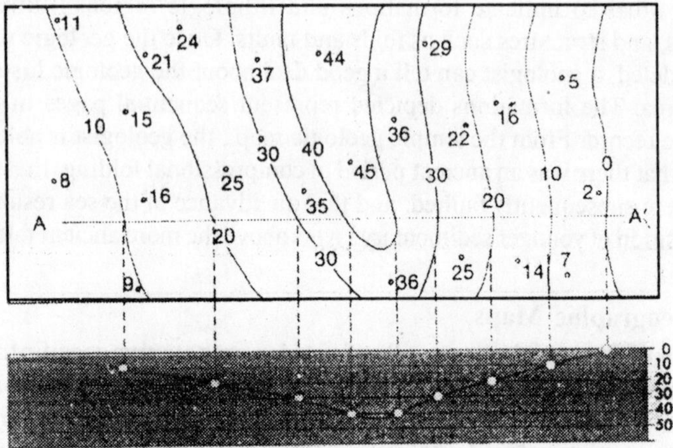

Fig. 6.19. Diagram illustrating the construction of a simple isopach map in an area of undeformed strata.

shorelines, and areas of uplift. The map indicates a semicircular center of subsidence in southern New York and Pennysylvania in which over 2000 ft of sediment accumulated. The isopach pattern further indicates a highland source area to the southeast.

Lithofacies Maps

Maps constructed to show areal variations in facies can provide additional details and validity to paleogeographic interpretations. Such graphic representations are called *lithofacies maps*. Geologists first correlate the formations. Then, assuming that the unconformity represents one time plane and the ash bed another, they define the time-rock unit as X. Paleontologic study of the rocks between the time planes confirm the validity of the time-rock unit. Geologists may now prepare the lithofacies map. Time-rock unit X is missing at well number 11; this may be the result of its not being deposited there or, having been deposited, of its being eroded away. It is logical that the sandy facies was deposited adjacent to a north-south trending shoreline.

figure lithofacies map of rocks deposited over 400 million years ago in the eastern United States. From this map, one can infer the existence of a highland area that existed at that time along our eastern seaboard and that supplied the coarse clastics. Detrital sediments from the source area become fine, and the section thins as one proceeds westward from the source highlands. Finally, as far west as Indiana, the map indicates that

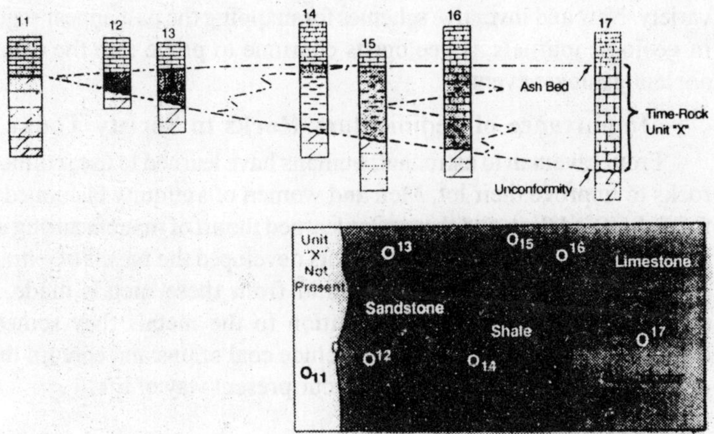

Fig. 6.20. Diagram illutrating the preparation of a lithofacies map from a subsurface time-rock unit. Well locations are indicated by small circles. Correlation of rock units between wells is indicated by dashed lines. Because of the few control points, the exact position of lithofacies boundaries on this map is somewhat arbitrary.

only carbonate precipitates were laid down. The conglomerates were probably the deposits of great alluvial fans built out from the ancient mountain system. Because the northern border of the time-rock unit cuts across the bands of facies, it is considered to be an erosional border and does not represent the original extent of the unit mapped.

The lithofacies maps just described provide a qualitative interpretation of areal changes in rock bodies. Quantitative lithofacies maps can also be constructed and are frequently used in the study of subsurface formations that are known primarily from well records. By means of contour lines, such maps show the areal distribution of some measurable characteristic of the unit being mapped. For example, contours may be drawn on the percentage of one lithologic component compared to the total unit or on the ratio of one rock type to the others within the unit. An isopach map is ordinarily the base map for any of the quantitative maps, since one must know the total stratigraphic thickness of the unit with which individual components are compared.

Perhaps the most important fact to remember about the mapping techniques used in deciphering earth history is that they are limitless in variety. New and inventive schemes for mapping the past appear regularly in geologic journals as geologists continue to probe into the details of ancient geologic events.

Importance of Sedimentary Rocks to Society Today

From caveman to astronaut, humans have learned to use sedimentary rocks to improve their lot. Men and women of antiquity fashioned tools from chert and flint, and they laater learned the art of manufacturing useful containers from clay. Their successors developed the means of extracting copper and iron from the rocks and from these metals made more sophisticated implements. In addition to the metals they sometimes contain, sedimentary formations include coal seams and contain the oil, gas, and groundwater important to our present way of life.

Mineral fuels

The mineral fuels-petroleum, gas, and coal- are our most important sedimentary resources. They are essential for heat and power and metal refining; they are also the source of many chemicals useful in the manufacturing of plastics and fertilizers. *Coal* is a brownish-black to black combustible rock that forms in beds from a few inches to many feet in thickness and is interbedded with shales, sandstones, and other sedimentary rocks. Extensive coal-bearing sequences characterize the Pennsylvanian and Cretaceous Systems. Pennsylvanian sequences of strata in the Applachians include over 100 individual beds of coal, each composed of the compressed and altered remains of land plants. Coal is abundant in the United States and will become increasingly more important over the next three decades as our reserves of petroleum are consumed.

Commercial accumulations of oil and gas require rather special geologic conditions. These conditions are found almost exclusively in sedimentary rocks. First, there must be a *source rock* for the petroleum. Ordinarily, this is a series of beds rich in the organic remains of unicellular organisms that accumulated along with the particles of sediment. Second, there must be a permeable reservoir rock such as sandstone or porous limestone to provide passage and storage for the gas and oil. The *reservoir rock* is covered by an impermeable *cap rock* to prevent the upward escape of hydrocarbons. Finally, there must be an oil-trapping structure so that the hydrocarbons can be concentrated in one place. Petroleum geologists seek out these structures in many ways. Long before drilling programs are begun, geologists conduct gravity surveys and seismic "reflective shooting" surveys to reveal clues to underground structures. Later, exploratory wells are drilled, and by careful analyses of electrical, lithologic, and paleontologic logs of these wells, a picture of the configuration of the underground layers is gradually developed.

Construction Materials

Other sedimentary materials useful to humans included clays for use in ceramics and bricks, limestones for building stones and cement, sand and gravel for concrete and glass, and evaporites for use in the chemical industry. Some sedimentary strata are rich in iron oxide. Those near Birmingham, Alabama, have been mined and smelted for several decades. Because minerals such as gold, chromite, diamond, cassiterite, and magnetite are heavier than quartz and other common silicates, they tend to accumulate in quiet areas of streams or to be concentrated by waves as placer deposits. Finally, there are sedimentary ores that form in place by the deep chemical decay of parent rock. The most important metal concentrated in this manner is aluminum. Bauxite, an almost pure hydrous aluminum oxide, is the ore mineral of aluminum. Bauxites oped in once humid, tropical regions as a result of the weathering of source rocks rock in aluminum silicates.

Limited supply of mineral resource

Any commentary on mineral resources would be incomplete without noting that ore bodies and oil fields are limited in extent and are the result of unusual associations of geologic conditions. Furthermore, it is not theory but fact that they are exhaustible and irreplaceable. Their effect upon the standards of living and society is so enormous that every citizen should become involved in political decision relating to the management of our natural resources.

Chapter 7

Fossilisation

Fossils owe their existence to a break in the natural cycle. Normally all of the material used in living organisms is recycled but fossilisation represents a transfer of material from the biosphere to the lithosphere. In the long term, of course, weathering of rocks may return material to the biosphere. The three stages of the process of fossilisation are mortality, biostratinomy, and diagenesis. The whole field is sometimes called taphonomy.

Mortality

Here we are concerned with the cause and consequences of death. In nature very few organisms die simply of old age. Far more die prematurely as a result of suffocation, thirst, inadequate light, severe temperature or pressure changes, poisoning, illness, parasites,; injury, or predation. The cause of death can only rarely be established in fossils. Examples include encasement in resin or amber, drowning in asphalt (Pleistocene of Rancho La Brea, California) or pitch (Pleistocene of Starunia, West Ukraine) and predation, when the material is preserved in coprolites. In other cases death may have resulted from a number of different causes, for example, an organism buried by sediment might die of asphyxiation, hunger, or pressure of overburden.

An abnormally high number of fossils is often attributed to mass death. At present such events occur where water is polluted by phytoplankton toxins or becomes chilled or oxygen deficient (for example, by heating in tropical lagoons or by upwelling of H_2S-rich water, or by being covered by ice for a long period). Care should be taken, however, when attempting to apply such modern observations to fossil occurrences.

Traces left by death-throes are very scarce but we can sometimes observe the attitude of death and the effects of rigor mortis where the contraction of ligaments and tendons may cause the head to be thrown back in the vertebrates.

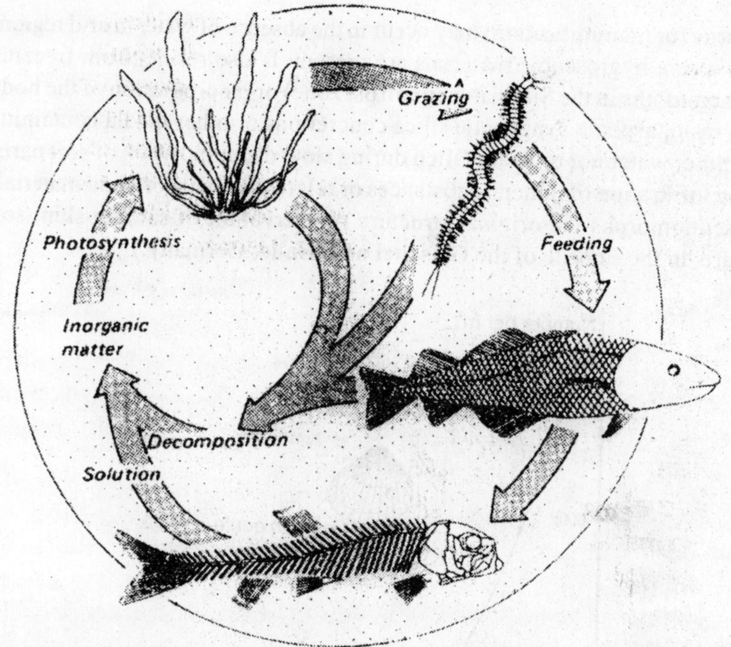

Fig. 7.1. The natural cycle. Decomposition of organic matter replaces the stock of inorganic materials.

Biostratinomy

Biostratinomy is concerned with the fate of an organism's body from the time of death until it is finally buried by sediment.

Soft Tissue

Among the soft tissue the most important organic components are proteins, fats, and carbohydrates. These begin to break down both chemically and bacterially immediately after death. The cause of this decomposition is controlled by environmental factors. In the presence of water and oxygen the organic substances break down into the simplest inorganic components such as CO_2 and H_2O under the attack of aerobic bacteria. Where oxygen is absent however, in stagnent environments, anaerobic bacteria break down the original molecules using some for their metabolism and converting the remainder into hydrocarbon mixtures of high molecular weight. This process may produce bituminous muds whose organic matter may subsequently convert to bitumens, oil, and natural gas, under the influence of higher temperatures and pressures. Stagnation also permits the preservation of organic matter. True preservation of soft tissue (or mummification) may occur in the absence of water in arid regions or where hygroscopic materials are present. It also results from freezing (mammoths in the Siberian permafrost zone) or incorporation of the body in resin, asphalt, syngenetic silica concretions or other media containing neither water nor oxygen. Often during slow decomposition of soft parts, the infiltration of mineral substances or relatively stable organic materials pseudomorphs the original structure (preservation of saurian skin, soft parts in the Eocene of the Geiseltal near Halle, Germany.)

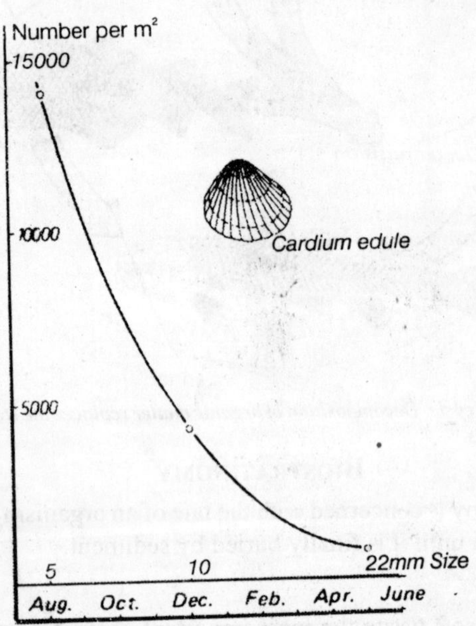

Fig. 7.2. ***Mortility of juvenile stages as shown by the bivalve Cardium edule from North Sea tidal flats.***

Skeletal material

Relatively few materials are available to the organic world for the formulation of protective and supporting hard parts. The most readily available are calcium carbonate (calcite and aragonite), calcium phosphate, opal, chitin and cellulose. Agglutinating organisms produce hard parts by cementing together foreign particles with an organic or inorganic cement.

Calcite is the preferred skeletal material of the archaeocyathids, octocorals, bryozoa, brachiopods, some annelids, polychaetes, many bivalves, pectinids, limids, ostreids, sonic cephalopod structures (nautiloid beaks, ammonite aptychi, belemmite rostra) several crustaceans (balanids, ostracods), echinoderms and red algae (Lithothamnia, Solenoporaceae). Calcite may include isomorphous $MgCO_3$ whose abundance increases with temperature. Precipitation of calcite is facilitated by warm, shallow water but by no means confined to that environment. Its solubility in pure water or in alkaline solutions is small (14 mg/l in pure H_2O), but in CO_2-saturated water its solubility increases to 1 gm/l; in acid media calcite is not preserved. In the modern oceans solution of calcite is particularly widespread in the cold depths of the oceans. In sediments, calcite is often leached from permeable strata but more readily preserved in fine grained and impermeable rocks.

Aragonite occurs in the hydrozoa, hexacorals, gastropods, most bivalve and cephalopod shells and the green algae. It is metastable in shallow marine environments but in fresh water it gradually alters to calcite at normal temperature and pressure. Its solubility is some 10% higher than that of calcite.

Calcium phosphate ($Ca_5(PO_4)_3(OH)$) is important to the vertebrates (bone material) and is also found in some brachiopods and arthropods (trilobites, crustacea). It is almost insoluble in neutral solutions (0,01 gm/l) and is well preserved in weakly acid or alkaline environments. In more strongly acid environments or where it remains in contact with acid for a long period (as in peat bogs) calcium phosphate dissolves leaving bones fragile and flexible.

Opal forms the iest of radiolaria, diatoms, siliceous sponges, and many flagellates. It is weakly soluble in water (river water (river water contains about 10 mg/l of S_1O_2 in temperate regions and 30 mg/l in the tropics), stable in acids other than HF and slowly soluble in alkalis.

Chitin, a nitrificated polysaccharide occurs in algae, fungi, lichens, cnidarians, priapulids, bivalves, annelids, onychophores, pentastomids, arthropods and tentaculates. It forms the skeleton of arthropods (crustaceans, tribolites, insects, etc.), graptolites, and some brachiopods. It is subject to decomposition like other organic substances but is more stable than most. Other organic substances that are involved in the building of skeletal material include proteins spongin (in some sponges) and keratin (horn, hair, scales, feathers, and claws of vertebrates).

Cellulose forms the cell wall of plants and thereby gives them a certain rigidity. It also appears in tunicates. In the presence of air cellulose breaks down to CO_2 and H_2O. Lignin (a benzol derivative) is an important structural constituent in the wood of pteridophytes and spermatophytes.

Decomposition of the soft tissue affects the preservation of the skeletal material since the gases evolved (CO_2, H_2S, NH_3 etc.) vary depending on environmental conditions and alter the pH by producing acids (H_2CO_3, H_2SO_4) or bases (NH_4OH) which may corrode or even dissolve calcium carbonate, calcium phosphate, or opal.

Disintegration of skeletal material

Articulated skeletons whose components are held together by organic tissue tend to disintegrate into their individual parts following death of the organism, the pattern depending on the type of skeleton.

Invertebrates

In bivalves, post-mortal relaxation of the adductor muscles allows the valves to spring apart. The ligament decomposes more slowly than the rest of the soft tissue but when it has done so the valves separate. The remainder of the fossilisation process may procede in various ways. Many ammonites possess an aptychus that was probably a mandible aperture. If the organism is in an upright position during decomposition of the soft parts, the structure tends to slip down into the bottom of the body chamber where it is often preserved. When the aptychus consists of two plates these separate along the symphysis only at a late stage. Like most arthropods, the trilobites had a segmented carapace which disintegrated after death. However, since the resulting fragments are identical to those produced by sloughing of the carapace during growth of the trilobite it is difficult to distinguish between the two. In many echinoderm species the test comprises individual elements that are rarely fused together. They are instead held together mainly by ligaments and cartilagenous material. Disintegration begins where this material is most readily accessible, that is, in distal parts of the body such as the tips of the arms.

Fish

Whether a dead fish floats to the surface or sinks to the bottom depends on the amount of gas in its swim bladder at the time of death. Where a fish sinks onto an oxygen-deficient bed, its skeleton may remain intact as it is entombed in sediment. The same thing may happen to fish stranded on the beach. Gas produced by putrefaction accumulates mainly in the central cavity of the body, the corpse therefore floats belly up with head and tail dangling. The belly later ruptures and as the gas gradually escapes the fish sinks, lands on its head or tail and then usually rolls over onto its side.

Fish with a weak axial skeleton may begin to disintegrate while still

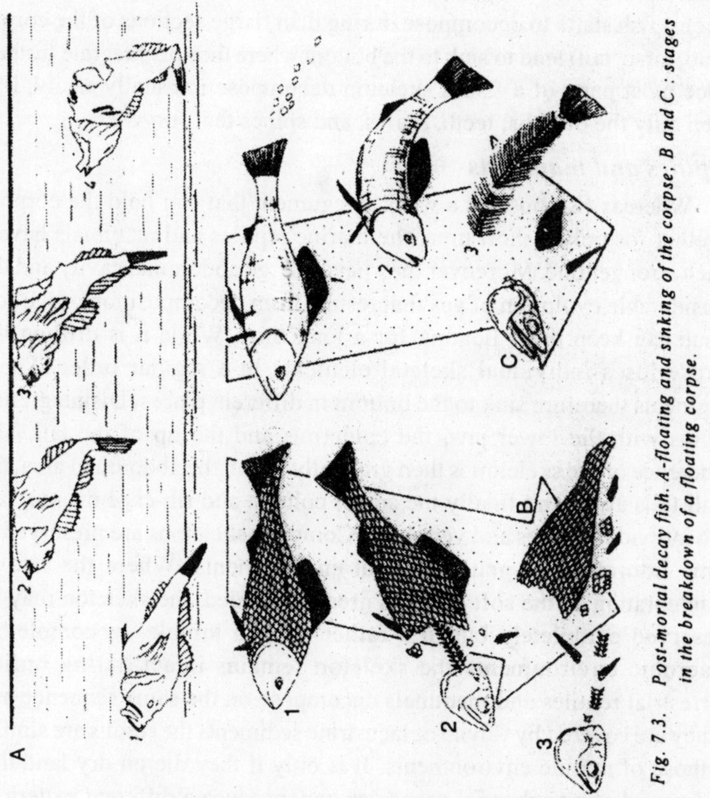

Fig. 7.3. *Post-mortal decay fish. A-floating and sinking of the corpse; B and C : stages in the breakdown of a floating corpse.*

afloat. In the ganoids with their overlapping armoured scales the otoliths are dropped first from the fishes ears. The scale- armour then separates from the skull and backbone which also fall apart fairly quickly. Disintegration of the skull begins with solution of the lower jaw. The scale-armour may remain intact for a long period - in Recent ganoids often for months but it then starts to corrode around the periphery and finally dissolves completely. In modern fish (without a scale-armour) disintegration again begins with the otoliths. They also soon lose their scales. Once the abdominal wall ruptures, the link between head and body weakens and they may separate completely. As in the ganoids, decomposition of the skull begins with the lower jaw whose components separate along their symphyses. The jaw joints come apart later as do the upper elements of the skull. The linkage of the tail-fin to the backbone also loosens or fails and finally the individual ribs and vertebrae fall apart. When a fish starts to decompose during drift, large sections of the corpse (head, torso, tail) tend to sink to the bottom where they disintegrate further. Since most parts of a fishes skeleton decompose unusually easily, it is often only the otoliths, teeth, scales, and spines that survive.

Reptiles and mammals

Whereas fish possess a weak integument that can hold the corpose together for only a short time, the marine reptiles and mammals have a much stronger one. Moreover they have a large abdominal cavity and the considerable evolution of gas that results from decomposition of the soft tissue can keep them floating for a long time. While it is drifting the corpse loses individual skeletal elements in a regular order. These fragments therefore sink to the bottom in different places. Disintegration begins with the lower jaw, the epidermis and the tip of the tail. The coherence of the skeleton is then gradually lost in the abdominal area, the skull falls away and finally the spinal column and rib-cage disintegrate into individual bones and vertebrae. Complete skeletons are preserved in some littoral or oxygen- deficient environments. Where the rate of disintegration of the soft tissue is greatly retarded, the skeleton may be preserved completely but in a rather tangled jumble. In completely anaerobic environments the skeleton remains intact during burial. Terrestrial reptiles and mammals decompose on the same sequence and if they are covered by fluvial or lacustrine sediments the results are similar to those of marine environments. It is only if they die on dry land that aridity and other subaerial processes may produce a different pattern of decay.

Birds

Because their feathers trap plenty of air and because their bones have air spaces, dead birds float on water for a long time. During this period, their skeletal elements are scattered over the sea floor. The down goes first, then the foot bones, then the head separates from the body although it may remain linked for a time by means of the tough trachea. Later, the pinions and tail feathers become detached from the decomposing periostreum and finally the torso disintegrates. From observations of modern gulls it would appear that complete skeletons are preserved only on land or on the beach, but whether these findings apply to all other Recent and fossil birds remain uncertain.

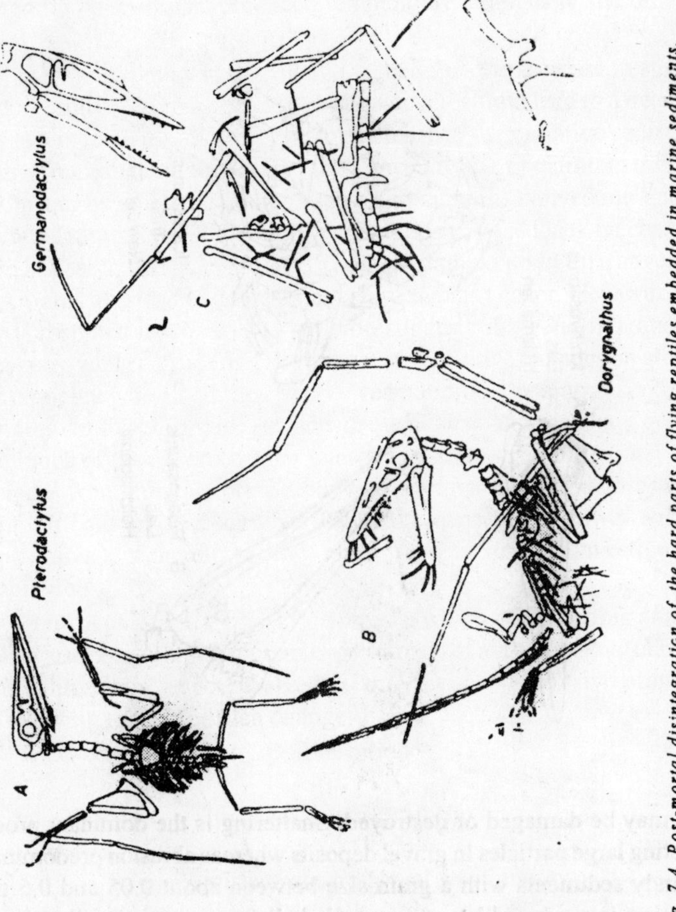

Fig. 7.4. Post-mortal disintegration of the hard parts of flying reptiles embedded in marine sediments.

Burial

The chances of *in situ* preservation depends on mode of life and whereabouts at death. Many benthonic organisms live under the sediment-water interface and are readily preserved in their growth position. Others living on the surface appear simply to have fallen over. In most cases, however, the organism did not live where we find it. A phase of transport intervened between death and burial, and during this period the organic remains were damaged, current-sorted, and aligned.

When organic remains undergo transport either alone or with sediment

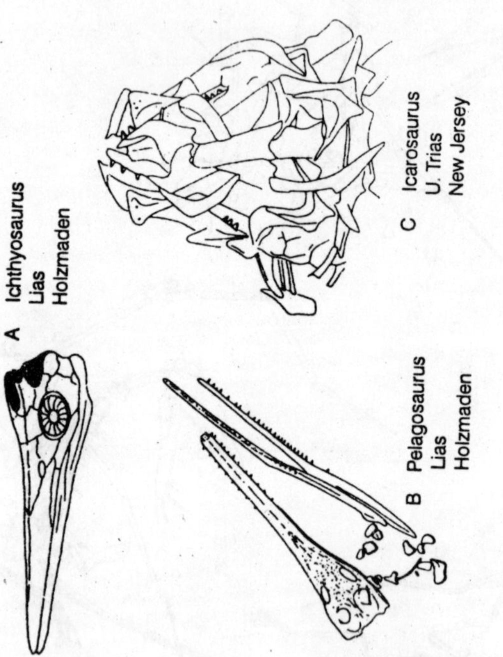

Fig. 7.5. Stages in the breakdown of reptiles skulls.

they may be damaged or destroyed. Shattering is the dominant process affecting large particles in gravel deposits whereas abrasion predominates in sandy sediments with a grain size between about 0.05 and 0.5 mm. Abrasion is produced by other small shell fragments as well as by the sand grains themselves. The slit and clay fractions have little mechanical effect. Where the fossil is being transported with a mass of shifting sand it is equally abraded on all sides whereas facetting is likely to result if the shell is lying on the surface of the sediment or anchored to a bed over which a uni-directional current is flowing. Bowl-shaped objects develop first a round and then a horseshoe shaped notch whose opening faces up-current. If the shell changes position or the current direction fluctuates several facets are developed. The results are similar to those seen in ventifacts. In areas of stronger currents or tidal flow where the fossils tip over and roll, all the projecting parts of the shell are abraded to produce shapes similar to those of shells abraded within moving sediment. Circular and horseshoe shaped pits are again developed. Glide facets are produced when the shell slides along an abrasive bed and has its base eroded.

Shattering and dislocation of skeletal material results not only from purely mechanical processes but also from organic activity - boring microorganisms such as algae and fungi, bivalves, sponges, and other animals all weaken the skeletal structure. Scavenging also plays a considerable part in biogenic disintegration.

The fate of bodies that lack any inherent buoyancy depends greatly on the ease with which they can be carried in suspension. Suspendibility can be calculated from the formula $S = 0/4G$ (where 0 = surface area in mm^2 and G = weight in gms). The higher the value of S, the more easily is the material transported. Organic debris which is easily suspended is carried largely in the turbulent zone above the bed whereas less easily suspended material is carried in the bed load. These two different modes of transport produce different types of wear. Buoyant bodies experience quite different conditions. They float until they are either washed ashore or lose whatever feature (gas, air chambers, fat droplets, etc.) confers that bouyancy.

During transport, organic debris is sorted according to its size, weight, shape, and resistance to abrasion. The strongest skeletal elements survive longest. The greater the range of suspendibility the more widespread the area over which the material is deposited. From their sorting curve we may determine whether the remains have suffered long or short transport.

The suspendibility of fossil material can be greatly affected by the presence of projections that act as anchors. Flat, disc-shaped bodies such as some gastropod opercula lie tight against the bed. They present only a

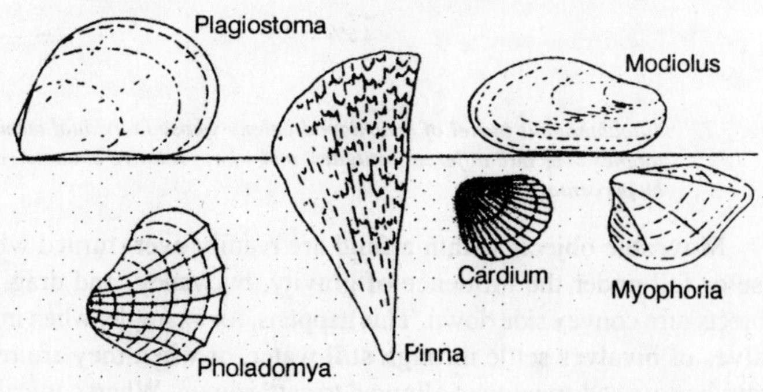

Fig. 7.6. Autochthonous burial of bivalves in the position of growth.

small surface area to the current and may therefore remain unmoved despite their high suspendibility while other larger objects are carried away. If the area dries out and is then recovered by water, such objects may be held up by surface tension and transported further than other material.

Current sorting should not be mistaken for other kinds of selective, post-mortal processes. All juvenile forms of a species may be killed off while the adults resist the attack and survive. The resulting fossil population would then only appear to have undergone size sorting. Selective diagenetic processes such as the solution of aragonitic tests and preservation of calcitic material may also be confused with current sorting.

Flow conditions in any medium (water, air, ice, sediment) affect objects within or at the surface of that medium. They may result in orientation of shell material. Movement about a horizontal axis may produce overturning or imbrication while rotation about a vertical axis produces alignment.

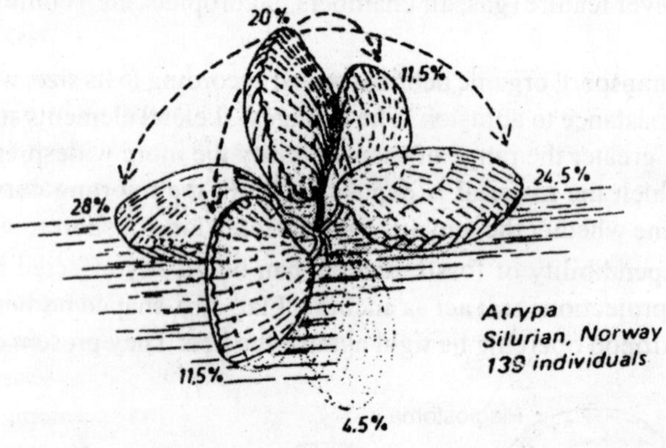

Fig. 7.7. ***Autochthonous burial of brachiopod colony whose individual members have topples over into different attitudes, and whose relative abundance is shown by percentage values.***

Moveable objects within a fluid are readily over- turned when they rise or fall under the influence of gravity, buoyancy, and drag. Curved objects turn convex side down. This happens, for example, when individual valves of bivalves settle through still water, or when they are reworked from bottom sediment then allowed to settle again. When conical objects such as gastropods are free to move within a bottom mud or other sediment whose consistency enables objects to be held in any position, they tend to come to rest point down where buoyant forces predominate but right way up where gravitational forces predominate, provided that a reasonable amount of vertical motion can take place.

Where the body being reoriented lies at the boundary between two media, its freedom of movement is partly inhibited by one of the media; the sediment in the case of a sediment-water interface, the ground in the case of a subaerial land surface. The restrictions imposed have considerable biostratonomic and palaeogcographic significance, because shells or other organic detritus tend to become overturned into the attitude where they offer least resistance to the current flow. This is particularly apparent in the case of cup-shaped shells. Here the rule is that in subaqueous environments with a sufficient current flow velocity, cup-shaped objects will normally come to rest and be buried convex side up. This fact affords an important indicator of the way up of a sedimentary sequence.

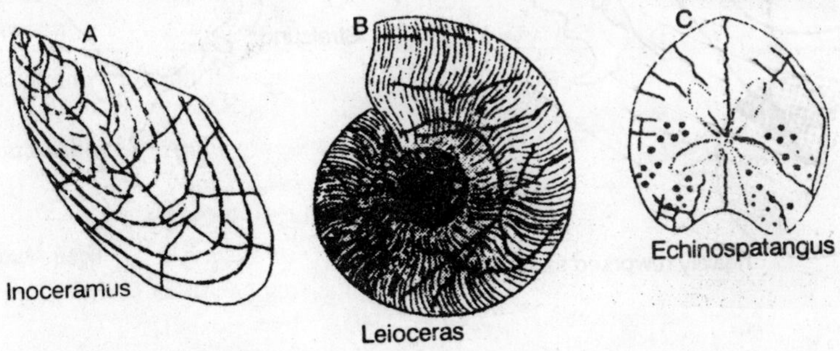

Fig. 7.8. Fracture patterns caused by mechanical stress and overburden pressure.

Exceptions to the rule are common when shells are able to sink into the sediment or are so closely packed that they mutually interfere. In the former case the shells often come to rest concave side up, while the latter situation produces random orientation. Irregularities in shape of the shell may also cause inversion or random orientation.

Where alignment occurs within one medium it may be described as 'free' whereas at the interface between two media it is termed 'limited'. It is best seen in elongate bodies, and most information is available when such bodies have differently shaped ends, for example, if they are elongate cones. When bodies of this shape are lying on a substrate over which a uni-directional current is flowing they roll into a position where they are

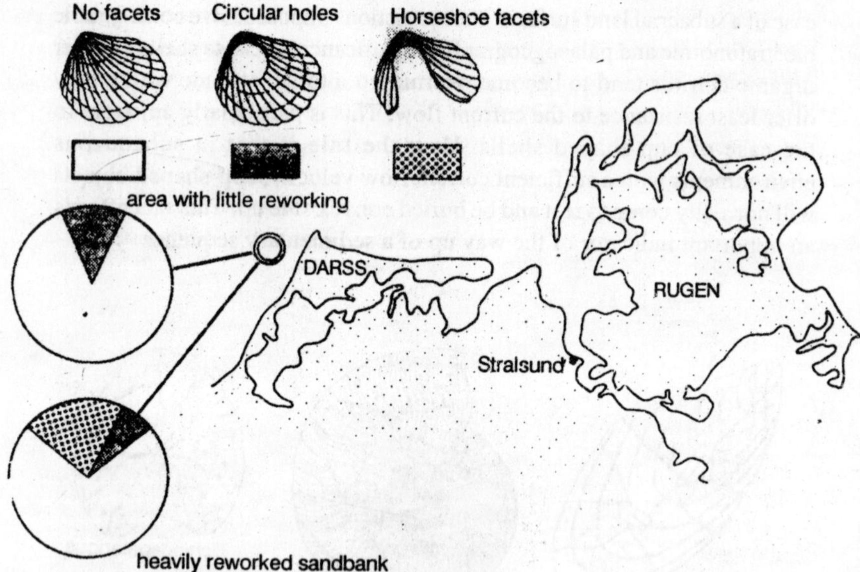

Fig. 7.9. Facets and their distribution in environments with different current strengths neat Darso in the western Baltic.

offering least resistance to the flow. This position occurs when the long axis of the body is parallel to the current and its pointed end is usually directed downstream although with open-ended shells such as turriform gastropods the pointed end may face up current. When such bodies are being rolled around by an oscillating current, for example, waves they lie with their long axis perpendicular to the flow. Spindle-shaped or cylindrical objects roll with their long axes perpendicular to the current. Preferred orientation of the most easily aligned shells requires current velocities in excess of 15 cm/s while a flow rate of over 40 cm/s may be needed in the case of large, heavy, or strongly ornamented shells. When the object has a projection that can serve as an anchor, the body pivots about it until the pivot point is directed up-current. A shell without such a projection can be pivoted in the same way if it is partly projecting out of the water or lying on a cohesive substrate.

Preferred orientation of elongate bodies can be analysed by means of a current rose. Symmetrical, bimodal distributions (propellorshaped) suggest orientation perpendicular to the flow. If the shells are conical we can then deduce that the current was an oscillating one. Such a deduction cannot however be made in the case of cylindrical objects. Uni-modal distributions indicate orientation parallel to a uni-directional current with, in the case of pivotable objects, the pivot end up-current. Non-anchored cones may, however, lie with their points upstream.

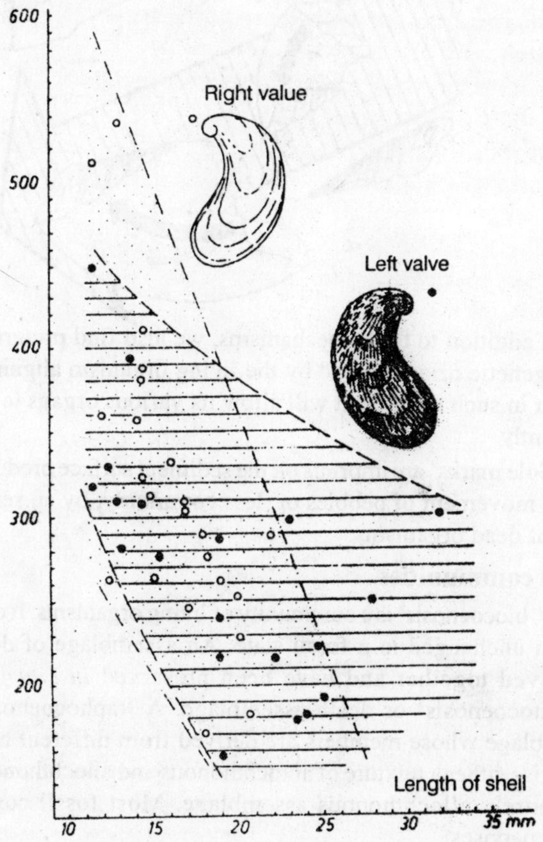

Fig. 7.10. Variation in ease of suspension as a function of shell size as shown by the Jurassic oyster Exogyra virgula.

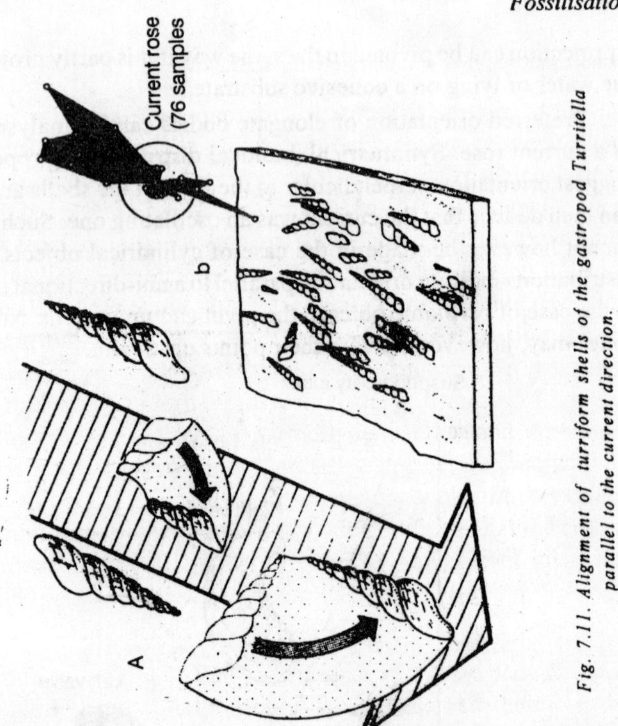

Fig. 7.11. Alignment of turriform shells of the gastropod Turritella parallel to the current direction.

In addition to these mechanisms, we also find preferred orientation of biogenetic origin caused by the living organism aligning itself in the current in such a way that will allow its various organs to function most efficiently.

'Sole marks' are imprints on the sediment surface produced physically by the movement of pebbles or, less commonly, by current-drifted hard parts of dead organisms.

Fossil communities

A 'biocoenosis' is a community of living organisms. It cannot possibly remain unchanged in a fossil state. An assemblage of dead organisms that lived together and have been preserved *in situ* is known as a 'thanatocoenosis' or death assemblage. A 'taphocoenosis' is a fossil assemblage whose members are derived from different habitats. It may comprise either a mixture of autochthonous and allochthonous individuals or a purely allochthonous assemblage. Most fossil communities are taphocoenoses.

Fossil assemblages are always preserved in sediment whose structures and texture enable us to distinguish various biofacies types. In the vital-

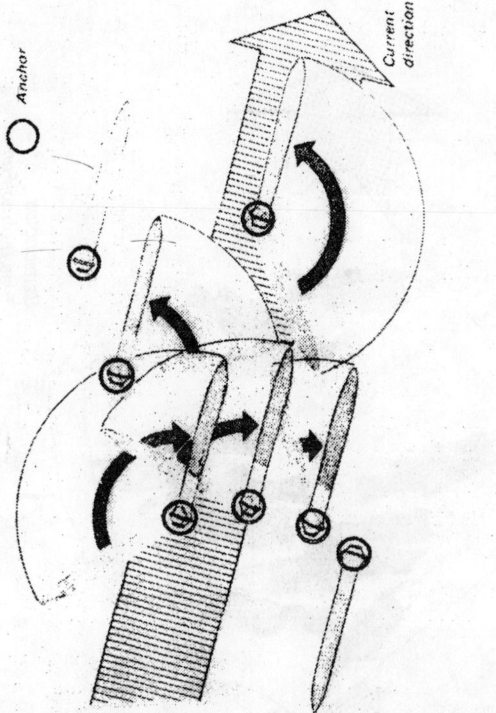

Fig. 7.12. Alignment of echinoid spines with their anchored ends upcurrent.

astratal biofacies, a single biocoenosis (now a thanatocoenosis) flourished there for a long period. It forms massive unbedded sediments, for example, reefs. The vital-pantostratal biofacies is characterised by the presence of an autochthonous thanatocoenosis in well bedded sediment. Remains of animals and plants foreign to the community may also be present. The vital- lipostratal biofacies displays many indications of reworking and sedimentary breaks. In it the remains of thanatocoenoses are supplemented by allochthonous taphocoenoses. The same sedimentary characteristics reappear in the lethal-lipostratal biofacies whose fossil assemblage is an allochthonous taphocoenois without any autochthonous organisms. Autochthonous life forms are again missing from the lethal-pantostratal biofacies whose assemblage again consists entirely of allochthonous forms. In this case, however, the bedding is undisturbed as the sediment has not been reworked.

Thanatocoenoses and taphocoenoses turn up in a number of frequently recurring guises the most important of which are shell banks, pavements, sorted pavements and bonebeds. Shell banks (lumachelles) are accumulations of skeletal remains (mostly shells) whose state of

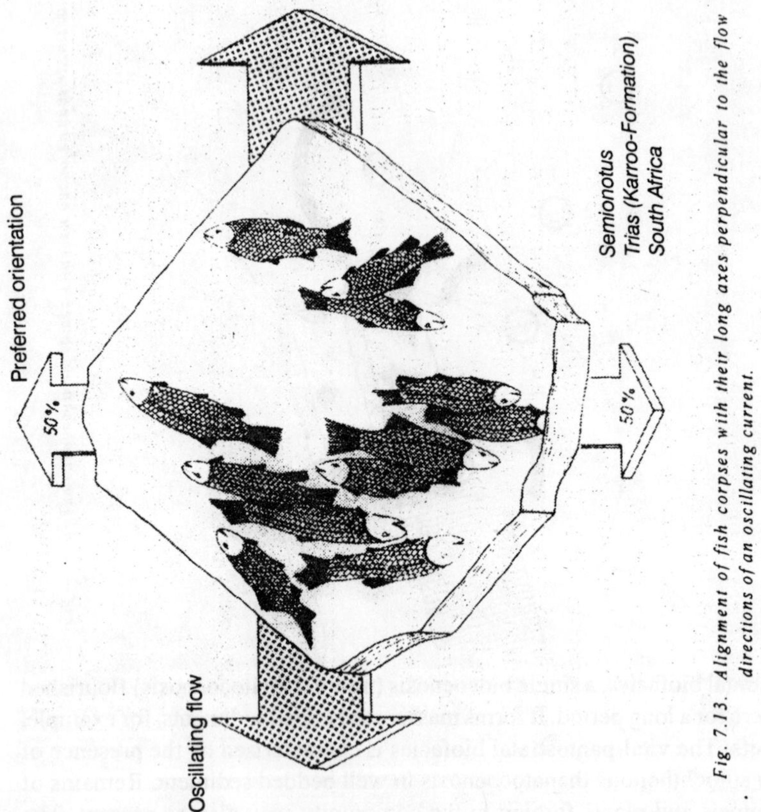

Fig. 7.13. Alignment of fish corpses with their long axes perpendicular to the flow directions of an oscillating current.

preservation ranges from intact through broken to shattered. Most shell banks are allochthonous taphocoenoses. They occur widely on shorelines and beaches, in estuaries, ahead of river deltas, on submarine ridges and on submerine dunes. Shells can also be piled up on the surface of reworked sediment as a result of the activity of burrowing organisms. In this case the assemblage is autochthonous. Shell pavements are bedding planes enriched in shell material. The density of shell cover may vary from sparse to almost complete. Pavements form in the surf zone either as allochthonous taphocoenoses or by winnowing of the autochthonous material. Most of the shells always lie convex side up. *Lesedecken* are pavements on which the shells have undergone size- and shape- sorting as a result of current activity. The long axes of the shells are commonly oriented parallel to the flow, for example, in belemite 'graveyards'.

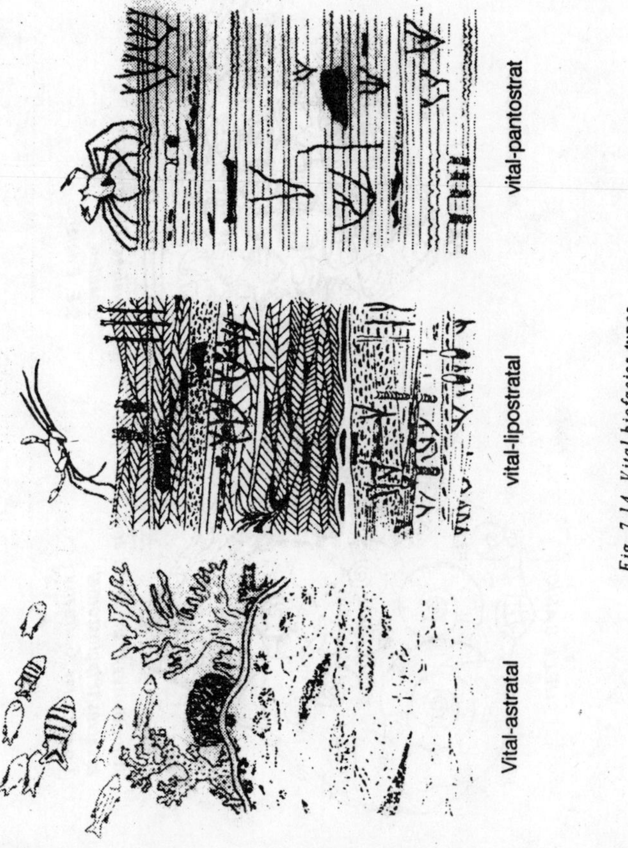

Fig. 7.14. Vital biofacies types.

Bonebeds are tabular enrichments of bones and teeth. Their components are always allochthonous and have often suffered considerable abrasion. Apart from the fissure fillings in karstified areas which also contain allochthonous taphocoenoses, bone beds are the most widespread sites of rich vertebrate assemblages. The famous localities in the lethalpantostratal biofacies, for example, Mansfeld Monte San Georgio, Holzmaden, and Solenhofen are exceptional cases.

Concentration of fossil material on a considerable scale can arise as a result of condensed sequences that form when sedimentation ceases for a time or when sediment is winnowed. The organic remains continue to accumulate at their usual rate during these periods giving enriched sequences that can be recognised by the differing stratigraphic age of the various constituents.

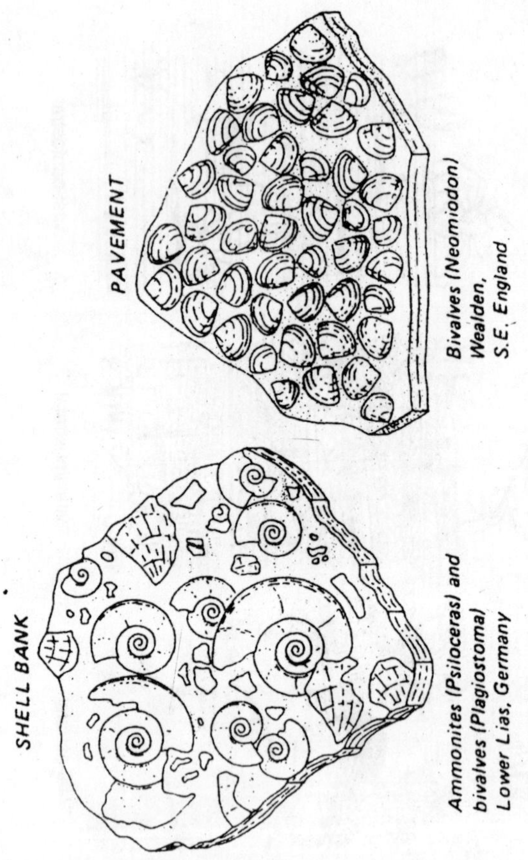

Fig. 7.15. Shell bank and pavement.

Concentrations may also arise by selective sorting (for example, placer deposits or bone beds) or by being washed into a cavity (for example, fissure fillings). Unusually well-preserved material occurs where decomposition of soft tissue is prevented or greatly retarded. Articulated skeletons whose elements are held together by soft tissue may then survive intact. Such conservation may occur in stagnant oxygen-deficient environments, for example, in bituminous shales, or in preserving media such as resin or peat, or in early diagenetic concretions, or in rapidly deposited sediments.

Diagenesis of Fossils

Diagenesis of fossils covers the fate of organic remains after they are buried in sediment. It is controlled largely by conditions of sedimentation and by the petrography of the sediment.

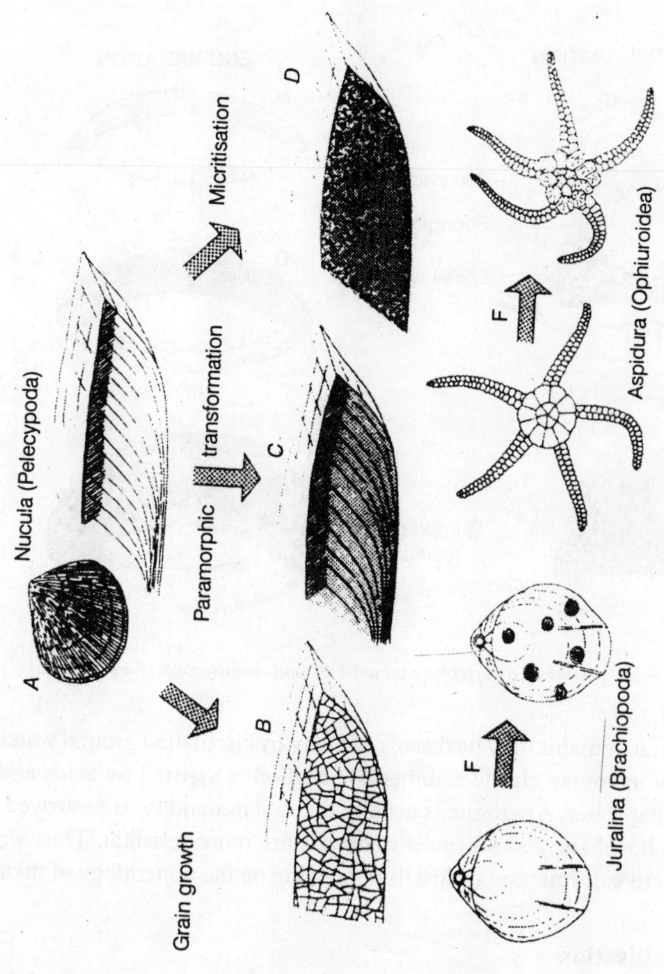

Fig. 7.16. A-D; patterns of recrystallisation shown by the aragonitic shells of the bivalve Nucula. E; Grain growth of skeletal elements in echinoderms.

Preservation of material

In the simplest case, the chemistry and structure of the organic remains does not change. Such fossil remains are fairly common in Recent sediments but with increasing age of the material the likelihood of some kind of charge increases. Original material is rarely preserved in Palaeozoic rocks. A sediment in which the circulation of pore water is reduced to a minimum is the main pre-requisite for preservation of such material.

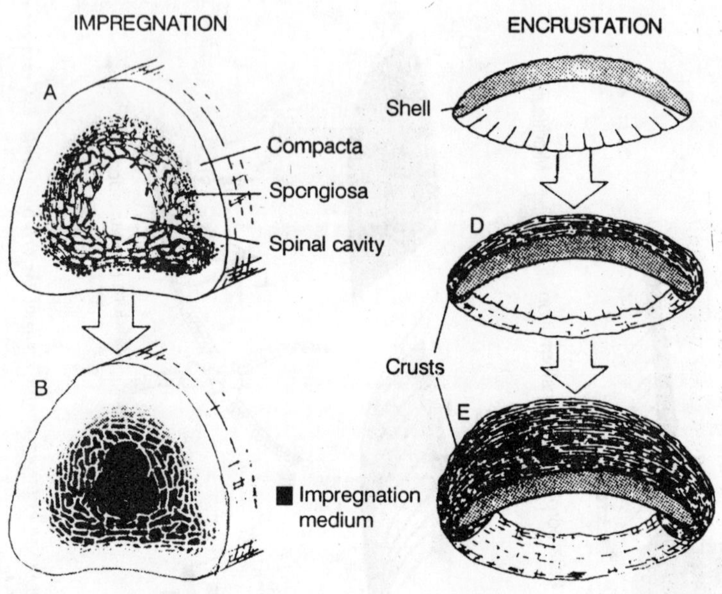

Fig. 7.17. Impregnation of a vertebrate bone (A-B) and encrustation of a shell(C-E).

Solution

Organic remains may be dissolved away by circulating ground water especially in course clastic sediments. Solution is assisted by acids and bases in that water. Aragonite is usually the first mineral to be destroyed; calcitic, phosphatic and siliceous materials are more resistant. Thus we get a selective destruction of fossils depending on the mineralogy of their skeleton.

Recrystallisation

Recrystallisation without change in the chemical composition of skeletal material can arise in a number of ways. Metastable phases of a polymorphic substance are transformed into stable phases in the course of time, for example, aragonite transforms to calcite. The shell structure may survive unaltered during this inversion although the finer details are usually lost. *Grain growth* involves growth of the larger crystals in the skeleton at the expense of the smaller ones and thus produces a completely new texture. The diagenesis of echinoid tests provides a fine example of this process. Here, the individual plates which in life are permeated by a network of cavities are each transformed after death into a single crystal

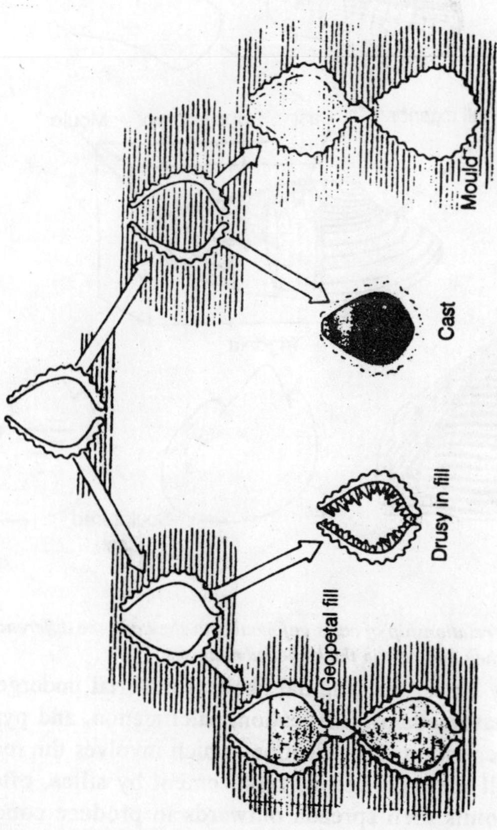

Fig. 7.18. Mode of formation of casts, moulds, cavities, drusty infills and geopetal fills.

of calcite with almost complete loss of the original structure. Occasionally, crystal growth does not stop at the shell margin but extends out into the sediment. Diagenesis of skeletal opal produces fine-grained quartz with the loss of water of crystallisation. Grain growth may or may not involve mineralogical transformations.

Micritisation involves the early diagenetic breakdown of skeletal material into a cryptocrystalline and usually structureless aggregate. Algae are usually responsible and aragonite is the mineral most affected.

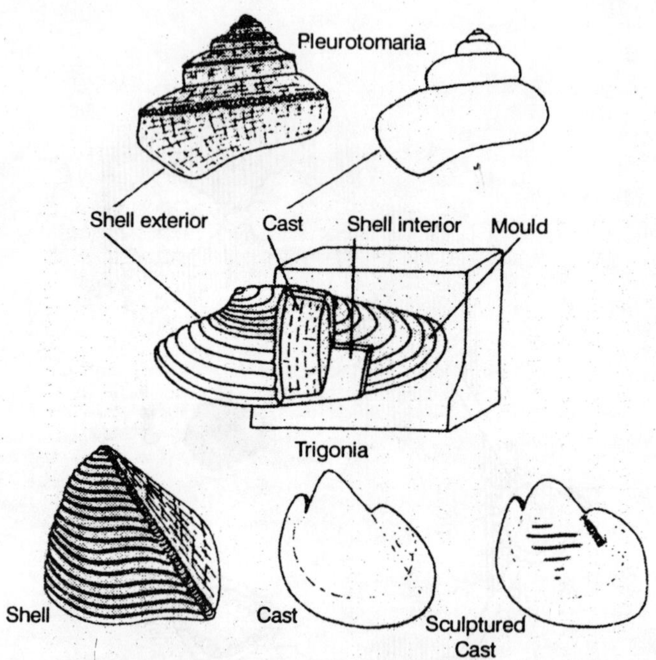

Fig. 7.19. The relationship of casts anf moulds to shell and the difference in ornament of shell and cast in thick-shelled molluscs.

In many cases, the original skeletal material undergoes chemical change (metasomatism). Silification, calcification, and pyritisation are particularly common. Silicification, which involves the removal of the original shell material and its replacement by silica, often begins at particular points then spreads outwards to produce concentric rings (beekite structure). It may occur during early or late diagenesis. Calcification affects mainly siliceous tests incorporated in alkaline, calcareous sediments, while pyritisation (involving the replacement of skeletal material by the iron sulphides pyrite and marcasite) is found particularly in fine clastic sediments deposited in reducing environments with stagnant pore water.

Diagenesis of plant matter such as lignin or cellulose can go in a number of directions but, in the absence of free oxygen, coalification involving a loss of O, N and H and a relative increase in C occurs. Methane, water, and carbon dioxide are released.

$$4C_6H_{10}O_5 \rightarrow 2\,C_9H_6O + 2\,CH_4 + 4CO_2 + 10H_2O$$

Under higher temperatures and pressures the reaction proceeds towards the production of almost pure carbon (anthracite and graphite).

Impregnation

Minerals are often precipitated in the pore spaces of skeletal material and thereby impregnate them. The minerals involved naturally depend on the chemistry of the ground water. Calcite, silica, and barytes are common.

Encrustation

Skeletal material may become surrounded by crusts, especially of calcite, produced either by algal activity or by chemical precipitation from supersaturated water (cf ooliths). Such material is sometimes incorrectly described as 'mummified'.

Internal Moulds

An internal mould (sometimes called a cast) is a replica of the inner surface of shells such as foraminifera, brachiopods, bivalves, gastropods, cephalopods, and echinoids. The material involved is usually derived from the surrounding sediment, although in the case of tightly closed shells that prevent the ingress of sediment, a crystalline fill (usually calcite) precipted from aqueous solution may be present. When the shell is only partly filled with sediment with the remainder either empty or containing crystalline precipitates the geopetal texture indicates which way up it should be like a 'fossil spirit level'. When no deposition occurs within tightly shut shells, and when the shell material itself is later dissolved after lithification, hollow moulds are produced. These may subsequently have a skin of crystals developed on their walls in the position of the original shell.

Internal moulds consisting of pyrite or marcasite often originate in anaerobic clays. They form in the same way as concretions and often infill only the most inaccessible parts of shells, for example, the innermost chambers of cephalopods or the tip of gastropod shells and so produce an illusion of stunted growth.

In thin-shelled organisms the inner and outer surfaces usually have similar shapes whereas in thick-shelled animals they are often very different. If such a shell (within which an internal mould has already formed) subsequently dissolves in still unconsolidated sediment the imprint of the external surface of the shell may by compaction become impressed on the internal cast to provide a 'sculptured cast'.

In ammonites, sediment can only enter the body chamber because the phragmocone chambers are hermetically scaled by septae. For this reason these chambers are often preserved empty or filled with later crystalline calcite. Since many other ammonite shells do, however, display internal moulds of sediment, the coarser-grained sediment must have entered through fractures in the shell, while fine-grained material appears to have passed in through the siphuncle. Where structural elements such as keels are separated from the interior of the shell by a partition (septate keels) they may remain empty when the internal mould forms to produce hollow keels that contrast with the filled keels produced where such partitions are absent.

Internal moulds are mostly formed during early diagenesis. Moulds on which epifaunas are present must have been reworked and have remained on the sea floor long enough for the epifauna to develop.

Concretions

Concretions result from the localised segregation of originally dispersed material. They may consist of calcite, siderite, silica, pyrite, marcasite, phosphate or other minerals and often contain organic remains. The concretionery mineràl frequently occupies only the pore space of the sediment (especially in calcareous concretions) or it may make room for itself by replacement (siliceous concretions) or by physical displacement of the host sediment (marcasite concretions).

Concretions may result either from the decomposition of organic matter or because of changing solubility of salts in rising ground water. Calcareous concretions form when the carbonate material present in most sediments segregates in an alkaline environment. Calcareous shells act as ideal nuclei. Siderite concretions occur where the O Eh level lies just below the sediment-water interface. Below it, iron dissolves in the pore water only to reprecipitate as it approaches the surface. Phosphatic nodules may either be pure or may grade into calcareous and ferriginous varieties. They are commonly found where phosphate-rich upwellings enter areas of slow sedimentation and are closely associated with organic remains and faecal pellets. Iron sulphides develop in acid or neutral-reducing environments by the reaction of iron and bacterially-produced H_2S. Both the stable form (pyrite) and the metastable form (marcasite) are found. Siliceous concretions (opal, flint, chert) derive their material from the dissolution of siliceous tests, or sponge spicules, present in the fine fraction of the sediment or from volcanic SiO_2. They often grow at a very early stage of diagenesis in association with organic remains. Mobilisation of silica is possible only in alkaline environments.

Early diagenetic concretions are very important in the preservation of fossils which become encased and protected before they can be destroyed. Fossils within concretions can be also undergo reworking without suffering damage.

Deformation

Deformation of fossils refers to shape changes that occur after the fossil is embedded in sediment. Such changes are caused by compaction that results from increasing overburden pressure and dewatering. If the fossil consists of articulated elements, these elements move relative to each other. On the other hand, shells, armour, or bones are rigid units that yield by fracturing. Regular radial, concentric and axial fractures appear along which relative displacements occur. Thin sections frequently reveal that shells that appear superficially to be intact are internally shattered.

Within skeletal material whose internal structure is so weakened by solution that individual crystals can move relative to each other, deformation can occur without fracturing. In this way curved shells can be squeezed flat and thick bones can be attenuated. Plastic deformation of internal moulds is a widespread phenomenon (pelomorphic deformation). The individual features of the cast are compressed vertically. The ratio V_2/V_1 (V_1 = original volume; V_2 = final volume) is known as the 'compaction ratio'. The ease with which deformation can be recognised depends on the original attitude of the mould.

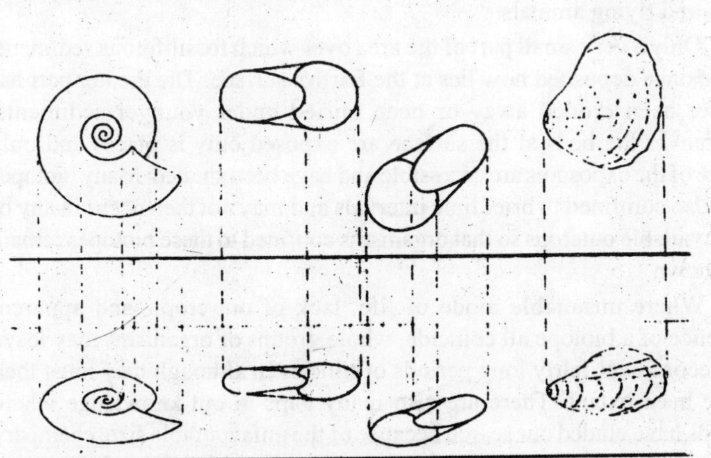

Fig. 7.20. Deformation of fossils resulting from compaction of the enclosing sediment.

Tectonic deformation also causes distortion, extension, and disruption of fossils enclosed in sediment but this is no longer to be regarded as diagenesis.

Corrosion

Corrosion involves partial solution of shells by water, acids (H_2CO_3, H_2SO_4), or alkalis (NH_4OH). It commonly occurs when buried fossils are re-exposed on the sea floor and frequently causes removal of those parts of the shell that project above the new surface. Such planar corrosion on the sea floor is called 'subsolution'.

Corrosion can also occur within the sediment when organic remains in unconsolidated sediment are attacked by rising pore water. In lithified sediments this can produce partings and stylolites. Weathering also produces corrosion mainly because of CO_2 dissolved in rainwater. The carbon dioxide released from plant roots also dissolves carbonate.

Gaps in the Record

Only a minute fraction (well under 1%) of all organisms are preserved as fossils and different groups fare quite differently. Completely soft-bodied animals and plants survive in only a few luckly cases whereas organisms with skeletal parts stand a better chance of preservation, although even then the record is very fragmentary.

Because of their mode of life, some organisms are hardly ever preserved. For example the plants and animals of the tropical rainforest decompose remarkably quickly after death as do organisms in turbulent seas and flying animals.

Only a very small part of the area over which fossiliferous sediments were once deposited now lies at the Earth's surface. The greater part has either been eroded away or been buried under younger sediments. Moreover the beds at the surface are exposed only is places and only some of the exposures are accessible and have been studied. Many biotopes are also comfined to brief time intervals and may not then occur in any of the available outcrops so that organisms confined to these biotopes remain unknown.

Where unsuitable mode of life, lack of out-crops, and apparent absence of a biotope all coincide, whole groups of organisms may leave no record over fairly long periods of time even although they must then have been extant. There are also many gaps in out knowledge where fossils have eluded our search because of the unfavourable size, chemistry or inconspicuous character. Other are so rare that only long and expensive investigations yield any material.

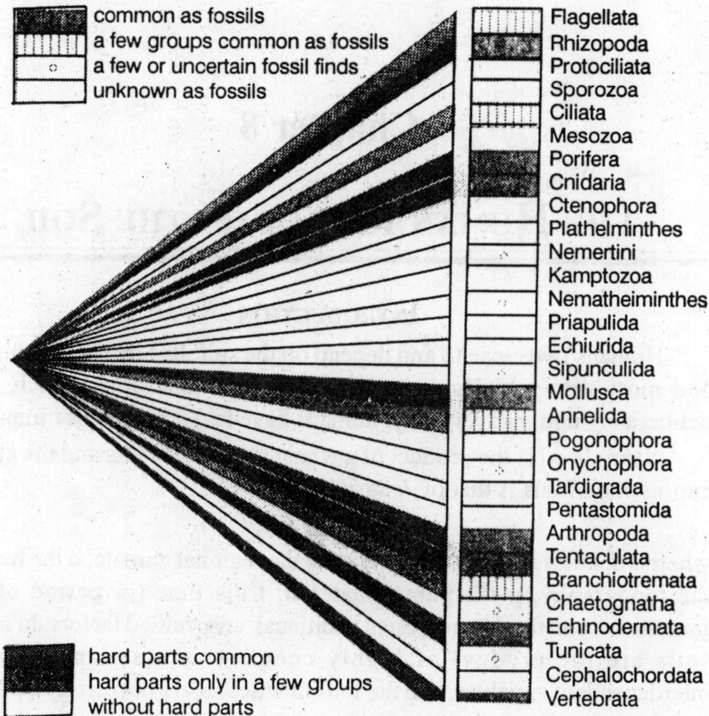

Fig. 7.21. Abundance of hard parts in different animal phyla and its influence on the fossil record because of the very limited preservation of soft-bodied organisms.

The smallness of the percentage of organisms preserved suggests that we can expect to find only the more common types as fossils. Representatives of rarer groups are found only in exceptional circumstances. Thus we observe only the peaks in the frequency curve of past life and it is astonishing how much valuable material they alone have yielded.

Chapter 8

THE HUMAN IMPACT ON THE SOIL

INTRODUCTION

Humans live close to and depend on the soil. It is one of the thinnest and most vulnerable human resources and is one upon which, both deliberately and inadvertently, humans have had a very major impact.

Natural soil is the product of a whole range of factors and the classic expression of this is that of *Jenny* (1941):

$$S = f\,(cl, o, r, p, t \ldots).$$

where s denotes any soil property, cl is the regional climate, *o* the biota, *o* the topography, p the parent material, t the time (or period of soil formation), and the dots represent additional, unspecified factors. In reality soils are the product of highly complex interactions of many interdependent variables, and the soils themselves are not merely a passive and dependent factor in the environment. None the less, following Jenny's subdivision of the classic factors of soil formation, one can see more clearly the effects humans have had on soil be it detrimental or beneficial. These can be summarized as follows (adapted from the work of *Bidwell* and *Hole*, 1965):

1. Parent Material

Beneficial: adding mineral fertilizers; accumulating shells and bones; accumulating ash locally; removing excess amounts of substances such as salts.

Detrimental: removing through harvest more plant and animal nutrients than are replaced; adding materials in amounts toxic to plants or animals; altering soil constitutents in a way to depress plant growth.

2. Topography

Beneficial: checking erosion through surface roughening, land forming and structure building; raising land level by accumulation of material; land levelling.

Detrimental: causing subsidence by drainage of wetlands and by mining; accelerating erosion; excavating.

3. Climate

Beneficial: adding water by irrigation; rainmaking by seeding clouds; removing water by drainage; diverting winds, etc.

Detrimental: subjecting soil to excessive insolation, to extended frost action, to wind, etc.

4. Organisms

Beneficial: introducing and controlling populations of plants and animals; adding organic matter including 'night-soil'; loosening soil by ploughing to admit more oxygen; fallowing; removing pathogenic organisms, e.g. by controlled burning.

Detrimental: removing plants and animals; reducing organic content of soil through burning, ploughing, over-grazing, harvesting, etc.; adding or fostering pathogenic organisms; adding radioactive substances.

5. Time

Beneficial: rejuvenating the soil by adding fresh parent material or through exposure of local parent material by soil erosion; reclaiming land from under water. Detrimental: degrading the soil by accelerated removal of nutrients from soil and vegetation cover; burying soil under solid fill or water.

Space precludes, however, that we can follow all these aspects of anthropogenic soil modification or, to use the terminology of *Yaalon* and *Yaron* (1966), of *metapedogenesis*.

We will therefore concentrate on certain highly important changes which humans have brought about, especially chemical changes (such as salinization and lateritization), various structural changes (such as compaction), some hydrological changes (including the effects of drainage and the factors leading to peat-bog development), and, perhaps most important of all, soil erosion.

Salinity: natural sources

Many semi-arid and arid areas are naturally salty. By definition they are areas of substantial water deficit where evapotranspiration exceeds precipitation. Thus, whereas in humid areas there is sufficient water to percolate through the soil and to leach soluble materials from the soil and the rocks into the rivers and hence into the sea in deserts this is not the case. Salts therefore tend to accumulate. This tendency is exacerbated by the fact that many desert areas are characterized by closed drainage basins (endoreic drainage) which act as terminal evaporative sumps for rivers.

The amount of natural salinity varies according to numerous factors, one of which is the source of salts. Some of the salts are brought in to the deserts by rivers, though it needs to be pointed out that most of these rivers do not have particularly high salt contents (generally less than 300 ppm). A second source of salts is the atmosphere - a source which in the past has often been accorded insufficient importance. Rainfall, coastal fogs and dust storms all transport significant quantities of soluble salts. This is shown by the data in table for some forested catchments in south-western Australia, where up to 130 kg ha^{-1} $year^{-1}$ of chlorides are introduced in precipitation. Further soluble salts may be derived from the weathering and solution of bedrock. In the Middle East, for example, notably in Iran, there are extensive salt domes and evaporative beds within the bedrock which create locally high ground-water and surface-water salinity levels. In other areas, such as the Rift Valley of southern Ethiopia and northern Kenya, volcanic rocks may provide a large source of sodium carbonate (trona) to ground waters, while elsewhere the rocks in which ground water occurs may contain salt because they are themselves ancient desert sediments. Even in the absence of such localized sources of highly saline ground water it needs to be remembered that over a period of time most rocks will provide soluble products to ground water, and in a closed hydrological system such salts will eventually accumulate to significant levels.

Table. 8.1. Soluble salt content of river in semi-arid areas

River	***Total dissolved solids (parts per million)***
Indus	250–300
Colorado	795
White Nile	174
Tigris-Euphrates	200–400
Niger	<60–80

A further source of salinity may be marine transgressions. At times of higher sea-levels, it has sometimes been proposed (see, for example, *Godbole*, 1972) that salts would have been laid down by the sea. Likewise in coastal areas, salts in ground-water aquifers may be contaminated by contact with sea water.

Human agency and increased salinity

It has already been stated that salinity is a normal characteristic of many desert areas. However, humans have increased the extent and degree of salinity in numerous different ways.

Table. 8.2. Irrigated area in major regions (in thousand hectares)

Region	*1961–5*	*1968*	*1978*	*% change 1968–78*
World	149 478	162 638	200 913	23.5
Africa	5 870	6 772	7 831	15.6
North and Central America	18 606	20 366	23 543	15.6
South America	4 862	5 403	6 663	23.3
Asia	100 363	108 184	130 950	21.0
Europe	8 957	10 266	13 670	33.2
Oceania	1 198	1 443	1 656	14.8
USSR	9 618	10 200	16 600	62.7

The extension of irrigation and the use of a wide range of different techniques for water abstraction and application, can lead to a build-up of salt levels in the soil through the mechanism of raising ground water so that it is near enough to the ground surface for capillary rise and subsequent evaporative concentration to take place. In the case of the semi-arid northern plains of Victoria in Australia, for instance, the water-table has been rising at around 1.5 m $year^{-1}$ so that now in many areas it is almost within 1 m of the surface. When ground water comes within 3 m of the surface in clay soils, but less for silty and sandy soils, capillary forces bring moisture to the surface where evaporation takes place (*Currey*, 1977).

Table. 8.3. Irrigation systems and methods

(a) Irrigation systems

(i) *Sources of water supply*

1. Rivers
2. Springs, artesian wells
3. Rain water
4. Ground water

(ii) *Methods of raising water*

1. Manual methods
   (a) Draw well, e.g. *shaduf* (Arabic), cigonal (Spanish)
2. Worked by animals
   (a) Inclined plane, e.g. *gird* (Arabic)
   (b) Geared wheel, e.g. *noria* (Spanish/Arabic), *nora* (Portuguese), *sakien* (Arabic)

3. Automatic devices
   (a) Impounding the flow of a river by a dam or weir
   (b) Kanat
   (c) Water wheels, e.g. *noria* (Spanish/Arabic), *naura* (Arabic)
   (d) Windmill pumps
4. Motor pumps
   (a) Diesel pumps
   (b) Electric pumps
   (c) Steam pumps

(iii) *Water storage*
1. Reservoirs
2. Ponds
3. Cisterns
4. Tanks
5. Water towers

(iv) *Water distribution* (*supply and drainage*)
1. Irrigation canals
   (a) Main canals
   (b) Secondary canals
   (c) Distributory canals
   (d) Furrows
2. Drainage canals
   (a) Main drainage
   (b) Secondary drainage
   (c) Collector drains
3. Levelling or terracing

(b) Irrigation Methods

(i) Surface irrigation
1. Dam or barrage
2. Dam/barrage and channel irrigation
3. Channel irrigation
4. Spraying

(ii) Underground irrigation

Second, many irrigation schemes require the addition of large quantities of water over the soil surface. This is especially true for rice cultivation. Such surface water is readily evaporated so that salinity levels build up.

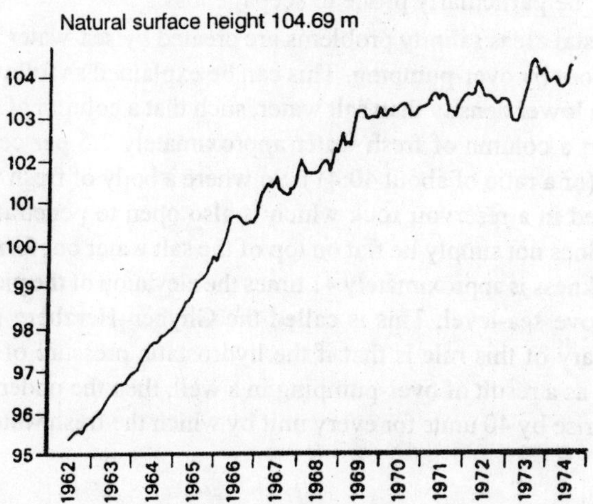

Fig. 8.1. Piezometer record to show ground-water level changes in the Murray Valley, Victoria, Australia, from 1962 to 1974 as a result of the extension of irrigation.

Third, the construction of large dams and barrages to control water flow and to give a head of water creates large reservoirs from which further evaporation can take place.

Fourth, notably in areas of soils with high permeability, water seeps laterally and downwards from irrigation canals so that further evaporation

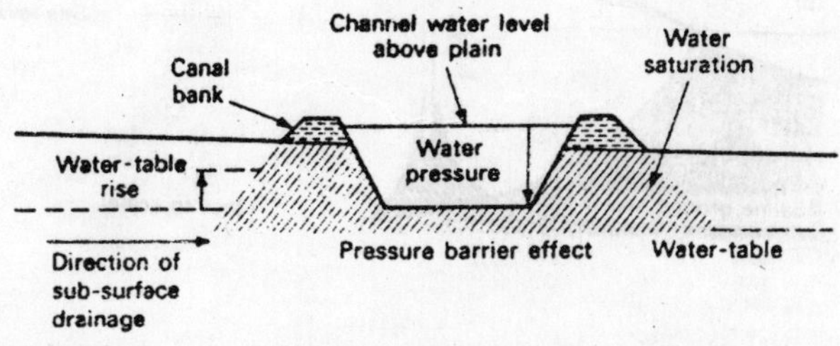

Fig. 8.2. The effect of an irrigation channel in causing a local rise in the water-table, through the development of a pressure barrier which influences the movement of sub-surface drainage.

takes place. Many distribution channels in a gravity scheme are located on the elevated areas of a flood plain or riverine plain to make maximum use of gravity. The elevated landforms selected are natural levees, river bordering dunes and terraces, all of which are composed of silt and sand which may be particularly prone to seepage loss.

In coastal areas salinity problems are created by sea-water incursion brought about by over-pumping. This can be explained as follows. Fresh water has a lower density than salt water, such that a column of sea water can support a column of fresh water approximately 2.5 per cent higher than itself (or a ratio of about 40:41). So where a body of fresh water has accumulated in a reservoir rock which is also open to penetration from the sea, it does not simply lie flat on top of the salt water but forms a lens, whose thickness is approximately 41 times the elevation of the piezometric surface above sea-level. This is called the Ghyben-Herzberg principle. The corollary of this rule is that if the hydrostatic pressure of the fresh water falls as a result of over-pumping in a well, then the underlying salt water will rise by 40 units for every unit by which the fresh water table is lowered.

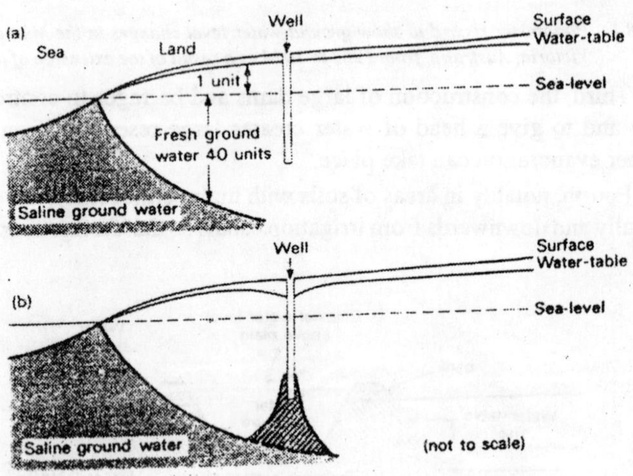

Fig. 8.3. (a) Illustrates the Ghyben-Herzberg relationship between fresh and saline ground water. (b) Illustrates the effect of excessive pumping from the well. The diagonal hatching represents the increasing incursion of saline water.

This problem presents itself on the coast of Israel, in California (*Banks* and *Richter*, 1953), on the island of Bahrain, and in some of the small coastal dune aquifers of the United Arab Emirates. A comparable situation arises in the case of the Nile Delta where, as a result of the construction of the Aswan Dam, ground-water levels have dropped downstream, leading to the intrusion of coastal salt water which has salinated the soil above, thus rendering it less suitable for cultivation. This is one of the prices which have to be paid for the undoubted gains brought by rationalizing the flow of the Nile so that little of the water is wasted by draining out to sea.

Table. 8.4. Hydrological and chemical data for south-western Australia, illustrating the effects of deforestation on ground-water recharge and river-water chemistry.

Catchment (type or name)	*Chloride input in precipitation (kgha^{-1} year^{-1})*	*Chloride loss in stream flow (kgha^{-1} year^{-1})*	*Recharge before clearing (mm/year)*	*Recharge with farming (mm/year)*
(a) Forested				
Julimar	53	78	—	—
Seldom seen	120	160	—	—
More seldom seen	120	140	—	—
Waterfall gully	110	180	—	—
North Dandalup	130	180	—	—
Davies	130	140	—	—
Yarragil	97	130	—	—
Harris	84	130	—	—
(b) Farmland				
Brockman	80	340	8	73
Wooroloo	78	420	4	61
Dale	24	460	0.8	24
Hotham	48	370	2	26
Williams	31	650	1	37
Collie East	50	740	2	60
Brunkswick	110	530	70	500

The problem of sea-water incursion as a result of over-pumping of aquifers is not, however, restricted to arid and semi-arid areas. It was noted as early as the middle of the last century in London and Liverpool, England, and there are now many records of this phenomenon in Germany, the Netherlands, Japan and the eastern seaboard of the USA (*Todd*, 1959).

Increases in soil salinity are not restricted to irrigated areas. In certain parts of the world salinization has resulted from vegetation clearance

(Peck, 1978). The removal of native forest vegetation allows a greater penetration of rainfall into deeper soil layers which causes ground water levels to rise creating seepage of sometimes saline water in low-lying areas. Through this mechanism an estimated 2×10^5 hectares of land in southern Australia, which at the start of European settlement supported good crops or pasture, is now suitable only for halophytic species. Similar problems exist also in North America, notably in Manitoba, Alberta, Montana and North Dakota.

The clearance of the native evergreen forest (predominantly *Eucalyptus* forest) in south-western Australia has led both to an increase in recharge rates of ground water, and to an increase in the salinity of the streams.

The spread of salinity

Anthropogenic increases in salinity are not new. *Jacobsen* and *Adams* (1958) have shown that they were a problem in Mesopotamian agriculture after about 2400 BC. Individual fields, which in 2400 BC Were registered as salt-free, can be seen in the records of ancient temple surveyors to have developed conditions of sporadic salinity by 2100 BC. Further evidence is provided by crop choice, for the onset of salinization strongly favours the adoption of crops which are most salt-tolerant. Counts of grain impressions in excavated pottery from sites in southern Iraq dated at about 3500 BC suggest that at that time the proportions of wheat and barley were nearly equal. A little more than 1000 years later the less salttolerant wheat accounted for less than 20 per cent of the crop, while by about 2100 BC it accounted for less than 2 per cent of the crop. By 1700 BC the cultivation of wheat had been abandoned completely in the southern part of the alluvial plain.

These changes in crop choice were accompanied by serious declines in yield which can also probably be attributed to salinity. At 2400 BC the yield was 2537 litres ha^{-1}, by 2100 BC it was 1460, and by 1700 BC it was down to 897. It seems likely that this played an important part in the break-up of Sumerian civilization.

Another area where salinization has posed a severe problem is the Indus Plain of Pakistan, where Sir John Marshall, the archaeologist, described the salt as 'a Satanic mockery of snow'. *Snelgrove* (1967) reports that of the 25 million hectares of arable land in the country, 4.6 million are now mostly waterlogged or poorly drained, 1.9 million are predominantely severely saline, 4.5 million have saline patches, and some 0.4 million are being lost yearly through the spread of these conditions. The problem has largely followed the rise of ground-water levels by 0.15-

0.60 m year^{-1} brought about by the building of major irrigation systems in areas of somewhat sandy, silty and permeable soils during the last hundred or so years.

In summary, it has been estimated that the percentage of salt- affected and waterlogged soils amounts to 50 per cent of the irrigated area in Iraq, 23 per cent of all Pakistan, 50 per cent in the Euphrates valley of Syria, 30 per cent in Egypt and over 15 per cent in Iran (Worthington, 1977: 30).

Consequences of salinity

One consequence of the evaporative concentration of salts, and the pumping of saline waters back into rivers and irrigation canals from tubewells and other sources, is that river waters leading from irrigation areas show higher levels of dissolved salts. These, particularly when they contain nitrates, can make the water undesirable for human consumption. Table illustrates the changes in total hardness levels that have been found for river waters in the USA.

Table. 8.5. Changes in water hardness brought about by irrigation

	Total hardness as mg/l of $CaCO_3$		
Location	***above irrigation area***	***below irrigation area***	***Increase***
Rio Grande, Texas	111	631	× 5.7
Yakima, Washington	33	134	× 4.1
Sunnyside, Washington	40	299	× 7.5
Arkansas River	212	890	× 4.2
Sutter Basin, California	72	480	× 6.7
		Mean	× 5.6

A further problem is that, as irrigation water is concentrated by evapotranspiration, calcium and magnesium components tend to precipitate as carbonates, leaving sodium ions dominant in the soil solution. The sodium ions tend to be absorbed by colloidal clay particles, deflocculating them and leaving the resultant structureless soil almost impermeable to water and unfavourable to root development.

The death of vegetation in areas of saline patches, due both to poor soil structure and toxicity, creates bare ground which becomes a focal point for erosion by wind and water.

Probably the most serious impact of salination is on plant growth. This takes place partly through its effect on soil structure, but more significantly through its effects on osmotic pressures and through direct toxicity.

When a water solution containing large quantities of dissolved salts comes into contact with a plant cell it causes a shrinkage of the protoplasmic lining. The phenomenon is due to the osmotic movement of the water, which passes from the cell towards the more concentrated soil solution. The cell collapses and the plant succumbs.

The toxicity effect varies with different plants and different salts. Sodium carbonate, by creating highly alkaline soil conditions, may damage plants by a direct caustic effect; while high nitrate may promote undesirable vegetative growth in grapes or sugarbeets at the expense of sugar content. Boron is injurious to many crop plants at solution concentrations of more than 1 or 2 ppm.

The expected yield reduction from salinity build-up is illustrated. The measure of soil salinity utilized is the electrical conductivity in mmho/cm of a saturated soil extract. The tolerances of different plants to salinity vary greatly, but all suffer from increased salinity.

Table. 8.6. Yield reduction for selected agricultural crops at different salinity levels, expressed by the electrical conductivity (mmho/cm) of saturated soil extacts

	% yield reduction		
Crop	***10***	***25***	***50***
Barley	11.9	15.8	17.5
Sugarbeet	10.0	13.0	16.0
Cotton	9.9	11.9	16.0
Wheat	7.1	10.0	14.0
Rice	5.1	5.9	8.0
Maize	5.1	5.9	7.0
Alfalfa	3.0	4.9	8.2

Reclamation of salt-affected lands

Because of the extent and seriousness of salinity, be the causes natural or anthropogenic, various reclamation techniques have been initiated. These can be divided into three main types: eradication, conversion and control.

Eradication predominantly involves the removal of salt either by improved drainage or by the addition of quantities of fresh water to leach the salt out of the soil. Both solutions involve considerable expense and pose severe technological problems in areas of low relief and limited fresh-water availability. Improved drainage can either be provided by open drains or by the use of tubewells (as at Mohenjo Daro, Pakistan) to reduce ground-water levels and associated salinity and waterlogging. A minor eradication measure, which may have some potential, is the biotic treatment of salinity through the harvesting of salt-accumulating plants such *as Suaeda fruticosa.*

Conversion involves the use of chemical methods to convert harmful salts into less harmful ones. For example, gypsum is frequently added to sodic soils to convert caustic alkali carbonates to soluble sodium sulphate and relatively harmless calcium carbonate:

$$Na_2CO_3 + CaSO_4 \rightleftharpoons CaCO_3 + Na_2SO_4 \downarrow \text{leachable}$$

Some of the most effective ways of reducing the salinity hazard involve miscellaneous control measures, such as less wasteful and lavish application of water through the use of sprinklers rather than traditional irrigation methods; the lining of canals to reduce seepage; the realignment of canals throught less permeable soils; and the use of more salt-tolerant plants. As salinity is a particularly serious threat at the time of germination and for seedlings, various strategies can be adopted during this critical phase of plant growth: plots can be irrigated lightly each day after seeding to prevent salt build-up; major leaching can be carried out just before planting; and areas to be seeded can be bedded in such a way that salts accumulate at the ridge tops with the seed planted on the slope between the furrow bottom and the ridge top (*Carter*, 1975).

Lateritization

In some parts of the tropics there are extensive sheets of a material called laterite, an iron and/or aluminium-rich duricrust (see *Maignien*, 1966 or *Macfarlane*, 1976). These iron-rich sheets result naturally, either because of a preferential removal of silica during the course of extensive weathering (leading to a *relative* accumulation of sesquioxides of iron and aluminium), or because of an *absolute* accumulation of these compounds.

One of the properties of laterites is that they harden on exposure to air and through desiccation. Once hardened they are not favourable to plant growth. One particular way in which exposure may take place is by accelerated erosion, while forest removal may so cause a change in microclimate that desiccation of the laterite surface can take place. Indeed, one of the main problems with the removal of humid tropical rain forest is that lateritization may occur. This tends to limit the extent of successful soil utilization and severely retards the re-establishment of forest. Although *Vine* (1968: 90) and *Sanchez* and *Buol* (1975) have warned against exaggerating this difficulty in agricultural land use, there are records from many parts of the tropics of accelerated induration brought about by forest removal (*Goudie*, 1973). In the Cameroons, for example, around 2 m of complete induration can take place in less than a century. In India, foresters have for a long time been worried by the role that plantations of teak (*Tectona grandis*) can play in lateritization. Teak is deciduous, demands light, likes to be well spaced (to avoid crown friction), dislikes competition from undergrowth, and is shallow-rooted. These characteristics mean that teak plantations tend to expose the soil surface to erosive and desiccative forces more than does the native vegetation cover.

One of the main exponents of the role that human agency has played in lateritization in the tropical world has been Courou (1961: 21-2). Although he may be guilty of exaggerating the extent and significance of laterite, Gourou gives many examples from low latitudes of falling agricultural productivity resulting from the onset of lateritization. It is worth quoting him at length:

On the whole, laterite is hostile to agriculture owing to its sterility and compactness. All tropical countries have not reached the same degree of lateritic 'suicide' but when the evolution has advanced a considerable way, man is placed in very strange conditions ... Laterite is a pedological leprosy. Man's activities aggravate the dangers of laterite and increase the rate of the process of lateritization. To begin with, erosion when started by negligent removal of the forest simply wears away the friable and relatively fertile soil which would otherwise cover the laterite and support forest or crops ... The forest checks the formation of the laterite in various ways. The trees supply plenty of organic matter and maintain a good proportion of humus in the soil. The action of capillary attraction is checked by the loosening of the soil; and the bases are retained through the absorbent capacity of humus. The forest slows down evaporation from the soil ... it reduces percolation and consequently leaching. Lastly the forest may improve the composition of the soil by fixing atmospheric dust.

Accelerated podzolization and acidification

There is an increasing amount of evidence that the introduction of agriculture, deforestation and pastoralism to parts of upland Western Europe promoted sonic major changes in soil character: notably an increase in the development of acidic and podzolized conditions, associated with the development of peat bogs. Climatic changes of the type envisaged by Blytt and Sernander and later workers (see Goudie, 1972a: 94) may have played a role, as could progressive leaching of Devensian (last Glacial) drifts during the passage of the Holocene. But the association in time and space of human activities with soil deterioration is becoming increasingly clear (*Evans* et al., 1975).

Replacing the natural forest vegetation with cultivation and pasture, human societies set in train various related processes, especially on base-poor materials. First, the destruction of deep-rooting trees curtailed the enrichment of the surface of the soil by bases brought up from the deeper layers. Second, the use of fire to effect forest clearance may have released nutrients in the form of readily soluble salts, some of which were inevitably lost in drainage, especially in soils poor in colloids (*Dimbleby*, 1974). Third, the taking of crops and animal products depleted the soil reserves to an extent probably greater than that arising from any of the manuring practices of prehistoric settlements. Fourth, as the soil degraded, the vegetation which invaded ~ especially bracken and heather - itself tended to produce a more acidic humus type of soil than the original mixed deciduous forest, and so continued the process.

Various workers now attribute much of the podzolization in upland Britain to such processes, and Dimbleby has concluded that ,although a few soils have been podzols since the Atlantic period, the majority are secondary, having arisen as a result of man's assault on the landscape, particularly in the Bronze Age' (see also *Bridges*, 1978).

The development of podzols, by impeding downward percolating waters, may have accelerated the formation of peats, which tend to develop where there is waterlogging through impeded drainage. Many peat bogs in highland Britain appear to coincide broadly in age with the first major land-clearance episodes (*P. D. Moore*, 1973; *Merryfield* and *P. D. Moore*, 1974). Another fact which would have contributed to their development is that when a forest canopy is removed (as by deforestation) the transpiration demand of the vegetation is reduced, less rainfall is intercepted, so that the supply of ground water is increased, aggravating any waterlogging.

However, the role of natural processes must not be totally forgotten, and Ball's assessment would seem judicious (1975: 26):

It seems to be on balance that the highland trends in soil formation due to climate, geology and relief have been clearly running in the direction of leaching, acidity, podzolization, gleying and peat formation. For the British highlands generally, man has only intervened to hasten or slow the rate of these trends, rather than being in a position to alter the whole trend from one pedogenetic trend to another.

Moreover, it would be plainly misleading to stress only the deleterious effects of human actions on European soils. Traditional agricultural systems have often employed laborious techniques to augment soil fertility and to reduce such properties as undesirable acidity. In Britain, for example, the addition of chalk to light sandy land goes back at least to Roman times and the marl pits from which the chalk was dug are a striking feature of the Norfolk landscape, where *Prince* (1962) has identified at least 27000 hollows. Similarly, in the Netherlands, Germany and Belgium there are soils which for centuries (certainly more than a thousand years) have been built up (often over 50 cm) and fertilized with a mixture of manure, sods, litter or sand. Such soils are called Plaggen soils (*Pope*, 1970). Plaggen soils also occur in Ireland, where the addition of sea-sand to peat was carried out in pre-Christian times. Likewise, prior to European settlement in New Zealand, the Maor- is used thousands of tons of gravel and sand, carried in flax baskets, to improve soil structure (*Cumberland*, 1961).

Another type of soil which owes much to human influence is the category called 'paddy soil'. Long-continued irrigation, levelling and manuring of terraced land in China and elsewhere has changed the nature of the pre-existing soils in the area. Among the most important modifications that have been recognized (*Gong*, 1983) are an increase in organic matter, an increase in base saturation, and the translocation and reduction of iron and manganese.

Soil structure alteration

One of the most important features of a soil, both in terms of its suitability for plant growth and its inherent erodibility, is its structure. There are many ways in which humans can alter this, especially by compacting it with agricultural machinery, by the use of recreation vehicles and by changing its chemical character through irrigation. Soil compaction tends to increase the resistance of soil to penetration by roots and emerging seedlings, and limits oxygen and carbon dioxide exchange between the root zone and the atmosphere. Moreover, it reduces the rate of water infiltration into the soil, which may change the soil moisture status and accelerate surface runoff and soil erosion (*Chancellor*, 1977). For example, the effects of the passage of vehicles on some soil structural properties are shown in table. Most notable of all is the reduction that is caused in soil infiltration capacity, which may explain why vehicle movements can often lead to gully development. Whether one is dealing with primitive sledges (as in Swaziland), or with the latest recreational toys of leisured Californian adolescents, the effects may be comparable. Grazing is another activity that can damage soil structure through trampling and compaction. Heavily grazed lands tend to have considerably lower infiltration capacities than those found in ungrazed lands. This is indicated for some American examples in table. The removal of vegetation cover and associated litter also changes infiltration capacity, since cover protects the soil from packing by raindrops and provides organic matter for binding soil particles together in open aggregates. Soil fauna that live on the organic matter assist this process by churning together the organic material and mineral particles. *Dunne* and *Leopold* have ranked the relative influence of different land-use types on infiltration as follows (1978, table after US Soil Conservation Service):

Table. 8.7. Rates of infiltration on grazed and ungrazed lands in America

	Rate of infiltration (mm/h)	
Site	***Ungrazed***	***Heavily grazed***
Montana	2.5-66.0	5.1-15.2
Oklahoma	134.6-309.9	40.6-83.8
Colorado	40.6-83.8	20.3-30.5
Montana	109.2-185.4	20.3-%.5
Wyorning	30.5-38.1	17.8-30.5
Louisiana	45.7	17.8
Kansas	33.0	20.3
Arizona	40.6	30.5

Source: processed by author from data in Gifford and Hawkins, 1978

Highest infiltration	Woods, good
↓	Meadows
	Woods, fair
	Pasture, good
	Woods, poor
	Pasture, fair
	Small grains, good rotation
	Small grains, poor rotation
	Legumes after row crops
	Pasture, poor
	Row crops, good rotation (more than one quarter in hay or sod)
	Row crops, poor rotation (one quarter or less in hay or sod)
Lowest infiltration	Fallow

In general experiments show that reafforestation improves soil structure, especially the pore volume of the soils (see, for example, *Challinor*, 1968). Ploughing is also known to produce a compacted layer at the base of the zone of ploughing (*Baver et al.*, 1972). This layer has been termed the 'plough sole'. The normal action of the plough is to leave behind a loose surface layer and a dense subsoil where the soil aggregates have been pressed together by the sole of the plough. The compacting action can be especially injurious when the depth of ploughing is both constant and long-term, and when heavy machinery is used on wet ground (*Greenland*, 1977).

On the other hand for many centuries farmers have achieved improvements in soil structure by deliberate practices, particularly with a view to developing the all-important crumb structure. In pre-Roman times people in Britain and France added lime to heavy clay soils, while the agricultural improvers of the eighteenth and nineteenth centuries improved the structure of sandy heath soils by adding clay, and clay soils by adding calcium carbonate (marl). They also compacted such soils and added binding organic matter by breeding sheep and feeding them with turnips and other fodder plants (*Russell*, 1961).

In the modern era attempts have been made to reduce soil crusting by applying municipal and animal wastes to farm land, by adding chemicals such as phosphoric acid, and by adopting a cultivation system of the no-tillage type. The last practice is based on the idea that the use of herbicides has eliminated much of the need for tillage and cultivation in row crops; seeds are planted directly into the soil without ploughing, and weeds are controlled by the herbicides. With this method less bare soil is exposed and heavy farm machinery is less likely to create soil compaction problems (see *Carlson*, 1978, for some of these methods).

Soil structures may also be modified to increase water runoff, particularly in arid zones where the runoff obtained can augment the meagre water supply for crops, livestock, industrial and urban reservoirs, and ground-water recharge projects. In the Negev farming was practised in this way, especially in the Nabatean and the Romano-Byzantine periods (about 300 BC to AD 630), and attempts were made to induce runoff by clearing the surface gravel of the soil and heaping it into thousands of mounds. This exposed the finer silty soil beneath, facilitating soil crust formation by raindrop impact, decreasing infiltration capacity and reducing surface roughness, so that runoff increased (*Evenari et al.*, 1971). Today a greater range of techniques are available for the same end: soils can be smoothed and compacted by heavy machinery, soil crusting can he promoted by dispersion of soil colloids with sodium salts, the permeability of the soil surface can be reduced by applying water-repellent materials, and soil pores can be filled with binders (*Hillel*, 1971).

Soil drainage and its impact

Soil drainage 'has been a gradual process and the environmental changes to which it has led have, by reason of that gradualness, often passed unnoticed' (*Green*, 1978: 171). To he sure, the most spectacular feats of drainage - arterial drainage - involving the construction of veritable

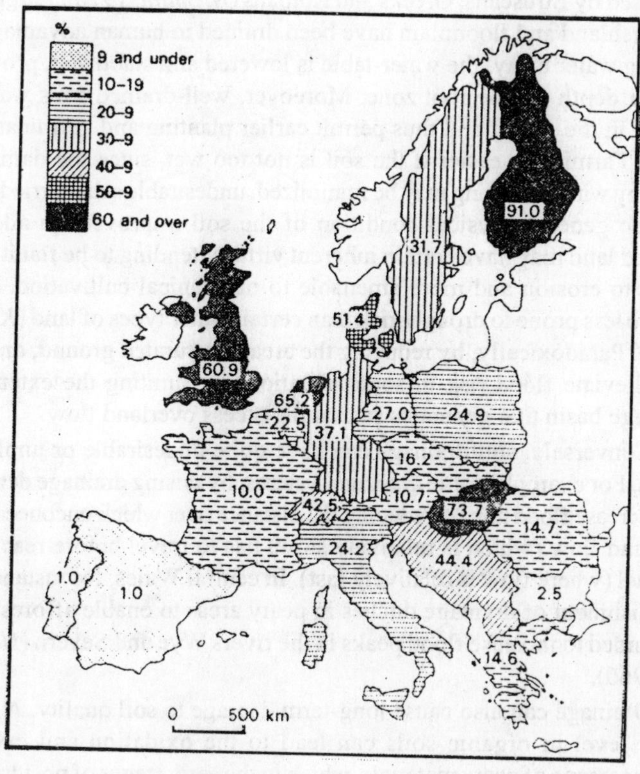

Fig. 8.4. Percentage of drained agricultural land in Europe. There are no data for the blank areas.

rivers and large dike systems, as seen in the Netherlands and the Fenlands of eastern England, have received attention. However, more widespread than arterial drainage, and sometimes independent of it, is the drainage of individual fields, either by surface ditching or by underdrainage with tile pipes and the like. *Green* (1978) has attempted to map the areas of drained agricultural land. In Finland, Denmark, Great Britain, the Netherlands and Hungary, the majority of agricultural land is drained. The drainage conditions of the soil have also frequently been altered by the development of ridge and furrow patterns created by ploughing (plate 4.2). Such patterns are a characteristic feature of many of the heavy soils of lowland England.

Soil drainage has been one of the most successful ways in which communities have striven to increase agricultural productivity; it was practised by Etruscans, Greeks and Romans (*N. Smith*, 1976). Large areas of marshland and floodplain have been drained to human advantage. By leading water away, the water-table is lowered and stabilized, providing greater depth for the root zone. Moreover, well-drained soils warm up earlier in the spring and thus permit earlier planting and germination of crops. Farming is easier if the soil is not too wet, since the damage to crops by winter freezing may be minimized, undesirable salts carried away, and the general physical condition of the soil improved. In addition, drained land may have certain inherent virtues: tending to be flat it is less prone to erosion and more amenable to mechanical cultivation. It will also be less prone to drought risk than certain other types of land (*Karnes*, 1971). Paradoxically, by reducing the area of saturated ground, drainage can alleviate flood risk in some situations by limiting the extent of a drainage basin that generates saturation excess overland flow.

Conversely, soil drainage can have quite undesirable or unplanned effecs. For example, some drainage systems, by raising drainage densities, can increase flood risk by reducing the distance over which unconcentrated overland flow (which is relatively slow) has to travel before reaching a channel (where flow is relatively fast). In central Wales, for instance, the establishment of drainage ditches in peaty areas to enable afforestation, has tended to increase flood peaks in the rivers Wye and Severn (*Howe et al.*, 1966).

Drainage can also cause long-term damage to soil quality. A fall in water level in organic soils can lead to the oxidation and eventual disappearance of peaty materials, which in the early stages of postdrainage use may be highly productive. This has occurred in the English Fenland, and in the Everglades of Florida, where drainage of peat soils has led to a subsidence in the soil of 32 mm per year (*Stephens*, 1956).

The soil climate of neighbouring areas may also be modified when the water-tables of drained land are lowered. This has been known to create problems for forestry in areas of marginal water availability.

Soil moisture content can also determine the degree to which soils are subjected to expansion and contraction effects, which in turn may affect engineering structures in areas with expansive soils (*Holtz*, 1983). Soils containing sodium montmorillonite type clays, when drained or planted with large trees, may dry out and cause foundation problems (*Driscoll*, 1983).

Some of the most contentious effects of drainage are those associated with the reduction of wetland wildlife habitats. In Britain this has become an important political issue, especially in the context of the Somerset Levels and the Halvergate Marshes.

Soil fertilization

The chemistry of soils has been changed deliberately by the introduction of chemical fertilizers. Sometimes these create environmental problems such as water pollution, while their substitution for more traditional fertilizers may accelerate soil structure deterioration and soil erosion. On the other hand, the use of synthetic fertilizers has greatly increased agricultural productivity in many parts of the world, and remarkable increases in yields have been achieved.

Table. 8.8. Quantities of fertilizers used by farmers in the UK expressed thousands of tons of plant food

Date	*Nitrogen (N)*	*Phosphoric acid (P_2O_5)*	*Potash (K_2O)*
1900	16	110	7
1913	29	180	23
1929	48	198	52
1939	60	170	75
1946	165	358	120
1956	291	386	305

The employment of chemical fertilizers on a large scale is little more than 150 years old. In the early nineteenth century nitrates were first imported from Chile, and sulphate of ammonia was produced only after the 1820s as a by-product of coal gas manufacture. In 1843 the first fertilizer factory was established at Deptford Creek (London), but for a long time superphosphates were the only manufactured fertilizers in use. In the twentieth century synthetic fertilizers, particularly nitrates, were developed, notably by Scandinavian countries which used their vast resources of water power. Potassic fertilizers came into use much later than the phosphatic and nitrogenous; nineteenth-century farmers hardly knew them (*Russell*, 1961). The rapid development in the use of the three main fertilizers - nitrates, phosphates and potash - in the first half of the twentieth century is shown in table.

Fires and soil

The importance and antiquity of fire as an agency through which the environment is transformed requires that some attention be given to the effects of fire on soil characteristics and on soil erosion.

Fire has often been used intentionally to change soil properties, and both the release of nutrients by fire and the value of ash have long been recognized, notably by those involved in shifting agriculture based on slash-and-burn techniques. Following cultivation, the loss of nutrients by leaching and erosion is very rapid (*Nye* and *Greenland*, 1964), and this is why after only a few years the shifting cultivators have to move on to new plots. Fire rapidly alters the amount, form and distribution of plant nutrients in ecosystems, and, compared to normal biological decay of plant remains, burning rapidly releases some nutrients into a plant-available form. Indeed, the amounts of P, Mg, K and Ca released by burning forest and scrub vegetation are high in relation to both the total and available quantities of these elements in soils (*Raison*, 1979). In forests, burning often causes the pH of the soil to rise by three units or more, creating alkaline conditions where primarily there was acidity. Burning also leads to some direct nutrient loss by volatilization and convective transfer of ash, or by loss of ash to water erosion or wind deflation. The removal of the forest causes soil temperatures to increase because of the absence of shade, so that humus is often lost at a faster rate than it is formed (*Grigg*, 1970).

Loss of soil humus, whether it be a result of fire, drainage, deforestation or ploughing, is an especially serious manifestation of human alteration of soil. As table indicates, humus has many beneficial effects on both the chemical and the physical properties of soil. Its removal by human activity can be a potent contributory cause of soil erosion.

Soil erosion: general considerations

In the late 1930s, towards the end of the so-called Dust Bowl years, *Sauer* conducted a campaign against what he called the 'destructive exploitation in modern colonial expansion' (*Sauer*, 1938. 497), and placed soil erosion squarely into the context of geography:

We may well consider whether the theme of soil erosion should not be moved up to the first category of problems before the geographers of the world. It is very important for the future of mankind. It has critical significance for certain chapters of historical geography. The physical processes involved are poorly observed and generalized and their study will undoubtedly shake somewhat the rather lethargic present position of geomorphology ... best of all the subject is suited to a 'hologeographie' approach in which the development of surface conditions of specific localization is examined as an interaction of identified physical and economic (i.e. Wirtschaft) processes.

That soil erosion is a major and serious aspect of the human role in environmental change is not to be doubted. There is a long history of weighty books and papers on the subject (see, for example, *Marsh*, 1864; *H. H. Bennett*, 1938; *Jacks* and *Whyte*, 1939; *Morgan*, 1979). Although many techniques have been developed to reduce the intensity of the problem (see *Hudson*, 1971) it appears to remain intractable. As *L. J. Carter* (1977: 409) has reported of the USA:

> Although nearly $15 billion has been spent on soil conservation since the mid-1930s, the erosion of croplands by wind and water ... remains one of the biggest, most pervasive environmental problems the nation faces. The problem's surprising persistence apparently can be attributed at least in part to the fact that, in the calculation of many farmers, the hope of maximizing short-term crop yields and profits has taken precedence over the longer term advantages of conserving the soil. For even where the loss of topsoil has begun to reduce the land's natural fertility and productivity, the effect is often masked by the positive response to heavy application of fertilizer and pesticides, which keep crop yields relatively high.

Although construction, urbanization, war, mining and other such activities are often significant in accelerating the problem, the prime causes of soil erosion are deforestation and agriculture. *Pimentel* (1976) has estimated that in the USA soil erosion on agricultural land operates at a rate of about 30t ha^{-1} $year^{-1}$, which is approximately eight times quicker than topsoil is formed. He calculates that water run off delivers around 4 billion tonnes of soil each year to the rivers of the forty-eight contiguous states, and that three-quarters of this comes from agricultural land. He estimates that another billion tonnes of soil is eroded by the wind, a process which created the Dust Bowl of the 1930s.

One serious consequence of accelerated erosion is the sedimentation that takes place in reservoirs, shortening their lives and reducing their capacity. Many small reservoirs, especially in semiarid areas, appear to have an expected life of only 30 years or even less. Soil erosion also has serious implications for soil productivity. A reduction in soil thickness reduces available water capacity and the depth through which root development can occur. The water-holding properties of the soil may be lessened as a result of the preferential removal of organic material and fine sediment. Hardpans and duricrusts may become exposed at the surface, and provide a barrier to root penetration. Furthermore, splash erosion may cause soil compaction and crusting, both of which may be unfavourable to germination and seedling establishment. Erosion also removes nutrients preferentially from the soil. Some damage may be caused by associated excessive sedimentation, while wind erosion may lead to the direct sandblasting of crops. Finally, extreme erosion may lead to wholesale removal of both seeds and fertilizer. *Stocking* (1984) provides a useful review of these problems.

Soil erosion associated with deforestation and agriculture

Forests protect the underlying soil from the direct effects of rainfall, runoff is generally reduced, tree roots bind the soil, and the litter layer protects the ground from rain-splash. It is therefore to be expected that with the removal of forest, for agriculture or for other reasons, rates of soil loss will rise and mass movements will increase in magnitude and frequency. The rates of erosion that result will be particularly high if the ground is left bare; under crops the increase will be less marked. Furthermore, the method of ploughing, the time of planting, the nature of the crop, and the size of fields, will all have an influence on the severity of erosion.

It is seldom that we have reliable records of rates of erosion over a sufficiently long time-span to show just how much human activities have accelerated these effects. Recently, however, techniques have been developed which enable rates of erosion on slopes to be gauged over a lengthy time-span by means of dendrochronological techniques that date the time of root exposure for suitable species of tree. In Colorado, USA, *Carrara* and *Carroll* (1979) found that rates over the last 100 years have been about 1.8 mm/year, whereas in the previous 300 years rates were between around 0.2 and 0.5 mm/year, indicating an acceleration of about sixfold. This great jump has been attributed to the introduction of large numbers of cattle to the area about a century ago.

This is based on data from tropical Africa, shows the comparative rates of erosion for three main types of land use: trees, crops and barren soil. It is very evident from these data that under crops, but more especially when ground is left bare, or under fallow, soil erosion rates are greatly magnified. At the same time, and causally related, the percentage of rainfall that becomes runoff is increased.

In some cases the erosion produced by forest removal will be in the form of widespread surface stripping. In other cases the erosion will occur as more spectacular forms of mass movement, such as mudflows, landslides and debris avalanches. Some detailed data on debris-avalanche production in North-American catchments as a result of deforestation and forest road construction are presented. They illustrate the substantial effects created by clear- cutting and by the construction of logging roads. It is indeed probable that a large proportion of the erosion associated with forestry operations is caused by road construction, and care needs to be exercised to minimize these effects. The digging of drainage ditches in upland pastures and peat moors to permit tree-planting in central Wales has also been found to cause accelerated erosion (*Clarke* and *McCulloch*, 1979), while the elevated sediment loads can cause reservoir pollution (Burt et al., 1983).

In general, the greater the deforested proportion of a river basin the higher the sediment yield per unit area will be. In the USA the rate of sediment yield appears to double for every 20 per cent loss in forest cover.

Soil erosion resulting from deforestation and agricultural practice is often thought to be especially serious in tropical areas or semi-arid areas (see *T. R. Moore*, 1979, for a good case study). However, recent measurements by *Morgan* (1977) on sandy soils in the English East Midlands near Bedford indicate that rates of soil loss under bare soil on steep slopes can reach 17.69t ha^{-1} $year^{-1}$, compared with 2.39 under grass and nothing under woodland. Water is not the only acitve process creating accelerated erosion in eastern England, though it is important (*Evans* and *Northcliff*, 1978). Ever since the 1920s dust storms have been recorded in the Fenlands, the Brecklands, East Yorkshire (*Radley* and Sims, 1967) and in Lincolnshire and they seem to be occurring with increasing frequency. The storms result from changing agricultural practices, including the substitution of artificial fertilizers for farmyard manure, a reduction in the process of 'claying' whereby clay was added to the peat to stabilize it, the removal of hedgerows to facilitate the use of bigger farm machinery, and, perhaps most importantly, the increased cultivation of sugar beet. This crop requires a fine tilth and tends to leave the soil relatively bare in early summer compared with other crops (*Pollard* and *Miller*, 1968).

Table 8.9. Annual rates of soil loss (tonnes per hectare) under different land-use types in eastern England

Plot	*Splash*	*Overland flow*	*Rill*	*Total*
1 *Bare soil*				
Top slope	0.33	6.67	0.10	7.10
Mid-slope	0.82	16.48	0.39	17.69
Lower slope	0.62	14.34	0.06	15.02
2 *Bare soil*				
Top slope	0.60	1.11	—	1.71
Mid-slope	0.43	7.78	—	8.21
Lower slope	0.37	3.01	—	3.38
3 *Gass*				
Top slope	0.09	0.09	—	0.18
Mid slope	0.09	0.57	—	0.68
Lower slope	0.12	0.05	—	0.17
4 *Woodland*				
Top slope	—	—	—	0.00
Mid-slope	—	—	—	0.012
Lower slope	—	0.012	—	0.008

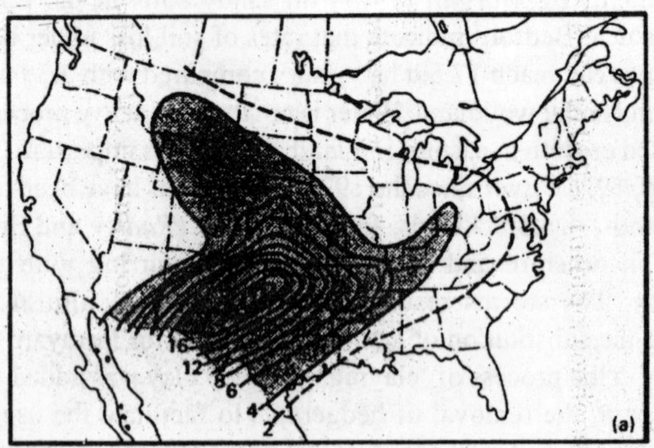

Fig. 8.5. The concentration of dust stroms (number of days per month) in the USA in 1936, illustrating the extreme localization over the High Plains of Texas, Colorado, Oklaboma and Kansas : (a) March.

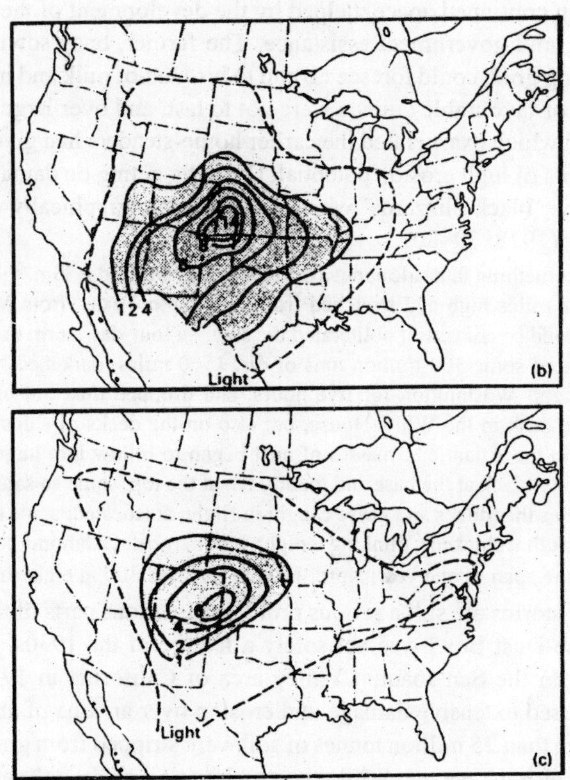

Fig. 8.5. The concentration of dust stroms (number of days per month) in the USA in 1936, illustrating the extreme localization over the High Plains of Texas, Colorado, Oklaboma and Kansas : (b) April, (c) May.

Nevertheless, possibly the most famous case of soil erosion by deflation was the Dust Bowl of the 1930s in the USA. In part this was caused by a series of hot, dry years which depleted the vegetation cover and made the soils dry enough to be susceptible to wind erosion. The effects of this drought were gravely exacerbated by years of over-grazing and unsatisfactory farming techniques. However, perhaps the prime cause of the event was the rapid expansion of wheat cultivation in the Great

Plains. The number of cultivated hectares doubled during the First World War as tractors (for the first time) rolled out on to the plains by the thousands. In Kansas alone wheat hectarage increased from under 2 million hectares in 1910 to almost 5 million in 1919. After the war wheat cultivation continued apace, helped by the development of the combine harvester, and government assistance. The farmer, busy sowing wheat and reaping gold, could foresee no end to his land of milk and honey, but the years of favourable climate were not to last, and over large areas the tough sod which exasperated the earlier home-steaders had given way to friable soils of high erosion potential. Drought, acting on damaged soils, created the 'black blizzards' which have been so graphically described by *Coffey* (1978: 79~80):

> there was something fantastic about a dust cloud that covered 1.35m. square miles, stood three miles high and stretched from Canada to Texas, from Montana to Ohio - a cloud so colossal it obliterated the sky ... a four-day storm in May 1934 ... transported some 300 million tons of dirt 1500 miles, darkened New York, Baltimore and Washington for five hours, and dropped dust not only on the President's desk in the White House, but also on the decks of ships some 300 miles out in the Atlantic ... masses of dust began to billow into huge tumbling clouds ebony black at the base and muddy tan at the top, some so saturated with dust particles that ducks and geese caught in flight, suffocated; some turning the sky so black that chickens, thinking it night, would roost. Oklahoma counted 102 storms in the span of one year; North Dakota reported 300 in eight months ...

Dust storms are still a serious problem in various parts of the United States: the Dust Bowl was not solely a feature of the 1930s. Thus, for example, in the San Joaquin Valley area of California in 1977 a dust storm caused extensive damage and erosion over an area of about 2000 km^2. More than 25 million tonnes of soil were stripped from grazing land within a 24-hour period. While the combination of drought and a very high wind (as much as 300 km per hour) provided the predisposing natural conditions for the stripping to occur, over-grazing and the general lack of windbreaks in the agricultural land played a more significant role. In addition, broad areas of land had recently been stripped of vegetation, levelled or ploughed up prior to planting. Other quantitatively less important factors included stripping of vegetation for urban expansion, extensive denudation of land in the vicinity of oilfields, and local denudation of land by vehicular recreation (*Wilshire et al.*, 1981). One interesting observation made in the months after the dust storm was that in subsequent rain storms runoff occurred at an accelerated rate from those areas that had been stripped by the wind, exacerbating problems of flooding and initiating numerous gullies. Elsewhere in California dust yield has been considerably increased by mining operations in dry lake beds (*Wilshire*, 1980).

A comparable acceleration of dust storm activity has occurred in the Soviet Union. After the 'Virgin Lands' programme of agricultural expansion in the 1950s, dust storm frequencies in the southern Omsk region increased on average by a factor of 2.5 and locally by factors of 5 to 6. Data on trends elsewhere are evaluated by *Goudie* (1983b: 520).

Soil erosion produced by fire

Many fires are started by humans, either deliberately or nondeliberately and because fires remove vegetation and expose the ground they tend to increase rates of soil erosion.

The burning of forests, for example, can, especially in the first years after the fire event, lead to high rates of soil loss. Burnt forests often have rates a whole order of magnitude higher than those of protected areas. Comparably large changes in soil erosion rates have been observed to result from the burning of heather in the Yorkshire moors in northern England, and the effects of burning may be felt for the six years or more that may be required to regenerate the heather (*Calluna*). In the Australian Alps fire in experimental catchments has been found to lead to a greatly increased flow in the streams together with a marked surge in the delivery of suspended load. Combining the two effects of increased flow rate and sediment yield, it was found that after fire the total sediment load was increased 1000 times (*Pereira*, 1973). Likewise, watershed experiments in the chaparral scrub of Arizona, involving denudation by a destructive fire, indicated that whereas erosion losses prior to the fire were only 43 t km^{-2} $year^{-1}$ after the fire they were between 50 000 and 150 000 t km^{-2} $year^{-1}$. The causes of the marked erosion associated with chaparral burning are particularly interesting. There is normally a distinctive 'non-wettable' layer in the soils supporting chaparral. This layer, composed of soil particles coated by hydrophobic substances leached from the shrubs or their litter, is normally associated with the upper part of the soil profile (*Mooney* and *Parsons*, 1973), and builds up through time in the unburned chaparral. The high temperatures which accompany chaparral fires cause these hydrophobic substances to be distilled so that they condense on lower soil layers. This process results in a shallow layer of wettable soil overlying a non-wettable layer. Such a condition, especially on steep slopes, can result in severe surface erosion.

Table 8.10. Soil losses fom burned and protected woodlands in the USA.

Location	*Forest cover*	*Years of record*	*Annual rainfall (mm)*	*Soil loss (ta ha–1 year–1)*
Holly Sping (Missoui)	Burned	2	1595	0.825
	Protected	2	1677	0.262
Guthie (Oklahoma)	Burned	10	765	0.28
	Protected	10	765	0.025
Statesulleo (North Carolina)	Burned	9	1162	7.7
	Protected	9	1162	0.05
Tyler (Texas)	Burned	9	1022	0.9
	Protected	9	1022	0.125
East Texas	Burned	1.5	–	0.512
	Protected	1.5	–	0.25
North Missourri (A)	Burned	Year 1	1627	1.27
		Year 2	1010	0.5
		Year 3	1262	0.125
North Missouri (B)	Protected	Year 1	1627	0.512
		Year 2	1010	0.255
		Year 3	1262	0.075

Table 4.11. Soil erosion associated with *Calluna* (heather) burning on the North Yorkshire moors

Condition of Calluna or ground surface	*Mean rate of litter accumulation (+) or erosion (–) (mm/year)*	*No of observation*
(a) Calluna 30–40 cm high. Complete canopy	+3.81	60
(b) Calluna 20–30 cm high. Complete canopy	+0.25	20
(c) Calluna 15–20 cm high. 40–100% cover	–0.74	20
(d) Calluna 5–15 cm high. 10–100% cover	–6.4	20
(e) Bare ground. Surface of burnt Calluna	–9.5	19
(f) Bare ground. Surface of peaty or mineral subsoil	–45.3	25

Soil erosion associated with construction and urbanization

There are now a number of studies which illustrate clearly that urbanization can create significant changes in erosion rates.

Table 8.12. Rates of erosion associated with construction and urbanization.

Location	*Land use*	*Source*	*Rate (t km^{-2} year^{-1})*
1 Maryland	Forest	Wolman (1967)	39
	Agriculture		116 – 309
	Construction		38 610
	Urban		19 – 39
2 Virginia, USA	Forest	Vice et. al. (1969)	9
	Grassland		94
	Cultivation		1 876
	Construction		18 764
3 Detroit, USA	General non-urban	Thompson	642
	Construction		17 000
	Urban		741
4 Maryland, USA	Rural	Fox (1976)	22
	Construction		37
	Urban		337
5 Maryland, USA	Forest and grasland	Yorke and Herb (1978	7 – 45
	Cuitivated land		150 – 960
	Construction		1 600 – 22 400
	Urban		830
6 Wisconsin, USA	Agricultural	Deniel et. al (1979)	<1
Construction			19.2
7 Tama New Town, Japan	Construction	Kadomura (1983)	c.400 00
8 Okinawa, Japan	Construction	Kadomura (1983)	25 000 125 000

The highest rates of erosion are produced in the construction phase, when there is a large amount of exposed ground and much disturbance produced by vehicle movements and excavations. *M. G. Wolman* and *Schick* (1967) and *M. G. Wolman* (1967) have shown that the equivalent of many decades of natural or even agricultural erosion may take place during a single year in areas cleared for construction. In Maryland they found that sediment yields during construction reached 55 000 t km $^{-2}$ year^{-1}, while in the same area rates under forest were around 80-200 t km^{-}

^{2} year $^{-1}$, and those under farming 400 t km $^{-2}$ year $^{-1}$. New road cuttings in Georgia were found to have sediment yields up to 20 000-50 000 t km $^{-2}$ year^{-1}. Likewise, in Devon, England, *Walling* and *Gregory* (1970) found that suspended sediment concentrations in streams draining construction areas were 2 to 10 times (occasionally up to 100 times) higher than those in undisturbed areas. In Virginia, USA, *Vice* et al., (1969) noted equally high rates of erosion during construction and reported that they were 10 times those from agricultural land, 200 times those from grassland and 2000 times those from forest in the same area.

However construction does not go on for ever, and once the disturbance ceases, roads are surfaced, and gardens and lawns are cultivated. The rates of erosion fall dramatically and may be of the same order as those under natural or pre-agricultural conditions. Moreover, even during the construction phase several techniques can be used to reduce sediment removal, including the excavation of settling ponds, the seeding and mulching of bare surfaces, and the erection of rock dams and straw bales (*Reed*, 1980).

Attempts at soil conservation

Because of the adverse effects of accelerated erosion a whole array of techniques has now been widely adopted to conserve soil resources, though some of the techniques such as hill slope terracing may he of some antiquity:

1. Revegetation
   (a) Deliberate planting
   (b) Suppression of fire, grazing, etc., to allow regeneration
2. Measures to stop stream bank erosion
3. Measures to stop gully enlargement
   (a) Planting of trailing plants, etc.
   (b) Weirs, dams, gabions, etc.
4. Crop management
   (a) Maintaining cover at critical times of year
   (b) Rotation
   (c) Cover crops
5. Slope runoff control
   (a) Terracing
   (b) Deep tillage and application of humus
   (c) Transverse hillside ditches to interrupt runoff

(d) Contour ploughing
(c) Preservation of vegetation strips (to limit field width)

6. Prevention of erosion from point sources like roads, feedlots
   (a) Intelligent geomorphic location
   (b) Channelling of drainage water to non-susceptible areas
   (c) Covering of banks, cuttings, etc., with vegetation
7. Suppression of wind erosion
   (a) Soil moisture preservation
   (b) Increase in surface roughness through ploughing up clods or by planting windbreaks

There are some parts of the world where terraces are one of the most prominent components of the landscape (plate 4.6). This applies to many wine-growing areas, to some and zone regions (such as Yemen and Peru), and to a wide selection of localities in the more humid tropics (Luzon, Java, Sumatra, Assam, Ceylon, Uganda, Cameroons, etc.). In areas subject to wind erosion other strategies may be necessary. Since soil only blows when it is dry, anything which conserves soil moisture is beneficial. Another approach to wind erosion is to slow down the wind by physical barriers, either in the form of an increased roughness of the soil surface brought about by careful ploughing, or by planted vegetative barriers, such as windbreaks and shelter-belts.

Some attempts at soil conservation have been particularly successful. For example, in Wisconsin, a study by *Trimble* and *Lund* (1982) showed that in the Coon Creek Basin, erosion rates declined fourfold between the 1930s and the 1970s. One of the main reasons for this was the progressive adoption of contour-strip ploughing.

Attempts at soil conservation have not always been without their drawbacks. For example, the establishment of ground cover in dry areas to limit erosion may so reduce soil moisture because of accelerated evapotranspiration that the growth of the main crop is adversely affected. On a wider scale major afforestation schemes can cause substantial runoff depletion in river catchments. Likewise, the provision of mulching is sometimes detrimental: in cool climates, reduced soil temperature shortens the growing season, whilst in wet areas, higher soil moisture may induce gleying and anaerobic conditions (*Morgan*, 1979: 60). Some terrace schemes have also had their shortcomings. They have been known to hold back so much water on hillsides that the soils have become saturated and landsliding has been induced. Similarly strip cropping, because it involves the farming of small areas, is incompatible with highly

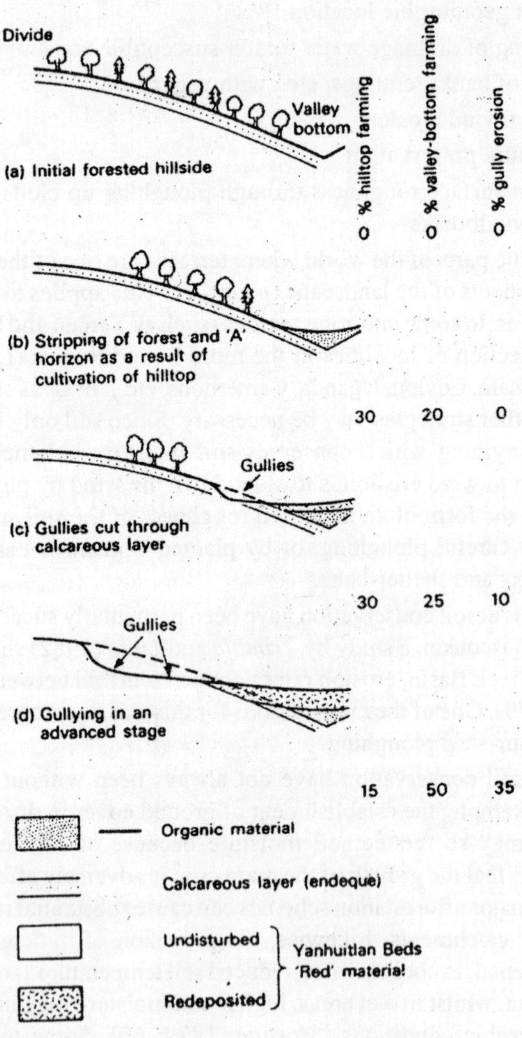

Fig. 8.6. Beneficial effect of gullying on production of agricultural land in Nochixtlan, Mexico.

mechanized agricultural systems, and insect infestation and weed control are additional problems which it has posed.

Soil conservation measures may not always be appropriate, for soil erosin can be a useful phenomenon. *Sanchez* and Buol (1975), for instance, have pointed out that in recent volcanic areas soil erosion has enabled removal of the more weathered base-depleted material from the soil surface, exposing the more fertile, less weathered, base-rich material beneath. Likewise, in the Nochixtlan area of southern Mexico, soil erosion has been utilized by local farmers to *produce agricultural* land. Severe gullies have cut in to steep valley-side slopes and since the Spanish Conquest an average depth of 5 m has been stripped from the entire surface area. The local Mixtec farmers, far from seeing this high rate of erosion as a hazard to be feared, have directed the flow of the eroded material to feed their fields with fertile soil and to extend their land. Over the past 1000 years the Mixtec cultivators have managed to use gully erosion to double the width of the main valley floors from 1.5 to 3 km and to infill the narrow tributary valley floors with flights of terraces. Judicious use of the phenomenon of gully erosion has enabled them to convert poor hilltop fields into the rich alluvial farmland below.

None the less it is undoubtedly true that manipulation of the soil is one of the most significant ways in which humans change the environment, and one in which they have had some of the most detrimental effects. Soil deterioration has led to many cases of what *W. C. Lowdermilk* once termed 'regional suicide', and the overall situation is at least as bleak as it was in the post-Dust Bowl years when jacks commented:

> The organization of civilized societies is founded upon the measures taken to wrest control of the soil from wild Nature, and not until complete control has passed into human hands can a stable super-structure of what we call civilization be erected on the land. (*Jacks* and *Whyte*, 1939: 17)

Chapter 9

The Human Impact on Climate and the Atmosphere

World climates

The climate of the world is now known to have fluctuated frequently and extensively in the three or so million years during which humans have inhabited the earth (*Goudie*, 1983a). The bulk of these changes have nothing to do with human intervention. Climate has changed, and is currently changing, because of a wide range of different natural factors which operate over a variety of time scales.

None the less, with the increasing human population and the rising level of technology, it is now apparent that over the last century human agency has probably become a significant factor in the variations in world climate which are taking place, but it remains extremely difficult to ascertain whether human influence or natural forces are responsible for observed trends. If human activity can be considered a factor then this is particularly because of inadvertent effects on atmospheric quality and on the albedo of land masses. Human influence on global climate can be summarized as follows:

Possible Mechanisms

CO_2 emission — industrial / agricultural

Chlorofluoromethane

Water vapour

Methane

Ozone

Krypton 85

Nitrous oxide

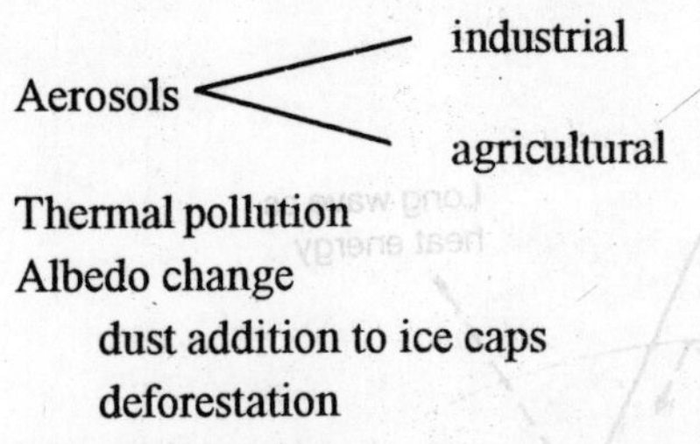

Thermal pollution

Albedo change

- dust addition to ice caps
- deforestation
- over-grazing

Alteration of ocean currents by constriction of straits, etc.

Diversion of fresh waters into oceans, changing the salinity, and, therefore, the freezing point of the sea water.

The CO_2 problem

Since the beginning of the Industrial Revolution humans have been taking stored carbon out of the earth in the form of coal, petroleum and natural gas, and burning it to make carbon dioxide (CO_2), heat water vapour and smaller amounts of sulphur dioxide (SO_2) and other gases.

The preindustrial level of carbon dioxide is a matter of some debate, but may have been as low as 260-70 ppm by volume (*Wigley*, 1983). The present level is over 330 ppmv, and the upward trend is evident in records from various parts of the world. Forecasts suggest that the level by 2065 will be about 600 ppm (Carbon Dioxide Assessment Committee, 1983). If fossil-fuel consumption continues at present rates, a concentration of up to 2000 ppm of CO_2 might be reached in two or three centuries from now. However, predictions are not without their problems, depending as they do on two major imponderables: the future rate of fossil-fuel consumption, and the way in which carbon dioxide may be absorbed by the oceans.

The prime cause of the release of CO_2 into the atmosphere is probably the burning of fossil fuels. Fossil-fuel burning throughout the world in 1981 released about 5.3 gigatons of carbon to the atmosphere as CO_2. The cumulative emissions from the mid-nineteenth century to 1981 totalled about 160 gigatons of carbon as CO_2. Fossil-fuel use for much of the post-war period averaged an increase of around 4.5 per cent per year, but because of the changing nature of energy provision resulting from the massive increases in the cost of oil, and other factors such as the adoption of nuclear power, it is now widely believed that energy consumption using fossil fuels will rise relatively more slowly in the near future, probably averaging about 2.5 per cent per year.

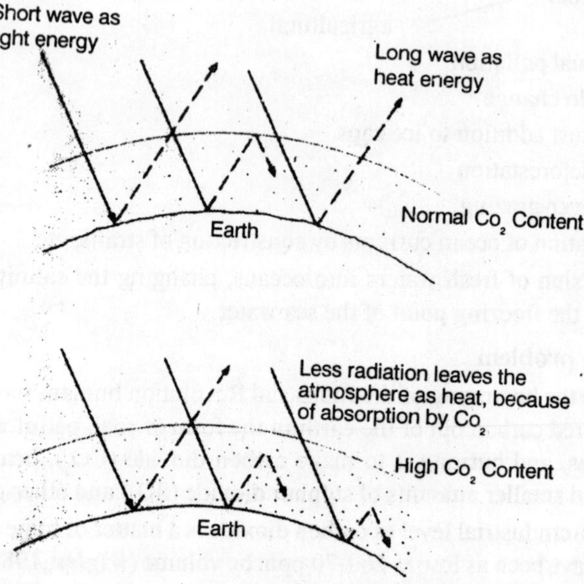

Fig. 9.1. The greenhouse effect: shortwave radiation strikes the earth's surface and is transformed into long-wave radiation(heat). Since CO_2 absorbs long-wave radiation, the greater the atmospheric CO_2 content the more heat is retained and the warmer the atmosphere becomes.

Another factor that may contribute substantially to CO_2 levels in the atmosphere is the burning of forests and changes in the organic levels in soils that are subjected to deforestation and cultivation (Wilson, 1978; Wong, 1978). *Woodwell* (1978) estimated that this source may be currently more important than the burning of fossil fuels, with deforestation releasing about 6 gigatons of carbon as CO_2 per year, and the decay of soil humus about 2 gigatons of carbon as carbon dioxide per year. However, there is considerable uncertainty about existing rates of deforestation, the proportion of deforestation that is caused by burning, the amount of carbon that may be kept stored up as charcoal, and the rate at which regrowth of vegetation consumes carbon. Consequently, the rates initially proposed by *Woodwell* have now been reassessed, and a current consensus value for the amount of carbon dioxide released by land- use changes is of the order of 2 gigatons per annum (*Clark*, 1982). Attempts have also been made to assess longer term release of carbon dioxide into the atmosphere by undertaking studies either of historical changes in land use, or by analysing $^{13}C/^{12}C$ ratios in tree rings. Both methods have given broadly similar results and indicate that since the middle of the last century human activities have released on average between 0.7 and 1.7 gigatons per year. From 1860 to the present, cumulative releases from changes in land use have been approximately equal to cumulative releases from the burning of fossil fuels.

The CO_2 levels in the atmosphere have an effect on the global heat balance, since CO_2 is virtually transparent to incoming solar radiation but absorbs outgoing terrestrial infra-red radiation; radiation that would otherwise escape to space and result in loss of heat from the lower atmosphere. This is called 'the greenhouse effect'. Consequently one would expect increased CO_2 levels to lead to an increase in surface temperatures. The degree of resultant change is the subject of debate, but it is thought that by AD 2050 when CO_2 levels have increased by 100 per cent over natural levels, mean surface temperatures might increase by between 1.5 and 3°C, with rather larger values being attained in high latitudes (*Hansen et al.*, 1981). In polar regions the temperature change may be more than three times the average: up to 10°C above present levels by 2050. Although the general consensus is that warming will occur, there are several investigators who doubt some of the premises upon which the climatic models are based (for example, *Idso*, 1982) and maintain that CO_2 increases could cause only slight increases or even negative changes in temperature.

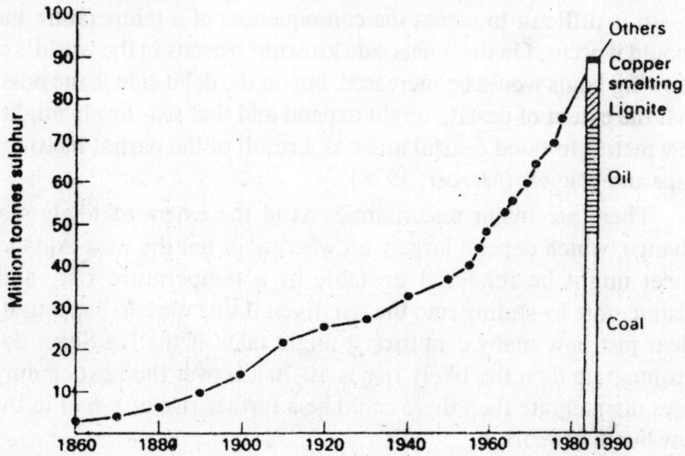

Fig. 9.2. Global SO_2 emissions from anthropogenic sources including the burning of coal, lignite and oil, and copper smelting.

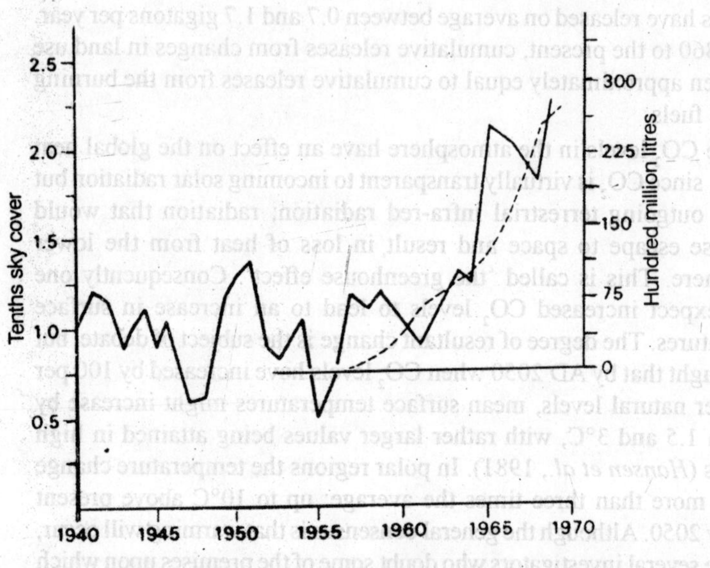

Fig. 9.3. The history of the annual high cloudiness at Denver, Colorado. The dashed line shows the growth in jet-fuel consumption by domestic commercial jet aircraft.

It is difficult to assess the consequences of a temperature increase should it occur. On the bonus side growing seasons in the world's cereal-growing lands would be increased, but on the debit side is the possibility that the extent of deserts might expand and that sea- levels might rise a few metres to flood coastal areas as a result of the partial melting of ice caps and glaciers (*Mercer*, 1978).

There are major uncertainties as to the extent of likely sea-level change, which depend largely on whether or not the west-Antarctic ice sheet might be rendered unstable by a temperature rise, and thus disintegrate by sliding into the sea. Even if this were to happen, it is not clear just how many centuries it might take. If the Ice Sheet does not disintegrate then the likely rise is 40-70 cm over the next century. If it does disintegrate then there could be a further rise of 5-6 m in the next few hundred years.

A carbon-dioxide increase could well have a profound effect on crop productivity and water-use efficiency. *Idso* (1983) has calculated that a

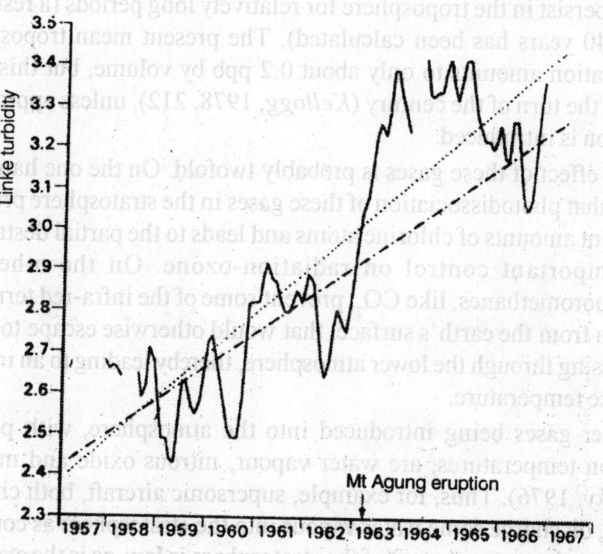

Fig. 9.4. Increasing turbidity at Mauna Loa Observatory.

doubling of the atmospheric CO_2 content could increase global vegetation productivity by 33 per cent, and a tripling by 66 per cent. Furthermore, because of its effect on stomatal closure in plants, he has estimated that a doubling of the CO_2 concentration could reduce vegetation transpiration by 34 per cent.

Woodwell (1978: 43) has stated: 'Carbon dioxide, until now an apparently innocuous trace gas in the atmosphere, may be moving rapidly toward a central role as a major threat to the present world order.' If temperatures do indeed rise by 1.5 to 3°C then we shall have conditions similar to those that existed during the warmest phases of the Holocene (the hypsithermal), and to those of the warmest portions of earlier Pleistocene inter-glacials.

Other gases

In addition to CO_2, other gases influence climate, and their rate of emission as a result of human activity is increasing, as illustrated for SO_2.

A recent contaminant of the atmosphere is a group of gases called chlorofluoromethanes (or freons), which are used both as refrigerants and as household aerosol propellants. These gases are extremely stable and can persist in the troposphere for relatively long periods (a residence time of 40 years has been calculated). The present mean tropospheric concentration amounts to only about 0.2 ppb by volume, but this could treble by the turn of the century (*Kellogg*, 1978. 212), unless appropriate legislation is introduced.

The effect of these gases is probably twofold. On the one hand, it is thought that photodissociation of these gases in the stratosphere produces significant amounts of chlorine atoms and leads to the partial destruction of an important control on radiation-ozone. On the other, the chlorofluoromethanes, like CO_2, prevent some of the infra-red terrestrial radiation from the earth's surface, that would otherwise escape to space, from passing through the lower atmosphere, thereby leading to an increase in surface temperature.

Other gases being introduced into the atmosphere, with possible effects on temperatures, are water vapour, nitrous oxide and methane (*Panofsky*, 1976). Thus, for example, supersonic aircraft, both civil and military, discharge some water vapour into the stratosphere as contrails. At present, the water content of the stratosphere is low, as is the exchange of air between the lower stratosphere and other regions. Consequently, comparatively modest amounts of water vapour discharged by aircraft could have a significant effect on the natural balance. It has been calculated that 400 supersonic aircraft, making four flights per day, would place 150 million kg of water into the lower stratosphere. This could, over a period of years, double the existing water content of the atmosphere, thereby leading to a small rise in temperature, perhaps 0.6°C (*Sawyer*, 1971).

However, statistics on the increase of cirrus levels as a result of stratospheric aircraft movements are still meagre (SCEP Report, in *Matthews et al.*, 1971: 39) and their statistical significance is not always proven. Yet studies at Salt Lake City and Denver between 1949 and 1969 do show an upward trend in cirrus cloudiness which paralleled the increase in jet aircraft activity. The expected rapid development of civil aviation in future decades may make this an important element of anthropogenic atmospheric modification. Nitrous oxide (which may, for example, be derived from supersonic aircraft and from the breakdown of nitrate fertilizers - *Hutchinson* and *Mosier*, 1979), ammonia and a number of other trace constituents which humans are adding to the earth's atmosphere, have infra-red absorption bands in the spectral region 7-14 gm and contribute to the atmospheric greenhouse effect (*Wang et al.*, 1976).

Methane, often called natural gas, is also increasing in the atmosphere. It is in part a normal constituent, arising from many biological processes and seepage out of the earth. Possible causes noted for the increase are a growth in the number of flatulent, ruminant farm animals, the presence of expanding numbers of termites as a result of vegetation changes in low latitudes, and an expansion in the area of rice cultivation. Like CO_2 its presence could lead to atmospheric warming.

Warnings have been circulated (*Boeck et al.*, 1975) about the possible role of a substance emitted from nuclear reactors, called Krypton 85. It is believed that its increasing presence will reduce the electrical resistance of the atmosphere between the oceans and the ionosphere. This in turn would affect the electrification of thunder- clouds and, through that, precipitation levels.

Aerosols

One consequence of the Industrial Revolution, which may be of equal significance to CO_2 emission, is the increased quantity of dust or smoke particles that are emitted into the lower atmosphere. A striking illustration of this is provided by the analysis of dust levels in glacier ice of known age in the southern USSR. Layers of ice dated AD 1800-1920 show a dust content of 10 mg/l, whereas by the 1950s, the figure had increased twenty times to 200 mg/l (*Davitaya*, 1969).

The average turbidity factor for the atmosphere (*Linke turbidity*) has increased by 30 per cent in a decade (the dot-and-dash line). It also shows the effect of a natural source of turbidity, the Mount Agung (Bali) eruption of 1963 (the single, continuous line). In the figure the dotted line represents the linear trend for the same period if the effects of the eruption are excluded from the computations.

However, not all investigations have demonstrated increases in atmospheric aerosol loadings on the regional or global scale. For example, studies by *Hoyt* and *Frohlich* (1983) at Davos in Switzerland, have provided no evidence for long-term changes in atmospheric transmission caused by this mechanism. They believe that trends in aerosol loadings from anthropogenic sources are local rather than regional. They suggest that changes in atmospheric transmission occur in urban and industrial areas, but believe that such changes are too localized to be the cause of hemispheric and global trends in temperature.

If an increase in atmospheric aerosols on the macro scale were to be proven, then they could be said to influence temperatures through their impact on the scattering and absorption of solar radiation. The exact effects, however, are still not clear, for whether added aerosols cause heating or cooling of the earth and atmosphere systems is a function not only of their intrinsic absorption and backscatter characteristics, but also of their location in the atmosphere with respect to such variables as cloud-over, cloud reflectivity and underlying surface reflectivity (*Weare et al*., 1974). So, for example, over ice caps 'grey' aerosol particles would warm the atmosphere because they would he less reflective than the white snow surfaces beneath, while over a dark reflecting surface they would reflect a greater amount of radiation, leading to cooling (*Peck*, 1975). Thus precise quantitative assessment of the effects of increased aerosol content in the atmosphere is hazardous, but *Rasool* and *Schneider* (1971) have suggested that a rise by a factor of four or five in global aerosol concentrations could be sufficient to lower temperatures by as much as 4.5°C.

Table 9.1. Estimated mass of global emissions of atmosphere particulate material, 1968 (million tonnes)

Source	*Diameter> 5μm*	*All sizes*
Sea salt	500	1000
Converted natural sulphate	335	420
Natural windblown dust	250	500
Converted manufactured sulphate	200	220
Converted natural hydrocarbons	75	75
Converted natural nitrates	60	60
Converted manufactured nitrates	35	40
Manufactured particles	30	135
Volcanoes	25	?
Converted manufactured hydrocarbons	15	15
Forest fires	5	35
Meteoric debris	0	10
Total	1530	2525+

Similarly, *Idso* and *Brazel* (1978) and *Brazel* and *Idso* (1979) point to the two contrasting tendencies of dust: the backscattering effect producing cooling, and the thermal blanketing effect causing warming. The second of these absorbs some of the earth's thermal radiation that would otherwise escape to space, and then reradiates a portion of this back to the land surface, raising surface temperatures. They believe that natural dust from volcanic emissions tends to enter the stratosphere (where backscattering and cooling are the prime consequences), while anthropogenic dust more frequently occurs in the lower levels of the atmosphere causing thermal blanketing and warming.

Industrialization is not, however, the sole source of particles in the atmosphere, nor is a change in temperature the only possible consequence. *Bryson* and *Barreis* (1967), for example, argue that intensive agricultural exploitation of desert margins, such as in Rajasthan, India, would create a dust pall in the atmosphere by exposing larger areas of surface materials to deflation in dust storms. This dust pall, they believe, would so change atmospheric temperature that convection, and thus rainfall, would be reduced. Observations on dust levels over the Atlantic during the drought years of the late 1960s and early 1970s in the Sahel suggest that the degraded surfaces of that time led to a great (threefold) increase in atmospheric dust (*Prospero* and *Nees*, 1977). There is thus the possibility that human-induced desertization generates dust which could in turn increase the degree of desertization by its effect on rainfall levels.

Any assessment of the likely consequences of human production of aerosols must bear in mind that natural production of aerosol materials is of a very much higher order. This is clear which shows the estimated mass of global emissions of atmospheric particulate material for 1968. None the less the data suggest that on a global scale human activity is now producing 280 million tonnes per year of small particulate matter into the atmosphere, compared to a natural rate of 1250 million tonnes per year, or a ratio of about 4.5:1.

The most catastrophic effects of anthropogenic aerosols in the atmosphere could be those resulting from a nuclear exchange between the great powers. Explosion, fire and wind might generate a great pall of smoke and dust in the atmosphere which would make the world dark and cold. It has been estimated that if the exchange reached a level of several thousand megatons, a 'nuclear winter' would occur in which temperatures over much of the world would be as low as -15° to -25°C (*Turco et al.*, 1983).

Thermal pollution

One consequence of the burning of fossil fuels is the production of heat. This is probably most important on the local scale where it can be identified as the 'urban heat island'. On a broader scale the amount of energy used by humans has been negligible, compared both to the resources of solar energy and to the energy of photosynthesis by plants. In global terms the total amount of heat released by all human activity is roughly 0.01 per cent of the solar energy absorbed at the surface (*Kellogg*, 1978: 215). Such a small fraction would have a negligible effect on the overall heat balance of the earth.

Vegetation and albedo

Incoming radiation of all wavelengths is partly absorbed and partly reflected. Albedo is the term used to describe the proportion of energy reflected and hence is a measure of the ability of the surface to reflect radiation.

Land-use changes create differences in albedo which have important effects on the energy balance, and hence on the water balance, of an area. Tall rain forest may have an albedo as low as 9 per cent, while the albedo of a desert may be as high as 37 per cent.

Table 9.2. Albedo values for different land-use types

Surface type	*Location*	*Albedo (%)*
Tall rain forest	Kenya	9
Lake	Israel	11.3
Peat and moss	England and Wales	12
Pine forest	Isreal	12.3
Heather moorland	England and Wales	15
Evergreen scrub (maquis)	Israel	15.9
Bamboo forest	Kenya	16
Conifer palantation	England and Wales	16
Citrus orchard	Israel	16.8
Towns	England and Wales	17
Open oak forest	Israel	17.6
Deciduous woodland	England and Wales	18
Tea bushes	Kenya	20
Rough grass hillside	Israel	20.3
Agricultural grassland	England and Wales	24
Desert	Israel	37.3

There has been growing interest recently in the possible consequences of deforestation on climate through the effect of albedo change. Ground deprived of a vegetation cover as a result of deforestation and over-grazing (as in parts of the Sahel) has a very much higher albedo than ground covered in plants. This could affect temperature levels. Satellite imagery of the Sinai-Negev region of the Middle East shows an enormous difference in image between the relatively dark Negev and the very bright Sinai-Gaza Strip area. This line coincides with the 1948-9 armistice line between Israel and Egypt and results from different land-use and population pressures. *Otterman* (1974) has suggested that the albedo affected by land use has produced temperature changes of the order of 5°C.

Charney and others (1975) have argued that the increase in surface albedo, resulting from a decrease in plant cover, would lead to a decrease in the net incoming radiation, and an increase in the radiative cooling of the air. Consequently, they argue, the air would sink to maintain thermal equilibrium by adiabatic compression, and cumulus convection and its associated rainfall would he suppressed. A positive feedback mechanism would appear at this stage, for the lower rainfall would in turn adversely affect plants and lead to a further decrease in plant cover. However, this view is disputed by *Ripley* (1976) who suggests that *Charney* and his colleagues, while considering the impact of vegetative changes on albedo, have completely ignored the effect of vegetation on evapotranspiration. He points out that vegetated surfaces are usually cooler than bare ground since much of the absorbed solar energy is used to evaporate water, and concludes from this that protection from overgrazing and deforestation might, in contrast to Charney's views, be expected to lower surface temperatures and thereby reduce, rather than increase, convection and precipitation.

Removal of humid tropical rain forests, which is proceeding at a fast rate has also been seen as a possible mechanism of anthropogenic climatic change through its effect on albedo. *Potter et al.* (1975) have proposed the following model for such change:

Deforestation

↓

Increaseci surface albedo

↓

Reduced surface absorption of solar energy

↓

Surface cooling

↓

Reduced evaporation and sensible heat flux from the surface

↓

Reduced convective activity and rainfall

↓

Reduced release of latent heat, weakened Hadley circulation and cooling in the mid and upper troposphere

↓

Increased tropical lapse rates

↓

Increased precipitation in the latitude bands 5-25°N and 5-25°S, and a decrease in the equator -pole temperature gradient

↓

Reduced meridional transport of heat and moisture out of equatorial regions

↓

Global cooling and a decrease in precipitation between 45-85°N and 40-60°S

However, more recent studies (*Potter et al.*, 1981) suggest that globally over the past few thousand years the climatic effects of albedo changes wrought by humans have been small and probably undetectable. Similarly, *Henderson-Sellers* and *Gornitz* (1984) have sought to model the possible future effects of albedo changes produced by humans and also predict that there will be but little alteration brought about by current levels of tropical deforestation.

Budyko (1974) believes that the present extension of irrigation to about 0.4 per cent of the earth's surface (1.3 per cent of the land surface) would decrease their albedo, possibly on average by 10 per cent. The corresponding change of the albedo of the entire earth-atmosphere system would amount to about 0.03 per cent; enough, according to Budyko, to maintain the global mean temperature at a level nearly 0.1°C higher than it would otherwise be.

Forests and rain

The belief that forests can increase precipitation levels has a long history (*Thornthwaite*, 1956), and it has been the basis of action programmes in many lands. For example, the American Timber Culture Act of 1873 was passed in the belief that if settlers were induced to plant trees on the Great Plains and prairies, precipitation would be increased sufficiently to eliminate the climatic hazards to agriculture. On the other hand, at much the same time, the view was expressed that 'rain follows the plough'. Aughey, working in Nebraska, for example, believed that, after the soil is 'broken', rain as it falls is absorbed by the soil 'like a huge sponge', and that the soil gives this absorbed moisture slowly back to the atmosphere by evaporation (cited by *Thornthwaite*, 1956: 569), and so increases the rainfall.

These two early and contradictory views illustrate the confusion that still surrounds this question today. Forests undoubtedly influence rates of evapotranspiration, the flow of streams, the level of ground water and microclimates, but there is little reliable evidence to suggest that regional rainfall is either significantly increased by afforestation or decreased by deforestation. Certainly schemes to augment rainfall levels on desert margins by widespread planting of forest belts are likely to achieve relatively little, for the aridity of deserts and their margins is controlled dominantly by the gross features of the general circulation, especially the subsiding air associated with the big high-pressure cells of the sub-tropics.

Although forests may not necessarily have a proven effect on regional or continental rainfall levels, they are far more effective than other vegetation types at trapping other kinds of precipitation, especially cloud, fog and moist. Hence deforestation or afforestation can affect water budgets through the degree to which they intercept non-rainfall precipitation. For example, in Hawaii, Norfolk Island Pines (*Araucaria heterophylla*), in an area where the annual rainfall is 2600 mm, condensed an additional 760 mm from heavy cloud. In the San Francisco area, *Parsons* (1960) recorded about 250 mm of drip from a pine tree on the Berkeley Hills during each of four rainless summers. In Japan this phenomenon has been used to good effect: trees are planted along the coast to intercept the inland drift of sea fogs.

There is one other land-use change that may result in measurable changes in precipitation; namely large-scale crop irrigation in semiarid regions. The High Plains of the USA are normally covered with sparse grasses and have dry soils throughout the summer; evapotranspiration is then very low. In the last three decades irrigation has been developed throughout large parts of the area, greatly increasing summer evapotranspiration levels. *Strahler* and *Strahler* (1973: 147) report that increases in July rainfall amounting to 20-50 per cent have been recorded over the main irrigated areas, compared with the average for the previous 60-70 year period. If irrigation is indeed responsible for rising precipitation levels the mechanism remains uncertain. One possibility is that the added water vapour resulting from the increased evapotranspiration heightens instability of the lower air layer and acts as a triggering device to set off more frequent and more intense convection in the air mass above.

The possible effects of water diversion schemes

The levels of the Aral and Caspian Seas in Soviet Central Asia are falling, as are water-tables all over the wide continental region. There are proposals to divert some major rivers to help overcome these problems.

However, this raises difficult questions 'because it appears to touch a peculiarly sensitive spot in the existing climatic regime of the northern hemisphere' (*Lamb*, 1977: 671). The low-salinity water which forms a 100-200 m upper layer to the Arctic Ocean is in part caused by the input of fresh water from the large Russian and Siberian rivers. This low-salinity water is the medium in which the pack ice at present covering the polar ocean is formed. The tapping of any large proportion of this river flow might augment the area of salt water in the Arctic Ocean and thereby reduce the area of pack ice correspondingly. Temperatures over large areas might rise, which in turn might change the position and alignment of the main thermal gradients in the northern hemisphere and, with them, the jet-stream and the development and steering of cyclonic activity. However, assessment of this particular climatic impact is still very largely speculative, and some recent numerical models indicate that the climate of the Arctic will not be drastically affected by Soviet river diversions (*Semtner*, 1984).

Lakes

It has often been implied that the presence of a large body of inland water must modify the climate around its shores, and therefore that artificial lakes have a significant effect on local or regional climates. Climatic changes produced by the construction of a reservoir are the result of a variety of factors (*Vendrov*, 1965): the creation of a body of water with a large heat capacity that reduces the continentality of the climate; the substitution of a water surface for a land surface and the rise of the ground-water level in the littoral zone supplying moisture to the evaporating surface (leading to a rise in wind velocity above the lake and in the littoral zone). Schemes have been put forward for augmenting desert rainfall by flooding desert basins in the Sahara, Kalahari and Middle East (see, for example, *Schwarz*, 1923). However, whether evaporation from lake surfaces can raise local precipitation levels is open to question, for precipitation depends more on atmospheric instability than upon the humidity content of the air. Moreover, most lakes are too small to affect the atmosphere materially in depth, so that their influence falls heavily under the sway of the regional circulation. In addition, one needs to remember that some of the world's driest deserts occur along coastlines. Thus a relatively small artificial lake would be even more impotent in creating rainfall (see *Crowe*, 1971: 443-50).

However, the climatic effect of artificial lakes is evident in other ways, notably in terms of a local reduction in frost hazard. In the case of the Rybinsk reservoir (c.4500 km^2) in the USSR, it has been calculated that the climatic influence extends 10 km from the lake and that frost-free season has been extended by 5-15 days on average (*D' Yakanov* and *Reteyum*, 1965).

Urban climates

It has been said that 'the city is the quintessence of man's capacity to inaugurate and control changes in his habitat' (*Detwyler* and *Marcus*, 1972). One way in which such control becomes evident is in a study of urban climates (*Landsberg*, 1981). Individual urban areas can at times, with respect to their weather, 'have similar impacts as a volcano, a desert, and as an irregular forest' (*Changenon*, 1973: 146). Some of the changes that can result are listed in table.

Table 9.3. Average changes in climatic elements caused by cities

Element	*Parameter*	*Urban compared with rural (–, less; +, more)*
Radiation	On horizontal surface	–15%
	Ultravoilet	–30% (winter); –5% (summer)
Temperature	Annual mean	+0.7°C
	Winter maximum	+1.5°C
	Length of freeze-free season	+ 2 to 3 weeks (possible)
Wind speed	Annual mean	– 20 to –30%
	Extreme gusts	– 10 to – 20%
	Frequency of calms	+ 5 to 20%
Relative	Annual mean	– 6%
humidity	Seasonal mean	– 2% (winter); –8% (summer)
Cloudiness	Cloud frequency+amount	+5 to 10%
	Fogs	+ 100% (winter); – 30% (summer)
Precipitation	Amounts	+ 5 to 10%
	Days	+ 10%
	Snow days	– 14%
Phenomenon		***Consequence***
Heat production (the heat island)		Rainfall +
		Temperature +
Retention of reflected radiation by high walls and dark-coloured roofs		Temperature +
Surface roughness increase		Wind –
		Eddying +
Dust increase (the dust dome)		Fog +
		(Rainfall + (?)

Compared with rural surfaces, city surfaces absorb significantly more solar radiation, because a higher proportion of the reflected radiation is retained by the high walls and dark-coloured roofs of the city streets. The concreted city surfaces have both great thermal capacity and conductivity, so that heat is stored during the day and released by night. By contrast the plant cover of the countryside acts like an insulating blanket, so that rural areas tend to experience relatively lower temperatures by day and night, an effect enhanced by the evaporation and transpiration taking place.

A second thermal change in cities, contributing to the development of the 'urban heat island', is the large amount of artificial heat produced by industrial, commercial and domestic users.

Table 9.4. Annual mean urban-rural temperature differences of cities

City	*Temperature difference (°C)*
Chicago, USA	0.6
Washington DC, USA	0.6
Los Angeles, USA	0.7
Paris, France	0.7
Moscow, USSR	0.7
Philadelphia, USA	0.8
Berlin, Germany	1.0
New York, USA	1.1
London, U K	1.3

In general the highest temperature anomalies are associated with the densely built-up area near the city centre, and decrease markedly at the city perimeter. Observations in Hamilton, Ontario, and Montreal, Quebec, suggested temperature changes of 3.8 and 4.0°C respectively per kilometre (*Oke*, 1978). Temperature differences also tend to be highest during the night. The form of the urban temperature effect has often been likened to an 'island' protruding distinctly out of the cool 'sea' of the surrounding landscape. The rural-urban boundary exhibits a steep temperature gradient or 'cliff' to the urban heat island. Much of the rest of the urban area appears as a 'plateau' of warm air with a steady but weaker horizontal gradient of increasing temperature towards the city centre. The urban core may be a 'peak' where the urban maximum temperature is found. The difference between this value and the background rural temperature defines the *urban heat island intensity* (ΔT_{u-r} (max)) (*Oke*, 1978: 255).

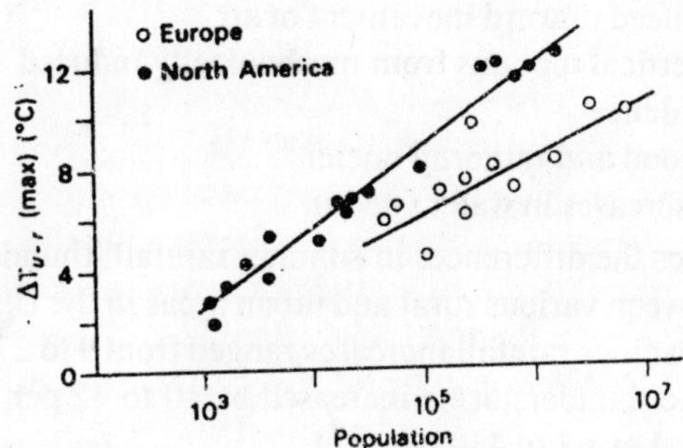

Fig. 9.5. Relationship between maximum observed heatisland intesity and population of North-American and Europzan settlements.

Table lists the average annual urban-rural temperature differences for several large cities. Values range from 0.6 to 1.3°C. The relationship between city size and urban-rural difference, however, is not necessarily linear; sizeable nocturnal temperature contrasts have been measured even in relatively small cities. Factors such as building density are at least as important as city size, and high wind velocities will tend to eliminate the heat island effect.

None the less, Oke (1978: 257) has found that there is some relation between heat island intensity and city size. Using population as a surrogate of city size $T_{u\text{-}r}$ (max) is found to be proportional to the log of the population. Other interesting results of this study include the tendency for quite small centres to have a heat island, the observation that the maximum thermal modification is about 12°C, and the recognition of a difference in slope between the North-American and the European relationships. The explanation for this last result is not clear, but it may be related to the fact that population is a surrogate index of the central building density.

The existence of the urban heat island has a number of implications; city plants bud and bloom earlier, some birds are attracted to the thermally more favourable urban habitat, humans find the added warmth stressful if the city is already situated in a warm area, less winter space-heating is required, but, conversely, more summer air-conditioning is necessary.

The urban-industrial effects on clouds, rain, snowfall and associated weather hazards such as hail and thunder are harder to measure and explain than the temperature changes (*Darungo et al.*, 1978). The changes can be related to various influences (*Changnon*, 1973: 143):

thermal induced upward movement of air
increased vertical motions from mechanically induced turbulence
increased cloud and raindrop nuclei
industrial increases in water vapour.

Table illustrates the differences in summer rainfall, thunder-storms and hailstorms between various rural and urban areas in the USA. These data indicate that in cities rainfall increases ranged from 9 to 27 per cent, the incidence of the thunderstorms increased by 10 to 42 per cent, and hailstorms increased by 67 to 430 per cent.

Table 9.5. Areas of maximum increases (urban–rural difference) in summer rainfall and severe weather events for eight American cities

	Rainfall		*Thunderstroms*		*Hailstorm*	
City	*%*	*Location**	*%*	*Location**	*%*	*Location*
St. Louis	+ 15	B	+ 25	B	+ 276	C
Chicago	+ 17	C	+ 38	A,B,C	+ 246	C
Cleveland	+ 27	C	+ 42	A,B	+ 90	C
Indianapolis	0	–	0	–	0	–
Washington DC	+ 9	C	+ 36	A	+ 67	B
Houston	+ 9	A	+ 10	A,B	+ 430	B
New Orleans	+ 10	A	+ 27	A	+ 350	A,B
Tulsa	0	–	0	–	0	–

* A—within city perimeter, B—8–24 km downwind, C—24–64 km downwind

One of the most celebrated examples of the effect of a city on local precipitation is provided by the Chicago area. At La Porte, Indiana, some 48 km downwind of a large industrial complex between Chicago and Gary, Indiana, the amount of precipitation and the number of days with thunderstorms and hail have increased markedly since 1925. There has been a 30-40 per cent increase in precipitation, and this seems to parallel the curve of increase in atmospheric pollution associated with the production curve of the Chicago iron and steel industrial complex. Moreover, peaks in steel production are seen to be associated with highs in the La Porte precipitation curve. Thunderstorms have also become more frequent, and since 1949 there have been 38 per cent more thunder-storm days at La Porte than expected on the data from surrounding areas. Similarly the incidence of hail days is 59 per cent greater over the total

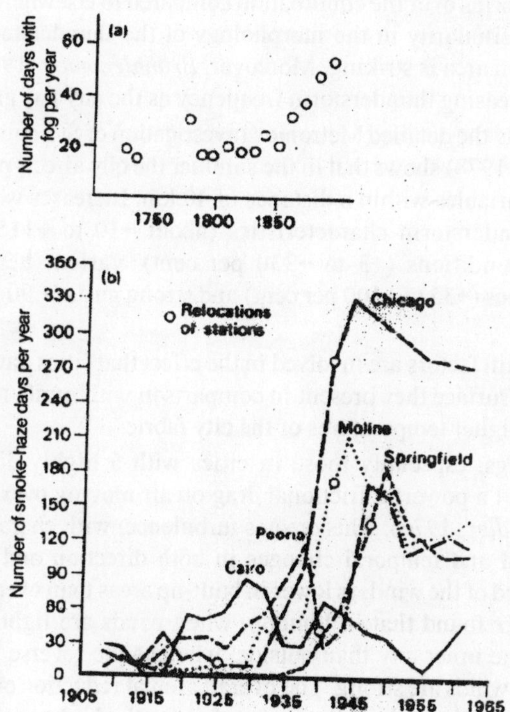

Fig. 9.6. (a) Number of fogs per year in London based on decadal means(after Brimblecombe, 1977); (b) Annual number of days with smoke-haze conditions in Illinois cities based on a 3-year moving average.

period since 1925, but reached 246 per cent higher in the period 1951-65. The industrial complex west of La Porte increases the number of condensation and freezing nuclei, the amount of water vapour and the air temperature (*Changnon*, 1968).

Another interesting example of the effects of major conurbations on precipitation levels is provided by the London area. In this case it seems that the mechanical effect of the city was dominant in creating localized maxima of precipitation both by being a mechanical obstacle to air flow, on the one hand, and by causing frictional convergence of flow, on the other (*Atkinson*, 1975). A long-term analysis of thunderstorm records for south-east England is highly suggestive - indicating the higher frequencies of thunderstorms over the conurbation compared to elsewhere (*Atkinson*, 1968). The similarity in the morphology of the thunderstorm isopleth and the urban area is striking. Moreover, *Brimblecombe* (1977) shows a steadily increasing thunderstorm frequency as the city has grown.

Similarly the detailed Metromex investigation of St Louis in the USA (*Changnon*, 1978) shows that in the summer the city affects precipitation and other variables within a distance of 40 km. Increases were found in various thunderstorm characteristics (about +10 to +115 per cent), hailstorm conditions (+3 to +330 per cent), various heavy rainfall characteristics (+35 to +100 per cent) and strong gusts (+ 90 to + 100 per cent).

Two main factors are involved in the effect that cities have on winds: the rougher surface they present in comparison with rural areas; and the frequently higher temperatures of the city fabric.

Buildings, especially those in cities with a highly differentiated skyline, exert a powerful frictional drag on air moving over and around them (*Chandler*, 1976). This creates turbulence, with characteristically rapid spatial and temporal changes in both direction and speed. The average speed of the winds is lower in built-up areas than over rural areas, but *Chandler* found that in London, when winds are light, speeds are greater in the inner city than outside, whereas the reverse relationship exists when winds are strong. The overall annual reduction of wind speed in Central London is about 6 per cent, but for the higher velocity winds (more than 1.5 m s^{-1}) the reduction is more than doubled.

Studies in both Leicester and London, England, have shown that on calm, clear nights, when the urban heat island effect is at its maximum, there is a surface inflow of cool air towards the zone of highest temperatures. These so-called 'country breezes' have low velocities and become quickly decelerated by intense surface friction in the surburban areas.

Smoke haze and photochemical smog

The emission of miscellaneous pollutants, especially into the atmospheres of industrial cities, increases the number of days with smoke-haze conditions as in eighteenth- and nineteenth - century London. The is also illustrated by the data for some Illinois cities. Chicago, the only major city in the group, was the first to show a sizeable increase, though the moderately industrialized cities of Moline, Springfield and Peoria also show considerable increases beginning in the 1930s. Cairo, a nonindustrial city with minimal twentieth-century growth, has had no great temporal increase in smoke-haze day frequencies (*Changnon*, 1973). In general, *Landsberg* (1970) estimates that on average the number of particles present over urban areas is 10 times greater than that over rural environs. The degree of pollution increases with city size. Many of these atmospheric particulates are hygroscopic and so tend to promote fog formation as water vapour readily condenses on them. However, although fog generally occurs more frequently in metropolitan areas, this is not true for very dense fog, for the heat island effect of greater warmth in the inner city often prevents the thickest night fogs from reaching the densities reported in the suburbs and outlying districts (see data for London).

Local dust plumes can create changes in precipitation. A notable example of this comes from a coal-fired power station near Boulder, Colorado where fly-ash aerosols inadvertently seeded supercooled fog and induced local snowfall. The shape of the plume and the area of snowfall were the same (*Darungo* et al., 1978).

Measures can be taken to control smoke haze. Edward 1 ordered a man to be tortured for burning coal and fouling the air in the fourteenth century, while more recently the clean-air acts in Britain have led to a reduction in smog in major cities. In London, emissions of smoke had, by 1970, been reduced to one-tenth of what they were in 1956, and in Manchester fog and sulphur-dioxide levels decreased, while sunshine levels went up. The downward trend in fog frequency since the introduction of pollution control measures is also demonstrated clearly for Oxford, central England (*Gomez* and *Smith*, 1984), where since the early 1960s fog has only been about half as frequent as it was in the preceding decades.

Table 9.6. Air pollution mechanisms

(a) Urban—rural air pollution gradients (concentration in μg/m³)

Pollution type	*Urban*	*Proximate*	*Non-urban* *Intermediate*	*Remote*
Suspended particulates	102.0	45.0	40.0	21.0
Benzene soluble organics	6.7	2.5	2.2	1.1
Ammonium	0.9	1.22	0.28	0.15
Nitrate	2.4	1.40	0.85	0.45
Sulphate	10.1	10.0	5.29	2.51
Copper	0.16	0.16	0.08	0.06
Iron	1.41	0.56	0.27	0.15

Manganese	0.07	0.02	0.01	0.01
Nickel	0.02	0.01	0.00	0.00
Lead	1.11	0.21	0.10	0.00

(b) Air Pollution related to city size

Population class	*Concentration (μg/m³)* *Total suspended particulates*	*SO_2*	*NO_2*
Non-urban	25	10	33
c. 10 000	57	35	116
10 000	81	18	64
25 000	87	14	63
50 000	118	29	127
100 000	95	26	114
400 000	100	28	127
700 000	101	29	146
1 000 000	134	69	163
3 000 000	120	85	153

Smog produced by the burning of coal is often sulphurous. The sulphur dioxide (SO_2) generated can oxidize in air to produce sulphur trioxide (SO_3), which reacts with water vapour (H_2O) in the presence of catalysts to form sulphuric-acid mist (H_2SO_4). The precipitation of such acid droplets with sulphate particles creates the so-called 'acid rain' which is liable to contaminate rivers and lakes. The acidification of fresh waters in Scandinavia may be caused by emissions from the industrial heartland of Western Europe, including Britain.

Table 9.7. Fog frequencies in London

Location	*Hours per year (based on four observation per day) with visibility less than* 40 m	200 m	400 m	1000 m
Kingsway (Central London)	19	126	230	940
Kew (inner suburbs)	79	213	365	633
London Airport (outer suburbs)	46	209	304	562
South-east England (mean of 7 stations outside London)	20	177	261	494

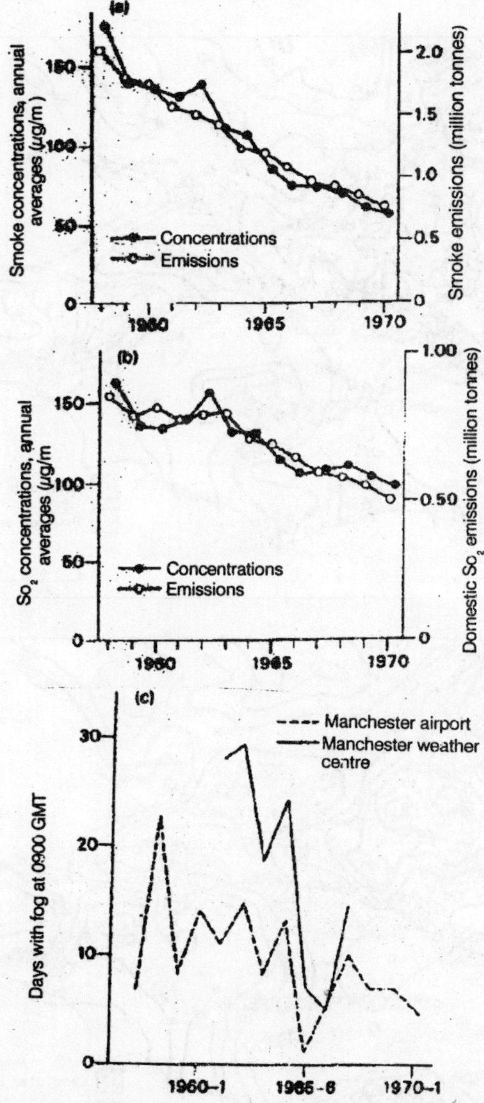

Fig. 9.7. Trends in atmospheric quality in the United Kingdom and in the Manchester area. (a) Trends in regional smoke concentrations and emmisions in the U.K.; (b) Trends in sulphur-dioxide concentrations and emmisions in U.K.; (c) Changing number of days with fog (visibility less than 1000m) in Manchester; (d) Comparative urban annual mean sulphur-dioxide concentrations; (e) Number of hours of sunshine Nov. to Jan. in Manchester.

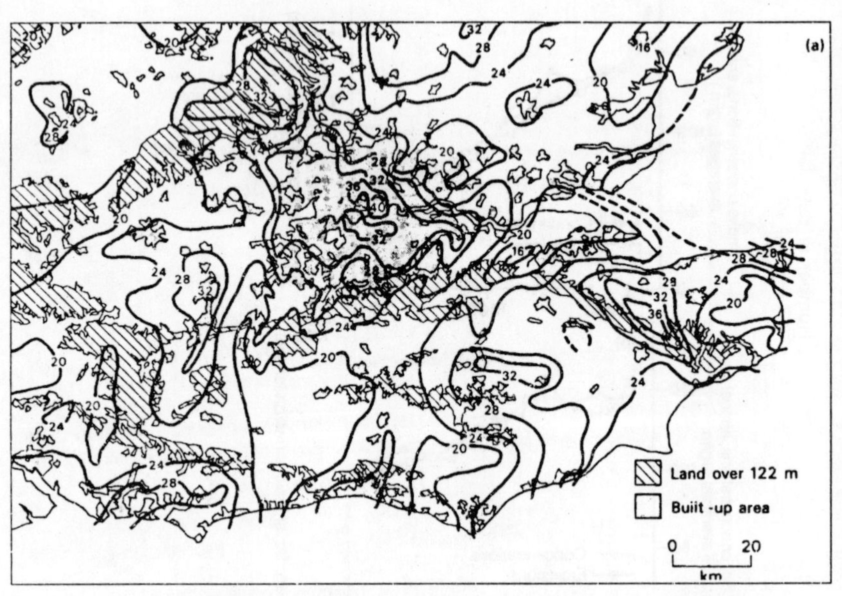
(a)
Land over 122 m
Built-up area
0 20
km

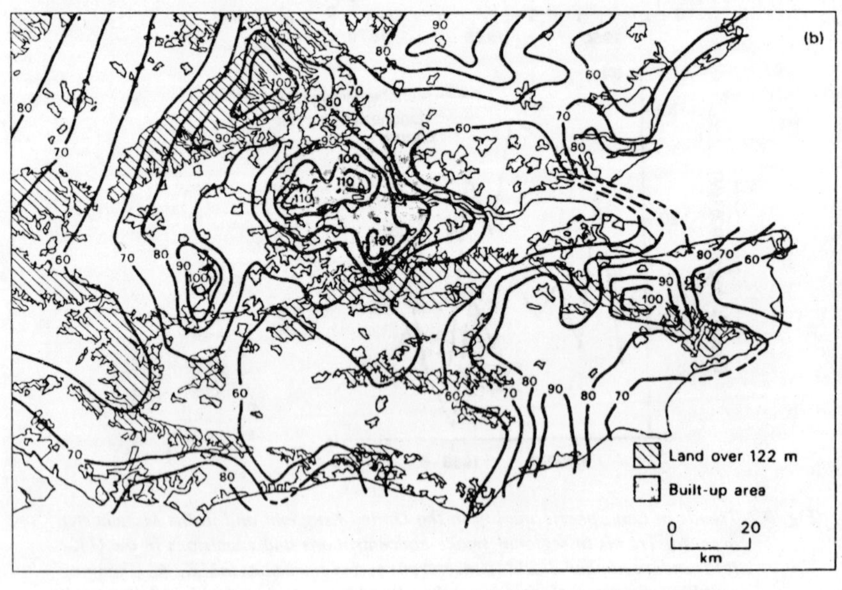
(b)
Land over 122 m
Built-up area
0 20
km

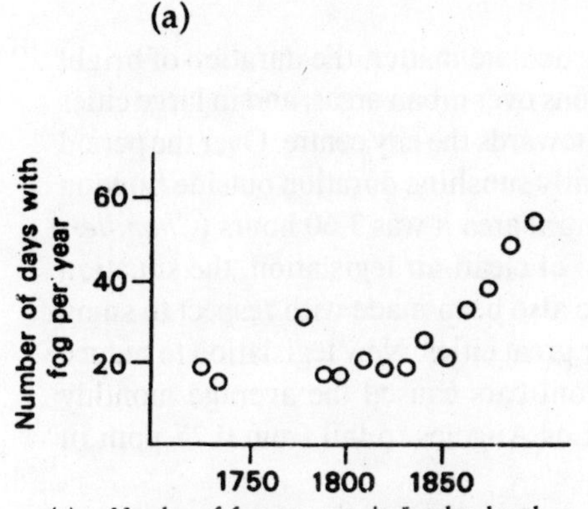

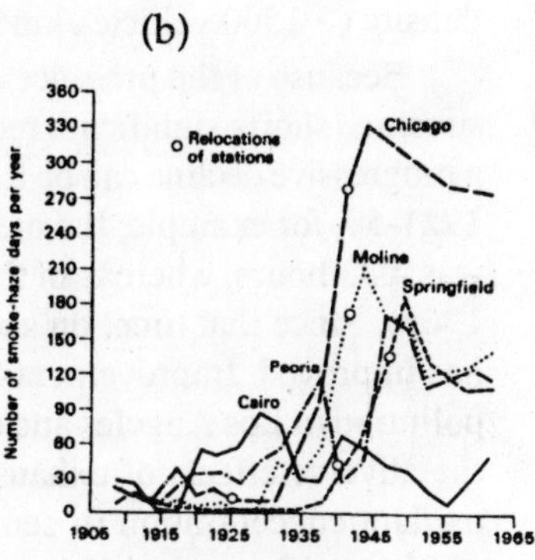

(a) *Number of fogs per year in London based on decadal means (after Brimblecombe, 1977.*

(b) *Annual number of days with smoke-haze conditions in Illinois cities based on a 3-year moving average (after Changnon, 1973.*

While smog produced by burning coal is common, there is a second widespread type: photochemical smog. The name originates from the fact that most of the less desirable properties of such fog result from the products of chemical reactions induced by sunlight (Cadle, in *Matthews, et al.* 1971: 340 et seq.).

Photochemical smog appears 'cleaner' than other kinds of fog in the sense that it does not contain the very large particles of soot that are so characteristic of smog derived from coal-burning. However, the eye irritation and damage to plant leaves it causes make it unpleasant. Photochemical smog occurs particularly where there is large-scale combustion of petroleum products, as in car-dominated cities like Los Angeles. Its unpleasant properties include a high lead content; also a series of chemical reactions are triggered by sunlight. For example, a photochemical decomposition of nitrogen dioxide into nitric oxide and atomic oxygen occurs, and the atomic oxygen can react with molecular oxygen to form ozone. Further ozone may be produced by the reaction of atomic oxygen with various hydrocarbons.

Photochemical smogs are not universal. Because sunlight is a crucial factor in their development they are most common in the tropics or during seasons of strong sunshine. Their especial notoriety in Los Angeles is due to a meteorological setting dominated at times by sub-tropical anticyclones with weak winds, clear skies and a subsidence inversion, combined with the general topographic situation and the high vehicle density (> 1500 vehicles/km^2).

Because of the presence of particulate matter, the duration of bright sunshine shows significant reductions over urban areas, and in large cities a progressive decline can be traced towards the city centre. Over the period 1921-50, for example, the mean daily sunshine duration outside London was 4.33 hours, whereas in the central area it was 3.60 hours (*Chandler*, 1965). Since that time, on account of clean-air legislation, the situation has improved. Improvements have also been made with respect to smog pollution in Los Angeles and other great cities. New legislation to reduce the adverse effects of exhausts from cars caused the average monthly oxidant concentration in central Los Angeles to fall from 0.27 ppm in 1965 to 0.17 ppm in 1974.

Rainmaking and other methods of deliberate climate modification

The most fruitful human attempts to augment natural precipitation have been through cloud seeding. Rainmaking experiments of this type are based on three main assumptions (*Chorley* and *More*, 1967: 159).

1. Either the presence of ice crystals in a supercooled cloud is necessary to release snow and rain; or the presence of comparatively large water droplets is necessary to initiate the coalescence process.
2. Some clouds precipitate inefficiently or not at all, because these components are naturally deficient.
3. The deficiency can be remedied by seeding the clouds artificially, either with solid carbon dioxide (dry ice) or silver iodide, to produce crystals, or by introducing water droplets or large hygroscopic nuclei.

These methods of seeding are not universally productive. Under conditions of orographic lift and in thunderstorm cells, when nuclei are insufficient to generate rain by natural means, some augmentation may be attained, especially if cloud temperatures are of the order of - 10 to - 15°C. The increase of precipitation gained under favourable conditions may be of the order of 10-20 per cent in any one storm. In lower latitudes, where cloud-top temperatures frequently remain above 0°C, silver-iodide or dry-ice seeding is not applicable. Therefore alternative methods have been introduced whereby small water droplets of 50 mm diameter are sprayed into the lower layers of deep clouds, so that the growth of cloud particles will be stimulated by coalescence.

Other techniques of warm cloud seeding include the feeding of hygroscopic particles into the lower air layers near the updraught of a growing cumulus cloud (*Breuer*, 1980).

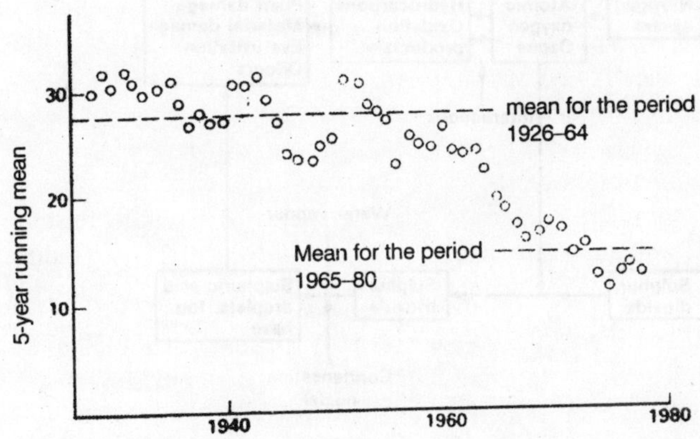

Fig. 9.8. Annual fog frequency at 0900 GMT in oxford, central England, 1926-80.

The results of the many experiments now carried out on cloud seeding are still controversial, very largely because we have an imperfect understanding of the physical processes involved. This means that the evidence has to be evaluated on a statistical rather than a scientific basis, so that although precipitation may occur after many seeding trials, it is difficult to decide to what extent artificial stimulation and augmentation is responsible. It also needs to be remembered that this form of planned weather modification applies to small areas for short periods of time. As yet, no means exist to change precipitation appreciably over large areas on a sustained basis.

Other types of deliberate climatic modification have also been attempted (*Hess*, 1974). For example, it has been thought that the production of many more hailstone embryos by silver-iodide seeding will yield smaller hailstones which would both be less damaging and more likely to melt before reaching the ground. Some results in Russia have been encouraging, but one cannot exclude the possibility that seeding may sometimes even increase hail damage (*Atlas*, 1977). Similar experiments have been conducted in lightning suppression. The concept here is to produce in a thundercloud, again by silver-iodide seeding, an abnormal abundance of ice crystals that would act as added corona points and thus relieve the electrical potential gradient by corona discharge before a lightning strike could develop (Panel on Weather and Climate Modification, 1966: 4-8).

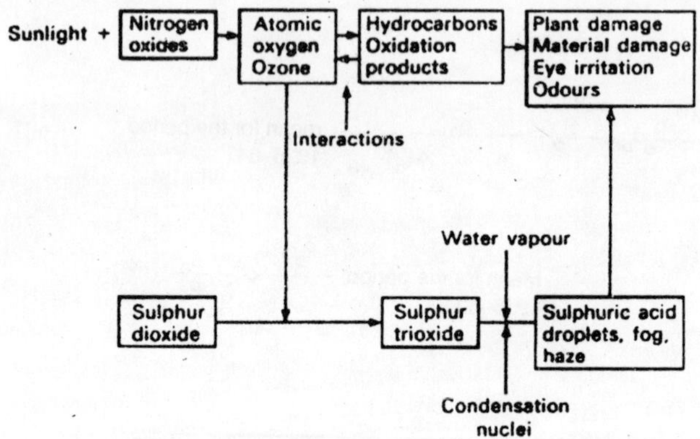

Fig. 9.9. Possible reactions involving primary and secondary pollutants.

Hurricane modification is perhaps the most desirable aim of those seeking to suppress severe storms, because of the extremely favourable benefit-to-cost ratio of the work. The principal once again is that of introducing freezing nuclei into the ring of clouds around the hurricane centre to trigger the release of the latent heat of fusion in the eye-wall cloud system which, in turn, diminishes the maximum horizontal temperature gradients in the storm, causing a hydrostatic lowering of the surface temperature. This, eventually, should lead to a weakening of the damaging winds (*Smith*, 1975: 212). A 1-5 per cent reduction in maximum winds is theoretically possible, but as yet work is largely at an experimental stage.

Much research has been devoted in the Soviet Union to the possibility of removing the Arctic Sea ice and to ascertain effects of such action on the climate of northern areas (see *Lamb*, 1977: 660). One proposal was to dam the Bering Strait, the-eby blocking off water flow from the Pacific. The assumption was that more, and warmer, Atlantic water would he drawn into the central Arctic, improving temperature conditions in that area. Critics have pointed to the possibility of adverse changes in temperatures elsewhere, together with undesirable change in precipitation character and amount.

Fog dispersal, vital for airport operation, is another aim of weather modification. Seeding experiments have shown that fog consisting of supercooled droplets can be cleared by using liquid propane or dry ice. In very cold fogs this seeding method causes rapid transformation of water droplets into ice particles.

In regions of high temperature, dark soils often become over-heated, and the resultant high evapotranspiration rates lead to moisture deficiencies. Applications of white powders (India and Israel) or of aluminium foils (Hungary) increase the reflection from the soil surface and reduce the rate at which insulation is absorbed. Temperatures of the soil surface and sub-surface are lowered (by as much as 10°C), and soil moisture is conserved (by as much as 50 per cent).

The planting of windbreaks is an even more important attempt by humans to modify local climate deliberately. Shelter-belts have been in use for centuries in many windswept areas of the globe, both to protect soils from blowing and to protect the plants from the direct effects of high-velocity winds. The size and effectiveness of the protection depends on their height, density, shape and frequency. However, the belts may have consequences for microclimate beyond those for which they were planted. Evaporation rates are curtailed; snow is arrested, and its melting waters are available for the fields; but temperatures may become more extreme in the stagnant space in the Ice of the belt, creating an increase in frost danger.

Traditional farmers in many societies have been aware of the virtues of microclimate management (*Wilken*, 1972). They manage shade by employing layered cropping systems or by covering the plants and soil with mulches; they may deliberately try to modify albedo conditions - Tibetan farmers, for example, reportedly throw dark rocks onto snow-covered fields to promote late spring melting; and in the Paris area of France some very dense stone walls were constructed to absorb and radiate heat.

Conclusion: the climatic impact

We can attempt to make certain general conclusions about the human impact on climate. The first is that humans are undoubtedly effective, sometimes deliberately, at the microclimatic level by altering the nature of the land surface. They are also causing highly important changes, mainly inadvertently, in the environment on the scale of the individual city. When it comes to a consideration of larger scales (regional plus global) there is much more controversy about the extent and direction of human influence, which is almost wholly unintentional.

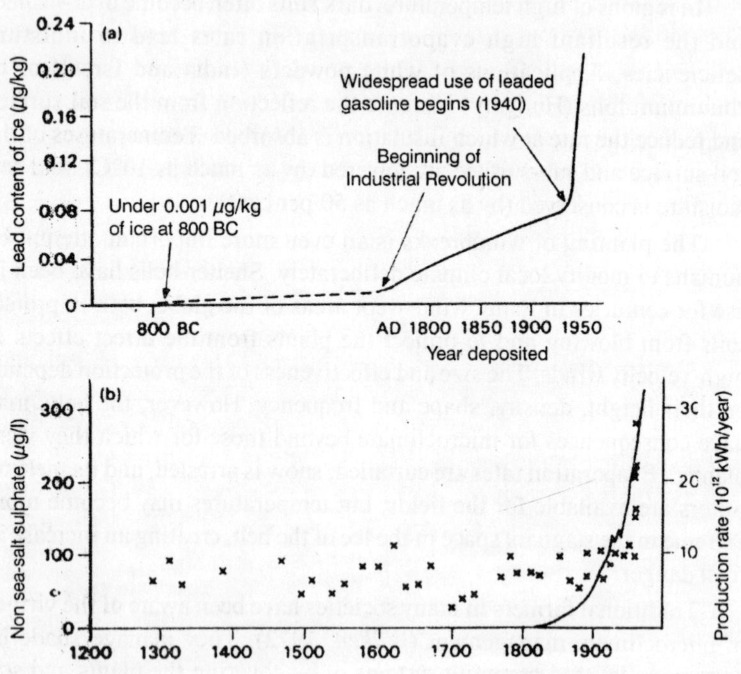

Fig. 9.10. Trends in atmospheric quality:(a) The chart shows the lead content of the Greenland ice cap due to atmospheric fallout of the mineral on the snow surface. A dramatic upturn in worldwide atmospheric levels of lead occured at the beginning of the Industrial Revolutionary of the nineteenth century and again after the more recent spread of the automobile.; (b) The suphate concentration on a sea-salt free basis in north-west Greenland glacier ice samples as a function of year. The curve represents the world production of thermal energy from coal, lignite and crude oil.

The fact remains that it is difficult to separate the effect of natural changes from those that may have been brought about by human actions. Moreover, we still know too little to be able to make deliberate climatic modifications of fully proven effectiveness, even on a local scale. Finally, as some of the examples discussed show, the possible feedback effects of some schemes for climatic or hydrological modification (such as the diversion of Siberian rivers into the Arctic) could be hazardous, given our present state of limited knowledge.

Such is the uncertainty surrounding the climatic future, that the *Global 2000* (Council on Environmental Quality, 1982) report considered three different scenarios feasible:

Case 1 (No change)

Yearly rainfall and temperature statistics would be similar to those of the 1941-70 periods, with occasional droughts in areas like the Sahel, India and the USA. This scenario might result if the warming trends induced by the build up of CO_2 were counteracted by natural cooling tendencies.

Case 2 (Warming)

Global temperatures would increase by 1°C, principally as a result of a warming trend caused by elevated CO_2 levels being sufficiently large to outweigh the effects of any natural cooling. Most of the warming would take place in polar regions and the higher middle latitudes, with only slight warming in the tropics. Annual precipitation would increase by 5-10 per cent on a global basis, but there would be more likelihood of US drought conditions similar to those of the Dust Bowl years of the 1930s.

Case 3 (Cooling)

As a result of changes in solar and volcanic activity, global temperatures would decrease by 0.5°C, with cooling reaching 1°C in the higher and middle latitudes. In general precipitation amounts would decline, and variability increase. Stormtracks, and the precipitation they bring, would shift towards the equator, improving conditions in the upper latitudes of the great deserts and worsening them on their equatorial sides. Severe monsoon failures would be more frequent in India, with severe droughts in the Sahel.

Air pollution: some further effects

This chapter has already made much reference to the ways in which humans have changed the turbidity of the atmosphere and the gases within it. However, the consequences of air pollution go further than either their direct impact on human health or their impact on local, regional and global climates.

First of all, the atmosphere acts as a major channel for the transfer of pollutants from one place to another, so that some harmful substances have been transferred long distances from their sources of emission. DDT is one example; lead is another. Thus, since the start of the Industrial

Revolution, the lead content of the Greenland ice cap, although far removed from the source of the pollutant (which is largely derived either from industrial or automobile emissions) has risen very substantially. The same applies to its sulphate content. An analysis of pond sediments from a remote part of North America (Yosemite) indicates that lead levels have also been raised as a result of human activities, being more than twenty times the natural levels. The lead, which came in from atmospheric sources, shows a fivefold elevation in the plants of the area and a fiftyfold elevation in the animals compared with natural levels (*Shirahata et al*., 1980). Some estimates have also compared the total quantities of heavy metals that humans are releasing into the atmosphere with emissions from natural sources (*Nriagu*, 1979). The increase is eighteenfold for lead, ninefold for cadmium, sevenfold for zinc, and threefold for copper.

A second example of the possible widespread and ramifying ecological consequences of atmospheric pollution is provided by 'acid rain' (*Likens* and *Bormann*, 1974). Acid rain is rain which has a pH of less than 5.65, this being the pH which is produced by carbonic acid in equilibrium with atmospheric CO_2. In many parts of the world, rain may be markedly more acid than this normal natural background level. Snow and rain in the north-east USA has been known to have pH values as low as 2.1, while in Scotland in one storm the rain was the acidic equivalent of vinegar (pH 2.4). In the eastern USA the average annual acidity values tend to be around pH 4 and the degree of acidulation appears to have been increasing. The acidity of the rain in turn leads to greater acidity in rivers and lakes. Studies by *Beamish et al.* (1975) demonstrated that between 1961 and 1975 pH had declined by 0.13 pH units per year in George Lake, Canada, and a comparable picture emerges from Sweden where Almer et al. (1974) found that the pH in some lakes had decreased by as much as 1.8 pH units since the 1930s.

The causes of this phenomenon are that increasing quantities of sulphur oxides and nitrogen oxides are being emitted from fossil fuel combustion. At present, roughly 60-70 per cent of the problem is due to sulphur-oxides emissions, and the balance to the nitrogen oxides. Additional quantities of these oxides are derived from the smelting of sulphide ores. These oxides are converted into strong acids (sulphuric and nitric) in the atmosphere and fall to the ground in rain and snow. How sulphate levels have increased in European precipitation. Two main factors contribute to the increasing seriousness of the problem. One is the replacement of coal by oil and natural gas. The second, paradoxically, is a result of the implementation of air pollution control measures (particularly increasing the height of smoke stacks and installing particle precipitators). These appear to have transformed a local 'soot problem' into a regional 'acid rain problem'. Coal-burning produced a great deal of sulphate, but was largely neutralized by high calcium contents in the relatively unaltered coal smoke emissions. Natural gas burning creates less sulphate but that which is produced is not neutralized. The new higher chimneys pump the smoke so high that it is dispersed over wide areas, whereas previously it returned to earth nearer the source. Some of the stacks are now enormous. One at the Sudbury copper-nickel smelter in Canada is 400 m tall. A possible subsidiary reason for some of the observed increases in acidity is that there may now be less calcium-rich dust in the atmosphere over North America since the passing of the Dust Bowl years (*Stensland* and *Semonin*, 1982).

The effects of acid rain are especially serious in areas underlain by highly siliceous types of bedrock (for example, granite, some gneisses, quartzite and quartz sandstone), such as the old shield areas of the Fenno-Scandian shield in Scandinavia and the Laurentide shield in Canada (*Likens et al.*, 1979).

The ecological consequences of acid rain are still the subject of some debate. *Krug* and *Frink* (1983) have argued that acid rain only accelerates natural processes, and point out that the results of natural soil formation in humid climates include the leaching of nutrients, the release of aluminium ions and the acidification of soil and water. They also note that acidification by acid rain may be superimposed on longer-term acidification induced by changes in land use. Thus the regrowth of coniferous forests in what are now marginal agriculture areas, such as New England and highland Western Europe, can increase acidification of soils and water. Similarly, it is possible, though in general unproven (see *Battarbee et al.*, 1985), that in areas like western Scotland, a decline in upland agriculture and the regeneration of heathland could play a role in increasing soil and water acidification. Likewise *Johnston et al.* (1982) have suggested that acid rain can cause either a decrease or an increase in forest productivity depending on local factors. For example, in soils where cation nutrients are abundant and sulphur or nitrogen are deficient, moderate inputs of acid rain are very likely to stimulate forest growth.

In general, however, it is the negative consequences of acid rain that have been stressed. One harmful effect is a change in soil character. The high concentration of hydrogen ions in acid rain causes accelerated leaching of essential nutrients, making them less available for plant use. Furthermore, the solubility of aluminium and heavy metal ions increases, and instead of being fixed in the soil's sorption complex, these toxic substances become available for plants or are transferred into lakes, where they become a major physiological stress for some aquatic organisms.

Fresh-water bodies with limited natural cations are poorly buffered and thus vulnerable to acid inputs. The acidification of thousands of lakes and rivers in southern Norway and Sweden during the past two decades has been attributed to acid rain, and this increased acidity has resulted in the decline of various species of fish, particularly trout and salmon. But fish are not the only aquatic organisms that may be affected. Fungi and moss may proliferate, organic matter may start to decompose less rapidly, and the number of green algae may be reduced.

Forest growth can also he affected by acid rain, though the evidence is not necessarily proven. Acid rain can damage foliage, increase susceptibility to pathogens, affect germination and reduce nutrient availability. However, since acid precipitation is only one of many environmental stresses, its impact may enhance, be enhanced by, or be swamped by other factors. For example, Blank (1985), in considering the fact that an estimated one-half of the total forest area of the German Federal Republic was showing signs of damage, referred to the possible role of ozone or of a run of hot, dry summers on tree health and growth.

Further useful information on the contentious issue of the effects or acid rain is contained in *Likens* and *Butler* (1981), *Hutchinson* and *Havas* (1980), and *Hornbeck* (1981).

It is perhaps worth concluding this chapter by reiterating the fact that the variability of air pollution in both space and time, while undoubtedly owing much to human action, is also highly dependent on natural conditions, and in particular on meteorological conditions (*Thompson*, 1978). This is brought out. Climatic facotrs control the efficiency with which effluents are diluted and dispersed away from primary sources, while local relief and microclimatic circumstances modify the interaction between the emission of pollutants and the atmosphere. Moreover, as we have already stated, not all pollutants result from human endeavour: the vast majority of nitrogen oxides are emitted by bacteria rather than by car exhausts, most chlorides in rain water come from the oceans, and a considerable proportion of atmospheric dust is injected into the air by such mechanisms as volcanic eruptions, and by dust storms removing fine silt from glacial outwash fans or desert basins.

Chapter 10

Volcanic Eruption

Introduction

From earliest times man has found volcanic eruptions mysterious and threatening. The hot lava, flickering light reflected from ash clouds, the violent eruption of volcanic bombs and ash, the smell of sulphur, and the accompanying rumbling and hissing sound all contributed to early man's concept of his world. The pitch-like appearance of some kinds of lava and the sulphurous smell contributed to the idea of a hostile underworld-a hell of fire and brimstone.

But even for modern man, volcanic activity is not always the subject of purely rational observation. A particularly well known example is the eruption of the volcano Paricutin in the state of Michoacan in Mexico which arose from a field of maize.

Egon Erwin Kisch has described the birth of this volcano; his report states: "It started in the maize field of Dionisio Perlido who lived in the township of Paricutin. On 20 February 1943 he arrived to work in his field and discovered a fracture in the ground. The ground rose, and began to smoke and rumble so that the man panicked and ran away. A crater formed and the field was soon covered by lava, volcanic bombs, and ash ... nothing remained of the maize field which will never yield a crop again. The continued eruption of scoria and ash formed a growing mountain with a crater at the top."

The Hamburg geologist *Dr. Franz Termer* reported in 1951 a visit he made to the volcano on 26 and 27 November 1949, about six and a half years after its formation. Whereas at first the volcano was characterised by explosive activity, by 1949 this had given place to an effusive phase, the main activity of which is the eruption of lava. The volcano had grown to a sizeable mountain which emitted large clouds of steam at 20 minute intervals. On 27 November a yellowish cloud of steam rose from the crater. It was both difficult and dangerous to climb the mountain. *Termer* then describes his ride along the edge of the lava field through layers of ash containing the burnt remains of trees. The flanks of the volcano become increasingly steep and are furrowed by channels eroded by water running off the cone.

Further progress was possible only on foot, past steep cliffs of older lava until a saddle-like plain is reached. Here, steam was being emitted quietly from gas vents called fumaroles, some of them having a characteristic sulphurous smell. Three hundred metres further on the base of the volcanic cone is reached. Dense clouds of steam arose from the crater and volcanic bombs and lapilli (Italian: small stone) fell: these are fragments of lava which solidify as they travel through the air, become partly or completely rounded by rotation. Some fall back into the crater, but others, often of considerable size, are thrown beyond the crater rim and roll down the flanks of the cone. There are many such large blocks, some several cubic metres in volume, at the base of the cone. In addition to bombs with smooth surfaces, there are some with an irregularly broken crust, and others—called breadcrust bombs-have the appearance of the crust of a freshly baked loaf.

The cone itself consists essentially of sharp-edged slaggy fragments of lava. The sides of the cone slope at between 32° to 35° making ascent very difficult and care is needed when on the crater rim because of falling ejecta. The inner walls of the crater fall steeply for 50 to 60 metres to the crater floor which consists of red-brown lava partially covered by greenish scum. The crater rim is about 300 metres in diameter, and that of the floor about 150 metres. There are two orifices (Italian: *boccas*) in the crater floor; when lava is not being erupted, the bocca is a white-hot shaft with liquid lava flowing down its walls. *Termer* reported a bluish flare above the mouth of the bocca.

The onset of activity is heralded by a dull rumble in the bocca, followed by bluish to reddish flames which shoot suddenly upwards, accompanied by a noise like the popping of a giant cork from a bottle. A cloud of yellowish steam is then emitted with a noise like loud thunder. Such explosions occur every 2 to 8 minutes and quantities of flowing fragments of lava are thrown up.

These fall on the inner and outer walls of the crater with a loud splat and, because they are still hot when they land, they become fused to the material on which they fall, and remain glowing hot for some time. This is a spectacular display at any time, but especially so at night. The bombs are thrown to a height of 600 metres and the larger ones become flattened in flight and from a distance they resemble birds because they shimmer in the hot ascending gases.

Apart from falling lava bombs, the visitor to the crater rim has to endure the smell and irritation of sulphuric and hydrochloric acid vapour which makes breathing difficult. Lava pted by the volcano forms a flow which runs down the - ink of the cone and quickly reaches a width of about 80 metres and flows over an older lava field where, some time earlier, a parasitic cone called Zapicho had formed. The lava flow glows impressively in the dark like a mighty red cascade with the flanks glowing a brighter red than the centre.

Kisch described the termination of such a lava flow thus: “I went towards this 12 metre high wall of lava, but I could not touch it, its radiated heat was too great. So I walked along the edge for several kilometres. The wall-like lava front made a noise like the rattling of iron chains, and some of the blocks in the wall became detached and fell down. Gradually the lava front crept forward like the edge of a wave. The lava front advanced 10 metres per day and always remained steep. Everything in its path is engulfed; large trees disappear without trace. I had always imagined lava to be a viscous, glassy mass like a stream, but what I saw here was a huge, rough, dark grey mass of boulders.”

Incidentally, the volcano Jorullo lies scarcely a two hours car journey from Paricutin. Jorullo formed in a similar way to Paricutin on 28 September 1759, and *Alexander von Humboldt* visited Mexico to see the volcano, among other things. He visited this volcano 44 years after its first eruption and was able, according to *Kisch*, to light his cigar at one of the small volcanic cones.

Nowadays the techniques of physics and chemistry are used in the investigation of volcanoes. For example, ‘the Academy of Sciences of the USSR has founded a large volcanological institute and observatory at Kamchatka. The temperature of lava in the bocca is measured and also that of the lava flow itself which soon falls to around 800°C. The amount, temperature and nature of volcanic gases and many other features are also recorded. Yet, though modern volcanology is becoming an increasingly exact science, many questions remain unanswered.

Volcanic activity is often accompanied by earthquakes, and the eruption of Paricutin was preceded by earth tremors. It became extinct in 1952 after it had erupted two cubic km of lava and tuff (lithified volcanic ash), and had produced about 40 million tons of steam, indicating that the lava contained about 1.1 % water.

There is also a large volcanic observatory in Hawaii, another active volcanic area. *Kilauea* is a large shield volcano in Hawaii and the research institute situated on its flanks is one of the most important in the world.

In Europe there is an observatory on Etna and information is also obtained of the activity of other volcanoes in the Italian volcanic province, especially Vesuvius which erupted catastrophically in A.D. 79, and has been intermittently active ever since.

The accounts of Pliny the Younger and Tacitus of the eruption of *Vesuvius* in A. D. 79 were the first detailed reports of an eruption. *Vesuvius* had been dormant since the Pleistocene ice age and, at the time of the eruption in A. D. 79, it was entirely covered with trees. Characteristically, the first eruption after a long period of dormancy is particularly violent. The towns of Pompeii and Herculaneum were totally destroyed and covered by thick layers of volcanic ash produced as a result of the violent, explosive nature of the eruption. Enormous volumes of gas under very high pressure blasted out the solid material filling of the volcanic vent, together with a large part of the volcanic cone. Towards the end of the main eruption a lava flow issued from a fracture in the flank of the volcano and poured over the coastal plain. Among the many casualties was Pliny the Elder, the uncle of Pliny the Younger; he was killed by the eruption it was his intention to observe. The fugitive components of eruptions, or volcanic gases, play an important role in many volcanic eruptions, particularly in their post-eruptive phase. It is probable that the greater part of the Earth's atmosphere was formed in this way over the long periods of geological time.

The gases emitted by modern volcanoes are predominantly steam and carbon dioxide but, in addition, there are varying but always small amounts of nitrogen (N), sulphur dioxide (SO_2), sulphur trioxide (SO_3) and hydrogen sulphide (H_2S) together with very small amounts of carbon monoxide (CO), hydrochloric acid (HCl), hydrofluoric acid (HF), hydrogen (H_2), argon (Ar), sodium chloride (NaCl), fluorine trichloride (F_2Cl_3), carbon oxysulphide (COS), and other compounds. Some of these gases can corrode rock, and native sulphur and sulphur compounds sublimate and give volcanic craters their particular yellowish and greenish colour. The fluidity and viscosity of a lava are to some extent determined by the amount of water and other gases it contains, though its silica content is of particular importance. Highly viscous melts are usually rich in silica and tend to behave explosively because they retain their gases. Such volcanic explosions can release more energy than an atomic bomb; in fact the energy released during the most violent eruptions is equivalent to that of 170,000 atomic bombs of the type dropped at Hiroshima. In contrast, the French volcanologist, *H. Tazieff* has filmed lava flows of such low viscosity that they flow almost as quickly as water. Individual volcanoes which constantly produce this kind of lava cover a very large area and are called shield volcanoes. In contrast, volcanoes erupting viscous, gas-charged lava form composite cones of classic "volcanic" form, made not only of lava flows but also of ash, bombs and lapilli thrown out during the eruption.

Such volcanoes, called stratovolcanoes, are those which cause the greatest destruction. *Vesuvius* for example, caused about 1,200 deaths in the eruption in A.D. 79. The eruption of Krakatau in 1883 was even more powerful; the greater part of the island Krakatau was blown away and the eruption and the resulting tsunamis caused the deaths of 36,417 people. The eruption of Mont Pelee in 1902 near the town of St. Pierre on the island of Martinique in the West Indies was especially catastrophic. An enormous glowing cloud of gas containing droplets of intensely hot lava in suspension was suddenly erupted and rushed over the town of St. Pierre killing all but two of its 26,000 inhabitants. A photograph of this glowing cloud, or *nuee ardente*, was taken from a ship and is quite a rarity for that time.

Vesuvius erupted again in 1906 and the cone was reduced in height by 105 metres and 100 people were killed.

In 1909 the volcano Kelut in Java erupted after lying dormant for 18 years during which time the crater had become filled with water. A secondary result of the eruption was that about 38 million cubic metres of water were discharged causing mud streams to form and killing 5,500 people.

In 1928 the Sicilian volcano Etna erupted both lava and ash, destroying the town of Mascali and killing 1,500 people; in this instance the eruption coincided with an earthquake so increasing the death toll. There have been several disastrous major eruptions of Etna between 1929 and 1950.

Low viscosity lavas can also cause enormous destruction particularly when the eruption is in populated areas as was the case with Heimaey in 1973 in Iceland when the speed at which the lava moved gave little time for precautions.